让我们的呐喊来唤醒

年轻的共和国

EDITED BY HAN MINZHU

ASSISTANT EDITOR HUA SHENG

Cries for Democracy

**WRITINGS AND SPEECHES FROM
THE 1989 CHINESE DEMOCRACY
MOVEMENT**

Princeton University Press | Princeton, New Jersey

Copyright © 1990 by
Princeton University Press
Published by Princeton University Press,
41 William Street,
Princeton, New Jersey 08540
In the United Kingdom:
Princeton University Press, Oxford

All Rights Reserved

Publication of this book has been generously assisted by a
grant from the World Journal Culture Foundation

Library of Congress Cataloging-in-Publication Data

Cries for democracy : writings and speeches from the 1989 Chinese democracy
movement / edited by Han Minzhu.
p.   cm.
ISBN 0-691-03146-0 (alk. paper)—ISBN 0-691-00857-4
(pbk. : alk. paper)
1. China—Politics and government—1976- 2. Students—China—Political activity.
3. China—History—Tiananmen Square Incident, 1989. I. Han, Minzhu.
DS779.26.C75   1990
951.05'8—dc20   90-31251

This book has been composed in Gill Sans and Sabon

Calligraphy on page i: "Let our cries awaken our young Republic!" From the
"New May Fourth Manifesto" of the Beijing Students' Federation,
May 4, 1989.

Princeton University Press books are printed on acid-free paper,
and meet the guidelines for permanence and durability
of the Committee on Production Guidelines for
Book Longevity of the Council on Library Resources

Printed in the United States of America by Princeton University Press,
Princeton, New Jersey
10 9 8 7 6 5 4 3 2
(Pbk.) 10 9 8 7 6 5 4 3 2

iv

CONTENTS

PREFACE

Yan Jiaqi

From April to June 1989, the Chinese Democracy Movement introduced a glorious chapter in China's history. Although the Democracy Movement would end prematurely, drowned in the blood and tears of the June 4 massacre in Beijing, it proclaimed to the entire nation and the entire world a fundamental principle of democracy: all of a state's power belongs to the people, and the power of the ruling party and government is not intrinsic, but flows from the people. This principle applies to all ruling parties; the Communist Party that claims to be the representative of the people is no exception. The people have the right to criticize and oppose the Party and the government, and to recall leaders of the country that do not enjoy their trust.

This book has collected a large quantity of big- and small-character posters posted on Beijing campuses and streets, declarations and announcements printed as handbills, and speeches from the Democracy Movement. From these rich and varied materials one can discern that the university students and people of China are no different from people in the rest of the world: they hold the same convictions about democracy, freedom, the need for rule by law, and human rights. Because present-day China's autocratic system is so firmly entrenched her students and citizens show tremendous, intelligent courage in challenging such rule. These valuable first-hand documents and materials are of great importance for understanding, and further research into, the Democracy Movement.

The Democracy Movement was characterized by one outstanding feature: demonstrators used only peaceful, rational, and nonviolent means to try to achieve their goals. In carrying out protests against the government with a nonviolent hunger strike, Beijing students completely exposed China's defects, allowing the Chinese people to see through "socialism's" pretty words, to grasp the true roots of China's defects, and to comprehend how autocracy constructed on expropriation of people's property savages and eliminates humanity.

Although this Democracy Movement was crushed by the machine guns and tanks of the Chinese Communist Party, the rage of resistance still smolders across all of China. It will not be long before the movement for democracy will once again burst out. And in the future, the 1989 Democracy Movement will be fairly evaluated and the slaughterers behind the June 4 massacre given their just sentences.

In addition to conveying to those outside of China the spirit of the 1989 Chinese Democracy Movement, the publication of this book also preserves for history many invaluable documents. For this, the students and citizens of Beijing, as well as all Chinese, are grateful to the editors and contributors of this volume who have dedicated much time and labor to making this book possible.

Paris, September 1989

One side of the famous "Triangle" (*Sanjiaodi*) at Beijing University, where hundreds of big-character posters, notices, and other posters were hung during the Democracy Movement. Credit: Ming Pao Newspapers, Hong Kong

In the latter half of May 1989, few surfaces in Beijing were safe from poster and slogan writers. Slogans were painted on storefronts or scratched on walls, and signs were draped from office buildings and across streets. This sign is affixed to a traffic police sentry box: "People, come [to Tiananmen] in the night; the students are depending on the people." Credit: Ming Pao Newspapers, Hong Kong

Throughout China, handbills posted on street poles and city walls were an important means of disseminating information and appealing to the citizenry for support. Credit: Melissa McCauley

Bus passengers in Shanghai grab for handbills being distributed by students. Credit: Tristan Mabry

Student posters and banners cover the walls of central buildings at Qinghua University in Beijing. Credit: Ming Pao Newspapers, Hong Kong

INTRODUCTION

Jonathan D. Spence

China in 1989 was deeply troubled. We all heard the rising chorus of disillusion and anger from those Chinese seeking some form of meaningful say in their government, and some chance of participation in the discussion that would decide the nation's future. We saw on our television screens or in person the massing of a million or more people to underscore these demands. We tried to chart—in anguish and perhaps sometimes with a kind of horrified fascination—the sequence of events on June 3 and June 4 that left so many innocent people dead. We watched as the Chinese security system and the party leaders tried to identify, arrest, intimidate, imprison, or execute any Chinese who were caught up as activists in the protests. And we noted how the Chinese government's blind and ugly response to the crisis it generated led to one thing the government certainly did not want or expect: the galvanization of Chinese opinion abroad and the formation of an overseas organization to marshal and coordinate the disaffected, the Front for a Democratic China, with its headquarters in Paris.

The texts in this book speak powerfully and directly to the hopes and goals of the Chinese who participated in the spring protests of 1989, and the accompanying commentaries and analyses by the editors give the context in precise detail. In this introduction, rather than repeat any of that material, I would like instead to reflect on how different strands from the past have impinged directly—even fatally—on the present. Of the numerous such strands, I will concentrate on four: the Chinese tradition of intellectual protest, the emergence of a new pattern of student protest, the reasons for governmental repression in China, and the problems posed by Western science and culture.

There has been an immensely long tradition inside China of intellectual protest against government inadequacies. Many of Confucius's own writings in the fifth century B.C. were focused on the problem of how and when to direct which kind of criticism at rulers and ministers, and on when and in what circumstances one would or should serve in a given government. Confucius himself was only one of many thinkers interested in such problems, and from his day on debate has almost never been stilled. The consequence has been that, under a series of dynasties and autocratic regimes, the intellectual-as-moralist has occupied an important place. Such men (until the late nineteenth century few women in China had the education or the opportunity to make their own views publicly known) saw it as their duty to speak out against injustice, even at grave personal risk. It was an obligation of being educated, of having absorbed the moral wisdom and values of the past, that one try to live by those values and help one's ruler also comprehend them. Those who died in the pursuit of this moral quest had a particular place of honor within the country's historical pantheon. By the late nineteenth century, the ideology of moral protest was integrated with Western strains of thought and constitutional government and democracy, and in some cases also linked to armed insurrection. The collapse of the Qing dynasty in 1912 in no way ended the tradition of moral and ethical protest by the educated elite against perceived abuses; indeed if anything it was strengthened during the agonies of the warlord period that followed the failure of China's republican government, and during the rule of the Kuomintang over much of China between 1927 and 1949.

What is especially significant is that such moral protest was also directed against the Communist Party by many of its own dedicated followers during the formative years of the party hierarchy in Yan'an from 1936 to 1945, and in Manchuria between 1946 and 1948. This same courage in maintaining a critical stance toward the inequities concealed within revolutionary rhetoric and activism never faded during the People's Republic either. Its most vibrant expressions came during the Hundred Flowers outpourings of 1957, the years of 1962–1965 just before the Cultural Revolution, at Democracy Wall in 1978, and in the renaissance of Chinese critical writing in the early 1980s. The hard thinking about democracy and its implications that surfaced in 1989 had, therefore, sprung from deep roots.

The idea of student protest has a different kind of pedigree. In the first place, the emergence of any such thing depended on a shift of values within Chinese society, such that the views of the young could be seen as mattering to the society as a whole—and this was not true of Chinese society before the nineteenth-century contacts with the West, and the changes in Chinese thinking that followed. Prior to that time, intellectual protest was the fruit of wisdom and experience—that was what gave it its significance. Those who were still young, and at a formative stage in education, were regarded as too ignorant to merit having their views heard.

There had to be, also, a forum in which youthful views could be expressed, and a set of issues around such views could be validly focused. The changing educational system and new modes of cheap mass-circulation publishing doubtless contributed more than anything else to this development. The Chinese students congregated in Japanese academies and universities in the late nineteenth and early twentieth centuries, and the dramatic growth in the number of colleges and universities within China itself after 1912, brought young students together in ways that had not existed before. They found mutual solidarity and moral support from within their own ranks, and no longer had to limit the expression of their views.

In terms of issues that galvanized the students, it is significant that in each of the major student demonstrations that had a major impact on China in the first half of this century—those of 1919, 1926, and 1935— the spark was anti-Japanese nationalism. Japan was perceived by the young as China's greatest enemy, and the need for a united national resistance against the Japanese was the students' central demand. The unwillingness or inability of either the warlords or the Kuomintang government to launch effective resistance against Japan was what drew the students together. The students knew that such acts of protest could lead to violent repression, and they were both bold and defiant. In 1919 and 1935 the protests were dispersed by police force without many casualties, but in 1926 dozens were shot to death and many more wounded by government troops.

The issue of nationalism in all these examples also edged over into a demand for more democracy, as the students realized that only some participatory concessions by the government would lead to policy changes. But democracy was, inevitably, a series of generalized ideas simplified into slogans, rather than a carefully thought-through plan for institutional reforms. Except for the few students who had lived and studied overseas, the concept of democracy was still an abstraction.

For many years after 1949, the CCP, in the name of revolutionary discipline and the interests of the one-party state, was able to mute any expression of student dissidence. Ambitious and able students were processed through the Communist Youth League, via the rare places in colleges and universities, into the CCP itself and specially assigned jobs. It took extraordinary courage and levels of dissatisfaction to speak out in such circumstances, though some students were startlingly forthright in the Hundred Flowers Movement. The use of the students by Mao Tsetung in the Cultural Revolution was an exceptional one, in light of the earlier pattern, for the students' awe of Mao and the presence of so many high-school students in the Red Guard ranks led to unthinking excesses of extraordinary violence, and to a complete absence of any specific nationalist element, despite the shrill anti-superpower rhetoric. But in the light of what happened in 1989, it does seem that many senior CCP leaders, humiliated, dismissed, and beaten up in 1966, responded to the huge chanting crowds of 1989 with anguished memories of twenty-three years before firmly in their minds.

Once the Cultural Revolution faded, a return to the earlier pattern of student protest reappeared: principled, linked to yearnings for the strength and prosperity of the nation, and imbued with hope for a participation in the decision making through some form of democracy. At Tiananmen Square in 1976, at Democracy Wall in 1978, at Hefei in 1986, students showed the same courage, the same intelligent awareness of the central issues, and the same bonds of solidarity that had marked their actions in the warlord and Kuomintang periods.

Why was it the case that all these political protesters, of whatever age and in whatever period, risked their lives each time they spoke out? The question is not a simple one, and an attempt to answer it probes at the heart of the Chinese state. From the first days of consolidated and unified empire, in the third century B.C., the Chinese emperors showed a tendency both to resent and to fear criticism. All sorts of rulers have done the same, in all sort of states, but in China the contrast between the actions of the rulers and their professed ideology seems particularly acute. In theory, an emperor represented a pivotal point between heaven and earth; he mediated between the two, and thus his own moral character was central to the well-being of all his people, and even to favorable weather for their crops and the absence of blights and natural disasters. A special office, the censorate, was designed and staffed to provide a nucleus of upright officials whose main function was to remind the emperor of his own moral obligations, and to point out his shortcomings to him. The existence of this avenue for criticism was enough to isolate other critics from the official policy process when the system was working effectively—as it sometimes did, for there have been many good and responsible rulers in China's long history. But when the system was flawed, or the temperament of the ruler hostile to any form of frank exchange, critical debate at any level became dangerous.

One of the tragic continuities of this situation was the absence of any concept of "loyal opposition" in Chinese political life. When things were going right, no criticism was needed. When things were going badly, no criticism was tolerated. Bold ministers did speak up, and educated men in office did express their feelings in poems and essays, but if their expressed views contradicted the dominant state view, they could and did lose their offices or their lives. Laws for treason were extraordinarily vague, and there was no protection for rights of assembly, association, debate, or expression. These freedoms were not granted in the new republic after 1912, either, since the first president, Yuan Shikai, took political dissent as personal criticism. Nor did they gain ground in the warlord years, or under Chiang Kai-shek. Chiang used Sun Yat-sen's concept of the necessity of an extended period of "tutelage" before the Chinese people could be ready for democracy as an excuse for heading off indefinitely any serious discussion—let alone implementation—of democratic structures.

The PRC in its turn, after 1949, could duck all notions of the need for democratic participation in government by claiming that China was a socialist state led by the Party, which itself represented the people. Nobody but class enemies, accordingly, had any cause to complain; and those who did complain were, therefore, obviously class enemies. At no period in Chinese history, furthermore, has there been any independent judiciary not subject to political manipulation or control by the center. There were some attempts to encourage such growth in the republican period, and brave, committed personnel ready to serve with integrity; but there were so many years of civil war, foreign invasion, and internal insurrection that "emergency" powers were constantly invoked by the state, making any coherent judicial growth impossible. One of the greatest ironies of the 1989 demonstrations was that many of the posters and banners carried by "disloyal" students simply listed clauses from the PRC's own Constitution that "guaranteed" rights to freedom of assembly and debate, rights that the state had never in fact permitted.

Cutting across these questions of value and repression were the problems posed for the PRC leadership by the power of Western science and culture. Since 1978, Deng Xiaoping had pledged that China would embrace elements from the West to develop its economy and strengthen the nation. And after the mid-1980s this process accelerated as China modified its control of industry and agriculture, opening them up to individual initiative and incentive. Inevitably this shook up the whole system of balances and trade-offs that had become an accepted part of state-socialist life in China. But Communist Party dominance of the economic world now became more problematic, and the problem of graft both deeper and more obvious. As the government sought to raise the level of China's pool of highly trained technical personnel by sending them abroad for advanced training, and to speed up levels of industrial production and energy exploration at home through joint ventures, it was inevitable that a sea of new ideas and influences came washing into the society. In the mid-1980s, Deng and other anxious government leaders (including both Hu Yaobang and Zhao Ziyang) had sought to isolate China from this contagion by launching mass campaigns against "spiritual pollution" and

"bourgeois liberalization," but with little success. The 1989 demonstrations were suffused with elements drawn from the West, just as they were
recorded by Western audio- and video-tape, and beamed by satellite to
viewers around the world. Yet in the crackdown after June 4, the leaders
vehemently insisted that they could separate out the intellectual and cultural side of the Western capitalist culture from its technological and scientific achievements.

This, I believe, is an impossible task. It is also an effort that has been
made before, with some tenacity, by the rulers of China in the late nineteenth century. At that time the Manchu rulers of the Qing, along with
many of their senior Chinese officials, tried to separate out what they
considered the heart of China's traditional moral and cultural values and
to protect them from the impact of Western ideas. Even with all the resources of a state-supervised educational system channeled through state-
run examinations, with the army and police at home, and Qing inspectors
and coopted student informants abroad, they could not stop the system
from unraveling. For each new technological development—military ar-
senals, steamships, railways, coal mines—led to unexpected spin-offs, to
a search for the ideas that lay behind the inventions, and to a need to
propagate the technologies themselves more widely. Thus did new
schools (including now those for women), newspapers and magazines,
debating societies, chambers of commerce, and translations of hundreds
of foreign books move in an accelerating cycle to circumvent all attempts
at closure.

If there is hope for today's China, perhaps it lies here. Not that we are
yet in one world, or that we all want one homogeneous world even if that
were possible. But certain forces of shared experience, vitality, and
change are entering international discourse, and China's rulers cannot
shut them all out. If only the leaders can come to see that those forces can
be benign as well as harmful, perhaps they will no longer need to gun
down their own people in their own streets. Perhaps they will read the
protestors' words instead, those words on which the writers spent much
time and thought. Such hopes are frail, I admit. But one of the graces of
this book is that we, at least, thanks to these skilful translations, can make
our own judgment as to whether the words were worth listening to, or
not.

EDITORS' FOREWORD

Youth are precious because of their purity, sensitivity, enthusiasm,
and courage. They are full of the new, sharp vigor of life. The
darkness that others have not felt they first perceive; the
filth that others have not seen, they first see; the words that others
will not and dare not utter, they speak boldly. Thus, while their criticisms may
be a bit excessive, they are not mere "grumbling"; their words perhaps are
not that balanced, but they are not necessarily mere "clamoring." From these
phenomena of "grumbling," "clamoring," and "restlessness," we should seek
out the nature of the problems that have given rise to them, and rationally
(note: rationally! youth are not necessarily always just "blindly raising
an uproar") eliminate the root causes of these phenomena.
Wang Shiwei, "The Wild Lily," Yan'an, 1942

China's youth spoke in the spring of 1989 with a purity and passion that
moved all but those who had the power to address the deep-rooted causes
of their grievances. They spoke to fellow Chinese and to all peoples with
peaceful protests whose images, caught by foreign print and television
journalists, transfixed the world: three student representatives kneeling
to offer a petition; hunger strikers lying weak and nearly motionless under a blazing sun; and the lone figure blocking a column of tanks from
advancing. Chinese students also expressed their hope, anger, conviction,
and dissatisfaction in thousands of posters, handbills, public statements,
and speeches. Powerful and provocative as these writings and words from
the 1989 Democracy Movement were, they did not reach the wide audience they deserve because they could neither be captured by the eye of the
lens nor be understood by non-Chinese speakers. *Cries for Democracy*
partially fills this gap by presenting in English translation a selection of
these writings and speeches.

The voices in *Cries for Democracy*, however, are not only student ones.
The power of the students' words and actions was such that millions of
supporters staged the largest pro-democracy, anti-government protests in
the forty-year history of Communist rule. Intellectuals and journalists
were particularly active during the Democracy Movement, and their pe-

titions, statements, and posters appear frequently here. Writings by other citizens, including a selection of pieces from workers' "autonomous" (nongovernmental) unions, also appear in the book. Finally, because the Democracy Movement can only be understood within the context of the Chinese Communist Party's and government's responses to the student and citizen protests, excerpts from major government announcements, as well as from crucial speeches by Party leaders, are included in every chapter.

The Democracy Movement was a drama, a celebration, and a tragedy whose story line could not have been predicted by anyone in or out of China. It is a story so compelling that we have chosen to present most of the documents in rough chronological order rather than thematically, and to supplement or introduce the selections with a narrative or commentary, as appropriate. We have been guided primarily by two criteria in our selection of materials: first, forcefulness or originality of thought; and second, diversity in terms of the views advocated and the events or issues addressed. The great bulk of writings from the Democracy Movement were spontaneous political and emotional expressions, often written in considerable haste; thus, literary merit has only been a factor in our choice of poetry, and then not always the deciding one. If there are relatively few selections that are critical of, or directly oppose, the pro-democracy protestors (other than government ones), this is primarily attributable to the fact that extremely few anti-protestor materials could be found in Beijing or other cities during the Democracy Movement, rather than to any unwillingness to insert them.

The materials in *Cries for Democracy* encompass big- and small-character posters, handbills (leaflets), open letters or public declarations that were circulated in Beijing and often released in Hong Kong, selections from people's (nongovernment-approved) Democracy Movement journals, a firsthand account of a participant in the protests, an excerpt from a television screenplay, transcripts of audiovisual or audio tapes, and copies of internal speeches or remarks by Party leaders. To aid readers faced with such disparate primary materials, we have placed an attribution at the end of each selection explaining the nature of the piece, its original location, and its approximate date; in some cases, however, this information was not available or is not complete. The main sources of the original documents have been our own photographs of such documents; photos contributed by American students or researchers who were in China in the spring of 1989; photos and their transcriptions by *October Review*, a Hong Kong journal; originals and copies of handbills, and newspaper or magazine transcripts of speeches and public statements. To the extent possible, we have verified the authenticity of materials chosen for translation; while we were unable to verify independently the authenticity of the internal speeches of Party leaders, they have been published in reputable Hong Kong and American sources. Aside from a few materials that appear in Chapter 6, the concluding chapter of the book, all the writings and speeches in *Cries for Democracy* were written or made in China.

Most of the materials listed above require no explanation. The big-character poster (*dazibao*), however, is a uniquely Chinese form of political expression meriting a brief introduction. The big-character poster is nothing more than a largish piece of paper, perhaps two by three feet, on which the writer has written his or her views, typically using ink and brush to make large-size characters legible from a distance. Some big-character posters may consist of a single sheet; others may extend over many sheets; the famous "Liyizhe" (a pseudonym) poster entitled "A Call for Democracy and Rule by Law," which caused a sensation after it appeared in Guangdong in 1974, went on for sixty-four sheets, or some 20,000 Chinese characters.

Simple in form, big-character posters have become the most famous and common mode of political expression in the Communist era. Their prominent role in political expression is traceable to pragmatic and historical factors. Posters are popular because they are one of the few outlets of expression available to Chinese who desire to make a dissenting political statement or to raise a personal grievance. At negligible expense, a big-character poster enables an individual to reach a large audience: posted at a prominent site, such as a university bulletin board or a city wall, a poster may be read by hundreds or thousands.

The special significance of big-character posters, however, stems from their historical background. As early as the late 1930s and early 1940s of the Yan'an period, when the young Communist Party led by Mao Tse-tung was struggling to build itself into a revolutionary force, loyal critics of the Party such as Wang Shiwei, an idealistic 36-year-old expert on ideology whose essay "The Wild Lily" probed the "darkness" of Yan'an, used big-character posters to voice their criticism. The power of the big-character poster already showed itself at this early time: a poster by Wang Shiwei censuring Party leaders for corruption and their intolerance of differing viewpoints created considerable excitement among young revolutionaries and sparked an intense debate among them about the Party's practices.

The institutionalization of big-character posters as a form of political expression did not come, however, until the Anti-Rightist Campaign of

1957, during which Mao Tse-tung encouraged his supporters to use big-character posters to respond to and denounce intellectuals who had criticized the Party. Mao further promoted the big-character poster as political weapon in the 1966–1969 Cultural Revolution. Believing that the mass media were controlled by his rivals, Mao urged students and his other adherents to use posters to arouse the masses to join the struggle against bourgeois enemies. During this period, the abuses possible with big-character posters also became evident: anonymous posters slandered individuals, basely attacked the Maoists' opponents, and incited violence.

Big-character posters were viewed by Maoists as such an effective means of expression for the masses that the right of citizens to draft the posters was enshrined in the 1975 Constitution, and included again in the 1978 Constitution. But by 1979, the classless "magic mirrors that show up monsters of all kinds" which had served Mao so well were being turned on the Communist leadership itself. During the 1979–1980 Democracy Wall Movement, posters questioned the authority of the Communist Party and demanded democratic rights. This challenge, and his own bitter personal experience as a victim of a massive poster campaign in 1975–1976, prompted Deng Xiaoping to have the right to write posters deleted from the Constitution in 1980.

Yet, Chinese citizens continue to write and post big-character posters. Student protests in the 1980s, whether large or small, have invariably been heralded by a flurry of indignant posters rallying students to action.

The spring of 1989 was no exception. Hundreds of big-character posters, and their cousins the "small-character posters" (*xiaozibao*), which we have rather unscientifically defined as posters whose characters are too small to be read from more than a foot or two away, went up on campuses at the very beginning of the pro-democracy protests. They drew thousands of readers, of whom many but not all were students and teachers; the sites where posters were most highly concentrated—usually at the students' dining hall and centrally located bulletin boards normally reserved for official use—became the gathering points for student demonstrators and announcements. Each development in the Democracy Movement brought a fresh wave of posters: reports on the latest events, analyses, calls to action, and new manifestos. Even in the second half of the movement, when the focus of activity had shifted away from campuses to Tiananmen Square, and increasing quantities of handbills were being produced, students never ceased to talk to each other and any others who cared to listen through posters to campuses.

The Chinese Communist Party in 1942 chose to silence Wang Shiwei rather than heed his words. Only a few months after urging Party leaders in "The Wild Lily" to consider why many youth and intellectuals at Yan'an complained in private of the indifference of Party bureaucrats, inegalitarianism, leaders' special privileges, and the Party's intolerance of dissent, Wang Shiwei became the target of fierce attack for these and other unorthodox views. Unlike other writers who had expressed critical views, Wang refused to admit any mistakes in his thinking. Unable to remold Wang, leaders of the Party did away with him: in 1947, Wang was secretly executed by decapitation.

Nearly half a century later, with a brutal military assault and a ruthless repression, the Chinese Communist Party once again has demonstrated that it finds it far easier to eliminate its critics than to face their criticisms. We the editors, who cannot at this time reveal our identities, know that our tears and anger will not bring back those who cried for democracy. Yet, we do not despair for China. Unlike Wang Shiwei, a victim of one of the Party's first purges, the youth who spoke out in 1989 were fully aware of the perils of doing so. The fear of Party retaliation did not stop them. Nor will it in the years to come.

Han Minzhu ("Chinese Democracy")
and Hua Sheng ("A Voice of China"),
Berkeley and New York, March 1990

ACKNOWLEDGMENTS

This book was made possible through the enthusiastic contributions of many people who generously provided assistance and resources, often on short notice. Unfortunately, the continuing repression in China makes it impossible to name here friends in Beijing who provided me with materials during the Democracy Movement.

One friend from Beijing who is now living in the United States can be directly thanked. He is "Hua Sheng," the Assistant Editor of this book. His knowledge, judgment, and dedication have been invaluable.

Many of the translations in the book are based on compilations of primary materials from the Democracy Movement published with great speed and accuracy by the Hong Kong journal *October Review*. I would like to thank in particular Chan Cheong and Zhang Kai of *October Review* for taking the time to respond to my numerous requests in connection with these primary materials. I would also like to thank photographer Franki Chan (Chan Muk Nam) for so selflessly donating the cover photograph as well as many other photos that grace this book. His generosity and trust are deeply appreciated.

The final form of many of these translations reflects the hard work of Wei Cheng. His ability to bridge the often perplexing gap between the Chinese and English languages has enabled the Chinese represented here to speak to Western readers that much more clearly and lucidly. Stephen Fleming's polishing of translations in Chapter 5 greatly improved the readability of selections in that chapter. Margot Landman spent many long evenings reviewing drafts of the manuscript, laboring to improve the prose of the commentary and translations, catching inconsistencies, and otherwise lending her energy and wisdom to this project.

A number of Americans and Chinese translated the original documents, often donating their time. Some of their translations were dropped in the final selection of pieces; many were revised. I trust that the translators will understand the personal preferences of this editor. My thanks to John Kiesch, James Dunlap, Chris Connery, Toby Feldman, Mary Scott, Dory Poa, Randy LaPolla, Wendy Locks, Dan Cole, Wu Ming, Ping, Nancy Murphy, Steve Davis, J. Wang, L. H. Murphy, Hilary Josephs, Bettina Schroeder, Jan Shelburne, Nicolas Howson, David Blumental, Stephen Fleming, and Wei Cheng.

A number of friends, old and new, in Hong Kong provided invaluable help in my efforts to collect materials for the book. These include Leung Mei Fun, Fan Cheuk Wan, Zhu Ren Lian, and Lai Pui Yee. Thomas Leung of Sing Tao Newspapers and Paul K. B. Cheung of Ming Pao Newspapers kindly gave me access to their newspapers' photo collections. And my thanks to G., S., and E. in Hong Kong and to T. in Beijing.

Nicolas Howson provided many insightful comments on Chapters 1 and 2. David Blumental, Toby Feldman, Marsha Wagner, and Melissa McCauley were wonderful and enthusiastic sources of information and contacts. The calligraphy that opens the book was done by Xiao Li. Jean and David, Shen Feng, Tristan Mabry, Wei Jiuan, Norman Kutcher, and the Center for Chinese Legal Studies at Columbia University also contributed to this book in a number of ways. James Anderson, Zhenya Erlij, and Steve Judd, eyewitnesses to events in Nanjing, furnished important materials from that city.

During the writing of this book two friends who had enthusiastically contributed translations tragically died: Yang Xiaoping in New York and Meng Xiaoping in Canada.

Joe Katz, Liu Yuan of the China Information Center in Newton, Massachusetts, Kim Fung, Huang Jingsheng of the Association of Chinese Students and Scholars in Stanford, and Yang Jianli of the Berkeley Coordinating Committee for China all assisted in getting this project off the ground last summer. Gene Young, John Major, and Linda Allen offered advice as I was writing the book proposal. Margot Landman, Jan Shelburne, Laurel, Ed, and Jocelyn were a crack team of proofreaders who generously donated their time in the crucial last stage of the book.

I am indebted to my firm for generously granting me a leave of absence to work on this book.

The man on the answering machine fortunately remains my closest and most patient friend despite eight trying months. Only his companionship and encouragement enabled me to meet what seemed to be an endless series of Federal Express deadlines.

Special thanks to my editor, Margaret Case, whose enthusiasm and support for this project has transformed an idea into a book. In addition to exerting tremendous efforts to bring this book out as quickly as possible, she has remarkably never lost faith that the next Federal Express package would arrive.

Han Minzhu

CRIES FOR DEMOCRACY

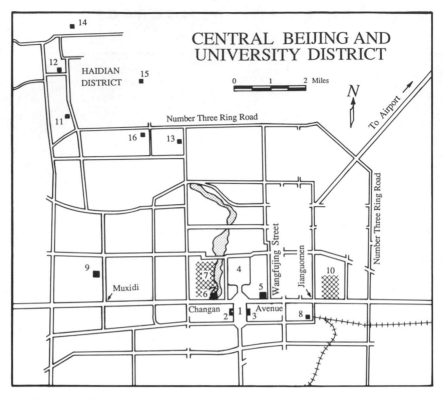

CENTRAL BEIJING AND UNIVERSITY DISTRICT

HAIDIAN DISTRICT

0 1 2 Miles

N

To Airport

Number Three Ring Road

Number Three Ring Road

Muxidi

Wangfujing Street

Jianguomen

Changan Avenue

1 Tiananmen Square
2 Great Hall of the People
3 Museums of the Chinese Revolution and Chinese History
4 Forbidden City
5 Beijing Hotel
6 Xinhuamen (rear entrance to Zhongnanhai)
7 Zhongnanhai (Chinese Communist Party compound)
8 Beijing Railroad Station
9 State Guesthouse
10 Embassy Area
11 People's University
12 Beijing University
13 Beijing Normal University
14 Qinghua University
15 Beijing Aeronautics Institute
16 University of Politics and Law

THE BIRTH OF THE 1989 DEMOCRACY MOVEMENT

"Those Who Should Have Died Live;

Those Who Should Have Lived Have Died"

April 15 – 22

"The process of democratization in China must be in accordance with national conditions; we cannot move too quickly."
Premier Li Peng, March 1989

"This disturbance was bound to come sooner or later. . . . It was definitely coming and was something that could not be diverted by man's will; it was only a matter of time and scale."
Deng Xiaoping, June 9, 1989

I've asked you over and over,
When will you come away with me?
But you always laugh at me,
For I have nothing to my name.

I want to give you yearnings,
And there too is my freedom,
But you always laugh at me,
For I have nothing to my name.

from pop song, "Nothing to My Name," by Cui Jian

"Carry out the behest of Hu Yaobang: advance the cause of democracy!"

C hina in early 1989 was a tinderbox of suppressed anger, mounting despair, and corrosive envy. Many Chinese were angry at rampant corruption in the government and the petty arbitrariness of Chinese Communist Party bureaucrats. Many were highly skeptical that the current leadership was capable of leading the nation out of its morass of corruption, double-digit inflation, stalled economic reforms, and a perceived breakdown in social order. And many were unhappy, though often they would not admit it, that a neighbor or some uneducated riff-raff down the street had become yet another one of the successful "10,000 yuan (dollar)" entrepreneurs of the vaunted reforms while their own state-fixed incomes remained at a few thousand yuan a year.

Nowhere was this potent combination of dissatisfaction and despair more evident than on China's university campuses. Here, the cream of Chinese youth studied amid appallingly crowded and uncomfortable conditions. A good number were not even interested in their studies: China's outmoded and inflexible educational system was characterized by static teaching and the peculiarity that many students, desperate to gain admittance to any university, enrolled in departments they were little interested in. And aside from those in fields that had become more important and lucrative under the economic reforms of the 1980s—disciplines such as international economics, English, some sciences, and law—students hardly looked forward to their future jobs. Seeing no answer to China's woes and little prospect of meaningful change, they turned cynical. Better to go abroad to study, they reasoned, or have a stab at making a bit of money while they could than to fret about matters beyond their control. Young teachers were no less disgruntled: they worked and lived under conditions that ranged from barely acceptable to dismal, while their freedom to teach was often restricted by arbitrary department heads or school authorities.

But then, as had happened in China in the past, the death of a popular leader jolted Chinese consciences and provided an emotional charge that ignited long-contained resentment. On April 15, Hu Yaobang, former head of the Party, collapsed while trying to get out of his hospital bed, where he was recuperating from a heart attack suffered a week earlier. Hu died at 7:53 in the morning. Within hours of his passing away, and before any official announcement had been made, Chinese campuses had come alive as students spontaneously began to express their grief for Hu.

Hu's premature death at the age of seventy-three touched a special chord with students because his tolerance of student demonstrations and unwillingness to wage ideological war on Western political and cultural influences had led to his fall from power in 1987. Outspoken and impulsive by nature, Hu had been a political liberal

5

who more than any other high Party leader had urged the Party to heed criticisms from youth and intellectuals. Yet he had paid a high price for his liberal views: in January 1987, following large student pro-democracy demonstrations across the country, he had been forced to resign by Deng Xiaoping, his erstwhile mentor. Although at the time Deng clearly acted under pressure from conservative Party elders who viewed dissent as politically threatening and ideologically unacceptable, there is also reason to believe that he had become disenchanted with his former protégé. Hu's sacrifice for the students, as well as his leading role in having intellectuals and others who had been unjustly attacked in the Cultural Revolution "rehabilitated," or their names and rights restored, had made him a deeply admired and respected figure among students and intellectuals.

Thus, at dozens of major universities in Beijing the reaction to Hu's death was swift. Numerous elegies and essays in Hu's memory were posted on the walls of central school buildings. By 4:30 in the afternoon, the first mourners had appeared in Tiananmen Square, the symbolic heart of Beijing and the country, where they laid at the Monument to the People's Heroes white paper flower mourning wreaths adorned with vertical strips of paper bearing elegiac couplets—a traditional Chinese manner of honoring the memory of a deceased. Over the next few days, many more processions of students spontaneously formed and marched from their campuses in the northwest district of Beijing some ten miles to Tiananmen. During these marches, they not only carried mourning wreaths and banners, but also shouted slogans and waved signs calling for an end to corruption in the government and for the introduction of democratic reforms.

Our exploration of writings and speeches from the 1989 Democracy Movement begins with a selection of elegiac couplets that appeared on campuses or in Tiananmen.

ELEGIAC COUPLETS

Those who should have died live,
Those who should have lived have died.

A sincere and honest man has died,
But the hypocritical and false live on.
A warm-hearted man has died,
Indifference buried him.

A star of hope has fallen[1]—China meets with calamity;
The ordinary people are angry; if they were not angry,
    what would be the way out?
    What a shame, what a shame!

One man who cared for all under heaven;
For one man all under heaven mourn.

Seeking self-governance for the people, attempting to make the country
    strong and prosperous,
What faults were these?
Upon hearing of the untimely death of an outstanding hero, upon seeing
    that the universe remains the same as before,
Who can remain unmoved?
    Yaobang, rest in peace.

Those with vested interests, obstinate, will not break;
When will the state's policies be accomplished?
Those who faced the darkness were banished and died in disgrace,
Where lies the path for our generation?

Old Mao fell, Old "D" fell,[2]
History will have its justice.
Elder Zhou has gone, Elder Hu has departed,[3]
We feel the same grief, we feel the same worries.

It is difficult for one man to illuminate the country,
But one man is enough to make the country perish.

National news, domestic news, all the news under heaven,
The news clouds the clear blue sky.

1. Many couplets used the metaphor of light or illumination because part of Hu's name,
"Yaobang," can be literally interpreted to mean "to shine on or to illuminate the country."
The writer may also be making an allusion to the belief in imperial times that a falling star
was an omen of misfortune.
2. "Old Mao" refers to Mao Tse-tung; "Old 'D' " refers to Deng Xiaoping.
3. "Zhou" refers to former Premier Zhou Enlai, a cosmopolitan statesman who died in
1976 and who is still highly respected by many older Chinese. "Elder" is used as a term of
respect for Zhou and Hu, in contrast to the rather familiar, slightly disrespectful form of
address of "Old" for Mao and Deng.

The sound of wind, the sound of rain, the sound of books being read,
Every sound calls out for a heroic soul.[4]

We sing a long song in place of weeping; we weep for a man only five
   feet tall.[5]
A man who crossed rocky lands and troubled seas!
Suddenly, we turn around to see a hundred million living souls
   awakening the heroic spirit of China.

"Down with Corruption! Long Live Democracy!
Long Live Freedom!"

Student discontent had been brewing for some time. Although no large-scale student unrest had occurred since the 1987 protests, pent-up dissatisfaction had already boiled over into street demonstrations several times during 1988. The immediate cause of the protests varied. In some cases, it was racial tension between
African and Chinese students. For example, at a dance at Hehai University in Nanjing in December 1988, a brawl between some African students and Chinese students and staff had led to angry protest marches denouncing Africans for allegedly
assaulting Chinese women and beating up other students. In other cases, the trigger
had been an attack on students by hooligans. Thus, in spring 1988, after three un-
employed youths killed a Beijing University student in a confrontation in a restaurant
near the campus, over a thousand Beijing University students marched to Tiananmen, demanding retribution and measures to improve school security and public
order. But in each instance, the underlying cause for the demonstrations, which
were disproportionately large and passionate compared to the original incidents,
was the students' feeling that education and intellectuals were undervalued by the
Party and government. Indeed, some of the Hehai students had expressed resentment that the Africans (who constituted the majority of third-world students studying in China on Chinese government scholarships) received far larger living stipends

4. The "heroic soul" refers to Hu Yaobang. This is an adaptation of a patriotic Ming dynasty couplet by Gao Panlong expressing the poet's concern for his country. The original
reads, "The sound of wind, the sound of rain, the sound of books being read / Every sound
enters my ears. / Domestic news, national news, the news of all under heaven, / I take all of
this news to heart." Shortly after Hu's forced resignation from the leadership of the Party in
January 1987, students expressed their sense of powerlessness by rewriting the poem, to
read: "The sound of wind, the sound of rain, the sound of books being read / And now dead
silence reigns / Domestic news, national news, the news of all under heaven, / But who gives
a shit about news anymore anyway."
5. Hu was a small man whose slight stature belied his energy and fieriness.

Illustration 1.1. Thousands of students applaud as a large oil portrait of Hu Yaobang by students from the Central Academy of Arts is placed at the Monument to the People's Heroes in the center of Tiananmen Square during the first week of mourning and protest demonstrations. Credit: Abbas / Magnum.

than they did themselves. Similarly, Beijing students who protested after the killing saw in it not just a larger breakdown in social order but also evidence of the government's failure adequately to safeguard intellectuals from rougher elements of Chinese society.

For these reasons, student response to Hu's death quickly moved beyond mourning to heated protests for democracy, an end to corruption in the Party, and freedom of the press. The most active and vocal students were those at Beijing University, China's most prestigious university, which boasted a rich tradition, stretching back to the May Fourth Democracy Movement, of spearheading student protests against government policies. Shortly after midnight on April 18—setting off from the campus this late so as to minimize the possibility of interference from authorities—three thousand Beijing University students, shouting "Long live freedom! Down with bureaucracy!" led a night march to Tiananmen; several thousand students from People's University joined them. In the dawn hours of the 18th, they attempted to deliver a petition containing seven student demands to the Standing Committee of the National People's Congress, China's nominal parliament, and to meet with a representative of the Standing Committee. The demands called for the government to: (1) reevaluate Hu Yaobang and his achievements; (2) renounce the

[1987] Anti-Bourgeois Liberalization campaign and the [1983] Anti-Spiritual Pollution campaign;[6] (3) allow citizens to publish nonofficial newspapers and end censorship of the press; (4) reveal the salaries and other wealth of Party and government leaders and their families; (5) rescind the Beijing municipal government's "Ten Provisional Articles Regulating Public Marches and Demonstrations";[7] (6) increase state expenditures for higher education; and (7) provide objective news coverage of the students' demonstrations.

To the students' frustration and anger, no representative of the Standing Committee came out to meet them, and they were forced to leave their petition with an office functionary. In the next piece, a poster from People's University, a student

6. The Anti-Bourgeois Liberalization campaign refers to the campaign against Western political ideas initiated in January 1987 by Party conservatives after the student demonstrations in the winter of 1986. It was short-lived; relatively few high leaders firmly believed in it, and lower-level Party officials reduced its impact with passive resistance, only perfunctorily implementing political study sessions and other measures called for by the campaign's proponents. Its forerunner in the Party's spasmodic battle against the encroachment of liberalism was the 1983 Anti-Spiritual Pollution drive, which similarly attacked Western values of individualism, freedom, and artistic license. The Anti-Spiritual Pollution campaign lasted for some five months, from October 1983 to February 1984, but was thwarted by the refusal of Hu Yaobang and other moderates to pursue it. Hu's failure to join the battle against bourgeois liberalization infuriated Party conservatives and contributed to his downfall in 1987.

7. The "Ten Provisional Articles Regulating Public Marches and Demonstrations," commonly referred to as the "Ten Articles," were a set of regulations hastily adopted by Beijing authorities after the outbreak of the 1986 student demonstrations. Under the regulations, groups wishing to hold a demonstration were required to apply at least five days in advance for a permit; no marches and demonstrations were permitted without the permit. Demonstrations were prohibited in the vicinity of the Great Hall of the People, Zhongnanhai (the Party compound west of Tiananmen Square), the state guesthouse, and the airport; Tiananmen Square was not specifically mentioned. The Public Security Bureau had great latitude for denying a permit: under broadly worded Article Six, permits could be denied if the authorities determined that the proposed demonstration could adversely affect "social order, work, education, scientific research, or day-to-day order." The requirement that the organizer of the march furnish his name, occupation, and full address had discouraged applications. Only three applications for marches were made after the regulations' promulgation, two of these by foreigners.

In the aftermath of the Democracy Movement, the Chinese government has taken steps to further restrict citizens' ability to stage demonstrations, particularly in Beijing and Tiananmen Square, promulgating the first national law on rallies, marches, and demonstrations on October 31, 1989. In addition requiring the filing of detailed applications for a permit, the law prohibits citizens from organizing or participating in demonstrations in cities in which they do not reside. New Beijing municipal government regulations, more detailed and restrictive than the original "Ten Articles," have also been enacted. Demonstrations and rallies are now explicitly banned in Tiananmen Square unless permission from municipal and national (State Council) authorities is first obtained.

who participated in the petition march recounts the students' feelings during the protest.

A RECORD OF THE APRIL 18
SIT-IN DEMONSTRATION

A little after midnight yesterday, more than three thousand students from Beijing University rushed out of the campus onto the streets. Some ten or so students were carrying a very large memorial banner on which had been written "Soul of China." When the marchers passed People's University, another several thousand students from People's University joined their ranks. Although many students returned to campus in the course of the march, two or three thousand students reached Tiananmen Square, where they began a sit-in protest, loudly chanting, "Long live democracy!" "Long live freedom!" "Long live rule by law!" "Oppose tyranny!" "Oppose dictatorship!" "Strictly punish government profiteering by officials!" and singing the "Internationale" and the "March of the Volunteers."[8] The momentum [of the moment] was magnificent.

At dawn, after a discussion, the students in the Square from Beijing University and People's University decided to present the demands of the greater student body to the Standing Committee of the National People's Congress (NPC).[9] However, they waited for a long time until finally someone who claimed to be a staff member of the preparation working group for Hu Yaobang's funeral came out. But he said that he could not answer any questions. The students' representatives negotiated with him. Then the deputy bureau chief of the Complaints Section of the Standing Committee came out. He agreed to convey the students' suggestions to the Standing Committee of the NPC and to forward them up to the Cen-

---

8. The "March of the Volunteers" is the Chinese national anthem. It was written in the 1930s by the famous composer Nie Er to inspire Chinese during the War of Resistance against Japan. Its words are as follows: "Arise, you who refuse to be slaves! Let our blood and flesh form a new Great Wall! The time of greatest danger for the Chinese people is here, from each one of us the last call to action comes forth: Arise! Arise! Arise! Millions united, braving the enemy's fire, march on! Braving the enemy's fire, March on! March on! March on!"

9. The National People's Congress (NPC) is China's nominal parliament. Although the Chinese Constitution provides that the NPC is the "highest organ of state power," it is essentially a rubber stamp that meets but once a year to ratify decisions already made by the Party. When the NPC is not in session, its powers are exercised by its Standing Committee.

tral Committee of the Party.[10] . . . He wanted everyone to leave the Square. A Vice President of Beijing University also urged the students to return to their schools. There was no response to the students' request to have a direct dialogue with one or two members of the Standing Committee of the NPC.

In our opinion, one or two members of the Standing Committee, even the Chairman of the Standing Committee, do not have the power to make any decisions about our demands. However, the representatives of the people have the duty and responsibility to receive and present the demands of the people. People have a right to meet with their representatives, a right that is guaranteed by the Constitution.[11] Furthermore, those students who participated in the sit-in demonstration agreed to return to their campuses so long as a member of the Standing Committee of the NPC came to receive their requests and agreed to present them to the Standing Committee. Why was not such a small request granted? We cannot help but ask: who, after all, does the NPC, the highest governmental organ, serve?

We were moved by the fact that many people gave the sit-in protestors both material support (providing them with tea, soda, ice-cream sticks, cigarettes, bread, and donations of money) and moral support. The students shouted loudly: "Long live the people!" and "Long live understanding!". . .

This afternoon at 4:00, when I left Tiananmen Square, there were still two to three hundred people sitting in protest in front of the Great Hall of the People.

Students of People's University: "What do you think of this event?" and "What are you going to do?"

—A witness from People's University,
afternoon, April 19
(poster at People's University)

10. Decision-making power in the Chinese Communist Party is concentrated in the Politburo, an elite group of twenty-odd high-ranking Party leaders. Within the Politburo, the first among equals is the Politburo Standing Committee, a group that in recent years has consisted of five or six persons who constitute the top leadership of the country. The Party Central Committee is a larger body of over two hundred members that is in itself not very powerful, but whose members hold leading positions in the military, government, and Party. As of 1989, however, the supreme leader of the country was not a Politburo member, but Deng Xiaoping, Chairman of the Party's Central Military Commission.

11. Article 76 of the Constitution states that representatives of the NPC "shall maintain close contact with the original units and people who elected them, and shall receive and relay on the views and demands of the people."

Although most students and intellectuals had not harbored much hope that Hu would make a political comeback after his 1987 ouster, his death nonetheless came as a psychological blow. In their minds, Hu had been the only high official who possessed the leadership ability and wisdom necessary to lead China out of its present plight: Deng and his generation of grizzled revolutionaries were too old and too conservative, both politically and economically; Premier Li Peng, incompetent and instinctively hostile to deeper economic reform or any political reform; and Party chief Zhao Ziyang, although a reformer, insensitive to the wishes of the people and tainted by suspected corruption in his family. The poster below, which appeared at the Monument to the People's Heroes, elaborates on such commonly held perceptions.

I'D LIKE TO KNOW

Comrade Xiaoping, I'd like to know:

You realized early on that it doesn't matter if a cat is black or white; as long as it catches mice, it's a good cat. Doesn't it follow that insistence on distinguishing between "red" [politically correct] and "yellow" [liberal or bourgeois Western] thinking shows a lack of careful reflection?

Reform in the political arena is an absolute necessity. But if we hear only words and see no actions, how will there be any results? Cars and residences, I want them all—and a computer to boot; so how is it that your policy of "getting rich together" has turned out to be nothing but the same old empty promises? Democracy and freedom, the people want; how can you claim that we are too childish by this much or that much? Massive disarmament you can achieve, so just what makes it so tough to clean up corruption in the Party?

Comrade Zhao Ziyang, I'd like to know:

How can the Party's interests be higher than the people's? They must be, or how do you explain the fact that a Party card is worth a three-year reduction in a jail sentence [for a Party member convicted of a crime]? There are more bureaucrats than public servants. How is it that if one wants to be an official, the secret to success is playing it safe: "no contributions, no mistakes"? A country of the people, the people would love; but with the Party treating the country like its private property, even if you were to wear out both feet slaving away, you wouldn't get anywhere. A country of the people, the people should run; so isn't entrusting only Party members to run it a bit inappropriate?

Comrade Li Peng, I'd like to know:

Are you or aren't you able to cope with the duties of a Premier? Running a nation and bringing it peace is no easy task; so why don't your political views ever come to light? While you equivocate, another generation grows old; who will win the race against time? The "Government's Work Report" you gave—who wrote it? You say the "Number Nines" [intellectuals] are only members of the working class; how can we possibly accept this?[12] A brain without knowledge can't be wise; a nation without intellectuals cannot be enlightened. In China's Four Modernizations, isn't progress in science and technology the most important?[13] So how is it that in the age of nuclear power being the son of so-and-so counts the most? I don't know how many white-collar professionals you'll drive to death. It's a cynical joke to mouth the great importance of education while treating the "Number Nines" as mere vassals.

Comrade Yang Shangkun, I'd like to know:

How many rubber stamps have you stamped? Maybe you ought to swap your rubber stamp for a metal one. If you really wanted to be an iron warrior serving the people, then what's the big deal if you lose your position as President of the country?

Mr. Yaobang, I'd like to know:

[Just as we stood] at the crossroads of reform, how could you have fallen? You appealed for democracy, cried out for freedom. How could all of this have been in vain? From the grave, will you be able to advise the people? Who will take the lead in shaping China's future?

12. The number nine has come to be associated with intellectuals in two ways. First, Mao Tse-tung used the phrase "Brother Number Nine" (laojiu) in the 1960s to allude to intellectuals; his inspiration was a line from the revolutionary model opera "Taking Tiger Mountain by Strategy," in which the protagonist, a People's Liberation Army soldier who joins a group of bandits to learn their ways, is called Brother Number Nine after his junior status. Second, the term "the stinking number nine" (chou laojiu) was used to refer to intellectuals beginning in 1968, when they were added to an existing set of eight bad social groups (landlords, rich peasants, counter-revolutionaries, bad elements, rightists, renegades, enemy agents, and capitalist-roaders); intellectuals became the ninth such group.

13. In 1975, at the First Session of the Fourth NPC, Premier Zhou Enlai announced China's agenda for the next years: the "Four Modernizations," or modernization of agriculture, industry, national defense, and science and technology. The Four Modernizations continued to be China's domestic policy rationale through the 1980s.

Compatriots, I'd like to know: where can we find China's way out? Who can definitely tell me: is there much hope for China, or hardly any at all?

—A student from Beijing
Industrial University
*(poster on Monument to the
People's Heroes)*

Hu's death brought campuses in Beijing, and to a lesser extent across the entire country, to life. The most visible signs of protest and regret were the marches on campuses and to Tiananmen, and the waves of posters that appeared on school walls. Less apparent but equally significant were the informal discussions that took place in packed dorm rooms concerning the need for democratic changes and the steps students could take to bring them about. These discussions rose spontaneously, but the natural leaders in them were a handful of students who had for some months already been politically active. These idealistic youth, who refused to subscribe to the prevailing belief that China was beyond redemption, had hoped to use May 4, 1989—the seventieth anniversary of the epochal May Fourth Movement, a period of student activism and sweeping cultural change symbolized by patriotic anti-imperialist student demonstrations on May 4, 1919—to prod their peers from their cynicism and self-centeredness. Now, in the middle of protests that were rapidly unfolding, they began to emerge as the core of the student leadership.

The most notable of this small group of activists was Wang Dan, a history undergraduate at Beijing University and son of a Beijing University professor, who was destined to become a top leader in the Democracy Movement. During late 1988 and early 1989, in addition to founding a journal on political reform whose name, *New May Fourth*, commemorated the May Fourth Movement, Wang Dan had organized "democracy salons" at Beijing University, where young students gathered to discuss topics as diverse as individual liberation, democratic reforms, and school conditions. Similar student activities, though on a smaller scale, also had taken place at other major universities in the capital such as Qinghua, China's leading institute of technology; People's University, in the past a sterile training ground for future Party apparatchiks but in recent years increasingly dynamic and diverse; and Beijing Normal University, the country's leading teachers' college. Though their numbers were small, the pro-democracy activists had sensed that many of their classmates shared with them a sense of oppression and a longing for change: isolated posters accusing the Party of autocracy and demanding democracy, precursors of the flood of posters that would appear once protests were under way, had turned up on various campuses during the winter of 1989.

Such student activism had been carefully monitored by school authorities.[14] Although university presidents were in some cases personally sympathetic to the student's grievances, they had to answer to Party authorities who kept a watchful eye on university campuses. As the democracy salons and related activities grew in popularity in February and March, Beijing University authorities had begun to take action, prohibiting certain speakers from appearing on campus and warning activists not to go too far. Wang Dan and other organizers had refused to be intimidated. On April 3, only twelve days before Hu's death would dramatically convert their lonely cause into a nationwide one, they had chosen to respond—and to make their case public—by putting up the poster below in the Beijing University "Triangle," the area where campus notices, unofficial and official, were customarily posted.

AN OPEN LETTER TO BEIJING UNIVERSITY AUTHORITIES[15]

President Ding Shisun, Party Secretary Wang Xuezhen, the University Party Committee, the Department of Student Affairs, and the University Youth League Committee:

This year marks the seventieth anniversary of the May Fourth Movement.[16] As the birthplace of this extraordinary movement of democratic enlightenment, Beijing University has always held high the banners of democracy and science [the two main rallying calls of the May Fourth Movement] and marched at the very forefront of our nation's progress.

14. Party watchdogs appear to have been extremely vigilant in noting all political activities on campuses during early 1989. The lengthy June 30, 1989, official report of Beijing Mayor Chen Xitong on the development and suppression of the Democracy Movement cites by title "anti-Party, anti-socialism" posters that appeared in the winter of 1989, most of which do not appear to have received much other attention in China or abroad. See *People's Daily*, July 7, 1989, pp. 2-3.

15. Title added by editors.

16. The May Fourth Movement, which spanned the years 1919 to 1921, was a broad movement both of student and intellectual political activism and of cultural reform. During this period, students and intellectuals initiated a nationalist, anti-imperialist campaign to strengthen China through modernization and social reform; their rallying cry was "Democracy and Science." Accompanying this political activism, which contributed to the birth of the Communist Party and other political organizations, was a vigorous literary and philosophical movement to embrace Western thought and reject traditional Chinese thinking and values. This period of social and cultural change is commonly referred to as the "May Fourth Movement," after historic student protests on May 4, 1919, against Chinese government capitulation to Japanese and other foreign powers' demands for colonial concessions. The movement still holds great meaning for Chinese students and intellectuals.

Today, as Chinese commemorate the May Fourth Movement, we, students of Beijing University, the hallowed ground of democracy, continue to hope that we will be able to carry on the distinguished tradition of Beijing University.

Thinking back seventy years, we recall how President Cai Yuanpei put the ideas of "democracy for governance of the school," freedom of thought, and tolerance of diversity into practice, fully ensuring that there would be academic freedom and freedom of speech within the school walls. Beijing University at that time could boast an unprecedented vitality in intellectual life, various scholarly trends, and many different schools of thought. In that environment, innumerable men and women of excellence, whose lives would later shine in the history of China, matured. This kind of democratic campus atmosphere still fills us with awe and pride. Yet we also note with great sorrow that today, seventy years later, this legacy of academic freedom and freedom of speech is in danger. One indication of this is the existence of many university restrictions regarding students' freedom to establish student associations, sponsor lectures, organize discussion meetings and salons, and other aspects of student freedom. We cannot help recognizing the fact that the "TOEFL School" [referring to students who spent all their free time studying for the Test of English as a Foreign Language, the standard test required of prospective foreign students at American universities] and "Mahjong School" [referring to students who spent their free time playing mahjong, the traditional Chinese game played with bamboo tiles and vaguely similar to gin rummy] are in vogue, and that business fever has suffocated all other interests. While there can be no doubt that this is the result of many social factors, it also is closely linked to the various kinds of restrictions on students' freedom of thought.

. . . It is our belief that seeking democracy requires more than opening one's mouth and yelling loudly; one must begin with concrete matters, . . . with matters that one has a stake in. Specifically speaking, we should begin by working hard to improve the democratic environment in school. It is our belief that in institutions of higher learning, such as Beijing University, there should be full freedom of speech and academic freedom. The unreasonable restrictions on these freedoms that have been imposed for various reasons should be abolished. Beijing University should serve as a special zone for promoting the democratization of politics; it should make a contribution to the progress of Chinese democracy.

We greatly treasure social and school stability and unity. Therefore, we would like to put forward the following suggestions, which stem from nothing other than a wish to establish channels for dialogue with the university leadership, from the desire to be open and honest with Party and Communist Youth League leaders of every level in the school, and to be treated likewise, and from our hope that with down-to-earth actions we can improve this learning environment of ours.

Beginning last semester and continuing today, from Activity Room 430 in Building 43 to the "democracy lawn" in front of the statue of Cervantes, thirteen democracy salons have been spontaneously organized by students concerned with the future of the country and the Chinese nation. These salons have provided the students with excellent opportunities for the exchange of ideas as well as for theoretical discussions. Recently, however, a few salons have run into interference from the Beijing Municipal Party Committee, the Party Committee of the University, the Security Department, and the Party branch in every academic department. Some students have also been personally subject to considerable pressure from authorities. We believe that these salons offer an opportunity to explore spontaneously various ideas; such forums greatly help to enliven the academic atmosphere and promote the exchange of ideas. And it is the wish of the majority of students to maintain the once-a-week democracy salons. Therefore, we suggest:

(1) That the university take the initiative to remove all types of pressure [on the students], lend its support to the sponsors of the democracy salons and similar activities, and grant them the freedom to invite eminent scholars to participate.

(2) The freedom referred to above should be precisely defined [by the following procedures]: two days in advance of a scheduled democracy salon, the organizers of these spontaneous meetings will furnish to university authorities for registration a list of the persons invited. In turn, university authorities should guarantee that they will permit all people to attend, with the exception of those who have lost their political rights.[17]

(3) That the university designate the "democracy lawn" in front of the statue of Cervantes as a regular meeting place for the democracy salons. The university may dispatch personnel to participate in the activities each time to help keep order, but this should not be used as an excuse for interfering in the activities.

(4) That the university guarantee it will not take any measures against

17. Articles 50–54 of the Criminal Law of the PRC provides that counter-revolutionaries and criminals convicted of serious crimes may be deprived of their political rights (which include the right to vote and stand for election and to hold a leading position in government offices, enterprises, or citizen's organizations), in addition to being sentenced to imprisonment, public surveillance, or death.

the organizers of these spontaneous activities, that it will not hold people responsible after the event, and that it will not prevent them from receiving their diplomas. . . .

We end this petition with the signatures that we have collected. We hereby appeal to all of the teachers and students of the university: please support our reasonable requests. We are confident that the wish to establish a real democracy first of all within the school campus is not the wish of only the signers of this petition, but also of all of the teachers and students. We therefore earnestly look forward to your support through your signatures.

> —Wang Dan and 55 other students,
>   April 3, 1989
>   (big-character poster at
>   Beijing University)

An important influence on students who took their role as fledgling members of the intellectual class seriously was a new boldness and vigor among China's intellectuals, which had become more evident with each passing month of 1988 and early 1989. The conservative backlash to the 1987 student demonstrations had had less impact and less staying power than many had expected; by mid-1988, with the Party's moderate elements, led by Zhao Ziyang, dominating national policy making once again, Chinese intellectual life was flourishing. For example, in art, young Chinese were experimenting with avant-garde forms. In journalism, the Shanghai *World Economic Herald* was breaking new ground with candid articles advocating more radical economic reform and new political reform, and "reportage literature"—aggressive exposé reporting in the framework of a story—had tackled topics previously considered taboo.[18] In economics, work on developing China's fledgling stock markets continued, despite the formalization in March 1989 of a slow-down economic policy of "improving and rectifying the economic environment" that favored increasing centralized control. Intellectuals across the country were busy as never before organizing unofficial discussion salons, founding new journals, expanding contacts with Chinese in Hong Kong and Taiwan, and participating freely in international

18. For example, in 1988, Dai Qing, a prominent reporter for the *Guangming Daily*, published two articles revealing for the first time many details about the persecution of two well-known intellectuals, Wang Shiwei and Zhu Anping, outspoken critics of the Party in the forties and fifties, respectively. The articles attracted considerable attention because neither of the two has been officially "rehabilitated" by the Party. Dai Qing was arrested in July 1989 for her activism during the Democracy Movement; several of the open letters she put her name to during the movement are included in this book.

cultural and scientific conferences. And some, aggressively marketing their works abroad, were even able to make tidy profits from their foreign contacts and travels.

That intellectual freedom, which ironically coexisted with a deepening sense of malaise among Chinese citizens, reached new heights in 1988 and early 1989 can be partially attributed to the Party's tolerant attitude. Of equal or greater importance, however, was the fact that many intellectuals had spun out of the Party's control and even out of the orbit of Party influence. As the bounds of intellectual freedom had expanded, so had the conviction that there should be no bounds.

Two highly significant developments in the intellectual world were to occur during this period. First, the attack on traditional Chinese culture reached a symbolic, if not intellectual, zenith with the nationwide broadcast of a controversial television essay, "River Elegy." Second, for the first time in the history of the People's Republic of China, well-established intellectuals would indirectly challenge the Party by initiating a national signature campaign for the release of political prisoners.

"River Elegy," a six-part series that first aired in June 1988, shocked many Chinese with its unreserved criticism of traditional Chinese culture and thinking, and in particular of three revered symbols of Chinese civilization—the Yellow River, cradle of Chinese civilization; the dragon; and the Great Wall. Using powerful visual images to underscore their points, its young principal writers, Su Xiaokang and Wang Luxiang, argued that the Yellow River, which unpredictably overflowed its banks, was as malevolent as it was kind to the Chinese who lived along it; that the dragon, associated with Chinese emperors, was essentially an icon of feudalism; and that even the Great Wall, long a source of national pride, had not served Chinese society well, since it had failed to keep out "barbarians" while encouraging Chinese insularity. Their sobering conclusion was that unless the Chinese decisively rejected these symbols as well as the traditional and complacent yet insecure culture they represented, China's modernization would be endangered.

"River Elegy's" basic message—that fundamental flaws in Chinese values were responsible for China's present-day backwardness, and that modernization depended on the adoption of Western values such as openness, competition, and democratic rights—was hardly new; since the early 1980s, numerous writers and thinkers had been arguing the same. But its unflinching yet emotional rejection of Chinese culture and its mass audience set it apart. Outraged conservative Party leaders and cultural commissars demanded that the film be banned, and forced the resignation of the head of China Central Television (CCTV). "River Elegy" survived, in part because Party chief Zhao Ziyang personally defended it. Ultimately, however, the conservatives would have their way: after Zhao's downfall and the suppression of the Democracy Movement in June 1989, "River Elegy" would be attacked anew and banned, Zhao's defense of it labeled "support of turmoil," Wang Luxiang arrested, and Su Xiaokang forced to flee the country. The following brief excerpts from "River Elegy" give some flavor of its iconoclastic spirit.

RIVER ELEGY
(excerpts)

History has proven innumerable times that the reason for a civilization's decline is not attacks from external forces, but the degeneration of its internal machinery. Toynbee said, "The most useful function of an external enemy is that when a society has committed suicide but still has not drawn its last breath, it delivers the final blow."

Over the last several thousand years, the Yellow River civilization has been many times the target of foreign attacks that have sought to subjugate it, yet it has never fallen. We have deeply admired this powerful capacity of cultural assimilation. But today, at the end of the twentieth century, although foreign attacks are no longer accompanied by cannons and cruel oppression, our ancient civilization can withstand them no longer.

It is already moribund.

It needs new cultural forces to reinvigorate it.

Ancestors of the dragon, what the Yellow River could give us, it long ago gave to our forefathers. The Yellow River cannot again bring forth the civilization that our forefathers created. What we must create is an entirely new civilization. It will not stream from the Yellow River. The sediment of the old civilization is like the sand and silt that has accumulated on the bottom of the Yellow River; it clogs our arteries. It needs a great flood to wash it away.

This great flood is already upon us. It is none other than industrialized civilization. It is calling us! . . .

The death knell of capitalism, which Marx prophesied a long time ago, has taken long enough to toll. Western industrialized civilization, which has miraculously burgeoned in two hundred years, displays all kinds of symptoms of morbidity, yet continues to readjust and renew itself despite its "predicament." The socialist countries that one after another broke free from the weakened links of the imperialist chain at the beginning of the century have now, one after another, begun to undergo large-scale social reforms. The arms control negotiations between the United States and the Soviet Union, the gunfire of the Persian Gulf, the endless coups in both Latin America and Africa, the waves of democracy movements in East Asia, the terrorists' activities plaguing affluent Europe, the rampant spread of AIDS—all have made our planet a jumbled mess.

Why are nature and society, the two foundation stones on which human civilization is built and sustained, so filled with scourges? Between nature's ravages and society's plagues, is there a certain connection?

For the Chinese, nowhere is there a flood more frightful than from the Yellow River. As early as the time of *The Book of Songs*,[19] the Chinese had sent forth their sigh:

> Till the River runs clear,
> How many life spans?

Throughout the entire history of our civilization, the Yellow River has been the "scourge of the Middle Kingdom."

Today, however, the Chinese sigh yet another sigh, deeper and heavier: why is it that our feudal era never ends, why is it as endless as the ceaseless floods of the Yellow River? It is a nightmare, one a great deal more frightful than the floods, whose fog rose, and continues to rise, from that great tomb under Mound Li [the tomb of the first emperor], pervading a two-thousand-year history. In the recent century, the Chinese tried, again and again, to bury their nightmare, to seal it in that tomb; yet again and again it came back alive.

As if on the track of an aged mill, history grinds on, slowly and heavily; in the riverbed which has accumulated silt and sand of the ages, the Yellow River flows on, as slowly and as heavily.

Is another flood coming?

Or is turmoil gone forever?

We are asking the Yellow River. We are asking history.

(screenplay from television series)

The second, far more startling manifestation of growing assertiveness in the intellectual world was the initiation at the start of 1989 of a signature campaign for the release of Wei Jingsheng and other political prisoners jailed a decade earlier for their involvement in the 1978-1979 Democracy Wall Movement. During 1977 and 1978, in a prelude to the movement, thousands of petitioners had flooded into Beijing seeking redress for wrongs suffered during the Cultural Revolution and other "leftist" campaigns—campaigns initiated by Mao or his supporters during the fifties and sixties to purge bourgeois ideology and elements from Chinese society, to carry on "continuous revolution," and to wage "class struggle." The actual half-year-long

19. The *Book of Songs* (also known as the *Book of Odes*) is an anthology of poems, dating from around 1200 to 700 B.C. It is the oldest extant collection of Chinese poetry.

"spring" of the Democracy Wall Movement had begun in November 1978 with the official reversal of the Party's verdict on the "1976 Tiananmen Incident,"[20] a sign of the ascendancy of the "rightist" Party leaders such as Deng Xiaoping who had been attacked during those campaigns. The announcement had prompted thousands of Chinese to gather at "Democracy Wall," a wall in downtown Beijing west of Tiananmen, to paste and read posters criticizing Mao (who had by then been deceased for two years), calling for the rehabilitation of his rightist opponents, and demanding political reform and modernization. Such a demonstration of popular sentiment bolstered Deng's position in the jockeying for Party leadership taking place at the time. Before long, though, Democracy Wall activists had intensified and broadened their criticisms: previously vague calls for political reform were sharpened into attacks on autocracy and the Party's authority, the banner of human rights was raised, and Deng attacked as well. Until then, Deng had been a crucial backstage supporter of the movement, encouraging its growth by leaking approving comments on the movement to Western reporters. By March 1979, he had abruptly reversed course, condemning the movement and ordering a crackdown.

One of the first to have been arrested, in March 1979, was Wei Jingsheng. Wei was a founder of *Exploration*, one of the most radical of the "people's journals" that blossomed during the movement, and author of several famous Democracy Wall writings, including "The Fifth Modernization—Democracy," "Do We Want Democracy or Do We Want Dictatorship?" and a sensational exposé about China's prison for top political prisoners, entitled "A Twentieth-Century Bastille—Qincheng: No. 1 Prison."[21] Wei was subsequently given a harsh fifteen-year sentence—reportedly on the direct orders of Deng—on charges of being a counter-revolutionary and revealing state secrets to foreigners. According to unofficial reports, Wei has spent much of his time in solitary confinement and now suffers from schizophrenia. An undetermined number of other Democracy Wall activists, including Huang Xiang, Chen Lu, and Xu Wenli, are also still in prison.

As 1989 and the tenth anniversary of Wei's imprisonment approached, a number of Chinese intellectuals decided that their consciences no longer permitted them to keep silent. The first to act was Ren Wanding, himself a former Democracy Wall activist and founder of the China Human Rights League, who had served four years in prison for his activities. In December 1988, Ren released a letter to international

---

20. The Tiananmen Incident is described below on page 61.

21. The title, "The Fifth Modernization—Democracy," alludes to the Four Modernizations; Wei maintained that China could not enter the modern era without a fifth modernization— democracy and human rights. In "Do We Want Democracy or Do We Want Dictatorship?" Wei was even bolder, directly accusing Deng of being an autocratic ruler no different from Mao.

human rights organizations urging an investigation into the condition and status of prisoners from the Democracy Wall period and 1987 student demonstrations. What attracted even more attention, however, was an open letter to Deng the following month by Fang Lizhi, China's internationally known dissident. In the letter, Fang, a fearlessly outspoken critic who had declared only months after his much-publicized expulsion from the Party in January 1987 that his next target would be Marxism, asked Deng to release Wei and others in the spirit of humanitarianism.

Ren's and Fang's public calls for clemency most certainly were great irritants to Deng and top Party leaders, including Secretary General Zhao Ziyang, a daring reformer in economic policy but no democrat. Their actions could be ignored, however, as the statements of two isolated dissidents. What could not be so discounted, and what therefore must have been a source of some surprise and worry, was the unified campaign by a varied group of well-established intellectuals that soon followed. On February 13, Bei Dao, a well-known poet and writer, and thirty-two other respected intellectuals sent a letter in support of Fang's letter to the Standing Committee of the Central Committee. The list of signatories ranged from the elderly Bing Xin, a writer whose best-known works were written in the 1920s and 1930s, to Su Shaozhi, former head of the Leninism–Marxism–Mao Tse-tung Thought Institute of the Chinese Academy of Social Sciences; many of the signatories went on to play active roles in the Democracy Movement. The signature campaign, paralleled by another one overseas and in Hong Kong, continued through the winter. Although most university students were too young to be familiar with Wei's case, news of the campaign caused a good deal of discussion when it reached campuses.

These public acts calling on the Party to free its political prisoners may not have achieved their objectives, but the acts themselves held great meaning. By choosing conscience over political safety, the petitioners stated unequivocally that the threat of Party retaliation would not dissuade them from acting in accordance with their beliefs.

Two of the letters from the petition drive—Fang Lizhi's and Bei Dao's—are presented below.

FANG LIZHI'S LETTER TO DENG XIAOPING

Chairman of the Central Military Commission Deng Xiaoping:

This year is the fortieth year since the founding of the People's Republic of China and also the seventieth year since the May Fourth Movement. There will certainly be many commemorative activities centering on these fortieth and seventieth anniversaries. However, in comparison to the past, there are many more people today than before who perhaps are concerned about the present and even more concerned about the future. They harbor the hope that the two commemorations will bring forth new hope.

In view of this, I sincerely suggest to you that upon the eve of these two dates a general pardon be granted nationally, and in particular, that Wei Jingsheng as well as all similar political prisoners be released.

I think that regardless of how one evaluates the acts of Wei Jingsheng, the freeing of this man, who has already served approximately ten years in prison, is a humanitarian act that will promote an excellent social atmosphere.

This year is also coincidentally the two hundredth anniversary of the French Revolution. No matter how one views this event, the freedom, equality, fraternity, and human rights it symbolizes have been accorded universal respect by mankind. Thus, I again sincerely hope that you will consider my suggestion, and in doing so, add new esteem to the future.

Respectfully submitted,
Fang Lizhi, January 6, 1989
(open letter)

OPEN LETTER TO THE STANDING COMMITTEE OF THE NATIONAL PEOPLE'S CONGRESS AND THE CENTRAL COMMITTEE

After learning of the open letter sent to Chairman Deng Xiaoping by Mr. Fang Lizhi, we were deeply concerned about this matter.

We believe that in the year commemorating the fortieth anniversary of the establishment of the Republic and the seventieth anniversary of the May Fourth Movement, a general pardon—in particular, the release of Wei Jingsheng and other political prisoners—would create a positive atmosphere advantageous to reform as well as be consistent with today's steadily growing trend across the world of respect for human rights.

> —Bei Dao, Bing Xin, Su Shaozhi, Lao Mu, Wu Zuguang, Mang Ke, Wang Ruoshui, Su Xiaokang, Yan Wenjing, Li Zehou, Jin Guantao, Zhang Dainian, Bao Zunxin, Chen Jun, and nineteen other intellectuals.
> February 13, 1989

"Special privileges, special privileges—the root of corruption."

Citizens' backing of the student protests, which began as sympathy, evolved into active support, and finally became outright defiance of the government, grew out of three powerful emotional sources: anger at the corruption of Party and government officials, and at the special privileges they enjoyed;[22] dissatisfaction with the economic situation, especially inflation; and alienation from the government, a feeling that government officials were solely concerned with protecting their own interests and totally indifferent to the wishes and needs of ordinary people.

Despite regular Party pronouncements of a crackdown on corruption, government corruption had seemed to spread unchecked over the past several years. It had assumed many forms, but could be generally described as Party officials' use of power and connections for personal benefit, whether to obtain foreign luxury goods, to accumulate large amounts of money (including foreign exchange), to travel abroad, to live in the best housing, or to send their children abroad. Of all corrupt practices, none was resented more than "profiteering by officials"—profitmaking by Party officials through the resale of valuable goods obtained illicitly or procured at a low, fixed state plan price (often several times less than the prevailing market price for the same product).[23] Official profiteering had become so commonplace

22. It is helpful here to understand the relationship between the Chinese Communist Party and the Chinese government. The government is the executive power of the state, with responsibility for the governance and administration of the country. In contrast, the Party is not in theory supposed to manage the affairs of the state; its role is to lead and supervise ideological work and to formulate basic policies that guide the country. In practice, the Party dominates all state matters and controls real power through a structure of Party "committees"; this system of control is summarized in Chapter 3, note 12. Whereas all government officials can be assumed to be Party members, not all Party officials serve in the government. For all practical purposes, however, and in the eyes of Chinese, there is little if any difference between the Party and the government. Thus, student and citizen dissatisfaction with the "government" was at the same time an attack on the Party, and "government corruption" or "profiteering by officials" refers to both government and Party officials.

23. Prior to 1980, the prices of commodities produced by state enterprises and collective enterprises were set by the state. In addition, raw materials and commodities in scarce supply, such as steel, rubber, fertilizer, and lumber, were produced by and supplied to factories according to the state plan and at state-set prices; enterprises were not permitted to exchange or sell these commodities among themselves. Beginning in 1980, the government introduced reforms under which a portion of the previously regulated commodities were gradually released from state regulation; enterprises were allowed to sell or purchase these deregulated commodities at market prices under certain conditions (enterprises were still required to meet state production quotas before selling any surplus at market prices). Market prices, although subject to a ceiling set by the state, are much higher than the state plan prices, which do not reflect the true cost of production or market demand.

This hybrid system, popularly known as the "dual-track price system," has created ap-

Illustration 1.2. The Democracy Movement was as much a protest against "bureaucratism"—in Chinese eyes, the arbitrary exercise of power or the abuse of power by Party officials—as it was a demand for democracy. This huge sign, made by workers at the Nanjing Municipal Advertisement Company, declares: "Democracy is the foundation for building the country; bureaucrats are the roots of corruption." Credit: James Anderson.

that a special term for it, *guandao* (literally, "officials engaging in reselling at a profit") has entered the Chinese vocabulary.

Knowing that an attack on corruption would be unassailable, students emphasized anti-corruption themes in their early public demonstrations, avoiding direct attacks on the Party or government. For many students, though, the emphasis on corruption was not purely a prudent tactical approach; they saw, and were firmly convinced of, a direct connection between corruption and the lack of democracy in

---

parently irresistible opportunities for profiteering. Government departments that are responsible for selling state-allocated materials to enterprises frequently deliver less than the plan-stipulated quantities, keeping the undelivered allocations for resale at a higher price for their own gain. Thus, any person or company that can obtain valuable commodities at state prices can reap enormous profits by reselling on the market. In one typical case cited by the *People's Daily*, the Beijing Agricultural Products Material Company, rather than selling plastic sheets (for use in greenhouses and crop protection) to peasants at the state-set price of 5,280 yuan a ton, sold the plastic to another agricultural company for the price of 5,745 yuan a ton; this company than resold it at an even higher price. The peasants were finally able to purchase the plastic sheets they needed at the price of 8,500 yuan a ton. In mid-1989, one yuan, or Chinese dollar, equaled approximately $U.S. 0.27.

China. The first selection below is a sarcastic introduction to the "ins and outs" of corrupt practices by Party officials and their sons and daughters. The second reflects the great skepticism of students and citizens about the government's commitment to fighting corruption and to reducing its expenditures on luxury items such as cars and hotels. The last piece explores the relationship between the spread of corruption and the lack of democracy.

SOLDIERS, LOOK HOW PROFITEERING BY GOVERNMENT OFFICIALS IS EATING YOU UP

Dear soldiers, please ask yourselves how come in these days of wild inflation, your food stipend remains at 1.65 yuan.[24] I suggest that you take a look at the the profiteering going on among government officials!

What does it mean when people talk about "profiteering by government officials"? To describe it simply, it refers to officials using their power to acquire things such as goods at low state-fixed prices, import and export licences (or documents), loans, and foreign currency at special low exchange rates, so that they can reap huge profits. These officials do business in the name of their companies. These companies can be categorized into two kinds: those run by the government and those run by the sons and daughters of high-level cadres [officials].[25] . . . The trading done by these companies can likewise be categorized into two kinds: domestic trade and foreign trade.

Now, let's take a look at the variety of ways these profiteering officials abuse their power to run their operations smoothly and suck the life-blood out of the people!

First, let's look at domestic trade. Now, our Crown Prince Deng Pufang [Deng Xiaoping's son], travel-worn [from his trips up and down the country], flies into the Northeast. . . . The Heilongjiang Province leadership, upon hearing of his lordship's arrival, wastes no time in taking him on a grand tour to Daqing [a major oil field in Northeast China]. Prince Deng is delighted to find Daqing has some profits he can dredge up: he buys, among other things, some tons of polyethylene and polypropylene

24. Although in the early 1980s one yuan was sufficient to buy a modest meal of noodles or dumplings, or a plate of meat, by 1989 it barely bought a small snack.
25. The Chinese term *ganbu*, or cadre, refers to all those who are state and Party officials, from low-level functionaries to the top leaders of the government and Party. Since the term *ganbu* does not carry the slightly pejorative meaning that "bureaucrat" has in English, it is generally translated here as "cadre" rather than "bureaucrat."

at the state-fixed price of about 3,000 yuan a ton, and then, after shipping them through the Shanhaiguan pass down to Beijing proceeds to resell them at 9,000 yuan a ton. Well, what a "piece of cake." Prince Deng has made a killing, doing practically no work while getting a hundred times' return. Money has poured into his pockets. Who wouldn't be gleeful in his shoes?

When it comes to foreign trade, well, things get a bit tougher. There are three conditions for success, and having only two just won't do. The first is the import / export licence. The second is the state-granted "right to engage in foreign trade."[26] The third is foreign exchange bought at the official state-fixed rate [in comparison to the market rate, which is nearly double]. Of the three, the import / export licence is the most important. But for those government lords, a licence is hardly an obstacle. They can always get one from their daddies or brothers who are big officials. And if their company has not been granted the right to engage in foreign trade, they can always find a company that does have the right to act as their agent. As for foreign currency, it's always available at the foreign exchange markets; it's only that they might have to buy it a higher price.

In late 1984 or early 1985, when Kanghua [Deng Pufang's company] had just begun operating, it already occupied as office space a compound on Gongyuan Street and a suite in the Overseas Chinese Hotel.[27] One day a certain businessman went up to one of these offices. There he was met by a Kanghua employee who showed him a thick pile of import / export licences (800 in all); there were licences for over a thousand cars and a few thousand color TV sets. The employee offered the licences to the businessman for a "service charge" of 3 percent. And by international trade custom, Kanghua could also obtain from the foreign manufacturers of those goods a commission ranging from 5 to 10 percent [for helping to

26. Chinese companies can only engage in foreign trade if they have first received authorization to do so from the government. This "right to engage in foreign trade" used to be limited to state trading companies, but in recent years, under decentralization of the trading system, a far wider circle of companies has been granted this much-coveted right. However, the vast majority of Chinese companies still do not enjoy this right.

27. Kanghua was a sprawling conglomerate headed by Deng Pufang, the son of Deng Xiaoping who was crippled when thrown off a roof during the Cultural Revolution. It had well over one hundred subsidiaries, many of them dummy corporations, not only in China but also in Hong Kong. It was closed down in 1988 after revelations of illegal conduct, including the evasion of income tax payments through the shifting of its revenues to a nonprofit organization for the handicapped run by Deng Pufang. Kanghua was but one example of the many "trading and investment" companies with branches in Hong Kong and abroad that are run by the sons and daughters of China's top leaders.

arrange their import]. Well, whether in the end this money went into the accounts of Kanghua company, or into the private pockets of Deng Pufang, only the devil knows. In this world of ruthless competition, all you need to know is how to act as the middleman, how to pull the right strings, so why worry that money won't reach your hands? The key to success is you have to hold onto your official's cap; with power in hand, licences come naturally.

Well, let me tell you, if you have power today, use it. Tomorrow you might not have the chance. And let me tell you, our lord officials are no monks who have taken a vow of abstinence. Who cares that the people are suffering hardships, who cares that there are urgent telegrams from disaster areas? You show them cash, their heads go dizzy. I'll give you another example: when the China National Coal Import / Export Corporation (CNCIEC)—where, by the way, Miss Deng [daughter of Deng Xiaoping] presides—exports coal, businessmen in Hong Kong pay officials a commission of U.S. $2 each ton (the price of coal is U.S. $41–45). And where is this money cached away? In Hong Kong.

Because Shen Tu [the former Director of the General Department of CAAC, the national airline] demanded from the Boeing Company some U.S. $500,000 in bribes for having CAAC purchase their 747s, he was promptly dismissed. Yet he still has three sons in America and a daughter in Europe. One of his sons came back to China just about a month ago, and said that he could obtain import licences for the following items [all of which are subject to state control and cannot be freely traded]:

1. Fish meal, 20,000 tons
2. Zinc-plated iron sheets, 20,000 tons
3. Fertilizers (including carbamide), 19 tons
4. Polypropylene
5. High-pressure polyethylene, 1,000 tons
6. Cold-rolled thin sheets, 1,000 tons
7. Cold-rolled planks, 1,000 tons
8. Copper plating
9. Palm oil, 6,000 tons . . .
16. Sodium hydroxide, 1,000 tons
17. Wood, 500,000 square meters
18. ABS resin, 2,000 tons

This Shen Tu junior has already lived in America for ten years, yet he still commands immense power in China. Thus it's small wonder that China's foreign debt has hit such an astronomical level—if only you realize that there are people who are fattening themselves out of all this.

Mind you, these profiteering officials are not nobodies. They have power and extraordinary IQs, and you name it, they know from A to Z the 1,001 ways to make a profit. Even in the area of foreign exchange, they don't miss a chance. For example, during the period 1984–1985, company X (let's not reveal its name here) bought a few million U.S. dollars at the official exchange rate. It then sold this foreign currency at an exchange rate of 1:15 [as opposed to the official rate of 1:3.72—even the rate at the officially sanctioned foreign exchange markets is only about 1:7] to companies that desperately needed it to purchase merchandise from abroad.

Turning your head to one side, you hear people with hungry stomachs complaining, and turning it to the other, you see others squandering money without a second thought. And the general state of economic depression persists alongside the ever-expanding pockets of a few individuals. Why is China's foreign debt so immense? Why is China's economy such a mess? Why does the daily stipend of a soldier remain at 1.65 yuan after all these years, despite rocketing prices? Nowhere else can one find the answer to these questions except in the word "official." One official takes the lead, another follows, and very soon each official acts as a protective shield for another's crimes. Now let me ask, in whose hands shall China crumble? "No corrupt officials, no revolt," as the saying goes. We want to build our country and we want to bring prosperity to the people, but allowing these corrupt officials to have their way will reduce all this to empty rhetoric. Trees must be chopped down when they are rotten, and parasites exterminated. My dear soldiers, let me ask you: if the people say no, if history says no, will you still allow this situation to go on?

(Beijing University handbill)

WHAT DO WE OPPOSE? WHAT DO WE NEED?
(excerpt)

. . . The second major cause for the student movement was the government's ineffectiveness in fighting corruption. The slogans of "improving and rectifying the economy" have appeared, with their main emphasis on the fight against corruption, but the only result has been a loud thunderstorm with a few drops of rain. This campaign resulted in only a reduction of the money supply [so that companies find it difficult to do business and expand]; the original intention of eradicating corruption has been forgottten.

Corruption in China falls into two categories: corruption that involves a violation of the country's laws, and corruption that goes on within the limits of the law; the latter is more dangerous.

During this student movement, many posters appeared depicting "revolutionary family trees" whose purpose was to expose leading Chinese officials who are profiteering through speculation. As citizens, the sons and daughters of leaders of course have the right to run a company; but since China is a country where officials stand at the center of the universe, they can use their power to obtain such advantages as discounted interest rates on loans and state allocations of [precious supplies of] low-priced raw materials. With a turn of the hand they can strike it rich. The Kanghua company, for example, grew rich by taking advantage of discounted interest rates: it paid only an annual interest rate of 3 percent on its loans, while the usual interest rate on deposits is 9 percent.

The anti-corruption campaign cited by State Council spokesman Yuan Mu is nothing but swatting at flies; by no stretch of the imagination could one call them taking on the rats or the tigers. . . .

Corruption is just like cancer in the body of our Party and our government. Throughout Chinese history there has been no dynasty which was not destroyed by corruption. The recent Kuomintang (Nationalist Party) government is an extremely good example.[28] In 1947, the decision made at the Third Plenum of the Kuomintang's Congress to carry out economic reform was based upon careful self-scrutiny. Tight and systematic economic and administrative reform measures were worked out. However, due to widespread profiteering by officials and rampant corruption, these measures that had been hammered out after extensive debate had an effect opposite to what was intended. This is a lesson worthy of our Communist Party's attention.

28. The Kuomintang (Nationalist Party) is the ruling party of Taiwan (the Republic of China). From 1945 to 1949, the Kuomintang, led by General Chiang Kai-shek, fought the Chinese Communist Party in a bitter civil war that culminated in the Communist triumph and founding of the People's Republic of China in 1949. The Kuomintang ruled a united China for one decade, from 1928 to 1937, before the Japanese invasion in 1937 threw the country into turmoil; the period of Kuomintang rule brought relative stability to China, but was also characterized by a steadily weakening economy and rampant corruption among Kuomintang officials. During the war against the Japanese, Kuomintang corruption reached new heights, expanding to include even army officials' speculation in contraband Japanese goods.

Since the beginning of the campaign to improve and rectify the economy, the work done by the government to fight corruption appears to be quite incompetent and ineffectual. One only needs to look at a few publicly known facts to see this.

First, the government has several times taken steps to streamline the swollen bureaucracy; yet somehow during the decade from 1978 to 1987, administrative outlays doubled, as did the number of administrative personnel. For example, take the case of the autonomous region of Inner Mongolia: out of 106 million inhabitants, 800,000 are administrative cadres; the annual personnel expenses (including wages, etc.) amount to 2.4 billion yuan, yet the annual revenue of Inner Mongolia is only 2 billion, not even enough to pay for taking care of all the cadres.

[Here is another example.] Issue No.16 of the periodical *Outlook* reported that according to an estimate by a deputy of the National People's Congress in 1987, recorded nationwide public expenditures on free meals, gifts, and purchases of luxury cars exceeded 53 billion yuan. In 1988, investment in nonmanufacturing projects such as the construction of buildings, halls, and hotels reached 51 billion yuan; this did not include costs for interior decoration, which add at least another 50 billion. According to incomplete statistics, in 1988 losses from defective products amounted to 18.32 billion across the country, which corresponds to 41 percent of the amount spent by the government on subsidies to state-owned enterprises to cover their deficits.

[And yet another example.] On March 29, the Chinese journal *Financial Times* reported that over the last three years in Sichuan Province, barely 1.56 billion yuan has been spent on agriculture; at the same time, cars ordered during that period consumed about 2 billion yuan. . . .

> *(published in student* News Herald,
> *No. 2, May 4, 1989)*

CHINA'S ONLY WAY OUT

(excerpts)[29]

. . . The government is facing bankruptcy. It has no money for education, no money for national defense, no money for energy, no money for trans-

29. The order of excerpts from this poster has been slightly changed from the original by the editors.

portation. It does not even have enough money to keep the living standard of ordinary state employees up to previous levels. Where has all the money gone? It has gone into the pockets of the corrupt officials, into the banking accounts of those big and small leaders who enjoy authority. The small amount of capital people have toiled to create has turned into Mercedes Benzes and Cadillacs—cars on the streets—and into hotels and restaurants [where these big and small leaders dine, stay, and entertain their relatives and friends for free]. . . .

Political corruption is the key problem [facing China]. The only weapon for smashing dictatorship and autocracy and ending all types of corruption that plague China is democracy. The power [presently] concentrated in individuals and a small portion of the people must be restricted; there must be some mechanism of checks and balances. The most basic meaning of democracy is that people themselves administer matters. In modern countries, direct democracy is not easy to implement; therefore, it is transformed into indirect democracy, that is, people entrust part of their power to others, and these people so entrusted are selected by the people. Since people are concerned that the people entrusted by them may abuse their power, they establish several institutions that counterbalance each other, and each institution is independently responsible to the people. This is the basic principle of democracy.

What does China have? Nothing. On hearing [calls] for democracy, the government says that the level of the people is too low for the implementation of democracy. But they have forgotten that when Chiang Kai-shek [the head of the Nationalist Party] ran the country under a dictatorship, one of his rationales was that the people were unenlightened and that they needed "instructive politics." When the Communist Party was fighting Chiang Kai-shek and the Nationalist Party, the Party was eager to demand democracy. How can it be that the Chinese people are, after forty years of communist leadership, still in the same ignorant condition as they were under Chiang Kai-shek's regime? If some old people over the age of fifty are unenlightened, this can be blamed on Chiang Kai-shek. But people under the age of fifty were all born "under the red flag and raised under the red flag"! How can it be that forty years of communist rule have produced a citizenship that is not even fit for a democratic society? Is this self-contradictory? On the one hand, the party boasts in its propaganda of forty years of achievements. On the other hand, it denies those achievements [by denying that the people are ready for democracy]. What kind of logic is this? There is no way out for China if we do not have democracy now.

Of course, we do not expect to achieve a perfect and beautiful democratic society at once; after all, the Chinese people have not had a single day of a free life. The dictatorship of thousands of years, particularly that of the last several decades, has made most people unable to adjust quickly to a democratic society. But this is no excuse for not having a democracy. Certainly, at least urban citizens, intellectuals, and Communist Party members are as ready for democracy as any of the citizens who already live in democratic societies. Thus, we should at least implement complete democracy within the Communist Party and within the urban areas. Furthermore, during the process of urbanization, we should see that people in those [rapidly developing] rural areas become acquainted with democracy.

. . . Chinese intellectuals still possess aristocratic airs: even in the revolutions for freedom and equality, they always give the impression of belonging to a class superior to others. Everyone is born equal; this issue was resolved during the Enlightenment. People's level of education may be high or low, and their contributions to society large or small, but they are all born as people and deserve the same respect. They all have the same right to pursue a good life. Intellectuals should not separate themselves from other classes and cannot claim special rights and interests. Intellectuals should be the spokesmen for the entire nation and the vanguard of social justice. The achievements of this movement that has been initiated by intellectuals will in the end be measured by the influence it has on the people. We should put our efforts into thinking about the future of the Chinese people. We should only be responsible to the people. Democracy and equality are like Siamese twins; one cannot have one without the other.

China's future rests on the shoulders of her one billion people. Only if we implement widespread democracy and more flexible economic policies will China have a way out. Democracy will check the hereditary system [that breeds corruption]; limited privatization will accelerate the development of the economy; freedom of speech and freedom of the press will provide effective supervision over the government; and equality will unite people into a greater force. But none of this will come to us: we must reach out and struggle for it.

(small-character poster at
People's University, April 24, 1989)

"Eliminate Networks of Personal Connections,
Wipe Out Petticoat Influence!"

To Party ideologues, China's huge problem of corruption was primarily attributable
to bourgeois Western thinking that exalted individualism, taught materialism, and
valued private ownership at the expense of socialist values of selflessness and collective interests. But the most important source of corruption did not lie in Western
materialism or any other foreign ideas. Rather, it lay in an explosive interaction of
new opportunity with ingrained practice. The practice of using personal influence
and connections (*guanxi*) to obtain goals and opportunities—whether a choice piece
of beef, train tickets, admission to a selective school, or a residence permit in the
city—had been pervasive well before Deng's reforms. With roots in Confucian values that emphasized family ties and loyalty, as well as reciprocity and the importance
of status, personal power and "connections" had grown even more important after
1949; in a planned economy of chronic shortages of goods and services, informal
barter and the trading of favors had become a necessary way of surviving. The
economic reforms had merely brought vastly expanded opportunities and incentives for exploiting one's status and connections. Dual-track pricing offered a quick
way to enormous profits, as did imports of foreign luxury goods; connections could
land one coveted hard currency, a phone at home, or a trip abroad—not merely a
bicycle or few days at a Chinese resort.[30]

In the following poster, the writer describes the mass of "webs of personal relationships" among the Chinese bureaucracy and traces their existence to the persis-
tence of feudal values.

UNLESS THE NET IS TORN, THE FISH WILL DIE

—Reflections on Reading "A Genealogy of the Contemporary Chinese Bureaucracy"

When faced with this huge network of personal connections, I find it hard
to believe that these people are really relatives, in-laws, parents, and children. I've tried convincing myself of the logicality of their relationships
with glib rationalizations: "the old man is a hero, his son a good fellow";
"distinguished families produce illustrious sons"; "there are no weak
troops under a strong general." However, the history of the latter days of

---

30. See note 23 above.

the Eight Banners will refute each and every one of these arguments.[31] I won't speak of the Banners at length, as former Premier Zhou Enlai used their example long ago.

Perhaps because of my old cadre background, though I could see all the smaller spiders busily and carefully weaving exquisitely intricate, far-flung webs of relationships from which they would extract benefits, it never occurred to me that the "proletarian revolutionaries, outstanding communist fighters, and excellent high-level leaders of the Chinese Communist Party" whom I so respected were also endowed with this instinct and talent for weaving webs, and indeed had, whether consciously or unconsciously, woven for themselves "magic webs." Our party is becoming ensnared in these spiders' webs, its vision impaired, its ears stopped up, its throat strangled, its strength sapped. The best and brightest are refused Party membership, while the dregs are admitted in droves. The Party is being manipulated by a bunch of "phonies."

These "spiders," having insinuated their way into the party, do nothing but spin and manipulate their silken threads, each devoting himself to the project of weaving his very own web. All that nonsense about the "Great Communist Endeavor," the "Task" entrusted to the Party by the proletariat, the "Great Social Enterprise" and the "Process of Democratization" has been nothing but fairy tales, bait to lure wealth into their webs. Never again will I believe in their saints and heroes. All that propaganda has been nothing but pretty lies, a gigantic hoax!

Perhaps I have to admit the great contributions of many older revolutionaries. They sweated blood for the people during the wars they fought in the name of revolution and democracy. But during peacetime, many of them lost the old resolute Party spirit and proletarian selfless virtue they had in the midst of war. They began to think of personal gain and to desire material comforts. They no longer wanted to be hard-working public servants; instead, they wanted to be the masters of the people, to have all kinds of privileges, to become the new gentry! How pitiful! How despicable! Our "heavenly guardians" have metamorphosed into stink-bugs (as soon as you turn your back on them, they release a fetid odor).

How could such a super-web have been woven in China? The reasons

31. The Eight Banners were military-administrative areas of the Manchu nationality in northeastern China, established in 1615. Following the Manchu conquest of China in 1644, the leaders of the Eight Banners were elevated to the aristocracy, and their families and descendants subsequently became renowned for decadence and corruption. Today, the expression "children of the Eight Banners" refers to the privileged, corrupt sons and daughters of high officials.

lie not only in the limitations and failings of the individual "spiders," but also in the profound influence of the old culture on the molding of their psychology. A look at history will reveal that they are nothing but puppets, albeit full of life and energy, manipulated by historical forces on China's grand stage, unable to break away from the ancient habits. In the early days of the revolution, when the Chinese nation faced danger, they were drawn toward the brilliance of truth by the fantastic magnetism of justice, and did great deeds for the people. However, under cover of the seemingly peaceful days that followed, the bureaucratic mindset and other seeds of feudalism that had been sleeping in the depths of their souls suddenly sprouted and grew, thriving in the greenhouse of the public trust, to the ever-increasing detriment of the people.

Perhaps some will ask: Could it be that the revolutionary will and mettle of China's proletariat was only half-baked? Having won the victory, would they refuse to entertain the proposition of democratic freedoms? Would they refuse to work toward China's advance from the realm of Nature to the realm of Freedom? The present situation shows that prospects of the party of China's proletariat are not as optimistic as Marx predicted!

Due to historical reasons, China's proletariat had the following inadequacies from the beginning: its members were few, youthful in age, and their level of education was low. The disseminators of Marxism-Leninism had the following inadequacies: many of the leaders of the proletarian revolution were not themselves of proletarian background, so in a certain sense, their revolutionary sentiments were not determined by their own will. Only under historical conditions posing a threat to the Chinese nation did workers, peasants, students, merchants, and soldiers come together to form a greater force which pushed the proletariat onto China's historical stage. Once the revolution succeeded, these deficiencies of quality gradually became obvious.

In the forty years since the founding of the People's Republic, the struggle against feudalism has never been interrupted, yet feudalism's ancient roots disappear only to reappear, tugging on people's souls. The older a person, the greater the accumulated power of the specter of feudalism in his heart. Mao Tse-tung's "love of the old" was a vivid example of this.

. . .

This is a creature of the times in China: [a man] draped in feudal robes and wearing feudal socks, intolerant of hereditary nobility, yet tolerant of the propagation of feudal-style nepotism; intolerant of the existence of the emperor, yet tolerant of continued despotism; intolerant of the clan system, yet careful to marry his children into families of status equal to his own; intolerant of lawlessness, yet utterly without regard for the sanctity of the Constitution! Enough! Enough!

Only on paper have I ever seen it said that "the freedoms of demonstration, assembly, and speech are the legal rights of the people"; never yet have I seen their existence legalized in society or heard a truthful report of their exercise! On paper, they are legal; on the streets, illegal. The government represents the Constitution, and the Constitution protects the government; the government ignores the opinions of the people, and the law of the Party supersedes the law of the country: this is China today, the result of China's marriage to Marxism, socialism in a potted landscape!

China's vast network of personal relationships and the widespread profiteering and nepotism of her officials have become one of the natural wonders of the world. We must rend the net asunder in order to advance the cause of democracy. We absolutely must not put our faith in those diehard feudal spiders, afflicted as they are with congenital AIDS. We must depend upon our ardent youth, who derive no nutrition from feudalism; youth is the true driving force!

Youth is the vanguard of history!

We will never again be deceived by any lie; we will nevermore be intimidated!

We will not submit to violence, nor will difficulties send us into retreat!

As long as we can see the truth, we will bravely press forward!

Truth calls to us, entreating us to persevere in the struggle! We must not allow our individual tragedies to become an historical tragedy!

> —The Imprecations of a Slave in the
> University's Education Department,
> April 30, 1989
> (big-character poster)

Special privileges enjoyed by Party officials, such as roomy apartments for themselves and their children, personal drivers, access to precious foreign exchange for the purchase of imported luxury items, trips to Hong Kong and abroad at state expense, and guaranteed first-class tickets galled ordinary citizens, who passed lives of an entirely different sort, an existence of cramped apartments shared by three generations, of long lines for seats on packed trains, and of a passport only upon application—an existence, in short, that reflected China's poverty and the government's control over citizens. Faced with such a sharp contrast between the life of the ordinary Chinese on the street and the Party official in his sedan, poster writers often

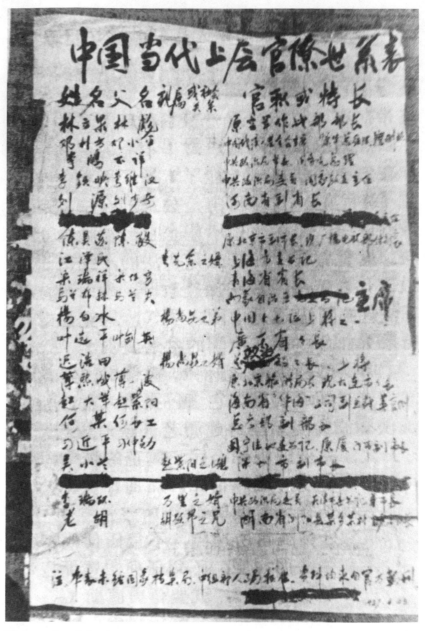

Illustration 1.3. "Genealogy of the Contemporary Chinese Bureaucracy"—a poster at Beijing University detailing the network of family relationships that exists at the top of the government. Many rumors about the background of high officials circulate among Chinese, but reliable information is difficult to come by. Credit: October Review.

found sarcasm the appropriate tool for conveying their anger and resentment. The next two pieces are examples of sarcastic treatments of the Party and its officials: the first is a litany of the special privileges enjoyed by Party officials, and the second a blistering attack on the hypocrisy of the Party.

A MEMORIAL AND TESTAMENT TO THE PRIVILEGED CLASS

The privileged class, "officials of the people,"
    you live a life to make the immortals envious;
Opening up, reform—what good opportunities—
    if you don't make money now, then you never will.
Children of officials violate the law and run wild,
    but the law barely touches them.
Although their sons and daughters are idiots,
    they can still chose between Beijing and Qinghua universities.[32]
These privileged accompany foreign guests, eating and drinking for free,
    And what's more, they receive a "subsidy" of hundreds of yuan.[33]
Not bothering to separate official business from private affairs,
    they ride gratis in airplanes and cars.
Everyone has a "special purchasing card,"
    which buys them high-quality products at low prices.[34]
Chartered planes and trains deliver gifts,
    delicacies from every land, fresh year round. . . .
The whole family happily resides in Zhongnanhai,
    their palatial second homes and villas scattered from the mountains to
    the sea.

32. [Footnote in original] An unwritten regulation stipulates that sons and daughters of officials with the rank of Vice Premier and above can enter universities without taking the national comprehensive examination.
33. [Footnote in original] It has been discovered that the monthly subsidies of senior officials who host foreign guests is over a thousand yuan.
34. [Footnote in original] "Special purchasing cards" not only allow one to buy scarce and desirable goods but also to purchase them at prices several times lower than at ordinary city markets. For example, hairtail fish of the highest quality costs only 0.60 yuan a half kilogram in Zhongnanhai. [Editors' note: After the suppression of the Democracy Movement, in an attempt to mitigate public anger at officials' privileges, the government announced that it had cancelled these special cards.]

Luxurious gleaming buildings, clubs, and hotels—
   the people can only look and sigh!
Well-known and clandestine "pleasure nests"—
   ordinary folks cannot even approach them in their lifetime.
A cluster of "public servants" for private masters,
   cooks, doctors, bodyguards;
"Staff workers" line up in front and back,
   beautiful ladies, "courtesans," await them on both sides.
"Limited-distribution movies" with sex and violence,
   only within the palaces are they not prohibited. . . .
The mighty Mercedes Benz moves through the staring red traffic light.[35]
Tourists and travelers are driven out from parks and beaches,
   only because some senior official has entered the park to play.
During their lives they enjoy to the hilt days of honor and glory,
   after death, they ascend to Babaoshan cemetery.[36]

*(big-character poster at
Beijing Normal
University, April 24)*

A SKETCH OF THE CHINESE COMMUNIST PARTY

Party leaders: Party chiefs. Personality cults, campaigns of myth-making, and a people conditioned by traditional culture have combined to transform them into godlike figures who through despotism, concentration of power, and imperious ways have become dictators over the people.

Party cadres: The servile ministers of the Party chiefs, paternalistic officials of the common people, arrogant and domineering new gentry. In-

35. [Footnote in original] The Mercedes Benz is the most luxurious car in the world. When senior officials travel through a city, the police open up a lane for them and they do not need to stop at red lights.

36. Babaoshan cemetery in the western outskirts of Beijing is the burial place for China's top military and political leaders.

sufferably overweening, they abuse their special privileges, use power to reap personal profits, take bribes, and pervert the law.

The Party organization: "Those who obey, prosper; those who oppose, perish." It co-opts those of similar mind and attacks those who disagree. An underworld gang organized along the lines of a patriarchal family.

The quality of the Party membership: Of the 47 million members of this "vanguard," as many as 75 percent have no more than an elementary-school education.[37]

Party spirit: Emasculated slavishness and ignorant loyalty from those who have lost the ability to think for themselves.

Party membership: Merely a card having utilitarian character and value as a currency of social exchange. Entry into the Party is a fashionable standard of progressiveness and a shortcut to material prosperity. Membership drastically changes the personalities of multitudes of individuals, who are transformed overnight into schizophrenic hypocrites. It severely twists the psychology of the nation's people and destroys the national character.

The will of the Party, the interests of the Party, the principles of the Party: Unopposable imperial edicts, totally meaningless "thou-shalt-nots." The Party's leaders were able to unleash, in the name of the principles, the nation-destroying living hells of the "Cultural Revolution" and the "anti-counter-revolutionaries campaign." The Party cadres used them to act as godlike authorities, gaining fame by deceiving the whole world. How many filthy exchanges have been carried out under the banner of sacred ideology!

The "Four Tendencies" of the Party: Toward formalization and idolization of the Party, toward the incontrovertible indispensability of the Party, toward proliferation of special privileges for those in the Party, and toward the corruption of Party cadres.

The Party: That leviathan of limitless power, the omnipotent lord of all under heaven. By merely issuing an order, the Party chiefs may set its vast machinery in motion; the Party's cadres and members are this machine's cogs and screws. How many of the people's most glorious heroes, pillars of the nation, has it strangled to death!

37. Under Marxist-Leninist theory, the Party is the "vanguard" of the working class, which is the representative of the advanced productive forces.

The "Greatness" of the Party: "It can correct its own mistakes."

Blood can wash clean the disgrace of autocracy, and can nourish a generation of true communists; or it can feed new feudal bosses and dictators.

(big-character poster at People's University)

One of the clearest messages of the entire Democracy Movement was that little in China remained sacrosanct after a decade of sweeping economic and social change and several years of steadily building discontent among the population. This was vividly demonstrated by student sit-in protests at the very heart of communist power—at the gates of Zhongnanhai, the Chinese Communist Party compound a quarter-mile west of Tiananmen, which housed Party offices as well as living quarters for many of the country's highest leaders. On the nights of April 19 and 20, student demonstrators, their numbers swelled by onlookers, gathered at Xinhuamen, the ceremonial main entrance to Zhongnanhai, calling for democracy and freedom. On at least one occasion, they attempted to deliver mourning wreaths and a petition to the compound, but were prevented from doing so.

On both dates, violent encounters between protestors and police guards stationed at the entrance to Zhongnanhai erupted during the early morning hours. Student and official accounts of the violence differed sharply: on the 20th, according to the students, peaceful demonstrators were suddenly set upon by police wielding belts and clubs who attempted to disperse the crowds, and numerous students were injured; according to the government, students shouted inflammatory anti-Party slogans and rushed the police, injuring at least four.

Angered by the police brutality and by the government's version of the the two Zhongnanhai clashes, students at Beijing University began boycotting classes on the 21st. Some of the students at other leading Beijing universities followed suit. The poem below, "Blood Stains," is dedicated to the "April 20 Incident." Composed by a student who had traveled to Beijing from Henan University, some 450 miles away, it calls on people to persist in their fight for democracy, anticipating that more blood would be shed on the way.

BLOOD STAINS
—In Remembrance of "April 20"

The throats of the heroic birds may all be slashed,
But dawn will continue to come.

Blood shed for freedom may have congealed,
Still there will be a new sun.
A black hand
Cannot block the light of the sky.
March on
Even though on the road ahead lies blood and death.
Life,
Life of freedom,
For these it will not be a wasted journey.

We may retain the tolerance of the sages,
We may have the honesty and purity of our ancestors,
We may assiduously struggle,
We may toil on in hardship,
But
No more shall we let the butcher's knife sacrifice us like helpless lambs.
No more shall we lend our cheeks to the kisses of humiliation and fraud.
March on!
Let us bravely bear high the banner of democracy.

Fear not a few devils,
Fear not villians,
The flame of truth can no longer be smothered,
Let it burn, let it burn all it can!

March on, free people!
Fear not that the journey will be rough,
Fear not that the road will be full of perils.
Even if ahead lies the end of our lives.
Our blood and our unconquerable souls,
Shall forever be in the annals of our nation!

> —A Voice from Henan University
> (*small-character poster,*
> *week of April 20*)

As in protest movements past, protestors frequently used poetry to voice their thoughts and emotions.[38] The poetry was not limited to the early memorial poems

38. During the mass mourning for Premier Zhou Enlai that led up to the 1976 Tiananmen

Illustration 1.4. Sit-in protestors at Xinhuamen, the main entrance to Zhongnanhai, the Communist Party headquarters, during the early morning hours of April 19. Clashes between the students and police would later break out. Credit: Franki Chan.

and couplets for Hu Yaobang; it appeared throughout the movement in all manner of places and forms, occasionally in elegant calligraphy on good paper, but far more often scrawled on a leaf of cheap notebook paper. Young Chinese obviously were drawn to poetry; even busy student leaders like Wang Dan had composed poems. This did not, of course, necessarily make them poets: much of the poetry publicly posted during the movement was mediocre, written without careful attention to meter, rhyme, or imagery, a kind of improvised free verse at best. Yet what shines through the mixed metaphors and awkward rhythms is the intensity of feeling that drove students to defy their government despite obvious danger to their safety and futures, and eventually to resort to a hunger strike. This intensity is all the more striking against the backdrop of cynicism smothering Chinese campuses before the movement's explosion.

Incident, many elegiac poems and couplets not only in modern but also in classical style were posted around Tiananmen. Collections of this poetry were later published and circulated. Poetry also comprised a significant part of the writings that appeared on Democracy Wall and in journals of the Democracy Wall movement. A carefully edited and introduced collection of the Democracy Wall poetry is *Beijing Street Voices* by David S.G. Goodman (New York: M. Boyars, 1984).

That students and others should use poetry in the midst of a highly action-oriented mass movement did not seem at all unnatural or inappropriate to the Chinese. China possesses a long tradition of poetry writing that stretches from the ancient *Book of Songs* (c. 12th-7th centuries B.C.), one of the cornerstones of classical Chinese studies, to the many contemporary poetry magazines. Poetry in post-1949 China has never been viewed as the domain of the specialist; on the contrary, an extremely wide range of Chinese, from workers to generals to statesmen, have written and published poetry. Poetry writing is viewed as evidence of one's education and mastery of language, and for this reason is a popular pastime among Chinese youth. And according to one traditional view, poetry's function is to offer social criticism—to reveal the grievances of the people and to remonstrate with their rulers. Certainly some of the poems printed in this book fulfilled this function. Perhaps most importantly, students saw poetry as a natural outlet for emotion and spontaneity, a means of expressing a sudden surge of feeling.

Two student poems from the early weeks of the movement are presented below.

EPITAPH

Black cloth wound tight on the arm,
Burying an episode of history for those to come;
Hatred will not drown
Those angry eyes in the black night.
Even if the dawn dies,
Stars will burn in place of tears;
Even if life is never again precious,
Time will be made a monument.

Thousands of years of silence;
In despair, hope decays;
How many times sorrow, joy, parting, and reunion—
China's song of hardship.
Again and again
Beating against the wall.
Use the lines of distress etched in the face
To smash the shackles and fetters.

(big-character poster,
circa April 22, 1989)

VESUVIUS VOLCANO
—In A.D. 78, Mount Vesuvius in northern Italy erupted, leaving the
once-prosperous city of Pompeii in ruins

Once, twice, countless times
I doused my raging flames;
Once, twice, countless times
I swallowed my boiling tears.
Deep in a nightmarish sleep, I dozed for centuries on centuries;
Look at the ice in my mouth, the snow on my face,
And the thorns on my arms and legs
   crawling with venomous scorpions.

O great Earth,
You are not a song, nor a psalm;
Look, great Earth—
My breast heaves, my lips crack with fury.
I want, with twenty-four hours of silent eruption,
To mourn the deathly silence of a hundred thousand hells.

I want to use my sulphur, my lava, my showers of stones
To destroy your colosseum, your temples, your cities;
To destroy your sun god, your moon god, your Supreme Being;
To destroy everything, everything that you have forced upon me.

> —A student at the Beijing Languages
> Institute, April 24, 1989
> *(published in student* News Herald, *No. I, May 2)*

At its inception, and until the government declaration of martial law on May 20, the
student movement did not seek to challenge the authority of the Party or the government. Indeed, students went out of their way to show the authorities and the
populace that they supported the Party and sought only change within it. Students
avoided anti-government and anti-Party slogans in their marches in April, and in the
mass student march of May 4 actually carried signs proclaiming "Support the leadership of the Communist Party." To a considerable extent, such pledges of faith
were hollow utterances intended to shield the movement from official criticism, for

Illustration 1.5. Students and citizens copy down poems and short essays pasted on the bas-relief walls at the base of the Monument to the People's Heroes. Credit: Abbas / Magnum.

many students either had completely rejected the Party or were indifferent to it. But at the same time, some expressions of support for the Party were genuine; despite great disappointment in its performance, a significant number of students still believed in the Party—or believed that no viable alternative to it would exist in the near future. This abiding faith in the Party's potential is shown, for example, in the long "open letter" below, in which the writer, though extremely critical of the Party and its leaders—even sarcastic at points—nonetheless looks in the end to the Party for change that will lead China out of its present plight.

AN OPEN LETTER TO THE CENTRAL COMMITTEE OF THE CHINESE COMMUNIST PARTY AND THE STATE COUNCIL OF CHINA

Honorable members of the Central Committee of the Chinese Communist Party, the State Council, and the Standing Committee of the National People's Congress:

We are very pleased that you have not taken harsh measures against the students marching and petitioning in Tiananmen Square. However, what right do you have to act otherwise? What right do you have to label the actions that students rightfully take to show their concern for the welfare of the country and its people "illegal activities incited and participated in by a small handful of bad people who aim to destroy the stability and unity of our country"? We think you must be aware that the people who have participated in the "events" are by no means "a small handful," nor are they only students from Beijing. Students in Shanghai, Wuhan, Jinan, and other medium- and large-sized cities have also taken to the streets at the same time. How can it be that a "small handful" of people have the influence to manipulate the entire country's students? No, we certainly have not been used by others. We act completely of our own accord! We act out of a true love of our Motherland and the Chinese nation! Our fervent hearts and our consciences do not allow us to keep silent any longer. We must rise up and come to the rescue of our homeland, which is afflicted with a multitude of ills.

At each student movement, the government invokes the same old refrain: "We must maintain a stable and unified political situation. . . ." In comparison to countries like Iran, Iraq, Israel, and Haiti, our country is stable and unified. Yet why doesn't the government use the dialectical method (of which Mao often reminded us) of "dividing into two" the great "whole," that is, why can't it see the other side of this heralded "situation of stability and unity"? If it did, then perhaps it would be able to grasp the problems facing our country. I feel that using the expression "rot coated with gold and jade" to describe the country's present situation is rather apt. Let us take a look at our country.

Officialdom is a stretch of blackness. Using the expression, "out of ten officials, nine are corrupt" to describe the situation of every level of the bureaucracy in our country is no exaggeration. This is especially true of cadres at the grass-roots level. They are "hick" emperors; during their term of office, the people have suffered, their waists growing narrower as officials' waists thicken. The forerunner of the Chinese democratic revolution, Sun Yat-sen, held that officials are supposed to be the "servants of the people," but what we have now is exactly the opposite.[39] Foreign presidents who come to our country are bewildered by the sight of police cars opening up a path for our state cadres when they venture out. Let's see what these foreign guests have to say: "Our people are the taxpayers, we all depend on them for our living, we dare not make the people yield the road to us." Perhaps some will say that this is false humility on their part, designed to win the people's support. But what about us? We are incapable of anything, even this type of "hypocrisy." A good portion of cadres only know how to issue decrees and orders, to attend endless banquets, to squander the wealth created by the people's sweat and blood, to cram the gold of the national treasury into their pockets, so swollen that no more can be stuffed in. Profiteering by government officials, bureaucratism, officials protecting one another . . . these phenomena are not unlike hordes of termites rotting the foundation of the socialist tower and invading the body of our motherland.

Our society is a mess. It has fallen into its most serious plight since Liberation.[40] Murder, violence, and robbery have become the norm rather than the exception. People who see others in danger do not go to their rescue. People who see money instead open their eyes and forget all else. . . . How many citizens are there who do not even possess a minimal level of morality? This only demonstrates that our country's laws are weak and ineffective, and that the government is incompetent. . . .

The contributions of the Chinese Communist Party to the Chinese revolution are undeniable, despite its errors. During the period of war [when the Party first joined the battle against the Japanese invaders and then liberated the Chinese from the corrupt rule of the Kuomintang], the peo-

39. Sun Yat-sen, often referred to as "father of the country," is a towering figure in both Communist Chinese and Kuomintang versions of modern Chinese history. While in exile, Sun founded the Revolutionary Alliance (T'ung-meng Hui), which launched a series of domestic revolts against the Manchu throne from 1905 to 1911. Although the roles of Sun and the Revolutionary Alliance in the Revolution of 1911, which finally precipitated the abdication of the emperor, has been disputed by some historians, Sun was indisputably a leading figure in the revolutionary movement of the 1920s that sought to end the rule of warlords and unite China. In fundraising speeches in the United States after the suppression of the Democracy Movement, top Chinese dissidents, heedful of strong anticommunist sentiment among many Chinese-Americans, but also clearly willing to cast themselves in the role of inheritors of Sun's revolutionary legacy, repeatedly quoted Sun—not Mao Tse-tung.
40. In Communist Chinese parlance, "Liberation" is the Communist liberation of China in 1949 from Kuomintang rule and oppression.

ple loved and supported the Party because it indeed brought the people benefits. But history has moved forward. Now as we approach the end of the twentieth century, what is the situation of the Party? It may be said that a great portion of the people no longer trust the Party. The reason for this is not a small handful of people who, wanting to overturn the rule of the Communist Party, spread rumors throughout the masses; rather, it is the corruption of the Party itself. Is the governance of the pyramid— the elaborate Party organization with its levels and levels—serving a positive or negative function? The peasants hate most the local county Party secretaries, for they are incapable of doing anything other than extorting money earned with the peasants' blood and sweat and gorging themselves until they are fat and their faces greasy and shiny. As for the workers, the faces they abhor most are those of the secretaries of the factories' Party Committees, because they only know how to preach lectures at endless meetings; they have neither the ability nor the knowledge to discuss technical matters. And as for university students, they dislike most those "administrators" [Party officials in the schools], because they only know how to conduct, gesticulating absurdly, "political study" classes.[41] If the entire society voices dissatisfaction with this stratum of officials who only feed themselves from the bowls the Party has secured for them without doing any work, the Secretary General of the Party should consider how to put an end to such a state of affairs.

The nature of the relationship between the Party and people is the same as the nature of the relationship between the army and the people. Just as fish cannot survive without water, the Party cannot survive without the people.[42] It was the people who created the Party and who made the Party's ranks grow. It is the people who raise and sustain several million soldiers and several hundred million cadres, big and small alike. But for

41. "Political study" classes are study sessions called and led by Party officials during which Marxist theory, the Party's recent policies, and important speeches by leaders are studied and discussed. In the 1980s, under Deng Xiaoping's policy of emphasizing economic development over class struggle and politics, political study sessions steadily became less regular. At leading universities such as Beijing University and People's University, most departments held study sessions only once every several weeks, whereas they had been held at least once a week during the late 1970s and virtually every day during the Cultural Revolution. In recent years a typical session would begin with the Party official reading portions of speeches or editorials from the *People's Daily* and soliciting comments. Discussion was often lethargic and extremely superficial; most persons at the sessions can best be described as apathetic. Since the suppression of the Democracy Movement, political study sessions have been revived.

42. A famous saying by Mao Tse-tung described the relationship between the Communist army and the people as that of "fish and water."

a long time now, the Party has put its interests and influence ahead of the government and the state; for a long time, it has touted itself as the "great Party," the "glorious Party," and the "correct Party." In its absolute rectitude and perfection, it calls on the people to "keep step with the Party Central Committee," and orders the people "to conscientiously carry out and implement the policies and decisions of the Central Committee" (regardless of whether they are correct or not). Whoever dares to raise a dissenting opinion is considered anti-Party and "anti-socialist." For these people, the Party does not hesitate to pick on their personal faults or problems, bludgeon them, or brand them with political labels. Do not believe that this type of thing only occurred during the Cultural Revolution. In 1987, there was Fang Lizhi, Liu Binyan, and Wang Ruowang; most recently, the investigation of and intervention in the *Science and Technology Daily* and the Shanghai *World Economic Herald* (two papers read by intellectuals).[43] The authorities' suppression of the students' constitutionally valid activities in Beijing and the use of electric prods on students by the Wuhan police—what are the differences between these incidents and the measures used in the Cultural Revolution against intellectuals, or the measures used by the Kuomintang in the late 1930s to repress student movements? If the Communist Party truly represents the interests of the people, the people will follow the Party without hesitation. But if the Party formulates policies that are inappropriate to China's situation, and issues mistaken orders, must the people still follow? The Party is not a god; nor is it a one-person organization. Yet, the Party has deified itself. . . .

In recent years the Party has changed to become more courageous than in the past. It is beginning to acknowledge that "nobody can be correct forever, the Party too is fallible, and therefore making mistakes is permissible." Indeed, whether committed by persons or by the Party, mistakes

43. Liu Binyan (an investigative journalist), Wang Ruowang (a writer), and Fang Lizhi were three outspoken liberal intellectuals expelled from the Party in the Anti-Bourgeois Liberalism campaign in 1987. Fang, a respected astrophysicist and vociferous critic of the Party who has openly challenged the merits of Marxism, was made one of the main scapegoats for the 1986 student unrest. Liu is best known for his pioneering pieces of "reportage literature," candid exposés of Party corruption and malfeasance, published in the late 1970s and early 1980s. He is currently residing in the United States, and in 1989 was one of the founding members of the Federation for a Democratic China (see Chapter 6). Wang Ruowang, a prominent figure in Shanghai intellectual circles, was labeled a bourgeois liberal for his criticism of the Party and its monopoly on power. In September 1989 he was arrested; he has since been accused of writing articles in support of the student protests and giving "counter-revolutionary" speeches in People's Square in Shanghai.

are unavoidable. This is obvious in the Party's past decisions to ignore population control, to initiate the Cultural Revolution, and to criticize, denounce, and ostracize our country's intellectuals. But these have gone beyond mere mistakes; they are crimes—against all of the people and against the entire Chinese nation! According to law, those guilty of murder must be sentenced to capital punishment. The consequence of the Party's crimes is not only the death of one or two persons, or a dozen or so people, but a threat to the existence of our entire state and our entire nation!

Yet no one has assigned guilt to Mao Tse-tung or to the Party. This is perhaps because our legal system is not sound, and our society is governed by the whim of the powerful. Despite the fact that we now have an established legal system, the Party remains paramount. The fact that when Party members commit crimes, Party discipline instead of law is used to sanction them is irrefutable evidence of this.[44]

Heraclitus of ancient Greece once said that "Man must fight for law, and be armed with the law in his struggles." During the Qin Dynasty, the great reformist Shang Yang[45] stated much the same. The point is that even ancient men realized the importance of law in governing a country. But, what is the present state of our legal system? Everywhere we see law replaced by power. For example, when a mayor's son breaks the law, he is

---

44. Disciplinary Inspection Committees established at all but the lowest levels of the Party hierarchy are responsible for investigating and disciplining Party members accused of violating Party discipline or breaking the law. Article 39 of the Party's charter provides for five types of punishment: (1) a warning; (2) a serious warning; (3) dismissal from Party posts and a recommendation to non-Party organizations to dismiss the wayward person from non-Party posts; (4) placement on probation; and (5) expulsion from the Party.

Party members who are suspected of having committed a crime are afforded special protection from legal prosecution by a number of factors. First, Party procedures call for a Party investigation before the matter is turned over to the police or procurator. Only after the Party Disciplinary Inspection Committee has concluded that the member has committed the crime and has stripped him of his Party credentials will the police or procuratorate step in to take the case. Because the Secretary of a Disciplinary Inspection Committee is subordinate to the Secretary of the general Party Committee at the same level, it is nearly impossible for him to carry out an investigation of the Party Committee Secretary or any persons the latter is shielding. Second, the "revolutionary record" of Party members or the fact that they have already been disciplined within the Party often mitigates the severity of legal punishment. Finally, courts will routinely consult with the Party Committee of the work unit of a convicted member before sentencing him.

45. Shang Yang (d. 338 B.C.) was a statesman and one of the earliest Legalists, men who believed that strong laws were essential to effective governance. Their advocacy of a strong, impartial legal system was not rooted in the desire to protect individual rights, however, but in the goal of enabling a ruler to maintain control over local populations.

not punished by the law, but by a private letter written by a provincial governor. This is the way all criminal activities committed by officials and their relatives are dealt with. Consequently, we have two systems for dealing with those who break the law—one for the average citizen, and one for Party members and their families. Furthermore, it is often the case that those who knowingly break the law go free if they have power, and often go on to punish the innocent. For those with power, good wine and cigarettes are effective problem solvers. And when a man has entered the circles of power, life suddenly becomes much easier for his friends and relatives as well. Although each year brings a plethora of new laws, the citizen is left wondering which should be taken seriously. Two thousand years ago, Shang Yang emphasized that "righteousness is important, but the law is even more important." He stressed that law should be applied without discrimination, regardless of an individual's status. Our forefathers understood the importance of law. . . .

However, the situation under our current system of law is quite different. The person who embezzles two hundred million yuan escapes the law because of his so-called contribution to the revolution. Consequently, the credibility of our system of law is seriously undermined. . . .

This is our "stable and unified" homeland! This "stable and unified" political situation is nothing but an exchange market for greedy officials and crooked clerks, an environment that generates official and private profiteers. It is a "stable and unified" one-party totalitarian government. Its continuation will surely lead to further corruption in our politics, and eventually to the country's damnation. What is there in this kind of "stability" and "unity" for us to value and fear losing?

The economic reform, though it promises some short-term achievements, does not offer fundamental solutions to the problems that ail our nation. Today and yesterday, in and out of China, one finds virtually no case where social reform depending entirely on changes of the economic structure of a given country has succeeded. China today faces a turning point in her history: it has been proven that the fossilized theoretical models derived from the classic works of Marx and Lenin, coupled with an imported political and economic system from the USSR, cannot bring prosperity to our country. But our country cannot turn to "complete Westernization."

The economic reforms that we have undertaken in the past ten years have left us worse off rather than better off; and the more reforms are proposed, the stronger resistance they meet, for the people's patience is nearly tried to its limit. The people remain tolerant not only because it is their well-trained habit to do so—a virtue much valued for centuries—

but also because they understand that the current reforms are meant to bring them a better life. They hope for a speedy solution to the problems that currently afflict our society. However, their tolerance is after all not endless. The past ten years of experience have made it clear that economic reform alone will not work, and that it is imperative to reform our political system. However, as political reform necessarily threatens the interests of the big shots as well as those of the middle-level cadres between the big shots and the common people, its implementation entails great risks. The very thought that this group of top and minor officials, if they feel cornered, might act in unison to launch a second Cultural Revolution is a realistic threat for those who have had the taste of the cowsheds [makeshift prisons] in the Cultural Revolution. It is no wonder that policy makers have been reluctant to promote political reform.

It has been said that "the establishment of democracy is a long and gradual process." This much we understand; yet we insist on asking: isn't forty years long enough? and, after these past forty years, what stage is Chinese "democracy" at? We have nothing, virtually nothing—except the legacy of our idolization of Mao Tse-tung, whose "one line" could change the world; the legacy of branding those who loved our country, and who dared to speak out, "rightists" and "counter-revolutionaries"; the legacy of the Cultural Revolution, which condemned our nation to hell; and the legacy of expropriating the political rights of those who call for democracy. At street corners, one often hears people say that the reason the people in power bear so much fear and hatred toward democracy is that democracy threatens to take away their authority and monopoly of power. As students in modern times, we did not believe such talk, but placed our trust in the government. We held great expectations for the Party and the government—but now we must face cold reality: the government and the Party have always let us down!

China simply has too many problems, and I will name no more. I also realize that, either in theoretical training or in practical experience, I have no more wisdom than does our current leadership, even less than our Party. I express these personal viewpoints simply as a Chinese citizen, and as one of the millions of college students. I have a loyal and patriotic heart, and I long for our country's prosperity and strength. Perhaps the statements I have made above sound deviant and radical, and perhaps some will incur denunciation as "counter-revolutionary statements" for which I may even be put in jail. But as I believe, at least for now, that what I have written are the right, patriotic things to say, and will be beneficial to our country. I hope that my words will reach the desks of Premier Li Peng, Secretary General Zhao Ziyang, and Senior Deng.

It is my hope that our senior leaders will go more often to visit the factories and the schools, the countryside and the army, not only because there are many problems demanding their attention but also because only there will they find the key to the solutions that will save China from imminent disaster.

Youth are the backbone of China!

—A student in the Auditing Department, Institute of Economics, Wuhan University, April 28, 1989
(*small-character poster*)

Other students neither had such faith in the Party and government nor assumed the Party to be the rightful leader of the nation. Their premise, reflected in the sarcastic essay below, was rather that the government was a servant (or as the essayist would have it, a pack animal) of the people—one that had to be mastered, since the Chinese had no other alternative to it.

BAI LE EVALUATES DONKEYS[46]
—Link up with the government

The government is in fact a type of donkey. Originally, we used it to pull the cart, but now it has changed into an animal that loves to eat and sleep, into a lazy bad-tempered worker that lashes out at will. It is impractical to sell it and buy another: there is no other donkey on the market. To kill it for its meat is even more unacceptable, and furthermore, its meat is too bitter. The only alternative we have is to train it with a carrot and a big stick!

The "carrot" is the support of the people; the "stick" is the resistance and protest of the people. At the moment, the stick is not yet big enough and hard enough to wield against the government, but what we can do is make the people wake up and act to protect their rights and interests.

Thus our goal is not to overthrow the government, but rather to supervise and prod it along and even assist it in moving forward. Our united

46. The title of the poster is a satiric modification of a Chinese saying, "Bai Le Evaluates Horses," which is based on the story of Bai Le, a man renowned for his ability to pick out the strongest and swiftest horses from a group.

front can include it, too! Don't forget that our dear Party joined hands with General Chiang Kai-shek during the "Xian Incident"![47] We should all have the spirit of generals!

There is an old Chinese saying, "Let you shame or embarrass a person too severely, he will only respond by becoming angry," which carries a lot of weight. We want the government to feel worried, to feel ashamed of itself and its actions, but we must have a good sense of timing and move carefully; we must work in stages. We don't want to enrage the Party, for this donkey will "jump" and kick out, and that would be a terrible mess!

. . .

Of course, this donkey is awfully difficult to train, so we must have patience, at the very least more patience than the donkey itself has. Don't forget: a donkey is after all a donkey, you can't expect it to behave and think like a person. So it's even more important to keep in mind strategy. Don't expect it to start behaving the way we want overnight, to go right away to the circus to perform and start making a lot of money. We have to teach it one step at a time!

And one last thing: pay attention not to get kicked by the donkey—it is really fat and strong.

—Son of the Earth, April 24
(*big-character poster at
People's University*)

If many students, disillusioned as they were, continued to support the leadership of the Party—at least until the declaration of martial law on May 20 and the violent suppression of the Democracy Movement, which may well have permanently destroyed the Party's credibility for students as well as many urban residents—then there were also many who did not. The students who totally rejected the Party's right to rule and blamed the Party for China's last forty years of turbulence and backwardness were often Party members. Indeed, many of the student and other pro-democracy demonstrators were Party members, a fact that was acknowledged by the present hard-line leadership in an unprecedentedly frank assessment of the

---

47. On December 12, 1936, Chiang Kai-shek, head of the Kuomintang government, was taken prisoner in Xi'an by one of his own generals who was unhappy with the Kuomintang's policy of waging civil war against the communists rather than resisting Japanese encroachments onto Chinese soil. Chiang was held captive for thirteen days until he agreed to call off the campaign against the communists and join them in a united front against the Japanese. From 1937 to 1945, the two parties cooperated in an uneasy alliance against the Japanese before turning on each other again upon the defeat of the foreign threat.

Party's problems after the crushing of the movement.[48] For many Chinese citizens, Party membership today does not mean that one recognizes the right of the Party to lead the country, believes in Marxism, or supports to Party policies. Rather, Party membership is a kind of necessary hurdle to professional advancement, and joining the Party, a concession to both practical realities and pressure from leaders in one's unit.

The anonymous poster below, one that completely rejects the legitimacy of the Party, cannot be considered typical. Yet it probably voices the thoughts of a good many Chinese who dared not to openly criticize the Party in such absolute terms. The poster was among those condemned in the official report by Beijing Mayor Chen Xitong on the quelling of the "counter-revolutionary rebellion" that appeared in the People's Daily on July 7, 1989. Two of the descriptions of the Party from the poster, "the most evil party of its time" and "the Party is on the verge of extinction," were specifically cited as anti-Party invective.

REFLECTIONS ON THE HISTORY OF THE CHINESE COMMUNIST PARTY

The history of the Chinese Communist Party positively informs us that it indeed deserves to be called the most evil party of its time. It only cares about its own position and pays no heed to the future of the country and the people. When the Chinese Communist Party was first founded, it attached itself to Sun Yat-sen's Nationalist party and thus quickly grew in strength. Taking advantage of the Japanese invasion of China and the Kuomintang unification of the country under the leadership of Chiang Kai-shek, the Communist Party prepared itself for a large-scale civil war; finally, after the war with Japan ended, the Communist Party positioned itself to challenge the Kuomintang Party. As soon as it was able to destroy the Kuomintang Party, it did so thoroughly and without hesitation. All the promises it made upon founding the country turned out to be nothing more than lies: private property was forcibly confiscated and converted into primary capital accumulation; all of the small parties that the Com-

---

48. In August 1989, Song Ping, Politburo member and head of the Party's Organizational Department, made what was a startling admission for the Party, conceding in public remarks: "Many of the people who incited and fomented this turmoil and rebellion were Party members" (see People's Daily, Overseas Edition, August 23, 1989, p. 1). Song Ping also noted that of the twenty-odd people who were named as major instigators of the "counter-revolutionary rebellion" in an official report on the protests by Beijing Mayor Chen Xitong on July 7, 1989, the great majority were Party members.

munist Party allowed to exist after the founding of the Republic gradually developed a father-son relationship with it; intellectuals met humiliation, exploitation, and repression; peasants' status and living standards did not rise; in particular, the people living in the old Party bases [the extremely poor rural areas where the Party developed its first stronghold] were deceived. The so-called "united front" was merely an infamous trick by the most evil party of its time [to create the appearance of a socialist democracy].

Other than wasting China's youth for forty years, the Communist Party has brought nothing to China. They have simply repeated history—they have just recycled the role of the Northern warlords and that of the Nationalist Party and revisited the historical development of socialism and capitalism. China still has not progressed. One hundred years ago, when China was in the period of the Tongzhi Restoration, it was keeping pace with the powerful Western nations; but today, China lingers at the same level as the poor African countries. Seventy years ago, a generation of elites held high the banners of democracy and science; today, our generation must raise them up again. In the last forty years, the Chinese Communists have produced 235,000,000 primitive illiterates; moreover, the modern illiterates are beyond count! The country's unification is far from being realized; on the contrary, nationalist separatism is on the rise once more. If things continue this way, China's days are numbered.

Mr. Jin Guantao [a well-known historian] has said, "Every organization, during the process of its development and maturation, will [inevitably] give birth to non-organizational forces [in response]. The mission of these non-organizational forces is nothing but to shake and destroy the existence of the organization." The Chinese Communist Party is an organization on the verge of extinction. The so-called "Cultural Revolution" launched by Mao Tse-tung and the so-called policy of "opening up and reform" led by Deng Xiaoping have given rise to the non-organizational forces that will eradicate it. Today, the Communist Party, especially its members who are government cadres, has already become a new privileged class of Chinese society. So-called "profiteering by officials," "engineering projects approved at the stroke of an official's pen," and "companies of princes" are just some of the Party's masterpieces; there's much more. The Central Committee's "Party of the Imperial Descendants" is even more powerful and frightening. Of course, actual power is in the hands of Deng Xiaoping and his relatives, disciples, sycophants, and card buddies. There are gangs and factions springing up all over and cliques forming across the country. Hoodlums freely form gangs without the army or the police taking action. Great turmoil across the whole of China is imminent. The Communist Party's day of reckoning is about to arrive. Readers, let's keep our eyes open and watch what happens!

(unsigned big-character poster
at People's University,
week of April 16, 1989)

For five straight days, from Sunday, April 16 to Thursday, April 20, Tiananmen Square had been the site of peaceful student demonstrations, the Monument to the People's Heroes in its center a stage for displays of mourning as well as of cries for democracy. The audience had been primarily university students, but each day brought out increasing numbers of Beijing residents. Many Chinese, including government officials, had initially dismissed the protests as a passing phenomenon, a case of students letting off steam. But by Friday, April 21, the first signs that this was no "ordinary student movement," as Deng himself would later put it, had appeared. Student demonstrations with thousands of participants had broken out in other major Chinese cities, including Shanghai, Nanjing, Wuhan, and Xi'an—considerably smaller than the Beijing protest, but one indication of how widespread student disenchantment with the nation's leadership was. Students in Beijing were boycotting classes. And Chinese intellectuals had begun to speak out: forty-seven prominent liberal intellectuals, led by the poet Bei Dao, one of the initiators of the early spring signature drive to free Wei Jingsheng, had delivered an open letter to the Central Committee supporting the students' demands.

All of this came to a climax on the evening of April 21 and the morning of April 22, the day of a state memorial service for Hu Yaobang. In preparation for the service, authorities had declared that the Square would be sealed off by early morning on the 22nd. However, in the first resounding triumph of student numbers and organization over state authority, tens of thousand of students gathered in Tiananmen in the evening of the 21st and announced their intention to remain there through the service. Masses of Beijing residents swelled the crowd to 200,000. In the end, no measures were taken to force the students out of the Square. But certainly many of those assembled there on the night of the 21st must have recalled the Tiananmen Incident of April 5, 1976, in which hundreds of thousands of mourners for Premier Zhou Enlai had been surrounded and attacked by the Beijing militia. At least several hundred, perhaps severalfold more, had died in that bloody assault. There were other parallels to the Tiananmen Incident that the assembled students could not have overlooked: as in 1976, the presence of so many in the Square was a thinly veiled protest against those in power, and the current mayor of Beijing,

Chen Xitong—like Wu De, the mayor in 1976—was a close ally of the targets of the protest.

In the poem below, a student airily speculates on the thoughts of China's highest leaders on the day of Hu's memorial service.

QUESTIONS AND ANSWERS BETWEEN THE BIGWIGS
—A record of an event at the Great Hall of the People on April 22

Li Peng, [Zhao] Ziyang,
Leading Wan Li [Chairman of the Standing Committee of the NPC],
Clambered onto the corner of the roof of the Great Hall of the People.
Hands behind their backs, they looked out of the corner of their eyes.
All they could see were ranks of petitioners,
Cries, shaking the skies, throngs covering the ground.
Ai! What's to be done?
Lo, Heaven will be overturned![49]

[Deng] Xiaoping asked, what means do we have?
[Yang] Shangkun replied,
We have millions of soldiers.
Don't you see the bright spring month of "April the Fifth [1976],"
The Square was covered with fresh blood.

We also have reserves.
If the Army is not enough,
Add the police.
No need to worry,
Heaven and Earth will not be turned upside down.

—To the meter of Mao Tse-tung's
"The Bird's Dialogue"[50]
(big-character poster)

---

49. According to traditional Chinese cosmology, the emperor was endowed with the mandate of Heaven. Thus the "overturning of Heaven" symbolized not only natural calamity but also a change in the political order.

50. "The Bird's Dialogue" was a poem composed by Mao in 1965, after China had broken off relations with the Soviet Union, in which Mao described Brezhnev as a short-sighted revisionist.

After the conclusion of the memorial service, students in the Square chanted for Premier Li Peng, the head of the government, to come out and meet with them. Three student representatives were allowed to pass through the line of paramilitary police blocking the approach to the western entrance of the Great Hall of the People, the massive building housing government offices and state meeting halls. In a dramatic gesture invoking the manner in which petitions were presented to Chinese emperors in times past, the three representatives knelt on the steps to present the students' petition, and the representative carrying the large scroll containing the petition raised it over his head. The three remained on the steps for about forty-five minutes; when it became apparent that neither Li Peng nor any other high official would emerge to receive the petition, they withdrew.

The representatives' gesture of kneeling in a plea to the government moved many onlookers, but also bitterly angered many students. These mixed emotions are reflected in the next two selections.

A PETITION SUBMITTED ON THEIR KNEES

At approximately 1:00 in the afternoon, a surge went through the crowds of students assembled in Tiananmen Square to demand government action. All peered forward. A solemn and moving picture appeared in front of them: three student representatives kneeling on the steps of the Great Hall of the People, the one in the middle holding a scroll of white paper high above his head, hoping in this way to move the "servants of the people" into emerging from the Great Hall to talk with the students. One minute after another passed. The student representatives became tired— so tired that they sagged down to the ground. Yet they continued to hold the petition above their heads. Approximately fifteen minutes [sic] passed; still they were ignored. Having no alternative, the students retreated down the steps. At this moment, the sound of weeping swept through the seated protestors. This solemn and moving scene was carved into every single person's heart. This memory, formed from drops of blood, will never be forgotten.

"Public servants," where has your conscience gone? Do you have any sense of humanity left? In the past, even Mao Tse-tung, Zhou Enlai, and Liu Shaoqi would come out in the middle of the night to meet with "rebellious little generals" of the Red Guards.[51] Now, with tens of thousands

---

51. In response to Mao Tse-tung's call in mid-1966 on the eve of the Cultural Revolution to purge bourgeois elements from all sectors of Chinese society, millions of high school and

of students sitting in front of you for more than ten hours, who, despite hunger and exhaustion, remained orderly, you not only ignored them, but also mobilized a force of the military police, intending to use bloody force to suppress the peacefully protesting students. Your actions have deeply wounded the hearts of a generation. Your actions have demonstrated to the entire world that you are a bureaucracy opposed to democracy and freedom. But there will come a day when history will mete out just punishment for your ruthless actions.

—Graduate students of Beijing University
*(big-character poster
at Beijing University)*

TRAGEDY OF THE AGE

Fellow students who participated in the April 22 petition protest will be unable to forget this scene: three representatives of the petitioners kneeling on the steps of the Great Hall of the People [in an attempt] to deliver the petition. Many of our classmates have expressed perplexity, surprise, and even anger at this action. We would like to testify that we respect the representatives' spirit in bearing the burden of such humiliation.

In the China of the eighties, during a march for democracy, people use a means of petitioning tainted with the stains of feudalism: kneeling! Is this not the tragedy of our age?

Did they disgrace us? Were they begging for freedom? Begging for democracy? No! They sacrificed their own self-respect and human dignity to fulfill a mission entrusted to them by tens of thousands of students. Think about it. As the representatives of tens of thousands of students, entrusted with so heavy a responsibility at such a critical moment, after the petition had been ignored over and over again, what else could they do but use the most provocative, most feudal method—kneeling? What self-mockery to use a feudal method of expression in a struggle for de-

---

college students formed Red Guard units that took over schools, and mercilessly criticized and physically attacked teachers, administrators, and other figures of authority. Initially Mao's proxies in the Cultural Revolution, the zealous Red Guards had spun out of control by early 1967, wreaking chaos with violent attacks on any targets that displeased them, and battling among themselves. Only with the intervention of the army later that year, at the direction of Mao and other Party leaders, was order gradually restored.

mocracy in present-day China! And what powerlessness and impotence it implies!

We want to express our understanding and respect to you, the bearers of our petition. Although your action may itself be controversial, it is indeed a microcosm of, a symbol of, the student movement of contemporary China!

—Geology Department, April 22, 1989
(poster)

2

THE FOUNDING OF THE BEIJING STUDENTS' FEDERATION AND THE APRIL 27 MASS STUDENT MARCH

"Mama, We're Not Wrong!"

April 22 – May 1

"These people have come under the influence and encouragement of Yugoslavian, Polish, Hungarian and Russian elements who [agitate for] liberalization, who urge them to rise up and create turmoil. Their goal is to overthrow the leadership of the Communist Party. They will cause the country and the Chinese people to have no future. We must take measures and act quickly, without losing any time."
Deng Xiaoping, April 24, 1989, in remarks to Party leaders

"The whole Party and the people of the entire country must ... unite and take a firm stand against turmoil. ... It is absolutely forbidden to establish any illegal organization. ... Illegal demonstrations are forbidden. Going to factories, to the countryside, and to the schools to link up with others is forbidden."
People's Daily editorial, April 26, 1989

"Academic credits are truly valuable, a degree worth even more; but without democracy, we don't want either!"
student slogan on eve of class boycott

"Pleading on behalf of the people is absolutely not turmoil!"
student placard, late April 1989

Student pro-democracy activism continued to gain momentum in the week after Hu's memorial service. As new posters urging students to expand their pro-democracy activities blanketed campus walls and began spilling out onto neighborhood walls and telephone poles, student activists focused on founding a united organization. What had been spontaneous outbursts of sorrow and frustration were rapidly metamorphosing into an organized movement for political reform.

Student leaders at universities across Beijing had two immediate goals: first, to set up at each school an independent organization that would supplant the official student union, and second, to maximize student strength by establishing a unified organization that would coordinate protests. The official unions, charged under the national student federation's charter with "implementing the Party's educational policies under the leadership of the school's Party organization," did little but organize Party-sanctioned activities such as sport days, Party propaganda campaigns, or anodyne commemorations of historical events. In most Beijing universities, the student union was supervised by a Deputy Secretary of the school Party Committee, together with union "representatives" nominated and chosen by school Party officials. For these reasons, few students believed the unions represented student interests; on the contrary, they suspected them of being government listening posts. Similarly, union leaders were regarded as ambitious politicos interested in strengthening their Party ties.[1]

Beijing University students were some of the quickest to challenge the official student unions. On April 19, activists put up a poster demanding their dissolution; the following day, they announced the establishment of an autonomous student group, the Beijing University Students' Solidarity Committee. The short poster below shows the contempt in which students held the official unions.

DOWN WITH STUDENT BUREAUCRATS

When the students are fighting for democracy and freedom, what are the student unions doing? Student unions ought to be organizations generated by the students themselves, serving the students. [Leaders of] the student union at Beijing University, however, by willingly playing the role of

1. Student union chairmen have frequently gone on to high Party posts. For example, Hu Qili, a Politburo member until mid-June and formerly Mayor of Tianjin and head of Party propaganda work, served as Chairman of the Beijing University student union in the 1950s. Similarly, Jia Chunwang, former head of the Ministry of State Security, had been chair of the student union while a student at Qinghua University.

running dogs of bureaucracy, and having become bureaucrats themselves, have betrayed the interests of the students. At the time of the election, they played games with one another and exchanged favors to win votes; after they were elected, they used public funds to pay off their personal debts. Now the chairman of the student union himself has gone so far as to tear down the big-character poster bearing the signature of "the [autonomous] student union." What did he do that for? He only did it for his personal interest, for fame and personal gain which will pave the way for his becoming a bureaucrat sitting comfortably above the people. In the middle of the student movement, [these leaders] hide inside the university, anxious as hell; yet they are not worrying at all about the student movement, but about the possibility that their positions might be in jeopardy. Yesterday, when the student demonstrators returned to campus, they tried with a cart of plain water to buy off our heroes who had been out there fighting for over twenty hours.

To do away with bureaucratism, we must first do away with these student bureaucrats!

—Students of Beijing University
(poster at Beijing University,
circa April 27, 1989)

Student organization took a major step forward on April 23, with the establishment of the "Provisional Students' Federation of Capital Universities and Colleges" ("Provisional Students' Federation"). Although Beijing University, by virtue of its prestige, its large number of student activists, and the early leadership of its Students' Solidarity Committee, would be the physical and symbolic center of the movement, the Provisional Students' Federation was a diverse alliance of over twenty Beijing institutions. Its first two leaders, Zhou Yongjun and Wuer Kaixi, hailed from two schools that would produce many activists: the University of Politics and Law and Beijing Normal University, respectively.

The Provisional Students' Federation did not lose any time before declaring a citywide class boycott of indefinite duration to protest the beating incidents on April 18 and April 20, the government's failure to respond to the student petition, and distorted press reports of the protests. In addition, it transmitted a letter to schools across the country, which led to the establishment of the "National Federation of [Autonomous] Student Unions of Universities and Colleges."

The first two notices below appeared at People's University on April 24. The third is an official release of the Provisional Students' Federation on April 26, summarizing major student positions and demands as protests entered their second week.

Illustration 2.1. A cartoon attacking the corruption of the present Chinese bureaucracy caricatures the bureaucrat as a corrupt, corpulent official from days past. The heading at the top states "Democracy—The Ideal Displayed on High." The couplet (vertical lines) reads: "A big belly that can hold [all] the democratic rights under Heaven" and "A laughing mouth that mocks the ignorant, lowly [ordinary] Chinese people." Credit: Han Minzhu.

ITEMS TO NOTE REGARDING THE CLASS BOYCOTT

1. Boycott classes, not studies.
2. During the class boycott please do not return home or march without authorization. Respect the normal school rules and daily schedules.
3. Further announcements of student activities during the class boycott period will be made.

> —People's University
> Provisional Autonomous Student Union
> *(big-character poster at
> People's University, April 24, 1989)*

PUBLIC NOTICE

Because the leadership of the original student union is inept, has sold out the students' interests during this April 22 protest movement, and is completely unable to represent the students' wishes, the People's University Provisional Autonomous Student Union has been established in response to the demands of the great majority of students following a meeting of the entire student body. It supplants the [official] student union. It will dissolve on its own initiative when conditions permit.

> —People's University
> Provisional Autonomous Student Union
> *(big-character poster at
> People's University, April 24, 1989)*

SPECIAL BULLETIN

—At nine o'clock this morning, the Provisional Students' Federation of Capital Universities and Colleges held a press conference for foreign and Chinese reporters in front of the gates of the University of Politics and Law to announce the establishment of the Federation and to release the "Letter to Compatriots throughout the Nation."

—Forty universities and institutes in the capital participated in the conference today. They have decided to unify their activities.

—The Provisional Students' Federation announced the major demands of this student movement:

1. We invite government leaders to engage in a dialogue with students concerning the demands that we have put forth.
2. We demand that Wang Fang, Minister of Public Security, search out the perpetrators of the April 20 incident in which students were beaten and identify the leaders directly responsible for this incident.
3. We demand that the managing editor of the Xinhua News Agency [China's official news agency] publicly apologize to students for the distorted reports and deceptive propaganda concerning this student movement that appeared recently, and guarantee that the press will speak the truth and report fairly from now on.

—The unified slogans of the Provisional Students' Federation are:

1. Support the Communist Party and socialism! Support reform!
2. Long live democracy!
3. Oppose corruption in government; oppose special privileges!
4. Pledge to defend the Constitution to the death!
5. Patriotism is not a crime!
6. The press must speak the truth—oppose slander!
7. Long live the people!
8. Stabilize prices!
9. Every person is responsible for the fate of the nation!
10. The people's army protects the people!
11. Oppose violence! No persecution!
12. Demand dialogue!
13. Reform, patriotism, enterprise, progress!

—The Provisional Students' Federation has set tomorrow [April 27] as the date for students from forty Beijing universities and colleges to march in demonstration and peaceful petition.

—Main questions raised by reporters: . . .

Q: If the government uses military force to suppress or interfere in the student movement, how will you respond?

A: We are convinced that the people's government will not use violence against the people. Regardless of what happens, this great and patriotic democracy movement must persevere. We will use only peaceful petitioning to press for our goals.

Q: Will you unite with workers for a strike?

A: We hope to win the understanding and support of society at large. Nevertheless, we support a smooth process of reform carried out in an environment of social stability and price stability.

Q: When will the student strike end?

A: As soon as we are assured that the government is prepared to discuss our demands and give us reasonable answers, we will immediately return to class. . . .

> —The Provisional Students' Federation
> of Capital Universities and Colleges
> *(big-character poster at People's University,*
> *written by the People's University*
> *Provisional Autonomous Students*
> *Union, April 26, 1989)*

From the outset of the student movement, Beijing students, with a keen appreciation of the importance of winning broad public support, displayed a sophisticated grasp of the art of public relations. Aware that the ordinary people of Beijing knew little of their motivations and goals, and that government control of the media could rapidly turn public opinion against them, student organizations moved without delay to set up propaganda and public liaison subcommittees. The next two statements, one prepared by students at Beijing University and the other by students at the Beijing Aeronautics Institute, are examples of the students' efforts in the early stages of the movement to gain citizen backing.

ANSWERS TO QUESTIONS FROM BEIJING CITIZENS

Q: What kind of illegal organization have you established? Do you have any conflict with the regular student organization?

A: The [undergraduate] student union and the graduate student union should represent the interests of the masses and protect their legitimate rights and interests. However, since they act as the royal tool of school authorities, they have totally lost any reason for existing. The preparatory committees in each school[2] and the Beijing Students' Federation [the successor to the Provisional Students' Federation] are the autonomous organizations supported by the overwhelming majority of students. And according to the Constitution, citizens have the right to freedom of assembly.

Q: What do the students hope Beijing residents will do?

A: We fervently hope that the people will understand our actions, support us, and show their concern. Our goals are your goals. However, we do hope that you all will continue to go to work and keep up regular production and daily routines.

Q: Did police really beat students in front of Xinhuamen [on the 20th]?

A: Yes. Many of the soldiers and police were brutal. Among the students there were people who suffered eye injuries or whose faces were beaten bloody. Who could actually believe that unarmed students would beat specially trained soldiers and police?

Q: Today the Xinhua News Agency reported that due to internal disputes among Qinghua University students, they did not go through with

2. During the first week of the student demonstrations, "preparatory committees" were established temporarily at each school for the purpose of organizing student activities and laying the groundwork for a permanent independent student organization.

the scheduled dialogue with the government. What do you have to say about this?

A: Qinghua University is a member of the Beijing Students' Federation. It neither has the power to suggest, nor did it, a separate dialogue with the government. All the Qinghua delegates have opposed all along this kind of simplistic dialogue; furthermore, no internal disputes exist. Xinhua News Agency has a habit of creating rumors to cause damage—its malicious intent is obvious to all.

Q: Aren't your actions harmful to [social] stability and unity?[3]

A: No! At present, bureaucrats are corrupt, prices are soaring, reforms are blocked—complaints resound everywhere. For some time, the people have been unhappy; the students' decision to take action is only the public manifestation of the people's [low] morale. As a powerful expression of public opinion, it will help the government vigorously deepen and push forward the reforms. It is not something that harms social stability and unity. Only by thoroughly eliminating this [corrupt] bureaucratic system will we be able to achieve our goal of stable rule and peace.

> —Beijing University Students'
> Autonomous Preparatory Committee
> *(poster at Beijing University, April 27, 1989)*

A LETTER TO CITIZENS OF BEIJING

Citizens of the capital:

We are students of Beijing Aeronautics Institute. Our sacred mission is to uphold the people's interests. We have no choice under the current

---

3. Since 1980, Deng Xiaoping's government has repeatedly attacked unapproved social movements and protests by alleging that they endangered social "stability and unity" (*anding tuanjie*). Thus in 1980 Deng stated: "We can never achieve the Four Modernizations without a political situation of stability and unity, because people cannot embark on modernization without peace of mind." And in 1987, in Party discussions about the winter 1986 student demonstrations, Deng declared: "We must let foreigners see for themselves that the Chinese political situation is stable. . . . We should not be afraid of damage to our reputation. . . ." Raising fears about social unrest was obviously meant to undercut public support for dissidents, but should not be regarded as only a tactic: Deng and his generation of veteran revolutionaries, having struggled through nearly forty years of upheaval that included two wars (the War of Resistance against the Japanese and the civil war against the Kuo-

circumstances. Under circumstances that have pushed our patience beyond its limits, we feel compelled by sadness and fury to declare: a class boycott will commence on April 24.

Our action is by no means an action of blind impulse; we have a feasible program, clear and definite objectives, and a well-disciplined and powerful organization. We will not accept the control or manipulation of any person, nor will we stoop to compromise. We have no selfish motives or hidden ambitions. Our actions these last few days sprang from our patriotic hearts, from our pure and loyal love for our great motherland. We do not "desire to plunge the world into chaos" [as has been alleged], nor are we a "small handful" of bad people with ulterior motives. All we want is to do our best to push forward the process of reform and democratization, to try to obtain for the people the most practical benefits possible.

Citizens, our interests are now closely bound together. We swear to stand with the people to the death, to struggle to the very end!

We ask for all the citizens of Beijing to give us their support! We are one with the people!

Down with bureaucracy! Down with BUREAUCRATS!

Long live China! Long live the people!

> —Beijing Aeronautics Institute Students'
> Federation, April 24, 1989

—Please understand and trust us! Please extend your hands in support!

> *(poster at Beijing Aeronautics Institute)*

Such appeals to the public often began as posters on campus, to be converted subsequently into a mimeographed handbill. Although big- and small-character posters were a favored and effective means of reporting news or expressing viewpoints on campuses (and later in Tiananmen Square and its vicinity), they suffered from one major drawback: fixed in one location, their contents could only be circulated and made known by word of mouth or by tedious hand copying (which was often done—and which blocked the posters from view while the copyist was at work). Recognizing that printed handbills were needed for wide, accurate, and rapid dissemination both of student organizations' positions and of news of protest activities,

mintang) and several mass campaigns of great pyschological and physical violence, must deeply and instinctively fear mass unrest. In particular, they saw in the appearance of big-character posters, the birth of independent student organizations, and student mobilization ominous parallels to the opening stages of the chaotic Cultural Revolution.

Illustration 2.2. Curious Beijing residents cluster around students from Beijing Normal University who are soliciting donations that will enable them to continue their pro-democracy, anti-corruption campaign. Credit: Reuters / Bettmann Newsphotos.

student groups made procurement of mimeograph machines a top priority; limited funds and state control of all publishing houses precluded publication by a press.[4] Using simple mimeograph machines, Beijing University students, assisted by students from other schools, began producing a new publication, the News Herald (Xinwen daobao). In all, some eight or nine issues of the News Herald would be published, the last on May 31. A multipage broadside rather than a journal, a typical edition mixed accounts of pro-democracy activities with statements of student grievances and positions.

The News Herald was only the first of some half-dozen "people's (nonofficial)

4. Students were apparently able to obtain mimeograph machines from school departments and outside businesses without much trouble—a sign of both liberalization in China and the widespread support the students enjoyed.

publications" to appear during the Democracy Movement. These publications fell into two categories. First, there were news-oriented publications whose primary purpose was to coordinate protest activities and / or keep students and other citizens abreast of news developments; these ranged from the Beijing Normal University student news bulletin, *Hunger Strikers' News Bulletin* (*Jueshi qingyuantuan tongxun*), which was sometimes released several times a day, to *News Flashes* (*Xinwen kuaixun*), a publication organized by people from Chinese intellectual, news, and cultural circles (but printed at Beijing University) in reaction to the news blackout imposed by the government. Second, there were journals devoted to theoretical articles or political essays; among these were *One Generation of People* (*Yi dai ren*) and *Democracy Forum* (*Minzhu luntan*), edited by students at People's University and Beijing Normal University, respectively. In comparison to the political and literary journals of the 1978-1979 Democracy Wall period, the 1989 publications were narrower in focus and their writings less accomplished, but the Democracy Movement was crushed before the fledgling publications had time to grow and mature. Although a limited number of underground journals have circulated in China in recent years, the harsh crackdown on Democracy Movement activists has made it highly unlikely that any journals survive in any form.

The excerpt below from the essay "What Do We Oppose? What Do We Need?" (which has also been excerpted in Chapter 1) exemplifies the expository writing that appeared in the *News Herald*. Primarily a call for democratic procedures within the Party, this essay is one indication of the nonradical nature of the student movement; rather than advocating the adoption of a Western-style democracy with a multiparty system, most students sought Chinese-style democracy—a political system in which the Party would continue to dominate, but characterized by greater openness, critical debate, and the replacement of power politics with democratic procedures within the Party.

WHAT DO WE OPPOSE?

(excerpt)

Our student movement was prompted by the death of Comrade Hu Yaobang. The fact that he passed away a victim of an unjust charge provoked loud cries by a great many students and other citizens for justice and democracy.

Hu Yaobang did not voluntarily resign [from his post as Secretary General of the Party]; rather, he was forced to step down at an informal meeting that was organized by people who were not even members of the Politburo. This was a fundamental breach of the Party's charter. Elder Hu's ouster gave birth to a saying: "throughout the history of the Party, none of its Secretaries General have left office in a legitimate way." Speaking objectively, this type of incident is no model for democratic practices in the Party.

The real reason for Elder Hu's ouster was not the student protests [of winter 1986]. What brought him to political grief was his proposal to follow through with the suggestion, first raised by Comrade Deng Xiaoping, to rejuvenate the leadership of the Party. . . .

Elder Hu's ouster, coming against the background of the Party's present campaign promoting democracy and rule by law, is yet another manifestation of the absence of any procedures for the smooth transfer of political power. As a result, the majority of cadres and Party members do not expect the leadership of the Party to be stable, and modify their own behavior to maximize short-term benefits. They are just like China's peasants, who worry that the Party's policies will change.[5] [In such an environment, where political winds are ever shifting,] how can anyone, whether at the top or the bottom, concentrate on doing a good job of building democracy and modernizing China?

This arbitrariness in the transfer of power at the Party's top levels causes the masses, who have no clear picture about what is really happening, to worry that a brutal power struggle like that during the Cultural Revolution will break out. . . . Moreover, once this intra-Party power struggle and political infighting starts, the *People's Daily* sounds the bugle call to battle, calling on the people to join the struggle. This is not appropriate. If the Party does not reveal the real reasons why Comrade Hu Yaobang was forced out, if it does not promptly reevaluate Elder Hu's entire record, we warn it that the people's anger will be difficult to appease.

We the student body mourn deeply the loss of Hu Yaobang. We hope that procedures for leadership succession and the transfer of power in the Party can be worked out, and that such stipulated procedures are followed. In this way, the true principles of Marxism and Leninism for

5. Beginning in 1979, the Party leadership introduced agricultural reforms decollectivizing farming and granting peasants the right to manage their own plots of land through a contract responsibility system that has enabled many peasants to prosper. From the start, however, peasants have been fearful that the Party would suddenly reverse its policy and force recollectivization, and so there has been a tendency to overwork their assigned plots of land in order to reap short-term profits.

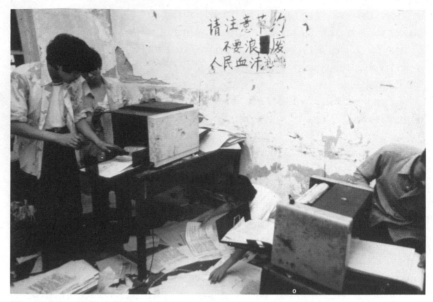

Illustration 2.3. A Beijing University dorm room converted into a mimeograph center. The writing on the wall states: "Please conserve. Don't waste the people's blood, sweat, and hard work." Credit: S. Franklin / Magnum.

building the Party can be realized. During the process of building the Party, Lenin suggested many times that the opposition faction be legalized. This is not only the practice of democracy. It is also the strongest guarantee that the Party's leadership will be stable. Only policies and approaches that have been forged through critical debate will truly be able to carry out the wishes of the broad masses of people and to obtain the greatest benefits of reform.

Although undergraduates, particularly freshmen and sophomores, composed the bulk of the student demonstrators, many graduate students also threw themselves into the movement. A portion of the graduate student activists were very young. Chai Ling, a key student leader from mid-May on, and her husband Feng Congde, a member of the Beijing University Student Solidarity Committee, were only twenty-three and twenty-two years old, respectively. Others, older and wiser in the ways of Chinese society—unlike undergraduates and graduate students fresh from college, who typically had never held a job, older graduate students had spent a spell of time working before returning to school—provided an important balance to their more impetuous classmates. And veterans of previous protests, such as Liu Gang, twenty-eight, served as behind-the-scenes counselors to student leaders.

Many of the most incisive and carefully composed posters that appeared on campuses were written by graduate students. The next two selections are posters written by doctoral students at People's University on April 23 and April 24. Beyond their important endorsement of the undergraduate-initiated protests, they propose a number of concrete actions for the students to take to strengthen their movement.

PROCLAMATION OF PH.D. STUDENTS (I)

1. We completely support the "seven demands" put forth by the university students of Beijing. We resolutely support the patriotic movement for democracy initiated by the students and people from all sectors of society.
2. Beginning today, all Ph.D. students will boycott classes.
3. The sincerity of asserting that there will be "collective responsibility" (Li Peng's words) for the "mistakes created by the collective policy decisions of the collective leadership" (Li Peng's words) can be proven with no other act than a collective resignation [of the top leadership].
4. We strongly demand the resignation of all Party, government, and military leaders who are over seventy-five.
5. Oppose violence. Protect human rights. The army must not participate in politics or interfere in domestic affairs.
6. Expenditures for the activities of the Chinese Communist Party should not be shouldered by the national treasury.
7. Remove restrictions on newspapers. Establish freedom of the press. Allow private papers, magazines, and radio and television stations.
8. We call for the establishment of a "Commission for Honest Government" by people from all sectors of society, which will conduct a thorough investigaton of the leadership of the Party, government, and military for evidence of corruption, and which will investigate and prosecute the illegal business activities of the children and relatives of high-ranking cadres, and make the results of these investigations known to the public.

Long live Democracy!

*(big-character poster at
People's University, April 23, 1989)*

PROCLAMATION OF PH.D. STUDENTS (II)

1. Because at present universities throughout the country still lack a united organization, we propose that [Beijing] students immediately establish a telephone and telegram network, with specified communication times and locations, with universities in each of the major cities in China; and that from May 4 on, students at universities throughout the country unify their actions, organizations, slogans, and objectives.

2. Because the student movement is currently still a "campus movement," and has yet to attain widespread understanding and support from all sectors of society, we propose that [Beijing] students: (1) draft and print large quantities of literature making clear our positions and the goals we are fighting for; (2) set up "democracy walls" outside the gates of their schools; and (3) form a large number of "special action groups" to distribute and post leaflets and organize public speeches at all train stations, theaters, hotels, and main commercial districts.

3. Because at present the student movement lacks powerful media of its own, we propose that: (1) the student autonomous committee at each university take over the school broadcasting station; (2) all universities publish and issue "student movement bulletins" of their own, which will facilitate communication among schools; and (3) all universities establish news release centers, hold on-the-spot press conferences, and report to the Chinese and foreign press, as well as to all sectors of society, the progress of the student movement.

4. Since during the student movement the personal safety and interests of the students have been seriously endangered, we propose that all universities join together to form a "lawyers' working group" that will immediately bring a lawsuit over: (1) certain distorted news reports regarding the "April 20 Incident" [in which students were beaten by police]; and (2) deliberate injury of students by certain police officers. This "lawyers' working group" should act to protect the legal rights of the students during the student movement.

5. Because the class boycotts at some schools are not doing well, and the students' actions are not unified, we propose that students: (1) reinforce the pickets at their universities and seal off classrooms; and (2) organize on-campus meetings for public speeches and reports [on student activities] in order to strengthen solidarity.

Long live the students!

*(big-character poster at
People's University, April 24, 1989)*

Deng Xiaoping and the conservative wing of the Party observed the student activism with a growing sense of alarm. On April 24, meeting in a special session to discuss the unrest, the Standing Committee of the Politburo resolved to take decisive action to prevent further student organizing. At their order, phone lines at Beijing University dorms were cut and telegrams to classmates across the country blocked by the Postal and Telegram Bureau. The next day, Premier Li Peng and Yang Shangkun, President of the Republic and Vice Chairman of the powerful Central Military Commission, the Central Committee's group in charge of military affairs, conferred with an angry Deng, who ordered army troops mobilized to suppress any additional demonstrations. Deng did not mince words. "This is no ordinary student movement," he declared, "but an episode of turmoil. We must take a firm stand and take effective measures in opposing and ending this turmoil. We cannot allow their objectives to be achieved." Li and Yang expressed their agreement; they would become the key advocates of the hard-line government position. Secretary General Zhao Ziyang, away on a state visit to North Korea, was not present at the meeting.

Deng's comments to Li and Yang were converted—some sources say paraphrased—into a front-page editorial in the *People's Daily*, the official Party paper, which condemned the student protests, labeling them "turmoil"—the official term for the disparaged Cultural Revolution. In the eyes of Party conservatives—who included not only the elderly generation of revolutionaries such as Deng, Chen Yun, the apostle of traditional Marxist economics, and Yang Shangkun, but also a younger generation of men such as Li Peng, Beijing Mayor Chen Xitong, and Shanghai Party chief Jiang Zemin—the editorial was a necessary measure that would slow down the snowballing student movement. The gap between these leaders and Chinese youth was tragically large; rather than imposing a measure of order, the editorial infuriated students and provoked a massive march in defiance.

The April 26 editorial appears in the first selection below. It is followed by one of the many scathingly critical student posters that quickly went up in reaction.

WE MUST TAKE A FIRM STAND AGAINST TURMOIL
(excerpt)

... During the period of mourning [for Hu Yaobang], a few abnormal phenomena also appeared. An extremely small number of people used the opportunity to fabricate rumors and attack leaders of the Party and state by name, and to deceive the masses into rushing Xinhuamen, [the entrance to] Zhongnanhai, the seat of the Central Committee and the State Council. There were even some other people who yelled out "Down with the Communist Party" and other reactionary slogans. In Xi'an and Changsha there were serious incidents of lawless elements smashing, looting, and burning.

Taking into consideration the broad masses' grief, the Party and government took a tolerant, restrained attitude to certain inappropriate words and actions of emotionally excited young students. On the 22nd, before the memorial for Comrade Hu Yaobang began, some students who had gotten to Tiananmen Square ahead of time were not cleared from the Square according to normal procedure. . . . The common efforts of all ensured that the memorial service went forward smoothly in an atmosphere of dignity and solemnity.

But after the memorial was over, an extremely small number of people with ulterior motives continued to take advantage of the young students' mourning for Comrade Hu Yaobang, fabricated all kinds of rumors, deceived people, used big- and small-character posters to slander, insult, and attack leaders of the Party and state, blatantly violated the Constitution, and encouraged opposition to the leadership of the Communist Party and to the socialist system. In some universities and colleges, illegal organizations were established and tried to grab power from the [official] student unions by force. Some even took over the schools' public address facilities by force. In some universities, students and teachers were encouraged to boycott classes; students were forcibly prevented from going to classes. Making unauthorized use of the names of workers' organizations, they distributed reactionary leaflets and everywhere linked up[6] with others, trying to create even more trouble.

These facts demonstrate that an extremely small number of people were not involved in mourning Comrade Hu Yaobang, were not trying to promote socialist democracy in China, and were not just a bit unhappy and letting off steam. [Rather], under the banner of democracy, they were trying to destroy the democratic legal system. Their goal was to poison people's minds, to create turmoil throughout the country, to destroy political stability and unity. This was a planned conspiracy, a riot, whose real nature was to fundamentally negate the leadership of the Chinese

---

6. The word used here is *chuanlian*, a term used in the Cultural Revolution to describe the activities of young people who went to factories and schools, and traveled by train free of charge, to make contact with other groups around the country and to spread "revolution."

Communist Party and to negate the socialist system. This throws down the gauntlet of serious political struggle before the whole Party and every nationality of the whole country.

If we take a lenient, permissive attitude toward this turmoil and just let it go, a situation of real chaos will emerge. What the people of the whole country, including the great mass of young students, hope for—reform and opening, austerity and rectification, development, control of inflation, a better life, opposing corruption, developing democracy and the legal system—will be reduced to nothing. Even the tremendous results achieved by reform over the last ten years could be totally lost. The great desire of the whole Chinese people—to revitalize China—will be next to impossible to realize. A China with great hope and a great future would become a China wracked with turmoil, a China with no future.

The whole Party and the people of the whole country must be fully aware of the seriousness of this struggle, unite, take a firm stand against turmoil, resolutely protect the political stability and unity achieved with such difficulty, and the socialist legal system. It is absolutely forbidden to establish any illegal organization. Any behavior which infringes on the rights of legitimate student organizations must be resolutely halted, no matter what its pretext. Those who deliberately create rumors and spread slander must be held criminally responsible in accordance with the law.

Illegal demonstrations are forbidden. Going to factories, to the countryside, and to schools to link up with others is forbidden. Those who smash, loot, and burn must be punished according to the law. The normal right of students to attend classes must be guaranteed. The great majority of students sincerely wants to eliminate corruption and to promote democracy. These are also the demands of the Party and the government. These demands can only be realized under the Party's leadership, by reinforcing [the recently introduced policy of] improving and rectifying the economy, by actively promoting reform, and by completing the construction of socialist democracy and the socialist legal system. . . .

(People's Daily *editorial,*
April 26, 1989)

A REVIEW OF THE *PEOPLE'S DAILY* EDITORIAL (APRIL 26)

Last night, before the April 26 edition of the *People's Daily* had come off the press, the China Central Television and China Central People's

Broadcasting, so anxious that they could not wait, broadcast the editorial more than ten hours early.[7] Yet, after listening carefully to the broadcast, we only felt deeply shocked, disappointed, and angry.

First, with one death blow, the editorial vilified the present patriotic movement as disorder and agitation. As we all know, from April 15 to 25, the students set off a democratic movement of unprecedented scale. From beginning to end, the goal of the students in this movement has been to accelerate the progress of democracy. In particular, they demanded freedom of the press and an end to corruption and graft. Many times the students took to the streets, marching, demonstrating, and petitioning. Their excellent organization and discipline won them the broad support of the citizens of Beijing; the students were certainly not incited by a "small handful" of individuals! However, even though the students' patriotic movement had already gained the enthusiastic support of the ordinary people, the *People's Daily*, which calls itself the newspaper of the people, came out with a disappointing position. What, may I ask, is the stand of this editorial of yours? After all, are you patriotic or unpatriotic?!

Second, the editorial appealed to the people to cherish the present situation of stability and unity, to work together to carry out reform, and so on. We students naturally treasure our youth; we also want to live and study in a stable and comfortable environment. But when we look around us, we see a country rotting in decline, in which the people are not masters of their own lives, in which the press has no freedom, yet in which officials are able to indulge in graft, corruption, and other misconduct. How long, may I ask, can this kind of "stability and unity" hold together our "people's republic"? Do we need this kind of confused "stability and unity"? Moreover, what kind of measures has the present government taken to address these grave problems? What kind of legislation has the government enacted to provide effective regulation? We have waited patiently for the past thirty years, but what have we gotten? Should we have to wait interminably and futilely? Should students who take to the streets to demonstrate only because they have no other means of expressing their concerns about their country and their people be accused of disrupting "stability and unity"? The best expression of promoting stability and unity would be for the ruling lords who hold power in the "people's re-

7. China Central Television is one of three national government-controlled television stations in China; China Central People's Broadcasting is the government radio station. Although there are also local stations operated by city or provincial authorities, no nongovernment radio or television stations exist.

public" to take positive, sincere, and effective steps to solve today's various social problems!

In summary, the entire editorial is without interest. There are no constructive suggestions to the government, but there is harsh condemnation for the patriotic movement. Intimidation coexists with pretended tolerance—a common ploy for this kind of editorial!

The greatest hope for progress in China is an awakened citizenry that strongly demands political participation. Whoever claims to represent the people's interest must have the courage to show himself and enter into a dialogue with the people!

The extremely negative tone of the editorial has really caused deep, deep shock, disappointment, and anger in the nation's citizens!

Since the government is not taking any constructive action, our movement must continue to the very end!

The indomitable youth of China is the hope of the Chinese nation!

—A young Chinese student, April 26
(big-character poster)

In the view of some students of Chinese politics, the tragedy of the Democracy Movement and its bloody ending was the inability of Deng and fellow Party elders to adapt their political instincts and tactics, honed over decades of fierce struggle and premised on absolute authority by the Party, into more flexible ones demanded by the changing nature of Chinese society in the 1980s. More and more Chinese were no longer content to follow government policies and orders unquestioningly. The development of private economic interests, loosening of work and travel restrictions, exposure to Western societies, and even the Party's campaign to instill legal knowledge had nurtured a growing sense of individual rights—and a budding belief that the government should be responsive to the people's wishes. According to this view, had Deng and the government adopted a more conciliatory and flexible approach at the beginning, agreeing for example to meet with representatives of the autonomous student union, the Students' Federation, and refraining from branding the demonstrations "turmoil," citizen sympathy for the students would have faded and a large-scale movement avoided.

Whether or not this would in fact have happened, it is undeniable that widely circulated reports of Deng's uncompromising April 24 remarks, particularly his comment, "What do we have to fear? . . . We have several million soldiers . . ." inflamed student and citizen anger at the government.[8] Furthermore, the government's tactic

8. In fact, Deng probably never used exactly these words. According to sources presently

of claiming that certain small groups of people were manipulating the students back-fired, causing the government to lose what little remaining credibility it had among the general citizenry, and generating great resentment among intellectuals and teachers, the alleged "black hands" behind the protests. In the next two essays, two Party members, reacting with disappointment to the Party's confrontational posture, reject support of the Party line in favor of their consciences.

PERPLEXITIES OF A PROFESSOR

(excerpt)

1. "They are only some hundred thousand people; we have three million soldiers."[9]

Apparently, "they" refers to us, the intellectuals. Well, with only some thirty, forty, or fifty yuan a month to feed ourselves,[10] we are really so feeble that a gust of wind would blow us over. The People's Liberation Army is invincible—one of its soldiers can fight ten enemies, right? Against a small handful of these sicklings and cripples, do they need to employ three million soldiers? . . .

3. "It is necessary to maintain the same line as the Central Committee."[11]

---

available, Deng said: "There are now 60,000 students boycotting classes; 100,000 students are not striking. We must protect and support those 100,000. Also, of the 60,000 boycotting, the majority can be won over. Workers and peasants side with us; cadres side with us, the democratic parties are also good. We have several million army troops! . . ."

9. Another inaccurate quotation of Deng's April 24 remarks. Since information about the latest developments depended on scattered posters, word of mouth, and rumors, it was common for several different versions of some comment or event to circulate, none of which was necessarily correct.

10. One yuan equaled approximately $U.S. 0.27 in 1989. A modest income by Beijing standards—adequate for basic living expenses but not enough for savings or purchases of good clothing or furniture—was about 125–150 yuan a month (including various transportation, housing, and food subsidies added to base salaries, which were generally very low). Intellectuals such as professors, researchers, writers, and so on, earned regular salaries of only 100-200 yuan a month. Thus for many it was only by taking on outside work that they were able to live modestly but comfortably. Food expenses as a proportion of income are relatively high in Chinese cities; one study has shown that approximately one-third of Beijing residents' income is spent on food. Intellectuals—and many factory workers and low-level state cadres—resent the fact that entrepreneurs, taxi drivers, and even some workers in profitable collective companies earn far more than they do, from several hundred to even 1,000 or more yuan a month.

11. According to the rules of most communist parties, although there can be internal discussion about a policy or program, once the party has reached a decision, all party members

. . . [From the Yan'an days in the thirties and forties through the Cultural Revolution, through an endless series of political campaigns,] we have always followed right behind the bearer of the Central Committee's flag. But what do we see again? The person in your crowd who has the highest decision-making power says: "Do not fear people calling us names; do not fear international opinion; do not fear that China's image will suffer."

How brazen are those words! How dark are your hearts! We old intellectuals and veteran party members shall keep our integrity in our later years. You have power, but we still have a shred of conscience. We could join in the "anti-unrest" bandwagon, but who can guarantee that after your death, this "unrest" will not be reevaluated as a "revolution"? Today's "anti-unrest" activities perhaps shall become a "counter-revolution" after you die. No more blind followers again. We are "veteran athletes" who have gone through all these political movements in the past and shall never be fooled again into taking part in any new movements. That is because only today did we realize that you subscribe to the three "do-not-fears" philosophy.

The expense for a single meal you consume is greater than what we spend to eat in a month. You don't know how to deal with the students, the workers, or the peasants, so you have to seize on the "beards" [teachers and professors who have influence over young students] to make an example out of us and to amuse yourselves. How we regret that, several decades ago, we didn't pick up the barrels of guns, but picked up pens instead. What was distressing then has only become worse. We lived in poverty to bring up generation after generation of scholars and military talents for your service; however, as for our rights, we still need to have children take to the streets to claim them. Your "cause" is a joke that shall cause you to perish without any sons![12]

These days, there are people who attribute your mess to the Communist Party. We, intellectuals and members of the Party, would die to be free of this great Party which has completely lost the backing of the people and which is controlled by a heartless, small handful. With your "three do-not-fears," are you really not afraid? We don't mind if you do not fear being sworn and cursed at. But one billion Chinese people and

---

must support the decision and refrain from voicing any dissenting or critical views of the decision. The exhortation to "maintain the same line as the Central Committee" is so familiar to Chinese ears that those who are skeptical of the Chinese Communist Party's policies tend to use it ironically.

12. To curse one to die without sons was one of the strongest imprecations in traditional Chinese society.

forty million Party members absolutely will not accept such nonsense as "do not fear international opinion" and "do not fear that China's image will suffer."

It's true you have three million soldiers. But who says there will not be some who will turn their guns back on you? After all, they are people's brothers and sons, not members of the Deng clan.

(unsigned small-character poster at Beijing University)

CHOOSING BETWEEN THE DEMANDS OF PARTY SPIRIT AND THE DICTATES OF ONE'S CONSCIENCE

—An Open Letter to All Party Members from a Party Member and Student at People's University

To All My Comrades in the Party:

Analysis of the editorials in the *People's Daily* and the general message from the Central Committee that was passed down to us at the recent Party members' meeting held on campus has made clear the hard-line attitude of the Central Committee: "Only sixty thousand of Beijing's students are boycotting classes; one hundred thousand of them have taken no action. We have three million troops, so what do have we to fear?" (words of Deng Xiaoping). It's quite apparent that the government may well use military force to suppress this Democracy Movement; the march and demonstration scheduled for tomorrow [the 27th] could very possibly turn into a bloodbath!

At present there are only two roads from which we may choose: we may act as conscientious Chinese and as conscientious Party members, and struggle for democracy and the prosperity of China; or we may act as "up-to-par Party members" and actively respond to the call of the Central Committee, in order to preserve our Party membership and secure our individual futures. How are we to choose?

I remember how Zhou Enlai once answered the question of a foreign friend by saying, "I am first and foremost a Chinese, and only then a Party member." For democracy and freedom, and for the cause of reform, there are some people who are even willing to shed their blood; are they worried about such small matters as their Party membership or future? In reality, the recent decision of the Central Committee does not represent the true feelings and voice of the majority of Party members. We must cry out as conscience-led communists!

Just look! Three student representatives are kneeling on the steps of the Great Hall of the People, under the imposing seal of the People's Republic of China, trying to submit a petition, but no one pays them any heed! Where is the leaders' Party spirit? Does the Party truly speak for the people? Who is destroying the Party, after all?

To handle the student movement for democracy and freedom, the government now has gone so far as to deploy three million troops whose sole function should be to protect the people. What kind of dictatorship is this, if not a dictatorship against the people?

As a Party member, I no longer wish to weep over governmental corruption and the apathy of the people. I only want to be a true communist, and to let my blood flow with the struggle for democracy and freedom.

I believe that history will bear me out. History will remember us: strugglers for democracy, true communists who fought for the good of our country.

(unsigned small-character poster
at People's University)

◦

"Those Who Lose the Hearts of the People Lose the Kingdom"

Despite ominous warnings from Beijing authorities that the mourning period for Hu had ended and that further demonstrations were illegal and strictly forbidden, on April 26 the Provisional Students' Federation announced a mass student march in protest of the *People's Daily* editorial. Its decision to carry through with the march was not made lightly: campuses were rife with reports that the 38th Army, an elite corps based not far from Beijing, had already taken up positions in and around the city. Under the mounting pressure and awareness that a decision to march could result in bloodshed or even loss of life, cracks in student unity appeared: leaders at Qinghua University declared their withdrawal from the newly formed federation. Though Qinghua students did participate in large numbers in the march the next day, the first sign of the factionalism that would plague the federation had already appeared.

Fearing violent encounters with the army or police, many students wrote their wills the night of the 26th. As more than 100,000 students strode out of their school

Illustration 2.4. On the morning of April 27, police lines seven to eight men deep are easily punctured when huge crowds press forward. Credit: Sing Tao Newspapers, Hong Kong.

gates on the morning of the 27th, they braced for the worst. But when the first rows of marchers formed by People's University students approached police lines seven or eight men deep, the unexpected happened: surging crowds of citizens who had turned out in support rushed the police lines—and the police did not fight back, but only linked arms in a futile attempt to hold back the huge crowds. With citizens running interference, the student marchers triumphantly made their way south to West Changan Avenue, then east toward Tiananmen Square. In a surprise tactic designed to minimize the possibility of any clash with the police, the marchers did not stop at the Square but continued east through the heart of Beijing. Large crowds cheered enthusiastically along the entire route; citizens threw food and drink to the exuberant marchers. Not until late at night did exhausted students return to their schools, after having completed a roughly twenty-mile circuit.

The march was a huge success and a public relations coup for the students, and a humiliation for the government: never before in the history of the People's Republic of China had there been such an anti-government demonstration. In the afterglow of the triumph, though, there were those who warned against complacency, and reminded classmates that none of their specific demands had been met or even addressed by the government. The two posters below appeared shortly after the April 27 march.

MY VIEWS ON THE SUCCESS OF
THE APRIL 27 MARCH

Whoever believes in the principles of democracy and who furthermore tries conscientiously to live according to those principles—such were the people who "went through the experience" [of participating in the April 27 march despite fear for their lives]. And those of us who went through the experience agree: the march was a great victory in the process of democratization in China, which began over forty years ago. It at least prevented the lords from acting at will. The writer, as a participant and "person who has been through the experience," would like to speak a bit about my own views.

How was the success of this protest march achieved?

First, to a great degree its success was due to the all-out support of the populace. One of the signs of success was that no military confrontation occurred. As all are aware, this was the problem that we were most uncertain about before we set out. During the march, as we saw police lines broken through one after another, our [pounding] hearts gradually calmed down. Only the organizers of the march and those many people who went through the experience can know what it was like to feel such fear and overwhelming relief.

Well, how were the police lines burst through? Almost all were broken through for us by citizens of the city! The writer, marching under the banner of the People's University graduate students (which was at the very front of the marchers' ranks), saw citizens walking with discipline in front of the marchers and opening up a path for them so that the students would not come into contact with the police. Every time we arrived at a key intersection, [supportive Beijing residents would crowd in toward the police and] banter with them, trying to make them understand why we were marching. They tried to persuade them with reason and to move them with emotion. All of a sudden, in a wave, they would start to press forward toward the police line. Once there was a breach in the line, they would expand it by linking arms and chanting, "Thank you, police!" Of course, we students, during the process, also chanted, "The people love the police!" and sang . . . to build up momentum. Thus the actual physical contact was made by citizens [rather than students]. Although some of the students also tried hard to persuade the police—some even cried very hard (extremely moving)—for some unknown reason, the police seemed to be very annoyed—so much so that they reacted against our efforts. If there had not been the people's wisdom and bodies, but only a few small megaphones and some slogans, how would we have made the "iron Great Wall" give up their duties?

In addition, the moral support the populace gave us was unprecedented. Their donations earlier, and [their support in] this march, seemed to convince our classmates that we occupied a place in the people's hearts and minds.

Well, what is the reason that this march was able to win the broad support of the citizens? (Let us leave aside the factor of popular desire.) My opinion is as follows: first, the educational work we did prior to the march was done relatively well—we took to the streets to explain our cause to the populace, we solicited donations, and using our thin and faint voices, shouted against China Central Television, which is equipped with modern satellite communications technology. The ordinary people saw this with their own eyes, and their hearts ached for us. They asked themselves: who are the students for? Aren't they doing this for us? (Now the students' intentions are known to the world.) Their consciousness was heightened; they wanted to lend a hand, but they had their families to take care of. This time, when the students declared that they would march, and the government stood firm, the citizens decided that no matter what, they would not let the students come to grief. "At least we should go to cheer for the students."

Second, as intellectuals, we made significant concessions in our banners and slogans. The original slogans that were suggested—"improve the treatment of teachers," and so on—were only shouted by some marchers from the teachers' colleges. The march's main purpose was changed to "petition for the people" and appeal for redress of wrongs suffered by the students. . . .

Third, there was no anti-Party or anti-government propaganda whatsoever. This reassured quite a portion of the populace, making them unafraid to speak for the students. No matter how much the populace may despise the authorities, once one touches upon the Party, their hearts hold some inexpressible feelings. This is a matter of emotion. It must be attributed to the Party's highest principles, some of the successes of the Mao Tse-tung era, as well as forty years of unceasing political education in schools. In sum, you may say that a mother acted wrongfully with good intentions, but you absolutely may not say that your mother is not your mother. Isn't this so? A mother, while listening to her children's tearful complaints, never forgets that her children have praised her in the past.

Another reason why this march produced some results: It was only a demonstration to tell the lords that we are not a "small handful." But there has been no progress in the substance of the democratization process (as stated before, this was just progress in form). This march did not have the goal of presenting a petition to the bigwigs, as was the case on the 22nd, so its object was simple and clear. There was none of the uncertainty of having to "cross the river by groping your way across the stones on the bottom" or to just "follow your gut feeling."[13]

Summarizing the above, we know that if we want to hold marches again and want to receive the support of the populace, then we must give up the satisfied air of victors. Again, we must appeal to the populace! Neither we nor the lords can afford any delay!

Perhaps we must expand our breadth of mind as well as think more coolly.

> —A student in the Computer Science
> Department, April 28
> *(small-character poster)*

LETTER TO PEOPLE'S UNIVERSITY CLASSMATES

Classmates:

Our protest on April 27 to publicize our cause was a great success.

At times of crisis, the will of the people decides their destiny. The actions of the students was reasoned, correct—and also permitted by the Constitution. Throughout the protest march, classmates combined enthusiasm with reason, thus enabling us to make the strongest possible show of force. We gained the broadest understanding and support of the people [that we could have asked for]. . . .

When the exhausted students of at least thirty-seven universities and colleges wearily passed through their campus gates, but with a fiery excitement that makes the heart leap, history wept, and history also smiled. People! We are speechless. Under such circumstances, we have no way of expressing our feelings, and there is no need for us to speak at length.

At the same time, we [must be aware] that we currently face the same kind of precarious situation that China faces whenever it takes a step

13. In emphasizing the need for flexibility in the course of China's ambitious and difficult economic reforms, Deng Xiaoping has used the expression to "cross the river by groping your way across the stones at the bottom" (*mozhe shitou guo he*). "Follow Your Gut Feeling" (*Genzhe ganjue zou*) was a popular Taiwan pop song in 1988 and 1989. Students often applied these two expressions to the floundering leadership of the Party's top leaders.

forward. We have achieved great success in publicity. We have seized the initiative. Nevertheless, before we can make any substantive progress, there is an even more difficult step ahead. We must prevent the appearance of various kinds of "restrictions and barriers" [thrown up by the government to intimidate us, turn the people against us, impede our organizing activities, and divide us].

For this reason, continuation of the class boycott is the only choice before us. We must actively prepare for a dialogue so that we can fully respond to the government's offer of a dialogue when it comes. We must present to the government the opinions of all the people, from workers to peasants to experts to scholars. We must allow the people—not just the students—to engage in a dialogue with the government. This is a requirement of a progressive republic. . . .

We hope that 1989 will not be like the year when "Bian Que was received by Duke Huan of Cai" [that is, the government ignores the diagnosis of the nation's ailments until they are beyond treatment].

> —People's University Provisional Students'
> Autonomous Committee, April 28
> (*big-character poster*)

"The *Enlightenment Daily* shows no enlightenment; the *People's Daily* has left the people; Central Television confuses black and white; and the *Beijing Daily* is full of nonsense!"

The call for freedom of the press, first raised by Beijing students in the seven demands of April 17, would emerge as one of the main themes of the Democracy Movement, on several levels. First, at a theoretical level, many students and intellectuals had identified an independent press, free from government control, as one of the foundations of a democratic society: thus the April 17 demands for a free press. Second, within days after demonstrations began, press freedom and veracity became practical issues: students found that the government-controlled Chinese press either failed to report pro-democracy activities or painted them in a negative light. Students were greatly angered by official accounts linking peaceful protestors to bad elements in society; this anger at perceived distortion by the press became a driving force behind the Democracy Movement. Third, student demands for freedom of the press brought into the movement many Chinese editors and reporters. During a ten-day "window" of press openness in early to mid-May, newspapers across the country carried sympathetic accounts, complete with photographs, of student and citizen demonstrations, enabling the growing Democracy Movement to carry its message to the hundreds of millions of Chinese living in smaller cities and in the countryside. Moreover, demonstrations by Chinese journalists in support of the students not only revitalized the movement at a couple of crucial junctures but also proved to the authorities that the students' complaints did not resonate solely within campuses.

To counter distorted or partial press accounts suggesting that in Beijing students and other pro-democracy demonstrators had attacked police at Xinhuamen, while in Xi'an and Changsha "lawless" bad elements had taken advantage of the student protests to riot on the day of Hu Yaobang's memorial service, citizens and students related the "real story" of the incidents in posters and handbills. An example of this genre of poster writing is the selection below, "Who Are the Thugs? Who Is Causing Disorder?" Writing to refute official press reports that on that day hoodlums had run wild, setting fire to vehicles and looting stores in downtown Xi'an before the police could restore order, the writer accuses the government of hiding the fact that police and paramilitary violence had incited the disorder. Though such posters contained their own inaccuracies, they performed the vital function of providing information otherwise totally unavailable.

WHO ARE THE THUGS? WHO IS CAUSING DISORDER?
—The Real Story of the April 22 Massacre at Xincheng Square in Xi'an

On April 22, after the rally in memory of Comrade Hu Yaobang had ended, students from various institutes of higher learning and residents from all walks of life in Xi'an assembled in Xincheng Square in front of the Shaanxi Provincial Government Building. Carrying wreaths with elegiac couplets, they gathered to express their grief at the death of Comrade Hu Yaobang.

By twelve noon, Xincheng Square was filled with students and Xi'an residents. At this time, several thousand paramilitary police stood in front of the provincial government compound; they appeared ready for combat. Forming a human wall, they blocked the gates of the east and west sides of the provincial government compound.

At approximately one o'clock in the afternoon, a group of twenty to thirty people carried a wreath to the entrance on west side. They talked to the paramilitary police guarding the entrance, requesting permission to bring the wreath into the provincial government compound. The policemen refused and shoved them out the gate. Urged on by the support of the crowd, this group once again carried the wreath up to the entrance and pressed in between the policemen standing there. The two groups began to clash. At this time, onlookers reported seeing policemen beating and kicking people in the crowd. Those of the crowd who had rushed forward were driven out of the gate once again. As a few persons in the crowd threw rocks and bricks at the police, several dozen policemen guarding the gate struck out at the crowd with their belts. The crowd fled in every direction. Then the policemen moved back to the gate. Once again, the crowd encircled the entrance. At this point two trucks were driven from within the compound to block the west gate and the policemen guarding the entrance retreated into the compound. Some members of the crowd rushed forward and set fire to the canvas covers of the trucks at the entrance. It was a small fire; a few policemen pulled off the covers and threw them on the ground, letting them smolder. Bricks were once more thrown at the policemen inside the compound, who in return charged the square, indiscriminately striking onlookers with their belts. The crowd backed away. But as soon as the policemen retreated, it surged forward. Police and crowd clashed like this three times; the atmosphere in the square became more tense.

At approximately two o'clock in the afternoon, contingents of student demonstrators from Northwest University, Xi'an Transportation University, and other schools arrived in succession at the square. They marched once around the square in an orderly fashion and then gathered at the center, forming a crowd that extended as far as the east gate of the compound. While the students were marching, the crowd and the police stopped fighting. The square quieted down temporarily.

At about two-thirty, a directive of the Xi'an municipal government was broadcast over the loudspeakers of the provincial government building. Following this, statements by the Deputy Party Secretary of Northwest University and the President of Xi'an Transportation University urging students to leave the square were broadcast several times.

At three o'clock a disturbance broke out once again at the west gate when individuals set fire to the reception office there. Paramilitary policemen within the compound who were close to the office did nothing to stop them and made no attempt to put out the fire. A fire truck arrived. As the fire was not serious, it was quickly extinguished. But the firemen did not withdraw. Instead, they turned a high-pressure hose on the crowd, knocking many students and observers down to the ground. The crowd resisted anew, and the earlier seesaw struggle was repeated. The two trucks, which had been driven away while the fire was being extinguished, were moved back to block the entrance. At that time, arson had already been committed. Why did they still use flammable vehicles to hold back an excited crowd? This can be explained by the words of an "insider": "They intended to have them burn the trucks." And in fact, soon the trucks were set on fire. Black smoke rose from the square.

Beginning from about three-thirty, a statement by leaders of the [autonomous] students' associations of Northwest University and the Xi'an Transportation University was broadcast several times over the loudspeakers. It declared that the provincial government had already accepted the student's demands and asked the students to leave the square. Seeing the tense situation, teachers from various universities also tried to persuade the students to return to their campuses. Under these circumstances, students began to leave the square. However, quite a few remained.

Some time after four o'clock, Governor Hou arrived at the command post at the provincial government building. The assaults by the police then intensified. Wearing steel helmets and wielding riot shields, a large group of riot police rushed out from the west entrance. In broad daylight they brutally whipped the unarmed, defenseless people with their batons and belts and bombarded them with stones and bricks. Many students and city residents were wounded and bleeding. It was a terrible sight. Comrades from the provincial level High Court and Procuratorate located in the west side of the compound saw what was happening. From the upper floors, some shouted, "Officers, don't beat people!" but they were cursed by some policemen below. The crowd in the square picked up stones and bricks and returned the attack. As the policemen fought their way forward, the crowd moved back, but the policemen did not dare hold their position amidst the enraged crowd. If they retreated even slightly, the crowd surged forward. Police and residents clashed thus four or five times. Some people were caught and brought inside the compound or the provincial government building, where they were brutally beaten. Some employees in the provincial government building witnessed a group of policemen using batons and belts wantonly to beat captives who were too weak to resist, beating them until they fell to the ground, then stomping on them with their heavy boots. Some people were beaten unconscious on the spot. A few cadres from the provincial government approached the police to ask them to stop their savagery. But the police, who could only see red, paid them no heed other than to shout back abuse.

At five o'clock in the afternoon, quite a few persons who had been beaten began to leave the square. However, many people now passing by after work, unaware of the situation, poured into the square. Their numbers kept swelling. In full public view, the police brazenly continued to assault the crowd. Their brutality enraged the people in the square, provoking them to fight back.

Beginning from six-thirty in the evening, the fighting intensified. The square was now in a state of chaos. The police could no longer control the situation. Some vehicles and rooms within the provincial Procuratorate building were set on fire.

At approximately eight in the evening, the paramilitary police began to seal off the square. Armed with batons, belts, and bricks, they beat anyone in their path. The crowd fled to the east, west, and south. It was in the ensuing confusion that the Tiantian Clothing Shop was "looted."

As to the truth about the looting of the Tiantian Clothing Shop, according to eyewitness accounts, policemen chased people to the intersection of Xihuamen. Those fleeing were blocked by crowds and, with nowhere to go, dashed into the still-open clothing store to hide. Once inside, they were trapped by police, who proceeded to beat them and arrest them as looters. The police were on the scene almost from the beginning. Nonetheless, one news report indicates that eighteen looters were caught in the act; yet another states that the clothing store was completely sacked. These inconsistencies expose some scandalous secrets.

The above is a description of the general course of events of the April 22 Xincheng Square incident. According to disclosures made by persons privy to inside information, eleven people were killed and several hundred people were wounded in this massacre. A bus driver was actually beaten to death by the police when he went out to inspect the road after his vehicle was blocked by the crowd. Even dozens of plainclothes policemen were beaten by policemen in uniform. Yet our newspapers claimed that no one died.

Before the April 22 massacre, the central government had clearly indicated that local authorities should not impede the mourning activities of the people, increase tension, or exacerbate matters. However, certain persons in the Shaanxi provincial government and police force openly defied the spirit of the central government directive. By deliberately provoking the incident and aggravating the situation, they caused one of the most appalling cases of bloodshed since the founding of our nation. This has seriously damaged the prestige of the Party and the government in the minds of the people.

Illustration 2.5. Copies of this photograph and the next one, of police beating demonstrators in Xi'an on April 22, were posted around Beijing in an effort to counter government accounts of the violence. Credit: October Review.

In truth, there were indeed bad persons who took advantage of the chaos to break the law. However, it was the police who created a situation of chaos by indiscriminately beating innocent people. What is most disturbing is that whoever was caught, whether a wrongdoer or not, became a target for combat practice. Even if they had committed criminal acts, they had already ceased their criminal activity and had lost their capacity to resist. They should have been handed over to judicial departments to be punished in accordance with the law. But the police started beating people as soon as they caught them, and even beat some people to death. The law of the Republic was trampled by these law enforcers. Their badges and collar insignia are covered with blood that cannot be washed away.

Today, the perpetrators of the April 22 massacre use the propaganda machinery in their control to hoodwink their superiors and subordinates and to misguide the public, claiming that the bloody atrocities they committed against the residents and students of Xi'an were "incidents of beating, smashing, looting, and burning committed by a handful of evildoers."[14] This is an attempt to cover up their crimes in order to deceive the people of this nation and the central government. But the truth cannot be concealed. These unforgivable crimes were viewed by over one hundred thousand people of Xi'an who were at the scene. Numerous witnesses and much evidence exist. Quite a few photographs of policemen commiting acts of violence are scattered among the people. This powerful evidence will ensure that the facts ultimately emerge.

The residents of Xi'an will absolutely not permit bloodied hands to smear the reputation of the city and will absolutely not tolerate the perpetrators of the massacre to continue their evil crimes.

With regard to a massacre of such exceptional scale, we strongly demand that:

1. the Central Committee of the Communist Party, the National People's Congress, the State Council, and the Supreme People's Procuratorate organize a special investigation team and immediately dispatch it to Shaanxi to ascertain quickly the truth behind the April 22 massacre (as interested parties, the Shaanxi Provincial Government and other government departments involved in the incident must not be permitted to participate in the investigation);

2. based on the findings of the investigation, the National People's Congress instruct the Supreme People's Court to form a special tribunal to investigate and try those implicated in the great massacre of April 22 in proceedings instituted by the Supreme People's Procuratorate;

3. the criminal liability of those who planned and directed the April 22 massacre be determined in accordance with the criminal law, the assailants be punished, and those who committed heinous crimes with no regard for human life be given the harshest sentence permitted under the law in order to quell the people's anger;

4. the *People's Daily*, China Central Broadcasting, and China Central Television announce the investigation findings and make known the facts to the whole nation. The ability of the central government to investigate and handle this case speedily is crucial to maintaining so-

---

14. These do not appear to be the actual words of the government reports, but they are close: on April 23, 1989, the *Beijing Daily* ran an article from Xinhua News Agency on rioting in Xi'an with the headline "Some Lawless Elements in Xi'an Surround and Attack the Provincial Government Building and Engage in Beating, Smashing, Looting, and Burning." This and other news reports (including television coverage) on the disturbance in Xi'an and Changsha were careful not to implicate students in the violence. Neither did they mention, however, any kind of beating of crowds by police.

Illustration 2.6. Xi'an, April 22, 1989. Caption on the original poster: "Take a look: how old were those who got beaten?!" Credit: October Review.

cial stability and unity in the Xi'an area. As residents of Xi'an, we wait with eager anticipation.

> —Faculty and students of universities
> in the Xi'an area, April 26, 1989;
> copied on May 13
> (*big-character poster*)[15]

In fact, a good number of editors and reporters were not inclined to speak for the government. Frustrated with the tight leash kept on the press by the Party, many shared the students' desire for political reform and an end to the special privileges

15. This poster may have been the one authored by Wang Jianxin, deputy director of the Historical Preservation and Museum Science section of Northwest University in Xi'an, who was arrested in September 1989 for drafting a wall poster account of the April 22 violence. Wang was also reportedly charged with sending letters demanding a government investigation of the incident to Central Committee members, the Supreme People's Court, and the Supreme People's Procuratorate, as well as organizing a protest march in May in Xi'an.

and corruption of Party officials. But tremendous pressure to run "correct" stories—articles with the Party's point of view—was exerted on journalists throughout the movement, with the notable exception of the two-week "window of openness" in early May. Nonetheless, in the first weeks of the protests, a few principled and courageous editors attempted to cover the protests from an independent perspective. On April 23, the *Science and Technology Daily* ran an entire page of news and photos about the student sit-ins at Tiananmen, going so far as to describe the movement as one for "freedom and democracy." The issue almost did not make the newsstands; authorities permitted it to appear only after a number of key editors and reporters threatened to resign. The *Science and Technology Daily* coverage was a milestone: since 1949, no major paper had dared to print an article so clearly against the interests of the Central Committee. (Chinese papers had in the past published articles or editorials attacking leaders; in these cases, however, editors acted with the direct or tacit backing of powerful figures who used the articles for their own political purposes.) After the June suppression, the paper's top editors were purged and replaced.

More draconian measures would be taken against the maverick Shanghai *World Economic Herald*. Its April 24 issue was confiscated at the printers on the order of Jiang Zemin, the urbane but politically hard-line Shanghai Party Secretary; the issue's transgression was a long account of an April 19 meeting in memory of Hu Yaobang in which leading liberal intellectuals alleged that Hu had been unfairly treated in 1987, and lamented that democracy in China had not advanced in a decade. Jiang not only halted distribution of the paper but also dismissed Qin Benli, the respected, seventy-year-old editor-in-chief of the *Herald*, known for his independence, on April 27. Nonetheless, copies of the banned issue found their way to Beijing, where they were posted on campuses. Qin's dismissal at the hands of Shanghai Party bosses became a cause célèbre for students and liberal intellectuals.

Two contrasting perspectives on the issue of freedom of the press are offered by the writers below. The first, an undergraduate who appears to have been actively involved in the student protests, maintains that the success or failure of the student movement, and of political reform in general, hinges on winning independence for the press. The second, undoubtedly more removed than the first from the protests, takes a longer-term look at the development of press freedom in China. His concern is not so much the lifting of restrictions on the press—which he assumes will necessarily follow from the tides of reform already washing through China and Eastern Europe—as the complete separation of news reporting and politics. This, he concludes, will only be realized when papers are commercialized— when they become the "enterprise of the [private] enterpreneur" who "will make not propaganda but promotion of sales the purpose of the newspaper." Such faith in the ameliorating effects of a capitalist system, whether justified or not, was a recurring theme of a good portion of writings in the Democracy Movement.

AFTER ALL, WHAT ARE WE FIGHTING FOR?

We are now facing a clumsy, decaying opponent which is making its last stand. In this last stand, in a sudden burst of clarity before its demise, it is setting up a trap. It is tragic that we have fallen into this trap. In arguing back and forth with our opponent about whether our demonstrations are "turmoil" or "legal," about the true facts of the April 20 incident, about the significance of kneeling when we submitted our petition [on April 22], . . . we have forgotten what our fundamental objective is (I do not deny that some of the issues cited above are substantive ones). The rules of fighting between gentlemen apply only to gentlemen. [The government's control over the media has given people across the country the impression that] the students are unreasonably and deliberately fomenting trouble. . . . [The government] is an opponent accustomed to perfidy and double-dealing. We should fight back in a very practical way for our real goals—freedom of speech and freedom of the press. We can demand no less and ask no more at this stage!

If we were to ignore the issue of freedom of speech and freedom of the press, all of our [other] goals would be nothing but wishful thinking. The government's distorted news reports and wanton slander, the [Beijing Municipality's] "Ten Articles" on public demonstrations, endless propaganda, and the reorganization of the Shanghai *World Economic Herald*—these are hardly isolated events. There is only one reason for all of them: the government will not allow the people to speak the truth. Recently, the Beijing Municipal Party Committee stated openly that it would put the [local] media under its control in order to turn around the government's present defensive situation. What a shameless warlord manner this is! It is obvious that media control is the only way they see for rescuing themselves: one after another, citizens are already moving to the other side. To win the hearts of the people, the government must conduct a thorough reform, but this is impossible for them to do at the present time. Therefore, the only recourse is to deceive and poison people's minds. The government fears most that students will take to the streets to distribute handbills, make speeches, and establish ties with workers and other citizens.

The government is making a last-ditch effort. Thus, we must focus on the critical point: taking the tools of public opinion presently controlled by them and making them the people's, for the people to use. . . . The downfall of many governments has occurred after they had lost control over the tools of public opinion, or, when prevailing public opinion was made known early on. The mass media has become the most effective weapon for people all over the world; unfortunately, up to the very present, we still cannot take advantage of it, and many people do not even appreciate its significance. This kind of misguidedness in our movement may very well lead to our defeat. And after we are defeated, the government will use the media to retaliate.

At the end of 1986, while we were struggling to realize true democracy and freedom, rights granted us under the Constitution, the Beijing Municipal government hastily adopted the "Ten Articles on Demonstrations." Its purpose was obvious: to restrict the freedom of citizens. Under the Ten Articles, all demonstrations must be registered in advance, and actual demonstration is not permitted until approval has been given by the authorities. This [set of regulations] is the object of universal ridicule! Freedom of demonstration and other rights are granted by the Constitution.[16] But now they cannot be exercised until they are approved by some aristocrats. In addition, as long as these aristocrats think a demonstration "may have some adverse impact" [on social order, production, etc.], they can always withhold approval. What an idea, this "may have some adverse impact"! Someone's subjective mind (intent on protecting its own interests and privileges) sets an unchallengeable standard that determines whether the people can exercise their own rights! A sad fact this is indeed! . . .

It is said that the Law on the Press will be promulgated at the end of this year [1989]. Based on the current situation, can we imagine what kind of law governing the press this will be? The Ten Articles have taught us a lesson already. Are there any people who can guarantee that the new press law will not become the shackles of "freedom of the press"? . . . Let me ask: how much freedom for the press can such a regulation bring? Thinking about this is enough to send chills down one's spine.

It is not hard for all to comprehend that press reform is the most appropriate breakthrough point for political reform. Public opinion functions as both a constructive and supervisory force. It is not for no reason that western nations call the public press the "fourth power [estate]." . . . Allowing people to speak the truth is the most fundamental feature of political reform. In the truth spoken by the people, we will be able to find an inexhaustible source of prosperity for our motherland and for the re-

16. Article 35 of the Constitution states: "The citizens of the People's Republic of China possess the freedom of speech, publication, assembly, association, and marching and demonstration.

vitalization of our nation. . . . Let us unceasingly continue our struggle for this objective until the people can truly speak frankly and without restraint!

—An undergraduate student, May 1, 1989
(big-character poster)

THE ROAD TO FREEDOM OF THE PRESS IN CHINA
(excerpts)

I. From Lifting the Speech Ban to Lifting the Newspaper Ban

. . . The "glorious revolution" of 1976 [the death of Mao Tse-tung and the fall of the "Gang of Four"—four ultraleftists, including Mao's wife— who had been the principal figures behind the Cultural Revolution, during which all spheres of activity were subjugated to politics and extreme violence justified in the name of class struggle] ended without bloodshed the era of speech prohibition. Emphasis on social "stability and unity" [rather than political struggle] and the rehabilitation of victims of unjust, false, or incorrect charges inevitably caused a reaction against Maoism and the end of idolization of one-man rule. . . . In a China that had freed itself of a phobia, criticisms of official personages and critical comments on national affairs began to be heard everywhere.

The development of this "free speech," however, has brought out people's desire for the freedom of the press, as is only natural. For those who are not to be satisfied by "just talking" but wish their points of view to reach and influence society, the best way to do so is of course with the help of the media. Now the grave problem is that in a country so vast, with over one billion people but very few news organizations, avenues for expressing oneself are crowded. Making things even worse is the policy that Chinese newspapers follow, one that looks not so much at the contents of the writings as at the status and position of the writer. It is only a matter of course that the opinions and wishes of the ordinary people are having a difficult time being heard.

Particularly problematic is the tradition of Chinese newspapers of serving politics; at the time when the "rightists" were attacked, no rightist could plead or defend himself or herself in the newspaper; now that it is "bourgeois liberalization" that one opposes, it follows that people like Fang Lizhi are not allowed to speak through the press. During the

Cultural Revolution Deng Xiaoping was personally attacked through the "Four Big Freedoms" [the four major rights of the people to speak out freely, air their views fully, hold great debates, and write big-character posters, which were guaranteed by the Constitution]. When he assumed leadership of the Party, he demanded in 1980 that the National People's Congress pass a resolution to abolish them [and they were dropped from the 1982 Constitution]. In actuality, however, the "Four Big Freedoms," although abused in the Cultural Revolution as means of slander, are not intrinsically wrong. Now that they have been outlawed, thrown out, so to speak, like the baby with bath water, one more channel of speech is obstructed. But "people have mouths, as the earth has mountains and rivers." What used to be expressed through big-character posters now finds expression in letters of grievance—many of which bear no name—trying to find their way up to the higher authorities.

The slogan of "Reforming China's Press" was put forward in 1979. More than a decade has gone by, but the Chinese press is still operating along essentially the same lines as before. People have cried out for a press law, to be built on the premise of "freedom of speech." Such a law is yet to come. The leaders of China have been extremely cautious about press reform, which is a sensitive topic: except for encouraging changes along the lines of business and professional efficiency, which have already seen progress, the leadership insists again and again on the outmoded "tool theory" and "mouthpiece theory"[17] as the ideological and institutional basis for China's media, and refuses to let go of its control over the newsman. Even worse is its reply to the public cry for the birth of nongovernmental newspapers; the leadership regards such activity to be a terrible offense and simply outrageous. Yet, if one looks at the changes, both international and domestic, that have occurred (many socialist countries are pushing for reform; Taiwan, which has been under martial law for a long time, has lifted its newspaper ban; on the mainland, a torrent of new ideas is pouring out of different social sectors), one hears the sound of a

---

17. The "tool theory" and the "mouthpiece theory" have developed out of debates over the class nature (alternatively, the "Party spirit") of news reporting and the press. They are instrumentalist theories that hold that the function of China's news organs is to be the mouthpiece of the Party and to further the implementation of its policies. Their origins can be traced to Mao Tse-tung's emphasis on the press's role as a political tool, and even further back to Lenin's statement that the basic principle of proletariat papers was to embody Party character. Hu Yaobang, despite his reputation as a liberal tolerant of dissent, reiterated such views in a major internal Party speech in February 1985. Since the suppression of the Democracy Movement, the Party has once again trotted out the theories to remind the press and the public of the limits to press freedom.

tide on the rise, growing louder and louder. Lifting the newspaper ban is only a matter of time now.

II. From Lifting the Newspaper Ban to the Pluralization of Politics

What would become of the Chinese news media if the ban were lifted?

. . . China's open policy has nurtured a group of people who are both politically and intellectually the very best. When the newspaper ban is lifted, they will step forth and, acting as spokesmen of different social classes and sectors [a role that, as explained above, we cannot expect the Communist Party's newspapers to play], will be the sponsors of newspapers. Representing a new productive force in China, they will be endowed with the ideology of equality and the drive for progress, qualities that will make it easy for them to gain influence in society, and that will form the basis of their position as leaders of public opinion. In time, they will become political leaders; their many newspapers will become many political centers and form many political forces.

But why will these unofficially sponsored newspapers, having been liberated from the straitjacket of politics, become political newspapers? In the first place, China has yet to experience a democratic enlightenment; the kind of "socialism" which China has implemented for the past few decades differs little from despotism. Whoever comes forth to run a newspaper, with even the least amount of political consciousness and the least sense of social responsibility, will necessarily employ the newspaper to campaign for democratic politics. In order to collect strength to combat autocratic ideology, to enhance the concentrated force of political colleagues and to reinforce their power for action, these newspapers will no doubt develop into political parties or merge with one progressive party or another into a unified entity, and thus become the mouthpiece of these parties. In the second place, the decline of the Chinese civilization has made the Chinese people feel an ever-increasing desire for reform. Granted, the Chinese have bitter memories about politics, and are disgusted by it at the bottom of their hearts; but at a time when the transition from the old to a new system is only beginning and when difficulties and obstacles are everywhere, people cannot but be pulled into the whirlpool of politics, and use political means to solve social problems. Soon after the birth of the bourgeois newspaper in England, America, and France, bourgeois revolutions took place in succession, and, as a result, the contemporary commercial newspapers quickly became papers of political parties. The newspaper of the proletarian class was political at its birth;

it is because at that time it was faced with the political task of utmost importance: to seize power.

The shift from one political center to many means moving away from the centralized toward a pluralistic politics. Such, beyond a doubt, is historical progress. Yet, the pluralization of politics cannot possibly come into being before the newspaper ban is abandoned. And without political pluralization, democratic politics will forever remain empty talk. Looking at the whole of human history, it is true that there has been no single dictator who did not say that he represented the people—so which autocratic system would say that it is against the people?

III. From Political Pluralism to the Freedom of the Press

Political pluralism signifies democratic politics, and a multiparty system is its basic form. . . . At the beginning, when such a system is being established and consolidated, the freedom of the press will remain immature. For on the one hand, when "Uniformity of Opinion" is replaced by the "Competing Voices of the Hundred Schools," parties and factions will be able to have newspapers of their own and freely express their points of view. On the other hand, however, these papers will not be free of biases; they will not publish news and editorials that are not in favor of the political parties to which they belong. Their views of events will frequently not report matters as they really are: [their inclination to search for facts to justify their views] will render objective, fair reporting difficult. True freedom of the press can only be realized when the age of the political paper ends. People's passion for political causes will grow and develop into a [broader] interest in the all-around development of man and society. Subsequently, the newspaper will become the enterprise of the entrepreneur who, adhering to the principle of neutrality, will make not propaganda but promotion of sales the purpose of the newspaper. It is only in this kind of newspaper, the newspaper of the advertisement, that people will be able to fully exercise their constitutional rights and freely express their ideas.

[IV] . . . To be sure, the realization of the freedom of the press depends on successful reforms of both economic and political institutions. While only a successful economic reform, one that clarifies the property rights of the news enterprise, can provide a base for the birth of newspapers of a new kind, it is only with successful reforms of political institutions that people will have the opportunity to participate in or criticize governmental affairs, to freely express their views for society to accept or reject.

The success of these also depends, however, on the reform of the press as a precondition. For the newspaper is where people's needs and wishes can be concentrated and reflected. As the mouthpiece of the people, China's press has the obligation to publish disagreements with the party in power, or send out warnings to the party so that it may effectively avoid making mistakes in the reforms. Before we break the "one-color" system of Party newspapers—the system which [as Hu Yaobang reminded us in 1985] must perform only one function: "to serve, under the leadership of the Party, the purpose of propagandizing the Party's guidelines and policies"—democratization of policy making cannot possibly be achieved. Neither will economic and political reforms succeed. The Chinese press must write clearly on its own banner: "Today, not tomorrow, we ask the government to expedite the lifting of the newspaper ban. Today, not tomorrow, we ask for the freedom of the press. . . ."

—"Han Hua"
*(article published
in journal)*

"A Dialogue with Youth Is No Different from a Dialogue with the Future!"

Student leadership throughout the Democracy Movement would be characterized by change and instability. In part, the frequent changes at the top reflected a fundamental problem of immaturity, inexperience, and factionalism; in part, however, they were due to the inherently reactive nature of the student movement, which had arisen spontaneously and would continually evolve in response to specific events. On April 28, the Provisional Students' Federation became the permanent Federation of Autonomous Student Unions of Beijing Universities and Colleges ("Beijing Students' Federation"). Zhou Yongjun, who had come under heavy fire for prematurely deciding to call off the April 27 march without consulting members of the steering committee, was replaced as chairman by twenty-one-year-old Wuer Kaixi, a first-year student in education at Beijing Normal University, of the Uighur minority. Wang Dan, the Beijing University activist, assumed a seat on the Standing Committee.

By now, close to the end of the second week of protests, the students' immediate goals had narrowed to government recognition of the Beijing Students' Federation and an open dialogue with the government. The protestors showed no intention of dropping their earlier demands for certain government actions to redress their grievances, yet what they clearly sought above all was the right to establish an organization free from government control and the opportunity to present their case to the government and public. In the eyes of the Chinese government, dialogue was not unreasonable, and could be pursued—but permitting a nonofficial political body beyond consideration. Thus, the government had made overtures to the official student union of Qinghua before the watershed April 27 march, using its initiative to foster division within the student ranks and to demonstrate its reasonableness. On April 29, government representatives, led by Yuan Mu, spokesman for the State Council, sat down to a three-hour dialogue it had asked the official National Students' Union and Beijing Students' Union to sponsor. With a few exceptions, the student representatives who participated were associated with the official student unions; the dialogue, which was subsequently televised in its entirety several times by China Central Television, proved to be a tame affair, occasionally becoming virtually a lecture session by the officials. A second "dialogue meeting" took place on April 30 with invited student representatives; it too produced few meaningful discussions.

At Beijing University, where expectations for a meaningful dialogue were particularly high, students were extremely disappointed with the cowardly performance of the Beijing University student "representative." Unsigned posters blasting him for selling out the students' interests soon appeared, a small but chilling reminder of the anonymous big-character poster denunciations of the Cultural Revolution. Student resentment at the government's careful choice of student representatives and the officials' avuncular attitude throughout the session is expressed in the first selection below. In the second piece, a student proposes concrete suggestions for avoiding a repetition of such an embarrassment.

WAS IT DIALOGUE—OR A LECTURE?

—An Evaluation of the "Dialogue" of the Afternoon of April 29

The government, bowing at last to the vigorous demands of more than one hundred thousand university students in Beijing, who have waged an arduous struggle in the form of class boycotts and demonstrations, finally decided to engage in dialogue with the students—or at least to put on the appearance of doing so. Instead of going through the autonomous students' union, which truly represents the just opinions of the masses of students, however, the government hand-picked a group of "student representatives," with whom on the afternoon of the 29th it made a great show of holding a "dialogue."

Even without dwelling on the fact that these "student representatives" whom the government had chosen were completely unable to represent the masses of progressive young students who have been active in the student movement, one look at the attitude of the [government] leaders suffices to show they had not the least intention of dealing seriously with the problems at hand. Realizing that the aspersions of "creating turmoil" cast in the *People's Daily* editorial of the 26th had failed to squash the students' [determination], and that the charges laid against them of being "anti-Party" and "anti-socialist" had not in fact set them quaking in their boots, the government decided to resort to other devious tricks. Summoning a few university students, they acted out their little "dialogue," which aimed to "reduce big problems to small problems and make small problems disappear altogether." Even though the scale of the dialogue was extremely limited, the [government] leaders used every means at their disposal to stall and vacillate, and to deal only in the most perfunctory fashion with questions of any real substance. They managed this by seizing and focusing on irrelevant details in an effort to buy time. Because the students [they chose] were not up to the task [of challenging the government], often their questions contained loopholes or flaws; when this was the case, several leaders would rush to attack the detail in question, falling over each other in their eagerness to display their bravery, while pointedly ignoring the real substance of the question. The most frustrating aspect of the whole affair was that the masses of brave young students who have risked their own safety in the pursuit of democratic reforms were made out to be nothing but a bunch of hot-headed, impertinent young whelps. Assuming grandfatherly airs, the officials uttered such [patronizing comments] as, "you're still young and easily excited," "you weren't born yet during the Cultural Revolution, were you?" and "we look on you as our own children." During this three-hour "dialogue," the leaders talked for more than 90 percent of the time. We have to inquire: was this really a dialogue between equals? or was it merely a father's lecture to his children?

The [government] leaders who took part in the dialogue are indeed tried and true veterans of bureaucratic conflict. With a single feint, they cleared a path right through a whole host of substantive questions, managing to skirt them all quite neatly. Their cheerful chatter served only to make the students squirm uncomfortably. But to these "grandfatherly public servants," so sure of the success of their little game, we now issue a stern warning: the time for clever antics has come to an end. The masses of students can see right through you. We hope you will act out of concern for the interests of the whole country, and recognize this huge patriotic student movement as the successor to the May Fourth Movement of seventy years ago. This movement should not be so much as mentioned in the same breath with the movement of the Red Guards [during the Cultural Revolution], who were manipulated and deceived by others. [We also hope that you] will cease to slander or attack the masses of progressive young students in any fashion, and that you will abandon your grandfatherly airs and, treating as equals the true representatives of the students, engage with them in a candid discussion of their demands.

[Government] Leaders, you'd better start showing a little good faith!

—Graduate Students at Beijing
Normal University, April 30, 1989
(handbill)

HAVE WE TRIUMPHED?—ON TACTICS

... It was amazing progress to go from antagonism to dialogue. This is unprecedented in the history of the Chinese republic. However, this "unprecedented breakthrough" not only gave us a sense of pride, but also presents us with a severe test. Considering how important the test that lies ahead is, the success that we have attained is only the beginning.

Negotiation and dialogue are highly skilled art forms. Prior to this movement, we were completely ignorant about them and totally lacked any experience in preparing for them. However, the people who we are trying to engage in dialogue are experts in it. Most of them are very familiar with student movements and are veterans at the negotiation table. In terms of slick talking and maneuvering for the right to claim to be the side that initiated dialogue, it has been all too apparent that these professional politicians who have been unworthily occupying places in China's officialdom are much more in control than the fresh-faced, green young students. In the so-called "dialogue" of April 29, their advantage in this respect helped them a great deal. We can see clearly how they quibbled [with us], avoiding the important and dwelling on the trivial, to gain time to think of ways to cover up the inconsistencies in their stories; how they wiggled out of embarrassing situations where they were unable to advance any further argument, and even managed to strike back; how they utilized the method of seizing on an isolated incident to turn the "dialogue" into a one-sided propaganda blitz and unjust accusation session. In short, this meticulously engineered farce tarnished the positive image of the student movement in the minds of all the Chinese people, a positive image that had been painstakingly worked for. It has caused bitter disappointment and indignation in a great many passionately committed students.

An even trickier matter lies within the student movement itself. On the one hand, because the Beijing Students' Federation and the preparatory committees of each university or college have not yet been legalized, the April 29 dialogue—or any other dialogue—could not be carried out with the representatives favored by the great majority of students. But on the other hand, when there is this kind of situation in which the student movement is in dire peril, unity and cooperation among students is easier to achieve. But [no matter what], if student representatives walk into the negotiation room (if we can call it negotiation) each with their own opinions, strategies, and working styles, then it is possible that all kinds of problems will surface. In addition, the possibility of being divided and demoralized is much greater in an atmosphere of negotiation than under the adverse conditions of demonstrations and sit-ins [that naturally promote a spirit of cooperation and determination]. The Qinghua dialogue of April 26 [in which the government tried to meet only with some Qinghua student representatives] and the enormous publicity about the [April 29] "dialogue" in the last couple of days have already proven this point.

In order that the effort of over a hundred thousand students is not wasted, in order that we live up to the support and the trust of the masses, and for the sake of the glorious dream that we have been seeking assiduously—democracy and science—we must make a dialogue produce more substantial results.

1. . . . The main condition for dialogue and the resumption of classes must be government recognition of the legal status of the Beijing Students' Federation. Dialogue should be carried out between the government and the Federation. Individual schools definitely should not participate in a dialogue on their own.

2. Representatives in the dialogue must be chosen for their eloquence, quickness in thought, and keen observational and analytical ability. The number of people should not be too many; all that is needed are five or six shrewd and capable people. These representatives should be picked by popular election within the Federation. Aside from possessing a spirit of sacrifice, unusual courage, and resourcefulness, they must also show that they do not get rattled by a quickly changing situation, and must be able to act as circumstances dictate without errors.

3. . . . The five or six people should be fully prepared; they should pay particular attention to being fully prepared in terms of factual evidence and statistics. They should complement each other in every question.

When the time for raising a crucial point arrives, they should be able to come quickly to the point and pursue it vigorously. They absolutely should not be evasive at any time.

4. The dialogue should not be turned into a disguised press conference or news announcement. Aside from raising questions, the student representatives should fully express and assert themselves. Through the media, they should reveal to the public the objectives and views of the students, as well as the true facts about the student movement.

Long live the spirit of liberty!

—Night of May 1, 1989.
(unsigned small-character poster)

The Democracy Movement was essentially a struggle of propaganda, of numbers against state power, and ultimately, of power politics at the very highest echelons of the Party. It did not involve any legal battles: no injunctions were issued and no lawsuits tried in Chinese courts. The reason that legal issues never took on any real importance in the movement, however, was not that they were never raised; rather it was that no real channels for legal action existed—a reflection of the fact that the Chinese legal system, despite significant strengthening over the previous decade, was still extremely fragile and had little actual force. Indeed, one of the notable aspects of the movement was the students' and other pro-democracy activists' attempt to use legal arguments and legal procedures for their cause. Several of the autonomous unions set up "law subcommittees" to research and present legal issues related to the movement; constitutional rights were frequently cited in defense of the demonstrators and in support of the demand for freedom of the press; the Beijing government's "Ten Articles on Public Demonstrations" were attacked as a violation of constitutional rights;[18] a major demand of the movement was passage of a press law guaranteeing the press a measure of autonomy; teachers and citizens threatened or actually tried to bring suits for libel against authorities; and, as related in more detail in Chapter 5, a number of prominent intellectuals attempted to have the Standing Committee of the National People's Congress convene an emergency meeting to rescind martial law and dismiss Premier Li Peng, in accordance with its constitutionally mandated powers.

In the end, though, no serious discussion of legal issues occurred in any forum. The students did not pursue their legal arguments with the government, in part because a dialogue between them and the government never materialized, and in

18. Students were not the only ones who thought of using the law to benefit: in his April 24 comments to Li Peng and Yang Shangkun, Deng said, "They are using constitutionally stipulated rights to challenge us. Beijing has the 'Ten Articles.' We must use them to restrict them."

part because legal issues began to fade in importance as the conflict sharpened. As for attempts to bring action in court, although complete details are not yet available, it appears that the efforts were stymied, as almost all expected they would be, by the courts' refusal to accept the suits. Finally, the petition drive to convene an emergency session of the Standing Committee of the National People's Congress was halted when Li Peng and the hard-line faction consolidated their power in the Party; initiators of the drive were arrested or, in more fortunate cases, severely criticized.

The posters below are two illustrations of how students and teachers brought analyses of citizens' legal rights to bear on the Democracy Movement.

OUR FATE IS IN LI PENG'S MOUTH

All are aware that the [April 26] editorial in the *People's Daily* characterized the current student movement as fundamentally an anti-Party, anti-socialist conspiracy. One may infer from this definition that whoever has been involved in the movement is also deemed to be a participant in this conspiracy, and thus inescapably bears responsibility for it. Moreover, this suggests that it would be totally appropriate to punish the organizers of the movement as counter-revolutionary criminals. Yesterday [the 29th], however, [State Council spokesman] Yuan Mu began the dialogue [with the students] with a message from [Premier] Li Peng, which went as follows: the *People's Daily* editorial was not directed at the majority of students, but only at an extremely small number of people who have violated the law. As this statement seems to have fundamentally overturned the definition given in the *People's Daily* editorial, it was greeted with the warm applause of the student representatives present at the meeting. Now, I would like to ask those student representatives who greeted the statement with "applause": did it ever cross your minds that whether you are a counter-revolutionary or not, whether you will be punished or not—all rests on a single statement from Li Peng! If the fate of the students lies in the hands of these fickle, unpredictable leaders, what about the fate of our country?

Similarly, when in the course of the dialogue one of the student representatives asked if the government would go after the participants of the movement and its organizers, [Vice Minister of the State Education Commission] He Dongchang's response was as follows: "The whole series of activities during the student movement was not legally permitted; they are prohibited by law. However, taking into account that the students support the Party and that they are acting out of patriotic enthusiasm, we will, therefore, not make the students liable for these activities." Yuan Mu then expressed absolute agreement with the way He Dongchang put the matter. What all this means is that, in their view, the students are legally liable for their unlawful acts, but our leaders can stand above the law and guarantee that the students will not be held responsible. Now, we cannot help inquiring, who was it that gave our leaders the right and power to surmount the law?

Is Li Peng and others like him practicing democracy or autocracy? Is this rule by law or rule by man?

—A Thinker
(big-character poster,
Shanghai, April 30, 1989)

INVESTIGATE AND DETERMINE THE LIABILITY OF NEWS ORGANIZATIONS IN ACCORDANCE WITH THE LAW—PROTECT THE RIGHTS OF CITIZENS BY LEGAL MEANS

It is common knowledge that news reports on the mourning and petitioning activities of the students during the past few days have either seriously distorted events, fabricated facts, or covered up the truth. Over the years, various student petitions and marches have all been the victims of distorted news reporting. This has had an extremely negative impact on society and has severely damaged the image of the students. This unacceptable, illegal behavior has seriously violated the legal rights of citizens.

According to the Article 38 of the Chinese Constitution, the personal dignity of citizens cannot be violated. It is forbidden to use any means whatsoever to vilify, slander, libel, or bring false charges against a citizen.

According to Article 131 and Article 138 of the Criminal Law of the PRC, the democratic rights of citizens cannot be unlawfully violated by any person or organization. It is strictly forbidden to use any method or means to bring false charges against cadres or the masses. All fabrication of facts and false charges against individuals (including criminals) will be punished as criminal offenses, and the perpetrator of the offense sentenced according to the nature, circumstances, and consequences of the offense and the legally stipulated punishment. All government personnel who bring false charges will be strictly punished.

In view of the above, we propose that:

Illustration 2.7. Protestors carry a placard citing Article 35 of the Chinese Constitution, which guarantees freedom of speech, press, assembly, and demonstration; and Article 37, which prohibits the infringement of personal freedom. The portrait is of Hu Yaobang. Credit: Ming Pao Newspapers.

1. A delegation be sent to the *Beijing Daily*, China Central Television, China Central People's Broadcasting, and other news organizations to demand that they explain their false charges [against the student protestors]; to make known to all sectors of society the real facts of the incidents; to guarantee that similar illegal acts will not recur; and to report anew the true facts about the students' demonstrations, their kneeling [in desperation] when submitting their petition to the government, and related matters.

2. If the demands of the delegation are rejected, we will go through legal channels and directly bring suit in the courts [to defend our legal rights].

> —[Names of forty-nine faculty members
> of People's University]
> (*big-character poster at People's University,
> circa April 24, 1989*)

Illustration 2.8. Ren Wanding draws a large crowd in Tiananmen as he speaks on the need for democracy in China. Credit: Sing Tao Newspapers Hong Kong.

An important aspect of the Democracy Movement was the cross-generational interaction between the young college students who led the student protests—the heart of the movement—and intellectuals one or two generations their senior. Leading liberal thinkers who participated in Beijing University democracy salons helped to shape student thinking with their analyses of China's problems and of the demise of Marxism, and encouraged students to engage themselves in the cause of reform. Furthermore, once the protests were under way, graduate students and young teachers in their late twenties and thirties quietly counseled their younger "revolutionary brothers" on tactics and strategy; some of these advisors were veterans of earlier, smaller-scale student protests in 1980 and 1987. Even before intellectuals started rallying as a group to the side of the students in the third week of the protests, certain well-known intellectuals were inspiring students by courageously stepping forward individually to embrace the student cause.

Two such bold figures were Ren Wanding and Chen Mingyuan. Ren Wanding, the founder of the China Human Rights League and Democracy Wall activist released from prison in 1983, is an exceptional figure whose unwavering commitment to his political convictions in the face of state intimidation distinguish him as one of China's relatively few committed dissidents. In 1988, Ren had published articles in Hong Kong and the United States attacking the Chinese political system. Unlike some establishment intellectuals who, at least until the ruthless June suppression, assumed that China was not ready for a multiparty system and favored change within the Communist Party first, Ren made clear in his numerous speeches at Tiananmen and campuses his belief that the only hope for China lay in the establishment of alternate political parties or forces. Ren refused to go into hiding when the government repression began, declaring that he had not violated any law. He was among the very first group of people arrested: on June 10, security police took him from his apartment. Ren was later cited in an official report as a major influence on the students and accused of delivering "slanderous and inflammatory" speeches.[19] However, as inspiring a figure as Ren may have been for students, it appears that he and other Democracy Wall activists may not have been as influential with the 1989 protestors as the government has contended: some students reportedly found their views, particularly their call for a multiparty system to challenge the Party's supremacy, too radical.

Chen, 48, professor of Chinese language at the Beijing Languages Institute, was a poet, mathematician, and authority on the Chinese language, a man noted for the breadth of his accomplishments. Some also knew Chen as the man who had been imprisoned in 1966 for passing off some of his poems as the work of Chairman Mao; his name had not been cleared until 1978, when it was established that someone else had been responsible for the fraud. Chen, unlike Ren Wanding, was not known to the public or Party for his political activities. Like Ren, however, he stepped forward during the movement to criticize the government acidly. In May, despite being ill, Chen insisted on issuing a declaration from his hospital bed supporting the students' hunger strike. He is believed to be in detention in Beijing. Excerpts from speeches by Ren and Chen follow.

A DISCUSSION OF THE HISTORICAL TASKS AND OBJECTIVES OF THE APRIL 1989 PEOPLE'S DEMOCRACY MOVEMENT

—A Second Look at the Transformation of China's Social Structure and the Historical Achievements of the People's Democracy Movement
(excerpt)

. . . In these thirteen years [from 1976 to the present], seven spontaneous mass movements, some large, others small, have erupted in China. That is an average of once every two years. Moreover, movements have often followed close upon the heels of one another. The frequency of such

19. In a speech by Beijing Party chief Li Ximing on May 19, 1989.

movements reveals to our people a truth: a people's Democracy Movement has been rapidly growing and gaining strength—and if the people have paid a high price for them, they have also gained a wealth of experience. In these movements, theories and programs have begun to take shape. The "Democracy Wall Movement" [1978–1979] presented political demands more mature than those of the April 5th Movement [in 1976, which was primarily a protest against leftist leaders] and pushed forward theoretical preparation for a democracy movement [by introducing the] concepts of people's rights, people's democracy, and a Marxism and socialism of the people. The Democracy Wall movement was also the earliest movement to raise the idea of reforming China's current social-political structure of unified, centralized leadership [by the Party]. Open political commentary and discussion replaced the poems of subtle dissidence of the April 5th Movement; manifestos and declarations replaced the simple banners and slogans; written reasoning replaced the shouting and clamoring; and groups organized on the basis of the right of assembly replaced the motley crowds.

The current April Democracy Movement, this university student movement, has also brought China's democracy movements to a new phase, one marked by the organization of an autonomous student association in each university, by the establishment of a unified federation of [autonomous student associations], and by the coordination of protest activities. The constitutional rights of citizens are being fully exercised and realized. The students have [defined their] issues, goals, and a short-term plan of action. Yet they have not assigned specific tasks, nor have they come up with long-term objectives. They lack a tight, strong organization and contingency measures.

[Yet, despite these shortcomings,] I wonder if our people have begun to realize that this time, the large scale and sophistication of the people's Democracy Movement are [in fact] proclaiming to our society that the leadership of a new political party or a new people's organization has appeared. This is the will of history. It is the will of the people. It is the will of society. The 1989 Democracy Movement will propel the birth of a new political party and new social organizations. Perhaps the movement will be strangled in its cradle, but if so, it will certainly be reborn in the next storm. I maintain that the long-term goal of China's democratic movement must naturally be the nonviolent reform of the present social-political structure of unified, centralized leadership by the Party [under which it controls all spheres of activity]. This structure must be supplanted by a pluralistic social-political structure, a pluralistic democracy, a pluralistic culture, and a pluralistic nation. These are the ideals of pluralism that [both] young and older scholars of social science have been discussing fervently and widely, that they so desperately yearn for. . . . If there are people who force us to shed blood, then let our blood flow! Traditional force must be met by traditional force if it is to be destroyed; material force must be met by material force if it is to be destroyed. This social-political structure of unified, centralized leadership is the result of China's long period of feudal society and our underdeveloped productive force. As the economy develops, as our productive capacity increases, and as our society opens up, this structure will disappear into history.

Do the Chinese people like, do they accept, the autocratic rule of unified, centralized leadership? Do the Chinese people like, do they accept, the dictatorship of such centralized leadership? No! This entire April Democracy Movement that we now see in front of us is the most conclusive denial of this [myth] that the Chinese people like "autocratic rule," that the Chinese people accept "dictatorship." Why then does the Communist Party insist on stuffing down the throats of the Chinese people things they dislike? Why does it call itself the sole and final representative of the interests of the Chinese people? Beside the fact that such a political party will do its utmost to protect its own interests, the answer to this question can also be found in what the Communist Party says, and what some people regularly say: at the present, who is able to replace the Communist Party?

Look, my friends, you have nothing to replace what you oppose. It is you yourselves who are not mature and strong enough. It is you yourselves who are not courageous, not wise enough. It is you yourselves who have not pushed yourselves to your limits! They have put you in check!

. . . My students, history's heavy burden rests on your shoulders. Now is the vital moment and opportunity to organize legal political parties and groups, to participate formally in the transformation of China's social structure. If you want me to speak the truth, I will just say these words of truth to the Communist Party and to all of you: I too have a wife and children, older and younger generations [to take care of]. I too have all the emotions and desires that everybody has. [But if we are to] call ourselves the pillars of the state, the brilliant heroes of the nation [I say to all of you]: intellectuals of all generations and young students, let us together make a valiant try. If we emerge from our books and strike while the iron is hot, we shall succeed. It is not that China does not possess the conditions for implementing a democratic political system. It is that oppression is too severe. If we free ourselves from this oppression, as you students defied [authorities'] orders not to march [on April 27th] and begin a class boycott, victory will come!

(speech by Ren Wanding in Beijing, late April, 1989)

EXTEMPORANEOUS SPEECH BY PROFESSOR CHEN MINGYUAN ON APRIL 23, 1989, AT THE "TRIANGLE" AT BEIJING UNIVERSITY
(excerpts)

My name is Chen Mingyan. [*Applause*] I would like to say that I did not come here for personal fame and gain, absolutely not. If there is someone in the audience who would like to report me to the authorities you may take my name right to the Public Security Bureau. [That's right! *Enthusiastic applause*] . . . I would also like to say that I did not come here to "spread evil words and delude the masses"; neither did I come with "ulterior motives." But the government, the news agencies, and our China Central Television station have already prepared these "caps" [political labels] and are dangling them over us. [Right! *Applause*]. [The government] is threatening us: whoever steps forward cannot possibly have good intentions, but [will be capped] with the charge of harboring ulterior motives, and so on and so forth. Under such circumstances, many people are made afraid; many keep in mind that there are parents and children to worry about, that they have a job, that they earn barely enough each day to meet daily expenses, that if they get thrown into jail how are they going to survive, and so on. I have never spoken in public before an audience this large, but today I feel I must step up to speak, for I can't bear it any longer. . . .

Whenever I mention "freedom," some people react as though the word "freedom" is taboo. Some say that "freedom" is a bad word; some others say that it ought to be avoided altogether. As you all know, Comrade Hu Deping [Hu Yaobang's son and Secretary General of the Party's United Front Department] once proposed that we cry "freedom" out loud. People have qualms about such a proposal, or they find the idea a vain attempt. But I feel that "freedom" is the most beautiful word in the world. Do I have to leave it to the possession of someone else? Why can not our great country and great people possess such a beautiful word? [*Applause*]

Yes, it's true that we are poor, we are backward, we are unenlightened, we pass our days in hardship. But we do have this one ideal—freedom and democracy! [Correct! *Extended applause*] Indeed, until the end of this century, until the end of my days and my children's days, we will live our lives impoverished, as we have been completely proletarianized. [*Applause*] But we have a one source of pride—that we have struggled for freedom and democracy!

It's not possible that this government will give us wealth. It's not possible that it will allow everybody to get rich. It can only allow a small bunch of "profiteering lords" to become wealthy. [Correct! *Applause*] But there is one thing that the government can do for our people, one thing the government can do to win over the people's hearts—give us our democratic rights! Give us freedom! [Correct! Give us freedom! *Applause*] And not lump us together with reactionaries! He who opposes freedom is a reactionary. [*Extended applause*] . . .

In addition, there's the issue of education, about which we have talked and talked until our tongues bled. Why can't we have education given top priority in the finances of the government? [Correct! *Applause*] Up to now, the government has behaved in the manner of squeezing tooth paste, and today our educational funds are no match for those of any other country in the world. The government has been crying that "we must reform," that "we must make China prosperous." But why is there always so little to spend on education? I would like to see a large-scale increase in our educational funds right away. [*Applause*] I would like to see all the properties of the "profiteering lords" confiscated, and used for education! [Yes! *Applause*] Because the government is always trying to explain about this or that difficulty: our industry is in difficulty, our agriculture is in difficulty, everything is in trouble. Even building houses for the provincial governors and county magistrates is very difficult. [*Laughter*] We have difficulty buying cars. But I think there is one thing that is not difficult at all—confiscating the unlawfully gained properties of the "profiteering lords," and putting them to use in education. [*Applause*]

My fellow students, I feel very excited and inspired. Our country has problems, all too many. However, I feel what I've so far said are the basic things we must demand. [*Applause*]

I suggest, my fellow students, that we organize investigation committees, that we act as the masters of our country and investigate corruption in our government. [*Applause*] In the meantime, we will praise those government officials who are men and women of honesty and integrity, officials who work for the people, even though honesty and integrity are the basic requirements for a government official and perhaps deserve no special praise. In the meantime, we will make known the facts about all corrupt government officials, and no matter how high their position, no matter how powerful they are, have them tried and sentenced according to the law.

Down with bureaucracy! [Down with bureaucracy!] Promote education! [Promote education!] Confiscate all unlawfully gained properties of the "profiteering lords"! [Confiscate all unlawfully gained properties of the "profiteering lords"!] Increase significantly funds for education! [Increase significantly funds for education!] Long live democracy! [Long live democracy!] Long live the People's Republic of China! [Long live the People's Republic of China!] Long live freedom! [Long live freedom!] Long live freedom! [Long live freedom!] [*Extended enthusiastic applause*] I would rather die than be without freedom! Long live our students! [Let Teacher Chen be an inspiration! Salute Teacher Chen!]

> *(recorded and transcribed by the*
> *Beijing University Students' Autonomous*
> *Preparatory Committee)*

"Mama, We're Not Wrong." So proclaimed a banner carried by young student pro-democracy demonstrators during their early protest marches in April. The theme of "Mama, We're Not Wrong (or alternatively, "Mama, I'm Not Wrong") was subsequently adopted by many different movement participants and found various forms of expression, ranging from display on T-shirts to poetry. For some of those who affirmed that "Mama, We're Not Wrong," "mama" was their motherland; for others, their mothers, who had beseeched them not to get involved in demonstrations; for others still, both motherland and mother. Yet for all those who marched, silently waited in sit-in protests, seized megaphones to speak their minds, wrote posters and banners, fasted or organized blockades of the army, neither "mama" could be heeded. As both a plea for understanding and approval and a statement of conviction, "Mama, We're Not Wrong" seems more than any other single expression to summarize the spirit of the 1989 Democracy Movement.

ANTHOLOGY OF "LAST WORDS"

On the 21st [of April], before the protest march, a certain six members of the same dorm room wrote their "last words" expressing their resolutions:

1. "Eldest Brother": For the future of Chinese nation, I have gone forth! History will prove our worth!

2. "Second Brother": For democracy, for freedom, I do not fear anything, not even death, but I will strive to return alive.

3. "Third Brother": For democracy and for freedom I will struggle, through fire and water; for the Chinese nation I will die, and die without regret! My fellow citizens, my fellow countrymen, when is China going to awaken from her slumber? When is China going to stand up and show the world her might? When?! When?!

4. "Fourth Brother:" Democracy will triumph, I will triumph. We will meet again in twenty years on this campus.

5. "Fifth Brother": For the future of the Chinese nation, for the hope of the nation, I have gone! I cannot listen to the words of papa and mama.

6. "Sixth Brother": For my homeland to emerge from its plight, I am willing to sacrifice my life, and die with no regret! Mama, this distant son has let you down. Let the son call you once more, "Mama!" You will not understand your son, but history will.

April 23:
   This time, they all returned alive . . .
   But . . .

(unsigned big-character poster)

"MAMA, WE'RE NOT WRONG"

I do not have the heart
To cast aside that quiet dark imploring of your silence,
and let melancholy brimming over
flow
to disturb the ripples of age, misery, and hardship
   collected beneath.

I do not have the heart
to allow the wailing wind and waves
to lash ruthlessly
at your aged sagging banks.
Although
maturity long ago sailed out to sea,
the orbit of dreams

still can in your gentle harbors
find the warmth of childhood.

On the streets
the solemn and stirring "Internationale"
is charging with all its might
through the unwieldy iron gates of silent midnight.
I can only wave farewell
And go to catch up with my courageous companions.

Perhaps
our youth will be flung onto
the gradually dimming embers of truth.
Perhaps
our raw throats will become hoarse
and for a time silent.
Perhaps our pure sincerity will be cut down by honest
misunderstanding
like a dead branch.
Perhaps
from the desert's vast stretches
the weary camels never will emerge.

But
please believe, Mama,
in history's deep, knowing valleys
will always be inscribed
my ringing echoes:
"Mama, we are not wrong."

—Ye Fu, May 1, 1989
(*big-character poster*)

3

THE SEVENTIETH ANNIVERSARY OF THE 1919 MAY FOURTH MOVEMENT

"Under Autocratic Rule, China Has No Future"

May 1 – May 13

"China must persevere in the policy of reform and opening to the outside world as the hope for solving China's problems. But a stable political environment will be needed. China has a huge population and everyone has his or her own views. . . . If young people all stick to their own views, then the kind of "all-round" civil war mentioned by Chairman Mao will occur. Civil war does not necessarily require guns; fists and wooden clubs will do. Democracy is our goal, but the state must maintain stability."

Deng Xiaoping, addressing President George Bush,
February 1989

"Do not believe in the 'stability and unity' of the dictators. Facist totalitarianism can only bring us disaster. Do not harbor any more illusions about them. Democracy is our only hope."

Wei Jingsheng, Democracy Wall activist, March 1979

The government had seized the initiative with the two nationally broadcast dialogues of April 29 and 30. Charges by student acitivists that the meetings had been a charade were buried by the government's massive propaganda machine; millions of Chinese were left with a picture of composed, reasonable government representatives who seemed willing to talk with students. But the Beijing Students' Federation, settling into its role as the representative of student protestors from all Beijing schools, rebounded quickly. On May 1, it denounced the talks as a ploy to sow division among students. The next day Federation leaders took to their bicycles to deliver a petition to the Party and the government, renewing their demand for a dialogue. The petition was precise: the Federation stipulated, among other things, that the dialogue be broadcast live, that Chinese and foreign journalists and other invited observers be allowed to observe, and that a joint communiqué regarding the outcome of the dialogue be issued to "guarantee the legal validity of the results of the dialogue." It was also brash: the Federation demanded that the government representatives to the dialogue be no less than members of the Politburo's Standing Committee, deputy chairmen of the National People's Congress Standing Committee, or deputy premiers of the State Council, who "understand various state matters and have policy-making power." Furthermore, noting that it reserved the right to proceed with demonstrations on May 4, the seventieth anniversary of the historic May Fourth Movement, the Federation asked the government to reply by noon the next day.

Only the most optimistic and naive of students could have expected a positive government response to such a petition. Federation leaders must surely have drafted it with one eye to history and one eye to maintaining pressure on the government to recognize their organization. They knew, as did China's leaders, that the calendar was their ally. The upcoming May Fourth commemoration would furnish the perfect occasion for a large demonstration; in addition, a protective cover of international scrutiny created by the imminent descent of a thousand bankers on Beijing for the annual meeting of the Asian Development Bank would soon protect peaceful demonstrators from violent repression.

As student organizational strength was gelling in the form of a stable Beijing Students' Federation, an opposite process of destablization had begun inside the Party. Secretary General Zhao, after returning from North Korea on May 1 and hearing his aides' reports on the student unrest, decided to adopt a more conciliatory line toward the unrest. Zhao's fateful decision to deviate from the hard-line Party posture adopted during his absence reflected both a more tolerant, liberal temperament and shrewd political calculation. Zhao was known for being relatively flexible and sympathetic to the demands of intellectuals for change. Although he was no political liberal—he had never aggressively pushed for political reform as he had for economic experimentation, and he reportedly supported the political theory of "new authoritarianism" in vogue in the late 1980s, which maintained that centralization of political power in a strong authority was called for if China was to modernize rapidly—he did value the contributions of intellectuals, and did not have the knee-jerk fear of dissent possessed by Party conservatives. Perhaps even more importantly, at this particular moment in time Zhao sensed that he could use the student movement to bolster his weak position in the Party. Since mid-1988, blamed for double-digit inflation and the country's other economic woes, Zhao had seen his power eclipsed by Li Peng's. Now he glimpsed an opportunity to parlay widespread citizen dissatisfaction into popular support that could help to restore some of his influence in the Party. Even more to the point, Zhao expected that success in resolving the unrest with his tactics of moderation would shift the balance of power in the Party back to him and his moderate supporters.

Zhao thus began to distance himself from the hard-line *People's Daily* editorial. According to an indictment of Zhao made by Yang Shangkun in an internal speech to top-level Party officials much later in the month, Zhao made it known within the Party's high circles that he did not support the April 26 *People's Daily* editorial, seizing on the excuse that the text of the published editorial differed slightly from the text of the piece he had seen and endorsed by telegram while in North Korea. On May 4, Zhao made an even bolder move. In nationally broadcast remarks to delegates of the Asian Development Bank, he declared that the student movement was patriotic, and that the students' grievances deserved to be seriously considered. Zhao's words would win him the support of a considerable portion of the students—but they would also be viewed by Party hard-liners as traitorous and an unforgiveable breach of Party discipline. The next selection presents an excerpt of Zhao's comments to the assembled bankers.

REMARKS BY SECRETARY GENERAL ZHAO ZIYANG TO DELEGATES AT THE ASIAN DEVELOPMENT BANK ANNUAL MEETING
(excerpts)

At this time, demonstrations by some students are still going on in Beijing and certain other cities. But I am firmly convinced that the situation will gradually quiet down. China will not experience any major turmoil. I am fully confident of this. . . . [Our guests] are all probably aware that recently some students have taken to the streets to demonstrate. Does this indicate that China's political situation is not stable? I would like to stress and point out that the basic slogans of the student demonstrators are "uphold the Communist Party," "uphold socialism," "uphold the constitution," "uphold the reforms," "advance democracy," and "oppose corruption." I believe these reflect the fundamental attitude of the majority of marchers toward the Party and government—both satisfaction and dissatisfaction. They absolutely are not opposed to our basic system; what they demand is that we rectify mistakes we have made in our work. They are very satisfied with the accomplishments of the reforms and national construction over the last ten years and with China's progress and development. But they are most dissatisfied with errors we have committed in our work. They demand that we correct mistakes and improve our performance. Moreover, affirmation of accomplishments, correction of mistakes, and further progress forward—these are just what our Party and government advocate. . . .

Are there people who seek to take advantage of or who are presently taking advantage of the students' actions? China is such a big country that naturally this is hard to avoid; there will always be people who wish to see turmoil break out in China, there will always be people who are ready to exploit [such a situation]. It's not conceivable that there won't be people who try to take advantage of it. Such people are extremely small in number, but it's worth warning about them. I think the overwhelming majority of students understand this point. . . .

I think that we must use democratic and legal avenues to resolve [the reasonable demands put forth by the students]. We should resolve them through reform and reasonable, orderly methods. If you analyze for a moment the specific situation, it becomes quite clear: what the students are most upset about is the phenomenon of graft and corruption. As a matter of fact, this is a problem the Party and government have been working on for several years now. But why are so many people critical [of our performance to date], and why are they so highly critical? There are two reasons. The first is that due to the imperfections of our legal system and to the fact that there is no democratic supervision [of the government], certain problems of corruption that in fact do exist cannot be promptly reported and tackled. The second is that because there is not enough openness in government, enough transparency, there are [unsubstantiated] rumors, or false charges, or gross exaggerations, or pure fabrications. . . .

At this time, we need to carry out consultative dialogues with all sectors of society, with students, with workers, with intellectuals, with each democratic party. Through democratic and legal avenues, and in an atmosphere of rationality and order, we should exchange opinions, increase our understanding of each other, and together explore ways of resolving the problems that are of common concern.

"Seventy years is too long; seize every minute"

As could be expected, the May 2 deadline came and went without any answer from the government. On May 4, seventy years to the day after patriotic students had marched to Tiananmen to demand an end to government capitulation to foreign imperialism, catalyzing a movement that in many ways marked China's break with her colonial and traditional past, students once again assembled at over thirty Beijing campuses for a mass protest march into the city. This time, though, the circumstances differed significantly from those of April 27. Now the mood was relaxed, not grim; the marchers buoyant rather than determined. Recent comments by Zhao and Yuan Mu, viewed as the alter ego of Li Peng, had indicated that authorities would not use force to break up the demonstration. The absence of any sense of urgency had also reduced the turnout considerably; whereas some two hundred thousand had marched on the 27th, there were now no more than one hundred thousand. But Beijing students knew that their steps would be matched by fellow students across the country, who were similarly massing to commemorate the May Fourth Movement. One of the successes of the Beijing Students' Federation had been the establishment of links with leading universities throughout the nation. Though these ties would be loose, hampered by the difficulty of long-distance communication in China and the embryonic state of student organizations, student activists at schools outside of Beijing would, from mid-April to the end of May, base their actions on events unfolding in Beijing. By the end of the day, demonstrations of over ten thousand students would occur in Guangzhou, Shanghai, Wuhan, and Xi'an; smaller but significant demonstrations would also occur in the metropolises of Changsha, Hangzhou, Nanjing, Chengdu, Chongqing, and even smaller cities like Changchun, Taiyuan, Lanzhou, and Xining. Beijing students also were aware that their movement had sparked student activism in Hong Kong; some Hong Kong students had already arrived in the capital to take part in the march.

If only to preserve some semblance of authority, Beijing officials ordered police to form human barricades at several points along the marchers' path; onlookers applauded and laughed in delight as officers offered only token resistance before yielding to the wave of marchers. Bearing banners that paid a tribute to the past— "Carry on the Spirit of the May Fourth Movement," "Democracy and Science"—as well as ones voicing their present grievances—"The Purpose of News Is Not Deception of the People," "Without Democracy, There Can Be No Stability," "Down with Corruption!" "Reform of the Government System Can Brook No Further Delay"—the protestors slowly advanced toward downtown Beijing. This time, they stopped to rally in Tiananmen, where they cheered each other as they entered the Square, and listened to Wuer Kaixi, chairman of the Beijing Students' Federation, read the "New May Fourth Manifesto," a program for the 1990s inspired by the "Manifesto of All Beijing Students" that student patriots had circulated seventy years previously on May 4, 1919. A rhetorical statement notable for its sense of historical calling rather than its ideas, the New May Fourth Manifesto undoubtedly held great emotional appeal for the students.

NEW MAY FOURTH MANIFESTO

Fellow students, fellow countrymen:

Seventy years ago today, a large group of illustrious students assembled in front of Tiananmen, and a new chapter in the history of China was opened. Today, we are once again assembled here, not only to commemorate that monumental day but more importantly, to carry forward the May Fourth spirit of science and democracy. Today, in front of the symbol of the Chinese nation, Tiananmen, we can proudly proclaim to all the people in our nation that we are worthy of the pioneers of seventy years ago.

For over one hundred years, the pioneers of the Chinese people have been searching for a path to modernize an ancient and beleaguered China. Following the Paris Peace Conference, they did not collapse in the face of imperialist oppression, but marched boldly forward.[1] Waving the banners of science and democracy, they launched the mighty May Fourth Movement. May Fourth and the subsequent New Democratic Revolution were the first steps in the patriotic democracy movement of Chinese students. From this point on, Chinese history entered a completely new phase. Due to the socioeconomic conditions in China and the shortcomings of intellectuals, the May Fourth ideals of science and democracy have not been realized. Seventy years of history have taught us that democracy and sci-

1. The "Paris Peace Conference" was the Versailles Peace Conference held in 1919 by the five allies (the United States, Great Britain, France, Italy, and Japan) after the defeat of Germany in World World I. As the conference began, many Chinese people, including intellectuals and students, expected that Germany's colonial claims in China, and particularly its claim to a large portion of Shandong Province under a ninety-nine-year lease forced on the Chinese government in 1898, would be annulled. The Chinese delegation's acceptance of an agreement between the Five Powers under which Japan took over Germany's colonial rights set off a bitter storm of protest in China, and was the immediate cause of the May Fourth Incident in which students protested in Tiananmen.

ence cannot be established in one fell swoop and that impatience and despair are of no avail. In the context of China's economy and culture, the Marxism espoused by the Chinese Communist Party cannot avoid being influenced by remnants of feudal ideology. Thus, while New China has steadily advanced toward modernization, it has greatly neglected building a democracy.[2] Although it has emphasized the role of science, it has not valued the spirit of science—democracy. At present, our country is plagued with problems such as a bloated government bureaucracy, serious corruption, the devaluation of intellectual work, and inflation, all of which severely impede us from intensifying the reforms and carrying out modernization. This illustrates that if the spirit of science and democracy, and their actual processes, do not exist, numerous and varied feudal elements and remnants of the old system, which are fundamentally antagonistic to large-scale socialist production, will reemerge in society, and modernization will be impossible. For this reason, carrying on the May Fourth spirit, hastening the reform of the political system, protecting human rights, and strengthening rule by law have become urgent tasks of modernization that we must undertake.

Fellow students, fellow countrymen, a democratic spirit is precisely the absorption of the collective wisdom of the people, the true development of each individual's ability, and the protection of each individual's interests; a scientific spirit is precisely respect for individual nature, and the building of the country on the basis of science. Now more than ever, we need to review the experiences and lessons of all student movements since May Fourth, to make science and rationalism a system, a process. Only then can the tasks the May Fourth Movement set before us be accomplished, only then can the spirit of May Fourth be carried forward, and only then can our wish for a strong China be realized.

Fellow students, fellow countrymen, the future and fate of the Chinese nation are intimately linked to each of our hearts. This student movement has but one goal, that is, to facilitate the process of modernization by raising high the banners of democracy and science, by liberating people from the constraints of feudal ideology, and by promoting freedom, human rights, and rule by law. To this end, we urge the government to accelerate the pace of political reform, to guarantee the rights of the people vested in the law, to implement a press law, to permit privately run news-

2. "New China" is the term introduced by the Party to refer to the new republic founded in 1949, and appears in the names of some official organizations such as the New China News Agency (Xinhua News Agency).

papers, to eradicate corruption, to hasten the establishment of an honest and democratic government, to value education, to respect intellectual work, and to save the nation through science. Our views are not in conflict with those of the government. We only have one goal: the modernization of China.

. . . Our present tasks are: first, to take the lead in carrying out experiments in democratic reform at the birthplace of the student movement—the university campus, democratizing and systematizing campus life; second, to participate actively in politics, to persist in our request for a dialogue with the government, to push democratic reforms of our political system, to oppose graft and corruption, and to work for a press law. We recognize that these short-term objectives are only the first steps in democratic reform; they are tiny, unsteady steps. But we must struggle for these first steps, we must cheer for these first steps.

Fellow students, fellow countrymen, prosperity for our nation is the ultimate objective of our patriotic student movement. Democracy, science, freedom, human rights, and rule by law are the ideals that we hundreds of thousands of university students share in this struggle. Our ancient, thousand-year civilization is waiting, our great people, one billion strong, are watching. What qualms can we possibly have? What is there to fear? Fellow students, fellow countrymen, here at richly symbolic Tiananmen, let us once again search together and struggle together for democracy, for science, for freedom, for human rights, and for rule by law.

Let our cries awaken our young Republic!

*(read by Wuer Kaixi at
Tiananmen Square
May 4, 1989)*

"The source of China's illness is 'centralized leadership'
[under the Party]; the solution is democracy."

For some observers of the student movement, the New May Fourth Manifesto encapsulated the nature of the students' protests: passionate, but vague and weak in ideas. Indeed, from the first week of the protests, otherwise approving sympathizers had expressed the opinion that the youth in Tiananmen lacked a clear concept of democracy and of the specific reforms China needed. Student leaders defended the generality of their slogans and public statements by explaining that broader, more abstract themes had greater mass appeal than narrower ones; the

Illustration 3.1. A student triumphantly waves a homemade flag of the Beijing Students' Federation at the Monument of the People's Heroes in Tiananmen Square on May 4, 1989, the seventieth anniversary of the May Fourth Movement. Credit: Franki Chan.

time and place for more precise demands were to be the dialogues with the government, as well as later exchanges. Putting aside for the moment the issue of whether the student organizations themselves followed democratic practices, the query still remains: how much did the protestors understand of democracy, their oft-proclaimed ideal? In terms of understanding how working democracies are structured and function, perhaps relatively little. Most students and other young intellectuals had a passing familiarity with the American and possibly European or Japanese political systems, but understandably no solid feeling for how they worked. This was one reason why few writings from the movement contained concrete suggestions regarding the institutional changes needed to bring about greater popular participation in the governance of the country. The proposals for structural change that were raised were only general propositions; rarely did they elaborate the actual steps for seeing such reforms into being. Pressed as they were against the face of autocracy, it is hardly unexpected that Chinese focused on the iteration of a few basic democratic rights, such as freedom of the press or the right to form their own organizations.

Yet, as the next several posters attest, if students and other young Chinese, with a few exceptions, could not or did not provide precise, comprehensive formulas for establishing a democratic form of government, they had clear ideas about what democracy represented and about what they desired: the right of people to have a say in their government's policies; the right of individuals to choose their own values, careers, and places of residence; the subjugation of personal power to the rules of law; and freedom of speech, assembly, and the press. And they did see lucidly how their country's present political system of Communist Party control and Marxist ideology had created a state of autocracy that was the antithesis of democracy—and which would absolutely deny the possibility of democracy. By early May, swept up in the heady success of the first two weeks of the protests, a number of poster writers were defiantly calling for the end of autocratic rule and the establishment of a multiparty system—though they carefully avoided directly calling for the Communist Party's ouster from power. Some Chinese, however, felt only depression: the sight of the thousands of students crowded in Tiananmen, chanting to a largely invisible government for democracy and reform, brought to mind similar images from 1919, and making them wonder if China was doomed to "wander in a cycle of feudal dynasties."

UNDER AUTOCRATIC RULE
CHINA HAS NO FUTURE

As early as seventy years ago Chinese intellectuals put forth "Democracy" and "Science" as revolutionary slogans. Today "Democracy" and "Science" remain the goals that a great many of our intellectuals seek and are fighting for. Forty years ago the Chinese people overthrew autocracy and dictatorship, only to meet, some forty years later, with new autocracy and new dictatorship. In the past we overthrew the old emperor; today new emperors live within Zhongnanhai, hoisting the flag of a "democratic republic," while sucking the sweat and blood of the people, pushing China toward the abyss of disaster. China is the peoples' China, and its future belongs to us. We will absolutely not allow new bureaucrat-aristocrats to ride on top of the people and indulge in their authority and wealth. We must overthrow bureaucratism. We must do away with the Confucianism that has made dogs of us. We must seize back the people's rights and power!

—A Youth from Liaoning, May 3
(big-character poster)

HOLD UP THE BANNER OF REASON

1. The Bewildering Cycle of History

The tragedy of Hu Yaobang is a tragedy of the Chinese people, and this kind of tragedy is one that permeates the history of the Chinese nation.

Suddenly compelled to look back into history, I am amazed, saddened, and thrown into utter despair. When Qin Shi Huang [the first emperor of China] established his one-man tyranny, it also marked the commencement of the dictatorial imperial dynasties.[3] The history to come followed this kind of trajectory: time and again peasants fought to overthrow corrupt dynasties, only to see a new tyrannical and dictatorial dynasty spring forth. The Chinese people entered a periodic and violent death cycle; in this way our great motherland has been tormented by periodic disasters, in this way our society's productive forces have periodically met with devastation and destruction.

At the time when some Western nations took the road of capitalism, ancient China continued to wander in a cycle of feudal dynasties. While Imperial China was self-drunken with the majesty of the "Celestial Kingdom," the cannons of the great Western powers began to fire on the great gates of China. Some progressive Chinese awakened then and began to realize that China could no longer afford to drift back and forth between the rise and fall of successive dynasties. So the revolutionaries of the bour-

---

3. Qin Shi Huang ruled the first Chinese empire from 221 to 210 B.C. Notorious for his order in 213 B.C. to burn all books except some texts on medicine and agriculture, in an attempt to enforce intellectual conformity and stifle dissent, Qin Shi Huang also advanced the development and unification of the country during his tyrannical rule with huge civic projects such as the construction of the Great Wall, roadbuilding projects, and the introduction of new standardized Chinese characters.

geoisie, represented by Sun Yat-sen, brought about the 1911 Revolution [against the Manchu emperor] and toppled the rotting Qing dynasty.

The people saw clearly, however, that Chiang Kai-shek [who assumed the leadership of the Nationalist Party after Sun's death and defeated various warlords to unify China in a republic under Nationalist rule] had not established in China a bourgeois republic, but a new, semicolonial autocracy.

[Moreover,] isn't the socialist system established by the communist-led revolution that overthrew Chiang Kai-shek still a tyrannical dynasty? We all know that in our country everything is directed by the Party, that everything serves politics, that in reality it is still the Chairman and Secretary General of the Party who direct everything.[4] The National People's Congress is only a stage prop, a flower vase, a rubber stamp, a fig leaf. Under the rule of this kind of dictatorship, which wears the cloak of Marxism-Leninism and socialism, the President of the country and other high-ranking leaders have been persecuted and assassinated;[5] personality cults and superstitions have spread like the plague to every corner of the land; and the Constitution of the Republic has been trampled upon. The word of only one man has the power of law.

And how has it been since the Third Plenary Session [of the eleventh Party Central Committee held in September 1978]? Have we left behind the bewildering turn of the dynastic cycle?

It was Deng Xiaoping who raised the slogan "reform of the political system," yet he lacks the wisdom and courage of George Washington, who, in order to establish a proper democratic tradition, refused to run again for President. Our political system is as it always was; the Chairman of the Military Affairs Commission [Deng Xiaoping] has become the

4. In fact, the post of Chairman of the Chinese Communist Party no longer exists, having been abolished by Deng Xiaoping in the early 1980s. The last post in the Party to carry the title of "chairman" is the chairmanship of the powerful Central Military Commission (CMC), the Central Committee's group in charge of military affairs. Deng was the Chairman of the CMC until November 1989 when, declaring his complete retirement from politics at the age of 85, he resigned from the position.

5. Top Party leaders have not escaped persecution and killing in the series of political campaigns that have wracked the People's Republic in its forty-five year history. In particular, the tragedy of Liu Shaoqi is often cited by Chinese as an example of the lawlessness and ruthlessness of inner-Party power struggles. Liu Shaoqi, President of the country from 1954 to 1968, was accused by Mao and his supporters in 1968 during the Cultural Revolution of "revisionism," and was imprisoned; he died in prison the next year. Many dozens of other top leaders have been subject to physical and psychological abuse during the purges that characterized Party politics from the fifties through the seventies.

behind-the-scenes manipulator. Deng Xiaoping's behavior somewhat resembles "directing the government from behind a screen," and he, Empress Dowager Cixi.[6]

My people, those who find democracy dear, after I tearfully survey our history, I see that rule by autocracy is the greatest obstacle blocking the road to reform!

2. My Grief and Indignation

Let us break through our narrow vision and closed-mindedness to look at the world, and to look at the world's history. The democratic fighters of the Renaissance unfurled the great flag of reason. The same banner also turned over a new page in the history of civilization.

What is reason? Reason is the point of contact between impulsive passion and knowledge. The great thinker Bacon said, "knowledge is power." I believe that the power of reason which combines knowledge and passion put together is inestimable.

Over the past few days, I have seen with sorrow that there is much impulsiveness and passion in the democracy movement at [Beijing] Normal University, but somewhat lacking in the students is knowledge—knowledge of democracy. It is precisely this that causes the movement to be short of knowledge. Where knowledge is insufficient, self-confidence will be lacking; insufficient self-confidence leads to a lack of courage, and as a result, organization is also very difficult.

We must have knowledge of democracy, or else we may fall into a state of blindness. Democracy primarily means a political system that strives for democracy; this in turn requires a rational kind of power structure, a highly efficient structure that will contain checks and balances.

One of the seven demands proposed by Beijing University students [initially on April 18 and again on April 22] was for "freedom of the press." However, they [the petitioning students] have forgotten the absolute condition necessary for the realization of "freedom of the press"—the elimination of the tyranny of one man. How is it that in America journalists dare to reveal the illegal actions of the President and his officials? If the American political system did not provide for the restraints that the Con-

---

6. Empress Dowager Cixi is a symbol to the Chinese of manipulative rule from behind the scenes. From 1861 to 1874, she controlled real power in China, directing the boy emperor Tongzhi from behind a screen located near the throne. After Tongzhi's death in 1874, the Empress Dowager managed to extend her rule by having an infant nephew named as his successor.

gress exercises on the President, and did not allow for criticism of the party in power by the opposition party [criticism that serves a supervisory function], then would journalists dare to do so?

China's Constitution has an article regarding freedom of the press, but it lacks the corresponding structural system that will guarantee this [right]. The National People's Congress is a rubber stamp, and the other parties [the eight "democratic parties"] don't dare to speak out.[7]

A movement that is struggling for democracy must follow the correct course. Our slogans [and objectives] must be substantive and address the basic problems existing in China today. And so I propose the following slogans [and objectives]:

1. Amend the Constitution, eliminate single-party dictatorship!
2. Allow every party and faction to contest elections openly!
3. Implement a parliamentary system, eliminate dictatorship!
4. Allow freedom of the press; enact a press law!
5. Separate the Party from enterprise management; eliminate special privileges!

> —A Beijing Normal University
> Professional Revolutionary,
> April 30, 1989
> (*poster at Beijing Normal University*)

ANOTHER DISCUSSION OF ONE-PARTY AUTOCRACY

"China," it has been said, "is following a capitalist road under the guise of socialism. Indeed, this is "socialism with Chinese characteristics":[8] a

7. The eight "democratic parties" are marginal, powerless "democratic parties" that are allowed to exist in China under the leadership of the Communist Party. They are historical relics of bourgeois and intellectual forces who accepted in 1949 the invitation of the victorious Communists to join in a "united front" that would form the government of the new People's Republic of China. Within a year of the founding of the new republic, however, the Communist Party forced the eight democratic parties to accept the leadership of the Party and agree to severe restrictions on their activities. Although frequently mentioned by the Chinese government as integral parts of the present-day system of "consultative leadership," the democratic parties are in fact no more than bit players. It is not unusual for a member of a democratic party also to belong to the Communist Party.

8. The phrase "socialism with Chinese characteristics" was used to describe China's flexible

handful of people have monopolized the political power of the central government and have been exercising a one-party dictatorship. . . . In this system, in order to secure their rule in perpetuity, this small group is allowed to manipulate the law as they please and rape the people's will. They can appoint their sons or grandsons to important offices, put the mass media under full control, and adopt an obscurantist policy of lying to the people. Or they may grant a portion of their power to "yes men," making them "agree to be chained, so as to put chains on others." In this system, they are able to ask the people of the whole nation to follow the Four Cardinal Principles [adherence to the socialist path, the leadership of the Communist Party, Marxism–Leninism–Mao Tse-tung Thought, and the people's democratic dictatorship].[9] Now, consider only one of the Four Cardinal Principles, "uphold the leadership of the Chinese Communist Party." It has fooled generations of Chinese people, and has left them with a very deep and strong inertia.

"Do whatever the Party asks you to do." This motto is a precise manifestation of the benightedness of the Chinese. And others such as "one hundred thousand people, all of one mind," or "ten thousand people with only one head" are but fairy tales from the Arabian Nights. A person with any sense of independence should have his own mind and own views, and should not blindly follow someone else's instructions. We may give full support to the correct leadership of the Chinese Communist Party, but we may of course choose not to follow misguided leadership. Changing the first of the Four Cardinal Principles to: "Support the correct leadership of the Chinese Communist Party" would, I feel, make it more appropriate.

The world of the future will be a pluralistic world, a world of coexistence; in that world, "a hundred schools of thought" will be able to contend in cultural and art forums, and many economic systems will be able to exist side by side. Thus, to claim that "unified leadership" [under the Party] is the only type of political system required undoubtedly violates the law of common sense. The Party has coined the euphemism of "the coexistence of pluralism with unified leadership." Such a creature is really hard to understand; "pluralism" in the hand of one-party leadership is

---

and unique approach to socialism (essentially, to rationalize the nation's move away from classic Marxist theory, centralized planning, and public ownership) by Deng Xiaoping in 1982 at the Twelfth National Congress of the Party, and has appeared regularly since then in major Party statements on reform policies. In recent years many Chinese have taken to using the expression in bemusement or sarcasm when discussing the state of Chinese society.
9. The significance of the Four Cardinal Principles is discussed at pages 162–63 below.

like a free man dancing in chains. If we do want democracy, it is necessary that we destroy the one-party autocracy or establish genuine democratic institutions capable of truly representing the interests of all social strata (such as nongovernment-controlled labor unions). And if we want democracy and freedom, the only thing to do is to give legislative power to the people. Only by following the principle of legislation by the people can there be true freedom of press and true freedom of speech.

I believe that the only way to change the current political situation in China is to fight for democracy—to emphasize that all people are equal before the law, and that no one is above the law. Political change requires that the right of legislation truly belong to the people. It means that laws will not be made by a small handful of government officials, and that they shall reflect the common will of the people.

The primary objective of legislation is freedom and equality. Only when people equally abide by laws that reflect their common wishes can there be freedom. Only when genuine rule by law replaces rule by autocracy, which is monarchy in disguise, can there be genuine democracy, and can it be possible for our society to overcome the defects of feudalism. The government is only an administrator of the people's sovereign will, an institution to which the people grant administrative power and entrust law enforcement power. If the National People's Congress is truly to reflect the people's will, the electoral procedures for its representatives must be changed.

In the absence of a genuine people's supervisory organ, a government [with unchecked power to] implement the law will become corrupt.

Let us greet the coming of a genuinely democratic, free spring with our actions!

> —By a Non-Revolutionary of
> Beijing Normal University, May 2, 1989
> (*big-character poster at*
> *Beijing Normal University*)

REFLECTIONS ON THE CHINESE COMMUNIST PARTY
(excerpt)

... Turning now to its organizational principles and methodology, the Chinese Communist Party has been an excellent carrier of the genes for

Illustration 3.2. The very real possibility of imprisonment or at least disciplinary action prevented many politically concerned students from becoming prominently involved in the student protests. Despite these risks and the presence of police with videocameras, these Shanghai university students address a crowd in front of the Shanghai Municipal Government headquarters at a May 4 rally. Credit: Tristan Mabry.

dictatorship and bureaucracy; the latter is not only a true-to-the-original copy of the former but also its logical extension. Today, after so many years, the Party still maintains the organizational form that existed when our nation had not yet been founded, a structure shaped by security considerations and based on military models. [This structure] stipulates that "the individual obeys the organization, subordinates obey their superiors, the entire Party obeys the Central Committee, and the Central Committee obeys one person (or a few persons)." In short, "to obey orders is a duty." How could this type of closed organization be anything but a breeding ground for dictatorships, patriarchies, and personality cults? Ours is a case of absolute nondemocracy (at times, the dictatorship of a single individual is realized through the tyranny of the majority, such as the Cultural Revolution and the downfall of Hu Yaobang), and all the dictatorships in China originate from within the Party (as in the case of Mao as well as Hua Guofeng).[10] In a country such as ours, it is not at all surpris-

10. Hua Guofeng was the primary rival of Deng Xiaoping for control of the Party in the

ing that, under the lengthy centralized leadership of a single party which founded itself on such principles and methods, dictatorship and bureaucracy should arise again and again. Nowadays, many people are placing their hopes in the possibility that one or two wise and capable individuals might arise from within the Party. The idea is absolutely terrifying; have we not had enough of handing over the lives of a billion people to one or two leaders? So many times has the Party said the simple phrase: "in the end, our great Party always brings order to chaos," but this is nothing but [a justification for] at the cost of several decades of their lives for hundreds of millions of people (half their lives); the cost of the lives of hundreds and thousands of others, and the cost of pushing history back several decades, or several hundreds of years (as did the Cultural Revolution in China, and Stalinist revisionism in the Soviet Union). Now, if a party has been committing unpardonable errors for most of its time, and yet we continue to place the fate of a billion people into its hands instead of their own, how does it differ from gambling? The Communist Party has always loved to drag out in the open a "handful of persons" outside its ranks. Why doesn't it expose the "large handful" within the Party itself? If 80 percent of the [nearly forty-seven million] Party members are good (and the standard for goodness is here measured by the ethical standards ordinary citizens ought to possess), how about the other 20 percent? Can nearly ten million people not be considered a "large handful"?

. . . When it comes to the political structure of the entire country, the Communist Party holds a rather dubious position. It was announced on October 1, 1949 [upon the founding of the People's Republic], that all the power resides in the people and in the National People's Congress composed of people's representatives, and that daily administrative affairs are the domain of the government. However, up to the present day in China we still have a system of unified leadership under the Party. The Party, instead of establishing its political program through national elections, and instead of having its will expressed through the mechanism of the National People's Congress, has placed itself high above what the Constitution has designated as the supreme organ of state power—the National People's Congress—and the supreme administrative body—the State Council. If the National People's Congress and the State Council are

period following the death of Premier Zhou Enlai and Chairman Mao Tse-tung in 1976. Hua, a moderate whom Mao had reportedly personally blessed as his successor, managed to take over the chairmanship of the Party after Mao's death in October 1976, but by late 1979 Deng and his supporters were dominating Party policymaking. In September 1980, Hua was replaced as Chairman of the Party by one of Deng's protégés—Hu Yaobang.

its machines, what's the point of adding the word "supreme" to them? And if the "representative assembly" that the people has elected is only the Party's machine, isn't the phrase "all power resides with the people" superfluous? Better just to get it over with and acknowledge that all power lies in the Party and the "Party's Gestapo." Indeed, when a few statements of a certain individual from the Party, who is neither an organ of state power nor an administrative body, can for a few years determine the directions or policy decisions of a country, does this not alarm us and make us bristle with anger?

. . . It is not that our nation does not need a nucleus; what is crucial is that this nucleus be chosen by the people. If a party or an organization has the people on its side, the people will elect it to power and make it possible for it to carry out its program. In brief, everything must be chosen by the people.

If, let us say, a citizen who has no right to speak up and express his opinions has no obligation to obey his government, then the people will have no need or obligation to support or heed a political party which, claiming as it may to represent the people, is totally devoid of a conscience and which has not been chosen by the people.

We should recognize that the people and the national government come first and that the Party comes last. It is absolutely not the other way round, where we recognize not the people and the government but a Party which represents nothing at all!

—May 17, 1989
(big-character poster
at Beijing University)

Political reform was not an issue that most Chinese citizens cared or knew much about. However, to many student activists and intellectuals, reform that would install some checks on the Party's absolute power, that would protect people from the arbitrariness of bureaucrats, was no less important than the fight against government corruption.

In economic policy, Deng the pragmatic nation builder had been more than willing to ignore the niceties of Marxist theory, and to abandon pure socialist economic structures for the sake of transforming China's economy (all undertaken under the rubric of "socialism with Chinese characteristics"); but in politics, Deng the authoritarian leader had been unwilling to entertain any challenges whatsoever to the Leninist theory of the Communist Party's leading role, and to implement reforms that would diminish the Party's control over political decision making.

This is not to say that Deng had always been hostile to the notion of greater citizen participation in the political process. In July 1979, despite his repression of the Democracy Wall movement, Deng had permitted the initiation of a set of political reforms that featured the introduction of direct elections for local People's Congresses at the county level (previously, direct elections had been used only at the lowest level, the commune) and established a system of more candidates than slots, with a more open candidate nomination process that made it possible for independent candidates from outside the Party apparatus to be nominated. Also introduced was new latitude for the press, which was given the go-ahead to diversify its coverage and engage in investigative reporting. However, these democratic reforms, limited as they were—the People's Congresses met only once a year and had no real power, and all media reporting still continued to be subject to review by Party officials—produced unacceptable challenges to the sanctity of Party authority and official ideology, instead of the tamer "masses' supervision" of the bureaucracy that Deng had envisioned. While the great majority of the county elections proceeded uneventfully, Beijing University and Hunan Teachers College in Changsha became the sites of heated campaigns during which leading candidates called for an independent press law, the separation of powers, the sharing of power among various political forces—or stated that Marxism should not be accepted blindly. Press exposés of corruption that specifically named high officials similarly created great unease at the top levels of the Party. By December 1980, Deng had delivered a speech sharply attacking "bourgeois liberalization"; during early 1981, new guidelines circumscribing press reporting were being circulated; and in the spring of 1981, the most outspoken student candidates were criticized and punished.[11]

The brief flirtation with socialist democracy ended, Deng, like many autocratic rulers, became over time less and less willing to yield political power to the people, although he did not completely abolish debate over political reform. Student unrest, driven in large part by the lack of any outlets for expressing dissatisfaction, only caused Deng and other hard-liners in the Party to retrench. In December 1986, as student pro-democracy protests spread, Deng warned through a *People's Daily* article that "reform of the political system can only be carried out under the leadership of the Party," and fiercely attacked advocates of "bourgeois liberalization" who were "trying to discard the leadership of the Party." Furthermore, while continuing pressure for economic efficiency provided the impetus for the announcement of new reform policies such as "separation of the Party from enterprise management," or "devolution of decision-making power to lower levels," these too were quickly doomed by the entrenched interests of Party officials, particularly those associated

11. For example, Tao Sen, a Hunan Teachers College activist, was expelled from school and reportedly sent to a labor camp. Wang Dan had good reason for requesting in his April 5 poster that Beijing University authorities not interfere in the graduation of student activists.

with the central government, and the reluctance of those at the highest echelons of the Party to shake up the pyramid of power on which their own power and positions rested. By the late 1980s, the Party's dismal track record in the area of political reform meant that few citizens took seriously Chinese leaders' periodic pronouncements that such reform was needed.

Thus, on the eve of the Democracy Movement, though the Party's influence had been indisputably eroded by social changes that had bestowed on citizens greater economic independence, and its stature battered by corruption, it still maintained a stranglehold over political power. No political reform of substance had occurred in a decade. Party officials controlled decision making at all levels, from individual factories up to the Supreme People's Court.[12] Virtually all decisions of import, from the appointment of cadres to the formulation of policy, continued to be made in the Party through internal, secretive processes dominated by the personal influence of the participants and elaborately constructed power alliances.

12. Party control over political power and indeed, all spheres of Chinese life, rests in a system of "Party and government merger into one body" (*Dangzheng heyi*) which has the following features: (1) A Party Committee or Party branch exists in all entities at various levels, whether economic (e.g., factories), military, administrative, judicial, cultural, or educational. The only exceptions to this organizational rule are religious associations and the "democratic parties"; even these, however, fall under the supervision of the Party's United Front Department. (2) The Party Committee or Party branch Secretary normally serves concurrently as the head of the entity; thus, the person with ultimate decision-making power in a factory or university is the Secretary of the Party Committee in the factory or school, not the factory manager or school president. (3) All important policy decisions are made through the hierarchal structure of the Party organization: decisions made at lower levels often must be approved by upper levels, and policies fixed at higher levels are transmitted to lower levels through Party documents and meetings for implementation. Participation in policy making is limited to members of Party Committees.

Such pervasive control is exemplified by the Party's involvement in the legal system. All judicial and criminal matters are supervised by Party "political-legal committees" established at various levels (such as county, municipality, provincial, or central); the secretary of each political-legal committee is either the deputy secretary or member of the standing committee of the general Party Committee at the same level. At each level, the Chief of the public security bureau, the President of the court, and the President of the procuratorate sit on the Party political-legal committee of that level. Unlike the public security Chief, however, the court President is usually not a member of the general Party Committee; thus, he is a low-ranking member of the political-legal committee with relatively little power. When political-legal committees meet to discuss the handling of important criminal and civil cases, their final decisions are invariably made by the secretaries of the committees. Those decisions are then implemented by the involved judicial and security officers.

In October 1987, proposals for separating the Party and government were raised for the first time. Such proposals, viewed as a fundamental aspect of political reform, called for less Party intervention in governmental and economic decision making. Little or no actual change, however, ever occurred, and the system described above remains intact.

In the next article, "Why Does China Need Democracy?" the author, a young teacher at People's University, dissects the current Chinese political power structure that has enabled the Party to maintain its grip on political power. In his analysis of why and how a system of centralized power has developed in China under Communist rule, the writer gives prominent mention to the "national character" of the Chinese people. Such examination—and condemnation—of national traits such as the willingness to entrust one's fate to those in power or the tendency to lapse into atomism upon the collapse of a strong central authority was typical of the thinking of young intellectuals in the 1980s.

WHY DOES CHINA NEED DEMOCRACY?
AN ANALYSIS OF THE CURRENT CHINESE POWER STRUCTURE
(draft)

. . . The essential characteristic of the current Chinese political system is a one-party, one-faction system of power. The Chinese Communist Party is the sole ruling party, and moreover, within the ruling party, no other factions are allowed to exist openly and legally. Such a political system inevitably leads to the concentration of state power in one person's hands, giving rise to a political system of "one party–one faction–one leader" ("Three Forces–One Entity"). This has been evidenced not only by the forty years of Chinese history, but also by the history of almost every socialist country.

How can a single man master and control the power of the entire state? Why is it that, to a certain extent, one single man can decide the destiny of one billion people? Is it because he is entrusted by God? Or because he is a talented statesman? Or because he is charismatic?

Based on my research, I think that such a political system of "unified, centralized leadership" [of one man and one party] cannot be sustained by a certain individual or a few people, but only by a unique system of power. This power system consists of the following four components:

I. A system of military force
This primarily refers to the military forces, police, plainclothes security personnel, courts, prisons, etc. There is a great man in China who once said that "political power grows out of the barrel of a gun," and that "without . . . the military, we would have . . . nothing."[13] Under this kind

13. The great man was Mao Tse-tung.

of system, whoever controls the military is the one with the greatest power. If no individual is able to control the military effectively, the whole country falls into chaos. However, even though this system is mainly built on military force, whoever has captured the power to rule the state will not be able to sustain its power by relying on force alone.

II. An ideological system

Every state tries to provide a complete ideological framework that justifies the ruler's control of power and his conduct. The ideology used to justify the "Three Forces–One Entity" system in China consists primarily of the following three components:

A. *Doctrine of class, class struggle, and the dictatorship of the proletariat.* According to this doctrine, the working class is the representative of the advanced productive forces; therefore, the entire society must be under the leadership of the working class—which takes the form of the leadership of the Communist Party, the vanguard of the working class. The Communist Party, meanwhile, is led by its "most authoritative, most influential, and most experienced" leaders (Lenin, *Selected Works of Lenin*, Vol. 4, p. 197). If you agree with this logic, then you will have to admit that the political system of "one party–one faction–one leader" is rational and unquestionable. If you do not agree, you can be made to "agree" through various means; for this purpose, the doctrines of class struggle and the dictatorship of the proletariat provide the theoretical tools. In looking back over forty years of Chinese history since 1949, one can see that every political struggle within and without the Party has been carried out under the rubric of the doctrine of class struggle and the dictatorship of the proletariat. Although nearly all of those who were subjected to "special treatment" during these struggles have been rehabilitated [their names and rights restored], one can figure that if this type of political system is to endure, it is bound to continue using the doctrines of class struggle and dictatorship of the proletariat to deal with dissidents, all in the name of sustaining "unity and stability" and "social stability." In theory, it is implied that this system of "Three Forces–One Entity" truly represents not only the interests of the working class, but also the interests of all the working people. But is this the reality? The crux of the problem is just this.

B. *Theory of socialist development by stages.* According to orthodox propaganda, socialism is a transitional period to communism, the highest goal of mankind; socialism will eventually prevail over capitalism; socialism is getting better and better, whereas capitalism is going to the dogs. Forty years of history have shown that as for determining what socialism really is, to date, there is probably no one who can say clearly. What was denounced as capitalistic yesterday could well be regarded as socialist today. Socialism, after several decades, has not yet entered its advanced stage; on the contrary, it has reverted to its elementary stage. The issue is not whether a clear definition of socialism should be worked out; it is that the authorities label the policies they have made or advocate "socialist" in an attempt to demonstrate that all their policies are correct and unquestionable; thus do they get the people to support and defend policies. In addition, those policies proven erroneous in practice could always be faulted for violating the principles of socialism. By so doing, the authorities can tell people again and again that a perfect and real socialism does exist, and also justify the legitimacy of what they are doing.

C. *Doctrine of Marxism-Leninism as the guiding doctrine.* Those in power claim that Marxism-Leninism is the greatest, most convincing theory of mankind, the universally applicable truth. They claim it is the theory that will lead the working people to their total liberation. They also claim that they are the most faithful disciples of Marxism-Leninism, the theorists and statesmen who possess a comprehensive, thorough, and complete understanding of Marxism-Leninism. By so doing, those in power can prove that everything they are doing is absolutely correct; in this way, they can justify requiring complete obedience from the people and can maintain political unanimity to the greatest possible extent. Those with dissenting views are censured and punished. Of course, the doctrines of class, class struggle, dictatorship of the proletariat, as well as the theory of socialism are only components of Marxism-Leninism. Because of their special functions, they have been analyzed independently here.

Even though this ideological framework is full of defects, it can justify itself through the strength of its "logic." Therefore many people, including a great many high officials, have believed in it and have also become its victims. . . .

The system of military force and the ideological system are the two main pillars of state power. They are complementary and indispensible. For some years, those in power have seen too that there are many defects in the ideological framework, even suggesting that Marxism can be further developed. But to protect and maintain the system of "Three Forces—One Entity," they absolutely will not permit people to analyze comprehensively and criticize openly this ideological framework. Yet it will be impossible to change the system of "Three Forces—One Entity" and have a new ideology if there is no new ideological framework available to re-place it.

III. An Organizational System

State power can only be sustained and exercised through a corresponding organizational system. This "conveyor belt" of power distributes and controls resources. The basic characteristic of the organizational system that supports the system of "Three Forces–One Entity" is the practice of appointing officials at various levels, especially at high levels, from above; this makes officials subservient to those above them. The present organizational system simply would not be able to endure without this practice. Under such a system, though some elections are allowed, they are confined to low levels or are not carried out in a meaningful way. [Political scientist] Yan Jiaqi has said that "in the elections for delegates of the Municipal People's Congresses, and the National People's Congresses, 99 percent of those on the 'candidate's list' that has been drawn up [by Party committees] prior to the convening of the Congresses are elected. But only 1 percent of the candidates who are nominated [from the floor] by more than ten delegates when the Congresses are in session can get elected. This happens not only in Beijing, but all over the country." With this type of system for state cadres, a certain extremely powerful ruler can subjugate the whole nation by effectively dominating a few subordinates. It is only natural that under such a system, political trickery has become highly sophisticated. There are typically two methods. One is "promotion and flattery." By promoting obedient subordinates or relatives to higher positions regardless of their rank or seniority, those in power trade power for loyalty and flattery, thus preserving their own power and ensuring their devotion. A second common method is to exploit conflicts [between factions] to maintain a political balance, or to take advantage of personal conflicts to defeat rivals one by one.

The three systems mentioned above, which can render the majority of the people psychologically or physically subservient, are the "hardware" of the national power structure that safeguards the system of "Three Forces–One Entity," and "social stability." According to my research, this power structure is essentially the same as that of feudal Chinese society save for differing ideologies. By comparing some of their characteristics, we find that although they are on the surface different, they are in fact essentially identical.

Comparison of the Present Power Structure
and Feudal China's Power Structure

	FEUDAL SYSTEM	PRESENT SYSTEM
Control of state power	by single emperor	by single person
Ideology	one only: Confucianism	one only: Marxism-Leninism
Doctrine regarding source of power	mandate of Heaven	class struggle
Power base	army	army
System of officials	appointed posts	appointed posts
Principles of organization	ruler guides subjects	the organization [the Party] directs the individual
	father guides sons	higher levels direct lower levels
	husband guides wife	the Central Committee directs the entire Party
Political tactics	highly sophisticated	highly sophisticated
Assumption about human nature	doctrine of inherent virtue	doctrine of the perfect proletariat
Status of the individual	none	extremely low

One major difference between the present political system and that of feudal society is that the economy of the present system is chiefly based on government ownership while the latter was based on private ownership. The question here is whether the change in the system of ownership has strengthened or weakened the centralized political system. As a matter of fact, through the nationalization of the means of production, the "one party–one faction–one leader" political system has come to control virtually the social existence of every single individual. Control over people by the state has become formidable in a way it has never been before; it reached an unprecedented peak in the period running from the mid-1950s to the mid-1970s. Therefore, under the crushing force of an autocratic political system—one that is essentially identical to that of feudal China—and the added factor of public ownership, even in situations of [extreme disaster] such as the great famine of 1959–1960 (during which approximately twenty million people died of hunger), the people have become too weak to rise up and create trouble, or "rise up in revolt."

Illustration 3.3. A large allegorical drawing at Beijing University, in which the massive rock of feudalism is crushing the Chinese people while officials plunder the land's riches. The drawing is entitled "The Eight Diagrams," after the ancient Chinese divination chart. Credit: Ren Daren.

By observing the present political system and the history of the past forty years, we can see that the "hardware" of this system of "Three Forces–One Entity" leads to three consequences:

1. No Freedom of the Press. . . . People are neither allowed to criticize government leaders and their policies openly nor even to discuss theories advanced by them. Why? Because the system's rigid structure [lacks the the resilience to absorb any challenges]. In this centralized system, if open criticism of the government were allowed, the government would lose its authority over society, and it would not be able to implement any of its policies. It is for just this reason that progress in formulating and promulgating a press law has been slow; the government is reluctant to allow any privately run papers.

2. No Real Right of the People to Vote. The people have no real right to vote, especially for leading figures in the government. They have to accept the government's nominations. The present political system would not survive if leaders on all levels were elected by the people.

3. No Legal Authority. Since political power is centralized, and the people cannot enjoy a free press or the right to vote, officials on all levels are only responsible to their superiors; they are not supervised and regulated

by the people. Thus, those with power are able at any time to resort to their own political power instead of the law. To take an extreme case, even the President of the country [Liu Shaoqi] was not protected by the law in the sixties. And in many matters, there is no justice in society, no distinction between truth and falsehood. Therefore, unless this social system is changed, law cannot have any authority; a society ruled by the will of a small group of people will never change into a society ruled by law.

IV. National character

Mao Tse-tung once said to Richard Nixon that Stalinist autocracy would never occur in the United States because Americans would not accept it. Likewise, it would be impossible to import the Chinese political system into America, for Americans would not accept it. The point is that political systems are sustained by compatible national characters.

The Chinese feudal autocracy of more than two thousand years has shaped the national character of the Chinese. And such a character has been sustaining and recreating such a political system. The political system and national character are Siamese twins that have developed together and have shaped each other. According to my research, the character of the Chinese consists of two outstanding traits: slavishness and sectarianism. That is, under strong political pressure most of the people resign themselves to adversity and stoop to compromise, and once they are out of the reach of the state they do things in their own arrogant, selfish, uncompromising, intolerant, and uncooperative ways. It is such a national character that has enabled the Chinese political system to survive for so long. Once this system breaks down, national chaos inevitably follows. After a period of chaos, the people find that they need a new authority to unify and stabilize society. Hence, for two thousand years the Chinese political situation has traced a vicious cycle of autocracy–chaos–new autocracy. . . .

Why is there such a mentality? The following is a brief analysis:

1. The Cult of Imperial Power. The people expect a certain "honest and upright official" or a "benevolent" emperor to safeguard their interests, rather than expecting to build a new political system that will support law as the ultimate authority. Because of the traditional doctrine of "inborn virtue" and the modern postulate of the perfect proletariat, the Chinese believe that man can make himself perfect in temperament, morality, and education. Thus they are inclined to entrust ultimate authority to a small group of people or a single person, without doing anything to regulate those persons' conduct. A survey of Chinese history shows that

many outstanding intellectuals in modern Chinese history have been stricken by this "cult of imperial power."

2. Slavishness and Passivity. People resign themselves to adversity, display the spirit of Ah Q,[14] stoop to compromise with the evil forces in society, and lie to each other. Because the political system possesses a powerful army and a tight social and political organization, the people never enjoy freedom of association, speech, and publication. The people, as countless physically and psychologically isolated individuals, are too weak to revolt. They have resigned themselves to adversity. As individual slavishness grows into collective slavishness, autocracy finds fertile soil in which it thrives.

3. A Bandit Mentality of "Each Man for Himself." In circumstances where they are not constrained by the iron rule of authority, Chinese display a type of "bandit" mentality of "each man for himself." The most conspicuous traits of this mentality are: conceitedness, self-centeredness, unwillingess to compromise, intolerance, warlords' battles, patriarchy, an attitude of superiority, factionalism, disunity, noncooperation, and the imposition of one's will upon others. The reasons for such behavior are: 1. The polarization of values [that is, good or bad, with nothing in between]. In a society characterized by such a polarization of values, people are simply divided into two groups—the extremely good and the extremely bad (the [sudden] rise and [equally precipitous] fall of leaders in certain countries exemplifies this). Therefore, everyone believes himself to be the best and others no good at all. Openly admitting mistakes is always regarded as a loss of face. Some people would rather die than admit their mistakes, even though they know they are wrong. 2. Chinese do not have freedom of association or freedom of the press, which are needed for the free flow and exchange of ideas. The antithesis of sectarianism is unity, cooperation, etc., but these can only be realized through organization [into groups, associations, clubs, etc.], frank exchange of opinions, and the exchange of information. 3. Appointment of officials through arbitrary, personal decisions. A person can be chosen to be an official on the basis of his ability—or [more likely,] his connections. The result is that officials neither listen to nor respect one another. 4. The idea that "the people can be told what to do, but not why" [has been drilled

14. "Ah Q" is the name of the pitiful, self-deceiving, eternal optimist in the "True Story of Ah Q," a short story by Lu Xun, the revered twentieth-century Chinese writer most famous for his biting depictions of Chinese society and the character of the Chinese people. Ah Q is a coward, a pathetic figure who rationalizes every injustice he suffers, finds victory in defeat, and picks on those far weaker than him.

into Chinese so thoroughly that] the majority of the people only care about their own interests, about what is right in front of their noses, and have no sense of social responsibility.

It is tragic that in its ideology, the political system of centralized power presumes the goodness of human nature, for in fact it is the evil side of men that that has been fostered and developed to its fullest extent by this system. For example, people tend to lie, fight among themselves—to be, in effect nothing but a heap of loose sand.[15] Moreover, the system has suppressed and attacked positive attributes of human nature such as honesty and creativity.

If a person lives under such a system for many years, he will inevitably acquire to some extent the negative characteristics described above; they will be so deeply embedded in his subconsciousness that even long after he has moved to a foreign country, this "quintessence of Chinese culture will still be a part of him." For many years now, people have been criticizing the tradition of Chinese culture. In my view, it is not necessary to repudiate totally Chinese tradition. What should be rejected are the components of the traditional culture that give rise to the ingrained negative habits of the Chinese. Should we carry out a reform of the "one party–one faction–one leader" system without concurrent transformation of national character, no one will be able to guarantee that China will be able to build a truly democratic political system, and that furthermore, there will not be a repeat of the vicious cycle of "tyranny–turmoil–new tyranny" that has characterized Chinese history for several thousand years. I believe that all Chinese citizens (including both those in power and ordinary people) must conduct self-examinations to see in fact how many of these deep-rooted negative habits they have acquired. Permit me to make a personal judgment: if, during the time we undertake a reform of the political system, we do not also initiate a movement to improve our national character through self-education and mutual education, then even if it is today's most resolute fighters for democracy who replace the people currently in power, there still is no guarantee that these warriors for democracy will not acquire new [dictatorial] powers.

We can see from the above analysis and a study of forty-five years of Chinese history that the political system of centralized power has created four unresolvable problems that have gravely impeded social progress:

---

15. A reference to a famous sentence by Sun Yat-sen who, lamenting the loyalty of Chinese only to their families or clans and their lack of national unity, likened them to "a pile of loose sand."

1. There is no guarantee that national decisions will be made, and when serious errors in decision making occur, they cannot be promptly corrected. . . .

2. Political corruption has become incurable. Although political corruption occurs in every society, it is a temporary phenomenon in societies with democratic political systems, and once it is discovered, it can be dealt with promptly before it becomes [so pervasive that it is] "environmental pollution" [which is slowly poisoning society]. But under the system of centralized power, corrupt phenomena such as exploiting power for personal benefits and bureaucratism are widespread. . . .

3. There has been a tremendous waste of human resources. It has always been strange and painful to see the phenomenon of a great poverty of material wealth exist next to a tremendous waste of human resources. The root cause for this phenomenon is the system of "Three Forces—One Entity" which, in order to ensure that power remain highly centralized and society remain stable, has not put the strongest men and the most outstanding minds to work on creating material wealth for society, but instead has diverted them into endless internal struggles in which they are preoccupied with critizing others as well as defending themselves from attack. The system must continually strike down one group of people after another, and then rehabilitate them one after another. With all this going on, who is in the mood to engage in the modernization drive? It is impossible to count how many brilliant people have been consumed and thrown away during the many large-scale political movements and struggles since 1949.[16] While other nations concentrate on economic development, we are feverishly busy tearing people down and then rehabilitating

16. A series of violent political campaigns since the founding of the PRC in 1949 have led to the imprisonment of millions and the execution, beating deaths, or suicide of about 900,000 Chinese. In the 1951 Campaign to Suppress Counterrevolutionaries, several million Chinese were sent to labor camps or thrown into jail, and by some estimates at least 700,000 executed. In the 1951-1952 "Three Antis and Five Antis Campaign" (against corruption, waste, and bureaucracy; and against tax evasion, fraud, bribery, industrial espionage, and theft of state property), targeted at bourgeois businessmen and entrepreneurs, fewer than 1,000 Chinese were executed, but over 30,000 were imprisoned. The third major political campaign in the 1950s, the 1957 Anti-Rightist Campaign (see n.8, Chapter 4, led to labor camp terms of twenty years or more for over 500,000 suspected rightists. These campaigns were followed by the 1966-1969 Cultural Revolution, in which at least 10,000,000 died and countless others persecuted. In the 1970s and 1980s no campaigns of comparable scale or violence occurred, but there were a number of bitter inner-Party power struggles in which the losers have been punished by arrest.

them. It is no wonder that our country has for so long been impoverished and backward!

Moreover, due to the phenomenon of bureaucratism in which officials abuse their powers for personal gain, people cannot, indeed dare not, speak their minds on many issues. "As time goes by, many people begin to assume an unconstructive attitude of indifference, no longer bothering their heads about what to say, what to think, or even to get angry," "on the surface, this phenomenon gives people the illusion of stability and unity. But such stability and unity are obtained at the cost of apathy and the suppression of true feelings" (words of Hu Jiwei).[17] In private, almost every person has complaints and bitter and painful feelings that cannot be expressed. . . .

4. It is impossible to prevent social turmoil. Purges are carried out constantly within and outside the Party to preserve the political system of unified power. Such power struggles that defy all procedural rules have created non-stop social turmoil. . . .

Due to the three unresolvable problems described above—continual errors in policymaking, corruption, and the low morale and apathy of the people—which have reduced China to a standing state of poverty and backwardness, and the added factor that there is no freedom of the press that can act as a "safety valve" (or, as some prefer to say, a "vent hole for anger"), discontent among the people is ever rising. Once it explodes, it will definitely lead to a confrontation with the authorities, similar to the April 5 Incident [the Tiananmen Incident of 1976] and other incidents that have broken out over the past few years across the country. Furthermore, since at present state power is concentrated in the hands of a person who is able to exert effective control over the army, who can feel confident that the entire nation will not erupt in truly major turmoil when [that man is gone and] there is no one able to assume his role? The worries about China's future that many persons have expressed are a reflection of their concern over this problem. By making a comparison of various countries, one discovers that in all democratic nations with a pluralistic political system, the political situation is relatively stable; moreover, it is always in nations in which power is highly centralized and concentrated [in the hands of a few] that political stability or frequent turmoil exists.

In summary, the primary function of the system of "Three Forces–One

17. Hu Jiwei, former editor-in-chief of the *People's Daily*, has long been an advocate of greater press freedom. Hu played an active role in the activities of intellectuals during the Democracy Movement. He was later removed from his position as a delegate to the NPC.

Entity" is to preserve the status quo—and to remove any guarantee that China will be able to keep moving forward toward progress. . . .

—XXX, Teacher at People's University
(*big-character poster at People's
University, May 12, 1989*)[18]

The ideological framework defining the limits of dissent during the Deng era has been the "Four Cardinal Principles": adherence to the socialist path, upholding the leadership of the Communist Party, upholding Marxism-Leninism-Mao Tse-tung Thought, and the people's democratic dictatorship. In the March 1979 speech attacking the activists of the Democracy Wall Movement in which he first laid down the Four Cardinal Principles (also known as the "Four Upholds"), Deng asserted that the Four Cardinal Principles were the "basic prerequisite for achieving modernization." Deng also declared: "The Central Committee considers that we must now repeatedly emphasize the necessity of upholding these Four Cardinal Principles, because certain people (even if only a handful) are attempting to undermine them. In no way can such attempts be tolerated. . . . To undermine any of the Four Cardinal Principles is to undermine the whole cause of socialism in China, the whole cause of modernization."[19]

Since their introduction, the Four Cardinal Principles have become an ideological straitjacket restricting free and candid debate over the merits of socialism, the Party's leadership, and Marxism. Viewed by Party conservatives as the bulwark against the advances of "bourgeois liberalism"—the Party's term for Western political thinking and its values of liberty, democracy, pluralism, and rights of the individual—the Four Cardinal Principles, which appear in a rephrased form in the preface of the 1982 Chinese Constitution, are far more than a political slogan; they represent a vision of Chinese society. Because of the danger of directly attacking the Four Cardinal Principles, most Chinese, even outspoken advocates of political reform, practice self-censorship when it comes to them. The poster below, although seriously flawed by major errors in its analysis of European history and oversimplifications of Marxist theory (some of which do not appear in the edited version that follows), nonetheless is an important piece, for it dares to challenge unequivocally the Four Cardinal Principles. And judging from the number of laudatory comments scrawled

18. This poster was subsequently published in the inaugural issue of the *Voice of the People* (*Renmin zhi sheng*), a Democracy Movement journal, on June 2, 1989.

19. Deng's speech, "Uphold the Four Cardinal Principles," was reprinted in the *People's Daily* on March 30, 1979. The translation quoted here is from the official Chinese government compilation entitled "Fourth Plenary Session of the CPC Central Committee," published by New Star Publishers, Beijing, 1989.

by readers on the poster, a good many young Chinese today similarly reject the political philosophy that their country's leaders and elders insist must be the foundation of their society.

THE FOUR CARDINAL PRINCIPLES:
LEVERS FOR REFORM, OR BARS TO CHANGE?

On April 18, two hundred brave students from Beijing University gathered outside of the Great Hall of the People shouting slogans from time to time. When someone yelled out: "Total Westernization!" not many echoed the cry. Then someone else stood up and said, "Anyone who shouts out slogans that conflict with the Four Cardinal Principles is no Beijing University person."

On April 26, the editorial in the *People's Daily* attacked the students on two charges: being "anti-party" and "anti-socialism."

On April 29, when [Vice Minister of the State Education Commission] He Dongchang was holding a dialogue with the students, he asked a rhetorical question: would the students have received the support and sympathy of the people of Beijing if they had marched under placards denouncing the Four Cardinal Principles?

The impression one gets from all of this is that everyone—students, members of the government, or ordinary people of Beijing—has a certain idea in his head; and that idea is that the Four Cardinal Principles are fundamental laws of nature, not subject to doubt or questioning, and that one simply cannot tamper with them.

I have turned this over in my own mind for quite a while, but I have not managed to find a convincing argument by anyone that the Four Cardinal Principles are some sort of divine revelation. Instead, I find it curious that, in this era of free speech and return to rationality there still seems to be a "forbidden zone" in people's thoughts. How can this be? The current reform, as it deepens, has called for bold theoretical inquiries. But if, in the midst of these inquiries, "decrees of Heaven" still exist— decrees not unlike the doctrines of the Catholic Church in medieval Europe that the earth was the center of the universe and that God created the world in a week, which one must simply believe and not question— then how can one hope for any real breakthrough in these theoretical inquiries?

"If it is real gold, it will not fear the smelter's fire; if it is just leftover snow, it will melt and disappear as soon as it is heated."

In that spirit, this writer has ventured into the "forbidden zone" and, having learned a few things there, has written it all down to await the benefit of my readers' criticism.

1. Concerning the Leadership of the Party

History cannot forget that in the mid-1930s, when the starving workers' and peasants' Red Army [of the Communists] broke through the siege of the Kuomintang and reached northern Shanxi, many ardent young people resolutely laid aside their secure city lives and went to the barren loess plateau of the northwest [where in Yan'an, the Communist Party was based]. Today, however, at the end of the 1980s, a group of privileged young party members on the campus of the People's University have put up manifestos declaring their wish to leave the Communist Party and found a new party!

What has happened to this group of young people? We will find—if we can bring ourselves to realize a single fact—that nothing has happened to them, and that there is still a little bit of conscience left in them, which gives them the courage to reject what is bad and follow what is good. That single fact is that the Communist Party has changed. . . .

Forty years have gone by. Now the Chinese people have discovered to their astonishment that corruption—the very thing that ruined the Kuomintang and besmirched its reputation—has crept into the Communist Party itself. Their "pal" has changed from one who once upon a time "would not take so much as a needle and thread from the people" to one who now skims the cream from the people's labor to build villas and purchase luxurious cars, going as far as to hoard what he has plundered in overseas banks. From the old motto of the Red Army soldier: "Do not take even half a penny," to today's veteran skilled in using his power and taking advantage of the loopholes of state ownership to engage in profiteering and speculation, thus wreaking havoc in our country and sending prices soaring, the Chinese people have discovered that the corruption of their "pal" has by far surpassed the corruption of the Kuomintang, who bore the burden of fighting in the War of Resistance against Japan.

Corruption such as embezzlement and bribery may occur in any country, no matter how democratic it is. In a democratic country, however, one is unlikely to find corruption as rampant as it is in China today, where nine out of ten government officials are corrupt. Besides, once corruption is exposed to the public, no one in a democratic country is able to stay outside the reach of the law, as the corrupt officials can in China.

What has caused Chinese intellectuals to despair is their realization that a single-party system has no immunity against corruption, that such a system is the breeding ground for corruption, and that as long as the Party's power is free of any check, any attempt by the Party to eliminate corruption from the top down will have no real effect. . . .

No organization or institution exists in China that can counterbalance the power of the Communist Party and independently investigate such corrupt members as official profiteers. Because of this, the few officials of integrity who dared to touch the untouchable have met with disaster. (In the city of Xuchang, Henan Province, a certain Party secretary uncovered a case of profiteering by officials, involving 1,050,000 yuan. In response to this, however, a member of the Xuchang Municipal Party Committee relieved him of his post as secretary, the reason given that the uncovering of profiteering of officials on such a large scale had made the people of Xuchang lose face.)

Alas! If the country's highest leaders or their relatives engage in profiteering, will there be anybody who dares to expose them? And if there are people who do come forward to investigate them, what if their bosses believe that the exposure of a top leader's scandal will cause all Chinese people to lose face?

This is where the "arrogance" of uncontrolled power lies. Under a one-party system, since the ruling party treats the exercise of state power as a forbidden zone into which no other organization can venture, it is impossible for those occupying the highest positions in the party's power structure to be subjected to any effective restraint. When leaders are not produced by democratic elections, but by the internal political struggles of a party, two consequences are unavoidable:

1. Power struggles aimed at seizing the highest position in the leadership have permeated the history of the Party from its early days right up to the present time. At times, such power struggles have even led to nationwide chaos—such as when Mao Tse-tung touched off the Cultural Revolution as an effort to oust Liu Shaoqi.[20]

2. Although in the early days of the People's Republic, Party leaders were still able to maintain their integrity, with the new emphasis on economic development and the concomitant decline of morality, the phe-

20. Liu Shaoqi was a prime target of the Maoists during the Cultural Revolution and its most prominent victim; however, it is inaccurate to state that Mao launched the Cultural Revolution in order to oust Liu Shaoqi. Mao's reasons for initiating the Cultural Revolution were complex; the elimination of top Party figures whom he did not completely trust, such as Liu Shaoqi, was a major but not exclusive motive.

nomenon of wholesale corruption has swept through society like the plague. . . . From the beginning, the historical record of one-party control has borne the mark of these twin brothers, "political turmoil" and "corruption." . . .

2 *On Marxism and Socialism*[21]

In 1825, European capitalism came down with malaria which, from then on, came on every eight or ten years. A Jewish doctor hastened to take the patient's pulse, and jumped to the conclusion that the disease was incurable. In the prescription he made in 1848 [in the *Communist Manifesto*], he claimed that capitalism was surely doomed, and just as surely, the final victor would be socialism. So he spent a lifetime diligently working at his alchemist's stove, trying to produce a magic elixir to save the world.

More than a century has passed. People have discovered to their dismay that all the patients for whom this doctor had pronounced the death sentence have turned out to be remarkably healthy; they are the embodiment of vigor and the spirit of life. Meanwhile, the primitives who had taken hold of the doctor's magic elixir and gulped it down—though unlike the Han Emperor Wu and the Tang Emperor Gao Zong,[22] who put an end to their lives with quack medicines of immortality—are feeling listless and sick to the marrow of their bones, without a single exception.

Perhaps someone will say that socialism has suffered so much misery and so many misfortunes simply because it was the result of "artificial insemination." However, there are developed countries that once tried socialist experiments in areas such as ownership. They did not see prosperity either, and it was the democratic political system in these countries that enabled them wisely to carry out rapid privatization.

Perhaps someone will say that Marx's theories are not wrong, but have been distorted by those who exercised them. This is the same as saying that the blueprints of a product are perfect, and it is only after it has been manufactured that the end product becomes a reject. One or two such rejects do not, of course, prove that the design for the product is flawed,

21. The writer addresses two of the Cardinal Principles in this section: adherence to Marxism–Leninism–Mao Tse-tung Thought, and adherence to socialism.

22. The Han Dynasty Emperor Wu (156–87 B.C.) turned in the later part of his life to superstitious practices and the mysticism of Taoism. Tang Dynasty Emperor Gao Zong (reigned 649–683) was a physically very weak and mentally infirm man; during much of his reign, the Empress Wu exercised control over state power.

but when it has failed to produce a single product that is up to specifications, then the problem is nowhere but in the design itself.

Marx advocated the use of violence to eliminate private ownership and the use of the "dictatorship of the proletariat" (which is one kind of violence) to sustain public ownership. It is this very argument that has entrapped the present-day socialist countries in a twofold dilemma:

First, although several decades of attempts to put socialism into practice has proven that public ownership has hit a dead end in all corners of the world, the "dictatorship" is still busy proclaiming the superiority of a system of public ownership. Although a "small handful" of outstanding intellectuals recognizes the hollowness of public ownership, they are still obliged to write articles using the unpersuasive euphemisms of "public ownership," "state ownership," or "a new-style public ownership," just to dodge the term "private ownership," as if mentioning it were "evil" itself because Marxism has so declared.

Second, even if the dictatorship also now realizes that our system of ownership will have to undergo reform, it still insists on maintaining the status quo, knowing that any attempt to reform ownership will endanger their own interests as the ruling class—the beneficiaries of the existing system. In other words, when reforms in the economic system reach a critical state at which a thoroughgoing reform in the political system is also required, the agents of the reform will become the very objects of reform. It is at this point that our reforms have stagnated. As a number of outstanding intellectuals bravely stepped forward to propose political reform, the old lords turned around and accused them of "making trouble," of "having no other motive than creating disharmony in society."

In discussing Marxism, one has to talk about the philosophical argument of historical materialism, which Engels claimed was one of the two factors that made socialism a science and not just an idle theory. This is a point that also has great practical relevance to the current reforms. . . .

I. Historical materialism maintains that the clash between productive forces and the relations of production [and the eventual advance of the productive forces] . . . provide the motive force in the development of society [and explain the general course of human history] . . . Given that every people must engage in the activity of producing material goods for survival, the question is, does the productive activity or economic life of one society provide the same kind of motive force for social development as it does in any other society? If the answer to this question is yes, then it follows that the civilizations that had an earlier start in history ought to enter modernized society earlier than the civilizations that began later. Now, is this what the record of world history shows?

The answer is no! The four ancient civilizations that were the first to thrive have either declined or vanished from the earth; none was the first society to enter modern society.

[As the history shows,] the true motive force for progress in human society is a free and democratic political system founded on a free and democratic spirit [rather than the economic dialectics posited by historical materialism]. This understanding has practical value in the cause of reform which China is currently undertaking. At present, simply playing with China's "economic base" cannot possibly make reform and modernization succeed. If China wants to move one step forward, it must radically reconstruct its "superstructure" and must, above all, democratize its political system. . . .

Historical materialism only examines a cross section of history. . . . As a matter of fact, such an attempt to locate the motive force for the development of society exclusively in socio-economic life is likely to lead to a kind of historical fatalism. Max Weber has ascribed the rise of western Europe to the push to power of a certain kind of spirit—the spirit of capitalism. His conclusion does ring true. That China has failed to get on its feet in recent years is precisely because it lacks the spirit of capitalism.

Marxism's major contributions are that it has had the unintended result of helping to hasten the perfection of the capitalist system, and that it has added to the treasury of human thought. But for the underdeveloped socialist countries that have looked upon it as a fount of wisdom and put it into practice, it has brought them nothing but disaster after disaster. . . .

3. *On the Democratic Dictatorship of the People*
On the surface, "the democratic dictatorship of the people" sounds far more elegant than "the dictatorship of the proletariat." And having "the democratic dictatorship of the people" explained as "democracy for the people but dictatorship against their enemies" sounds even more appealing to the ear.[23] However, we would do better to have "dictatorship

23. The term "dictatorship of the proletariat" was dropped from the Chinese Constitution and replaced with the expression the "people's democratic dictatorship" as part of the revisions leading up to the promulgation of the 1982 Constitution (the current one). The change was made because "dictatorship of the proletariat" (the working class) was felt to be too narrow in light of China's actual conditions—a relatively small working class and a

against their enemies" changed to "sanctions, authorized by laws embodying the will of the people and which are the products of democratic procedures, against criminals (including criminal offenders and corrupt officials)." And better still would be to change the Cardinal Principle of "uphold the democratic dictatorship of the people" to "uphold the democratic political system of the people." For the ideas "democracy" and "dictatorship" are as incompatible as ice and hot coals. Besides, whoever has heard of the Stalinist terror will shiver upon hearing the word "dictatorship"; whoever has witnessed the horrors of the Cultural Revolution will feel the trembling of his heart upon seeing the word "dictatorship."

At the same time, if we are not merely playing word games, we must take notice of two things:

1. The "democratic dictatorship of the people" today is somewhat different from the "dictatorship of the proletariat" of the Marxist-Leninist era. In Marxism and Leninism, the main point of "the dictatorship of the proletariat" is not that it is "democracy for the people," nor is it "dictatorship against their enemies"; rather, the concept refers to a political system created to facilitate the establishment and protection of an economic system based on public ownership. In such a political system, political decision making means unanimity, and administrative power is held by a single party. In essence, this is a form of autocracy. From the Soviet Union to China, from Czechoslovakia to Kampuchea, not a single socialist country has been exempt from the terror that accompanies this kind of autocracy. If, say, the degree of success in the economic reform in any socialist country depends on the degree to which it departs from the Marxist model of ownership and on the degree to which its political system is democratized, then the degree of success in the reform of the political system in all of these countries depends on the degree to which they can escape from the trap of Marxist-Leninist "dictatorship."

2. In present-day China, the "people's democratic dictatorship" still exists as a form of government. And under this form of government, the "legislative assembly" (the National People's Congress) cannot serve any

---

large peasantry. The more expansive term "*people's* democratic dictatorship" permitted peasants, intellectuals, and overseas Chinese to be included in the class exercising political control. The word "democratic" was added to underscore the fact that the people enjoyed democratic rights, while the bourgeoisie were subject to the dictatorship of the people. Thus, in the words of Mao Tse-tung, the "people's democratic dictatorship is a combination of democracy toward the people and dictatorship toward the reactionaries."

real function. . . . In a political environment in which power is not subject to restraint, corruption is a natural and inevitable consequence, and there is no way to get rid of it.

It is apparent that political democratization and economic freedom will necessarily touch on the Four Cardinal Principles. Unless we completely redefine the Four Cardinal Principles (how future society might be labeled we do not care; our objectives, which we do not hesitate to announce, are political democratization and economic freedom), not only will they fail to be levers for the advance of our society, they will also act as four bars blocking our way to progress.

China is facing the danger of being expelled from the world community, which is enough to make every one of us who has still any feeling of self-respect as a Chinese feel ashamed. There is no course open to us except to rise in a struggle for reform. A century has gone by since the Reform Movement of 1898, and it seems we are still stuck at the starting line, trying to change our old ways and make our country strong. I seem to see Tan Sitong, the vanguard of reform, who "drew his sword and sent his laughter into the sky," raising his arms and calling out to this generation: "Burst through the net!"[24]

> —A graduate student in the Law
> Department, Beijing University, May 9
> (*small-character poster at*
> *Beijing University*)

"A 'small handful' of people equals 1.1 billion times 99.9 percent."

Among the hundreds of student posters on campuses were also dozens of posters written by nonstudents. Most nonstudent posters were the work of young teachers; the rest came from a variety of Chinese citizens, not all associated with the schools where the posters appeared. Whether expressions of support for the protestors, self-reflections, or words of advice, such writings were mirrors for the students, a reflection of how they appeared to the outside world. Such views from the outside

---

24. Tan Sitong, a symbol of youthful courage and political conviction, was a young radical activist in the reform movement of the late 1890s which sought to restore Chinese sovereignty (in the face of growing Japanese dominance) through political, educational and philosophical reforms, including the introduction of a reconstituted, new Confucianism. Tan was executed in 1898 at the age of 33 by the Empress Dowager Cixi.

Illustration 3.4. A female student from a Shanghai university stands up to speak to citizens and students gathered in People's Square, the site of large rallies in Shanghai. Relatively few female students assumed leadership roles in student organizations. Credit: Tristan Mabry.

were supplemented by posters penned by students themselves, purporting to be passing along the reactions of ordinary Chinese with whom they had chatted. Two of the five posters below, "An Exchange of Views with Two Workers" and "Let's Listen to the Words of a Peasant," belong to this category. Although there is no specific reason to question the veracity of these accounts, their authorship should be kept in mind.

APRIL OUTLINE
—My Views on the Present People's Government
and the Student Movement

Age: 30
Education: Master's degree
Profession: stage director

Political situation: Party member

Political belief: communism

Premise of this article: the present student movement and the people's government have become antagonistic.

Basic views:

1. Our government is not a reactionary government. It is the people's government. We support it. But the government needs to be whipped, especially when it does not listen to the voice of the people. Then it should be lashed ruthlessly. The best whip is to take to the streets and demonstrate, for demonstrating is the simplest and most convenient [way of expressing discontent]. You have legs attached to your body, you have a mouth in your face. As you march on the streets, open your mouth and shout out loudly to let the people hear your dissatisfaction with the government.

2. The Party and its members: the Party is the mother and the Party member is the son. The Party and the people: the people are the mother and the Party is the son. In their relationship with the people, the Party and its members are equal. If the Party does not listen, Party members have the right and the duty to stand up and point out where the Party is at fault.

3. When an antagonistic conflict arises between the government and the people, the problem always lies with the government. The people are always correct.

4. Not every aspect of the student movement can be affirmed, but the movement should be affirmed as a whole.

5. In this world, there are no reactionary student movements, there are only reactionary governments. The fomentors of turmoil have always come from the government, not from the students. The government criticizes the students for creating turmoil, a pure reversal of reality. This has been the case without exception in modern and ancient times, in and outside of China.

6. Do not have overly high expectations for this student movement. To deal with a "disturbance" by the students, any government will either adopt deceptive measures (such as insincere dialogue) or resort to bloody suppression. The great significance and historical value of the student movement cannot be based on whether or not it attains a complete and thorough victory.

At this time, I am neither a student nor a teacher. I am much less a government official. In this movement, I play the role of a "third party." I

swear on my conscience that I am not partial to any side. But I saw everything with my own eyes, I felt everything myself, I experienced everything.

What I saw was real, what I felt was vivid, what I experienced was
extraordinarily profound. I thus arrived at my own true judgments and
thoughts, which perhaps do not accord with the wishes of the Party, the
government, or the students. However, they reflect the truth in my heart.

Since the Party asks that I tell the truth and the students abhor lies, I
am going to speak only the truth. . . .

[Sir Francis] Bacon, the great thinker of eighteenth-century England,
told the people that whenever the citizens bear a grudge against the government, no matter what kind of law the government promulgates or policy it formulates, whether good or bad, it will not be able to implement
it. Complete opposition by the people is an omen, a sign that the government will collapse. This is not the fault of the people, but the fault of
the government. Looking back over the record of our government, it is
only fair to say that in the past several years, the government, including
the present one, has had many good policies. But the citizens do not see
it this way, for without mentioning rampant official corruption and
skyrocketing prices, the patriarchal system of the Central Committee
bosses and nepotism have enraged the people and stirred them to rise in
protest.

This is not the fault of the Chinese people. The government must examine its conscience and ask itself why the people oppose it!

By demonstrating in the streets and shouting slogans, the students are
actually warning the government of danger, of the fact that the people are
resentful and dissatisfied. This offers the government a chance to make
certain changes before it is too late and to make great efforts to avoid its
collapse. The students' actions are for the benefit of the government; the
government should not confuse good intentions with malicious ones and
should not turn things around by saying that this is a plot that has been
underway for a long time. . . .

If raising the slogans "Oppose profiteering by officials" and "Oppose
corruption," and shouting out "Long live democracy" and "Long live the
people" is not patriotic but rather anti-government, then does this mean
that if one is patriotic, one cannot oppose profiteering by state officials
and corruption, that one cannot desire democracy and embrace the people? And isn't it the case that the government is announcing to the world
that it is despoiled by its officials' profiteering and corruption, that it neither wants to see democracy nor cares about the people? As to the claim

that there are people who have been yelling, "Down with the Communist Party," I think that the government should not make an issue over a few people. To do so is meaningless. The Party should have some self-confidence. If it is doing well, a few bad people will not be able to bring it down. It should be even less afraid of others' rebukes. The Party cannot be overthrown by mere rebukes. . . .

It seems as if the government has never planned to apologize to the people. In the past ten years, the silence and submissiveness of the people has fostered an abnormal attitude in the government: "The old man is always correct. How can anyone oppose me? How dare the people not obey me?" Thus, whenever it wants to give the people a lesson, it flies into a rage, never showing the least bit of respect for the people's feelings. Moreover, it never leaves itself a way out, a way to back down [from its extreme position]. Once the people begin to revolt, it becomes even more alarmed and does not know what to do. In a great fury, it rolls up its sleeves, swings its arms, and slaps the people in the face. The April 26 editorial in the Party newspaper was such a slap!

The people's government has lost its self-control!

Now let's see what it will do.

Suppression [of the student movement] is a plunge toward death; recognition of its errors, a move toward new life! . . .

What are "normal channels"? It is not that the people have not gone through normal channels to express their demands. Forty years, alas! Forty years of experience have taught us that "normal channels" have become abnormal and useless. Without even freedom of the press, how can there be normal channels? Today, the people have already arrived at the point described by the Englishman [Bertrand] Russell: they feel extremely fed up with all slow and incremental methods. They are infuriated!

Don't go out to demonstrate?! Can the progress of Chinese history afford to be slowed down even more?! . . .

Premier Li Peng has been wronged. The students have called for Li Peng to come out and meet them several times. It seems as if he has become the target of this student movement. Actually, Premier Li Peng is pretty good. Since he has taken office, he has actually worked sincerely for the people. At least, he thinks he has. But I do not know why he has left such a bad impression on the students. In my view, Li Peng's problem is that he lacks ability and commits mistakes. But in reality, his power is limited. Many things cannot be blamed on him. He is quite pitiful. To be fair, he is a very young man on the political stage.[25] We should encourage him, make more allowances for him. Today those who control the fate of a billion people are neither Li as Premier, nor Secretary General Zhao, but the "senate of elders" composed of the old generation of proletarian revolutionaries and headed by Comrade Deng Xiaoping. The entire root of our problems is right here. Students, don't make the wrong ones the targets of your attack.

The elder statesmen have rendered unforgettable service in the liberation of the Chinese people and the building of our nation. But this is history . . . despite its radiance, history cannot illuminate the present, not to mention the future.

Political life should be based on natural life. When one's natural life begins to decline, one's political life should immediately end. The tragedy of China is really that the natural life of the elder statesmen in the "senate of elders" has already declined, but their political life is still vigorous—how vigorous!

China in the eighties of the twentieth century is not Rome and Venice of the sixteenth and seventeenth centuries. There should not be a "senate of elders." Li Peng cannot lie in swaddling clothes in this senate any more. . . .

Suggestion: since the government has made "concessions," we should also make some "concessions." Any negotiation involves conflict, but the objectives of both sides are only attained gradually. The demands of our students can only be achieved step by step; expecting to achieve a complete victory is not terribly realistic.

The government is still our government.

If Li Peng can act like a gentleman and engage in a dialogue with student representatives (representatives of the autonomous federation), then there is some basis for arguing that he is a good premier. If he obstinately refuses to engage in dialogue, well, there is basis for arguing that he is a bad premier!

At present, it is unrealistic to repudiate the leadership of the Communist Party, for there are neither any theoretical nor actual grounds for doing so. Communism will certainly be realized (if the Earth doesn't explode). Only the Communist Party can lead the people toward communism. However, this is an extremely slow and long process. In the lengthy process leading to communism, must the Communist Party always hold

25. Li Peng was sixty-one in 1989; Deng and the "group of elders" that continue to control the Party are octogenarians. Zhao Ziyang was seventy in 1989.

on to political power alone, without interruption? In China, can other political parties be allowed to assume power once or twice?

These questions are indeed worth thinking over.

—XXX, An Observer, April 30
(small-character poster)

THE CONFESSION OF A YOUNG TEACHER

Teachers in China have always been known for their "other worldliness," their "genteel poverty," their "slender" physique and "long-suffering" temperament. In the eyes of the West, however, these epithets merely tell a story of pedantry and impoverished pedagogues, of pale, anaemic faces and weak personalities.

They pass their days conscientiously and quietly, but actually have quite a few complaints. They leave their lives to benevolent or heartless hands, and have little but tears to swallow. They dare neither to be angry nor to speak out. When angry, they do not venture to show it; when voicing their opinions, they watch the reactions of the listener. And they shed tears of gratitude when their superiors ease up a bit. Coming home from work with a rumbling stomach, they sink into deeper depression as they count the coins in their pockets, take a glance at the food on the table and then at their crowded, shabby dwelling. Other things make their hearts sink, too: living apart from their wives or husbands [because their schools have no jobs and no space for their spouses], they prepare late into the night, staring at a solitary lamp to see their own shadow.

And yet, when the critical moment suddenly arrives for him (or her) to become personally involved in the struggle for better living conditions, he will either withdraw into his shell like a snail, lest his face be seen, or esteem himself too other-worldly to "riot" with the students. Now he will put on an air of worldly wisdom, so that his wide experience and profound wisdom will be felt; secretly, however, he is hoping that the students will go a little further this time and put more pressure on the government. "That way," he thinks to himself, "the government might raise my salary, which would bring me up two or three steps on the ladder. My wife and child might also join me, perhaps even in a bigger apartment."

This is no normal state . . . this is what lasting suffocation has done to our teachers. There are statistics which show that virtually all teachers pass an existence of varying degrees of repression. You can see it in their faces.

I have been "fortunate" enough to become a teacher myself, and in three years' time, I've learned a great deal. As a colleague, I would like to pose a few questions to our teachers: do you suffer from this kind of complex? Do we, even more than the students, understand the urgency of democracy and freedom, or not? How much democratic consciousness have we communicated to the students in our lectures? As we single-mindedly try to give them knowledge, and as we undertake their political education, is it our aim to let them use the knowledge we give them to create wealth that will fill the pockets of corrupt officials? Isn't today's self-inspired student movement a monumental mockery of the clumsy method of our so-called political education? When the students in the Square were fighting hunger, not only did we fail to send them some kind of warmth; even worse, we lay asleep in our holes. When the students dragged their exhausted bodies back to campus, rather than greeting them with a warm welcome, we just stood on the sidewalks acting like a street crowd. And when the students were shouting "Long live the teachers!" did we cry out "Long live the students!"? As mentors for the students, we, the whole bunch of us, cannot even be compared with those old ladies by the side of the street who give their popsicles to the students. The hearts of our teachers are colder and harder than those popsicles. Take a look at those poor students—hungry, cold, sleepy, and exhausted—they still knelt down in front of the Great Hall of the People for half an hour! Their sincerity does not entertain doubt or abuse. Granted that they were a bit immature, perhaps—all the more should we have given them a hand, instead of leaving them there, alive or dead. Is it their lot to be beaten up, to shed blood, and ours to sit tight and wait to benefit from their gains? Now, if you do think that the students are just "making trouble," whose fault is it when your students make mistakes? It is you who live off salaries and who have produced this bunch of "troublemakers." Little wonder that people do not take us seriously. We have taken such pains to give the students a proper political education, which is now all gone in a second to God knows where. It would be only fair if Old Man Deng [Xiaoping] decided to jail this bunch of teachers and give them a good flogging!

Faced with the simple, selfless, almost childish enthusiasm of the students, I feel ashamed! Before them, I no longer feel that I am their teacher, but their student. Really, it should have been us to awaken the democratic spirit in their hearts. Instead, it is the students who have awakened us. Indeed, compared with theirs, our longing for democracy hardly comes out as sincere and ardent. They dare to laugh or cry; they are brave enough to love and to hate; they are not at all inhibited from letting their tears flow. When it comes to us, the so-called "profound" teachers, we look as though we wear a rubber mask, unable to laugh or cry, and incapable of showing emotions. Ours is a numb and indifferent face, pale and lifeless from "anaemia," typical of the pedagogue.

For the past three years, I thought I had matured. It is only during this student movement that I am beginning to realize that my mind and my heart have aged rapidly, that I have become versed in the ways of the world. As though afflicted by a virus, I also carry the air of a self-indulgent pedagogue—a pretty disgusting sight that makes one puke. Though only twenty-six years old, my heart has ceased to be young. The blood vessels of my heart harden each day; before long, I will be suffering from arteriosclerosis.

Nowhere could I have found and regained the passion of my youthful years, had it not been for the students whose ardent slogans plucked the dusty, spent strings of my heart. As I stood among the ranks of the students, hand in hand, and sang the "Internationale," my eyes could not help but brim with tears. The many years of frustration and dejection now erupted, as though a stone were lifted from the opening of my heart. What relief!

Now the older teachers might still grumble that I am still too immature. But to these older teachers, I have my advice to offer: don't be too hard with your lives. Don't you now enjoy disco dancing, the same disco which, only a couple of years ago, you thought would bring the end of the world? Why repress what you were born with? Why devastate yourselves? Is our life not bitter enough already? Overloaded with work, taking a minimal salary, undernourished, with numerous difficulties in earning a livelihood—you name it. Can we do nothing but depend on our students to strive on our behalf for improved conditions? Having advanced in years or lacking the vigor and impulse of youth are no excuses for letting our minds age. We should look up to the example of Mr. Hu [Yaobang], who was "an old man but young at heart" and who was always full of youthful vigor, and act as understanding friends of youth. Our knowledge, our years, and our experiences bid us take a stand ahead of our youth; they bid us always to remember that we are teachers, we are mentors, and that we have a responsibility to take our students by the hand, to lead them, instruct them, and protect them. When they act wrongly, we should criticize them, but when they have done the right thing, we must do all we can to support them. It is time that we teachers changed our image. Just think how Lu Xun [the famous writer] treated his students! It is time that we ceased to be weak personalities and "wise" pedagogues.

Let us tighten the strings of our hearts. Let us apply fresh rosin to the strings that once played the song of youth. Together with our students, we will carry forth the spirit of the May Fourth Movement. Let us begin ourselves to exercise true socialist democracy.

Give us science! Give us education! Let us invite democracy and freedom to settle down in the land of China!

> —A Young Teacher Who Knows What
> Shame Means, April 29
> (big-character poster)

OFFICIALS FROM THE PUBLIC SECURITY BUREAU, THE PROCURATORATE, THE COURTS, AND THE MINISTRY OF JUSTICE SUPPORT THE JUST ACTIONS OF OUR STUDENTS

Over the last several days, we have heard and seen with our own ears and eyes the determined, just actions the university students of the capital have taken to push forward democratization—acts that move us to song and tears. Deeply moved and inspired, we extend to the students on this occasion our most sincere respect.

Students, believe us, all officials from the judicial administration departments [such as the courts, the Public Security Bureau, and the Procuratorate] who possess minds, who possess a sense of justice, who have a desire to see China develop and prosper, will not blindly follow the baton of rigid thinking opposed to the people so that we become your antagonists.

Due to the particular circumstances [of our work and our sensitive positions], it is not yet appropriate for us to act in the same way that you have and become involved in this powerful, sweeping movement. But we absolutely will not act against the tide of history, nor will we passively just sit and watch [your struggle]. Already, reporting the situation faithfully, we have informed our colleagues about your program, slogans, and actions; we have also used whatever means we can, given our situations, to show support for you.

Without any qualms, we cast our lot with you—the outstanding heroes of our time who, for the sake of building a democratic and prosperous

Illustration 3.5. Posters cover the walls of a dining hall which stands in the Beijing University "Triangle." The characters at the top warn, "Those who suppress the student movement will definitely come to no good end." Credit: Ren Daren.

new China, bravely throw your lives into the struggle for democracy. History will be a testament to you!

> —Chinese Communist Party
> Members, Officials in Judicial
> Departments
> *(big-character poster at
> People's University, May 3)*

AN EXCHANGE OF VIEWS WITH TWO WORKERS

... I wish here to reveal to you, my classmates, the content of a conversation I had this afternoon [April 29] with two workers. Along the way I will touch on the sincere hopes that citizens, that is to say "the people," have for our patriotic movement.

The two workers are from two different units.[26] They are both college

26. Every individual in China belongs to a "unit" that bears overall responsibility for that

graduates. One of them resigned from a position "bestowed" on him by the government, choosing instead to operate two restaurants on his own. The other is a researcher in a certain scientific research facility. The central topic of our conversation might be called: "the support given to the student movement by citizens and workers"—that is how it was described by one of the workers. They related several anecdotes as examples. At one of their units, workers were organized to study the *People's Daily* editorial [of April 26]. After reading the editorial, the boss who organized the meeting asked workers to express their views and opinions. The workers then raised a series of questions that he could not answer. Most views were nothing but complaints, of course, over unfairness in job assignments, long work days, the low level of social welfare, the insecurity or even impossibility of workers' receiving continuing education, and so forth and so on. The boss—a low-level cadre in the Party—listened to the workers' complaints and expressed his sympathy, "Never mind all of you, even we are dissatisfied!" (notice the subtle sarcasm).

One of the workers told me that when he went to a meat market to buy some ribs, the shop assistant at the market said that they were saving the ribs to give to college students. When a number of city residents who had also come to buy ribs heard this they said, "Well, then give them the ribs. They need the nourishment." This worker also said that he hoped students would go to all units and collect contributions because it would certainly be a success. The workers are all waiting for us. He also added that all the workers in his unit said the same things and are waiting for us to come.

He told me, "Students, your actions have been recognized by all of the society. The people hope that you can carry through with this movement. Don't give up half way, or the people will be disappointed. What you lose will then be even more. The government lost the support of its people long ago. If, in the course of this struggle, even a drop of the students' blood is shed, workers throughout the city will unite and express our opposition—even to the point of going on strike."

---

person and maintains a dossier on him or her. The unit, which may be a factory, a school, a government organ or office, or a neighborhood organization (in the case of the very young and elderly), assigns its members housing, issues identification cards, makes job assignments (including approval of a transfer to another unit), distributes grain coupons, and so on. In the biggest factories or offices, the unit is virtually a self-contained community. In recent years, the importance of the unit has declined slightly, as economic reforms have created a new class of self-employed entrepreneurs and increased job mobility, allowing a limited number of Chinese to become less economically dependent on their work unit.

Finally, the two workers repeatedly urged me to convey the outcries of citizens and the aspirations of workers to all dedicated young people. Workers hope that we will explore theoretical problems and use our minds to break through the scheming and deception of the government.

When we separated, the two workers once again gave us the "V" [victory] hand signal and, raising clenched fists, shouted, "The people will thank you, history will remember you. Fight! Be resilient! Victory belongs to you. Victory belongs to the people."

—A Revolutionary from the Foreign
Languages Department of Beijing
Normal College, April 29
(poster at Beijing Normal
College)

LET'S LISTEN TO THE VOICE OF A PEASANT

A few days ago, this writer made a short trip to the outskirts of the city. On the train, I met a peasant from Nanpi County in Hebei Province who had come to Beijing to seek medical treatment. We talked for two hours. The following are the main points of what we talked about.

Graduate Student [hereafter GS]: Where are you from? Why did you come to Beijing?

Peasant [hereafter P]: I'm from Nanpi County in Hebei [Province]. I came to get medical treatment for my child.

GS: Did you see the students' demonstration?

P: I arrived in Beijing on the 2nd of May, so I missed the April demonstrations, but I witnessed the May 4 one. I was staying with a relative in Haidian [the university district]. Having heard on the 3rd that they were going to demonstrate, I went out to the street early the next morning to watch. I saw students from People's University, Beijing Agriculture University, and Beijing University go by, and then I followed them. Along the way, I saw more and more universities represented; aside from students from Beijing schools, a number were from out-of-town ones. I also saw a journalists' group near Tiananmen Square. So reporters are having a tough time too, eh? Along the way there were several hundred thousand ordinary folks. I think they all supported the students, and helped the students to get along with the policemen. According to my relatives, the crowd was even bigger on the 27th of April. I was really surprised.

GS: What do you think of this demonstration?

P: Government officials these days are ridiculous; they've made a complete mess of the country. In the past, people didn't dare to speak out, but now they do. I completely agree with what the students' slogans say. These students are terrific. They poke right at the sore points of the government officials. It made me feel that I had let out my own anger! I heard that before the previous demonstration a number of students wrote their wills. They are all very young. They don't have any other intention than to speak for the people, and to try to improve the country's situation. To tell you the truth, at that time I cried.

(At this point, the peasant became choked up and on-lookers sighed with emotion for quite a while.)

GS: How is your life now?

P: I am just barely hanging in. It was very good during the first three years of the reform [in the early 1980s]. I was netting 3,000 yuan a year, but now I'm only making 2,000. Though it's only a 1,000 less, the money then was worth five times more. The newspapers are always reporting that the reforms are bringing material benefits to the peasants. This was true a few years ago, but not any more. Recently, the standard of living has gone down quite a bit. My second child is sick, and this has cost me 3,000 yuan, which is several years of my savings.

GS: How would you rate the economic status of your family in the area where you live?

P: We are among the better-off. I'm very healthy and I can work hard.

GS: At present how much do you invest in your land every year?

P: About 100 yuan per mu [approximately 1/6 of an acre]. The prices for production inputs have doubled; if I could just maintain the same level as that of the previous years, that would be O.K. Originally fertilizer imported from the U.S. was 20 yuan per sack, but now it has gone up to 50 yuan. Some of the fertilizer was even adulterated. Pesticides have also gone up, and there are a lot of fake ones. Someone in the village attempted to commit suicide by taking pesticides but because the pesticide was fake the person did not die. Our town produces cotton. In the past we sprayed pesticides at most three times a year, but now there are many fake ones, so we have to spray seven to eight times. And the insects aren't afraid of the pesticide anyhow. Aside from this, the cost of electricity is also high. The price of diesel oil is high too, and you can't get it at the state price but only at the free market price of over 8 mao [80 Chinese cents] per liter.

GS: In the countryside at present, is it the case that if a person's educational level is higher, he can make more money?

P: Yes.

GS: Is it convenient for students to go to school in your town?

P: It's all right. Zhang Zhidong, a high-level military strategist of the Qing dynasty came from our county, and he built a middle school for his home town. It's really pretty decent.

GS: Do peasants often read the newspaper?

P: There are two copies of the newspaper in the village. Because I'm the head of the village, I read one copy, and there's an old man who reads the other. The rest of the people don't bother to read. They say that there is nothing that is true in the newspaper.

GS: Are you saying that the peasants are not concerned at all with current events?

P: We are concerned about them. We are close to the city; whenever someone returns from [the city], everyone will go to his house to find out what was going on outside.

GS: Do you think the students are right?

P: Absolutely right. It's about time to make some noise. The officials are just too much. Right now, township [officials] are not doing anything for production, but every township government has one or two cars, and not a few have sedans. It takes more than 20,000 yuan a year to maintain a car, and this is all at the expense of us peasants.

GS: Do you think it is possible to wipe out [corruption among] government officials engaged in business and profiteering?

P: I think it's pretty tough. County court officials are also not honest. They accept gifts and pull strings. The government is not so great either; the big officials are engaged in big corruption, and the little officials are engaged in small corruption. I think China must go through some big changes. How can a government like this not collapse? "If Qing Fu doesn't die, the crisis in Lu will not end (original words of the speaker)."27

---

27. Qing Fu was an official of the State of Lu in the Spring and Autumn Period (770–476 B.C.) who stirred up much turmoil with his political machinations, which included the murder of two state monarchs. The saying "until Qing Fu is done away with, the crisis in Lu will not be over" today means "unless the prime culprit or chief offender is not eliminated, the country will not see peace."

GS: What kind of government do you think should be established?

P: Presently, nobody can watch over the government. They keep saying that the people supervise [the government], but the people don't have any power (original words)!

GS: Are you trying to say that there should be separation of powers?

P: Right. There should be a three-way division of power (original words).

GS: How old are you now? What is your educational level?

P: I'm 36 years old. I only attended six years of school. But I read the newspaper every day. On this trip to Beijing I even went to Beijing University to read big-character posters.

—Reported by a graduate student, May 6, 1989
(Everything written here is true, the writer is willing to take full responsibility.)

(small-character poster)

Beijing and its universities were quiet for several days following the May 4 demonstration. Students at most campuses had returned to classes, their energy and emotion seemingly spent by the tension and physical strain of the previous three weeks. Yet the decision to end the class boycott had been controversial and had led to yet another change in leadership, if only a temporary one, among the students. More radical student leaders, fearing that the resumption of classes would further drain the already ebbing enthusiasm for marches or demonstrations, argued that the government would not consent to a dialogue on acceptable terms without further pressure. They were backed by significant portions of the student bodies at Beijing University and Beijing Normal University, who refused to end the boycott. They were outnumbered, however, by more moderate leaders who felt that further disruption of their studies was counterproductive and unnecessary; citing Zhao's conciliatory remarks on May 4, they pointed out that the government seemed to be taking earnestly the demand for a dialogue. Further evidence of this was the fact that the country's papers, taking their cues from Zhao, had begun to report the protests more objectively: on May 5, the *People's Daily* ran its first balanced account of the Democracy Movement protests.

To facilitate the arrangement of a dialogue, on May 3 a group of moderate students founded a new student organization, the Students' Dialogue Delegation of Beijing Universities (the "Students' Dialogue Delegation"). By establishing an organization composed of elected representatives from Beijing universities but without any ties to the Beijing Students' Federation, these students hoped to surmount the primary obstacle to a dialogue: the government's hostility toward the Federation. Having labeled the Federation as an illegal organization that had usurped the authority of the official student unions, and fearful that any softening of their attitude toward it would encourage workers and other disgruntled Chinese to form similar political organizations, most Party leaders refused even to consider recognition of the Federation. On May 6, the Students' Dialogue Delegation submitted a petition to the Central Committee, the NPC Standing Committee, and the State Council. Considerably simpler in its terms, and thereby more realistic, than the May 2 petition, this petition set forth only two basic conditions for the dialogue: first, that the students choose their own representatives; and second, that the meeting be broadcast live on television and radio. In remarks to reporters, chairman of the Students' Dialogue Delegation, Xiang Xiaoji of the University of Politics and Law, expressed confidence that the government would reply by the Delegation's May 8 deadline.

During the week of the 4th, moderate government leaders did attempt to find some common ground for a dialogue. What Xiang Xiaoji and other student leaders could not have anticipated, however, was a growing schism in the Party that pitted Zhao and his moderate faction against hard-liners, who included not only Deng, Li Peng, and the Beijing Municipal Party Committee but also the extremely powerful "group of elders"—aged revolutionaries of Deng's generation who dominated Party politics even though they had retired from most posts in the Party or government. Dismayed by Zhao's remarks on the 4th and similar overtures to students during other public appearances, Beijing Mayor Chen Xitong and Beijing Party Secretary Li Ximing accused Zhao at a hastily convened Politburo meeting on May 8 of "betraying" them by implicitly faulting their hard-line approach to the student unrest. An angry Zhao rebuffed them. At about the same time, the "group of elders" also met secretly to discuss Zhao's challenge to the hard-line position. During their meeting (or meetings) this powerful but shadowy group of veteran communists agreed that the April 26 editorial could not be repudiated, thereby guaranteeing that at least one of students' fundamental demands—retraction of the April 26 editorial—would not be met.

The internal discord in the Party rendered impossible a timely government response. On May 8, government functionaries—to date, representatives of neither the Beijing Students' Federation nor the Students' Dialogue Delegation had been received directly by high officials—assured the Dialogue Delegation leaders that the government was planning to initiate "broad contacts with workers, peasants, intellectuals, students, teachers, and persons outside of the Party," but informed them that the government would need until the 11th to give a specific answer to the petition.

Disappointed but not discouraged by the delay, the Students' Dialogue Delegation took advantage of the extra time to prepare for the dialogue they still expected. The following report from the student *News Herald* suggests that they went about this task with organization and care.

A SUMMARY [OF THE ACTIVITIES] OF THE BEIJING STUDENTS' DIALOGUE DELEGATION [AND ITS OBJECTIVES]

In order to facilitate the carrying out of a dialogue between representatives from the Central Committee, the Standing Committee of the National People's Congress, and the State Council and the masses of Beijing university students, student representatives from more than twenty Beijing colleges who were elected through democratic procedures met on May 3 at the University of Politics and Law to establish the Beijing Students' Dialogue Delegation. After its formation, the delegation focused on two tasks: first, it drafted a petition demanding a dialogue addressed to the Central Committee, the NPC Standing Committee, and the State Council. Second, it [did basic preparatory work] by setting up its organizational structure, holding discussions at the University of Politics and Law regarding the contents of the dialogue, conducting interviews with several dozen news agencies from China and abroad, and gathering the opinions of people from all walks of life throughout China.

At the May 3 organizational meeting, the representatives from the various colleges democratically recommended that representative Xiang Xiaoji from the University of Politics and Law and representative Shen Tong from Beijing University serve as the conveners for delegation meetings. On May 5, three topical groups were formed within the delegation, and the conveners appointed a core member for each group based on people's interests and background.

The first group's focus of discussion is the current student movement. . . . The second group's focus is how to carry out further reform. . . . The third group's focus is Article 35 of the Constitution [the right of Chinese citizens to freedom of speech, of publication, assembly, and so on]. . . .

Beginning on May 6, the topical groups [of the delegation] held discussions for three consecutive days. A summary of these discussions follows:

In the first group's discussion, the representatives unanimously agreed that . . . the basic causes of the movement are the lag between reform of the political system and reform of the economic system, and the lack of continuity and stability in economic reform policies. . . .

The second topical group focused on the issue of reforms [needed by

China]. Members of this group thought the system of lifetime political appointments, autocratic rule, profiteering by officials, [other] corruption, and various other crises were the manifestation of defects in [China's political and economic] structures. All of the representatives thought that during the dialogue with the Central Committee and the government emphasis should be placed on several concrete issues in order to assist in a practical way the Central Committee and government in carrying out economic and political reform.

The third topical group focused on the citizens' three basic rights—freedom of association, freedom of speech, and freedom of demonstration—provided in Article 35 of the Constitution. The group would like to hold a dialogue with the Central Committee, the State Council, and the NPC Standing Committee to discuss three issues: the legal status of the Beijing Students' Federation; correcting the erroneous treatment of Qin Benli, the editor-in-chief of the *World Economic Herald*, by the Shanghai Party Committee; and the abolishment or amendment of Beijing's Ten Articles on Marches and Demonstrations. . . .

> —News Herald reporter
> *(published in student* News Herald *No. 3,*
> *May 12, 1989)*

"We Want to Speak the Truth; Don't Force Us to Cook Up Stories"

The Shanghai authorities' heavy-handed intervention in the *World Economic Herald* had effectively stifled a major forum of liberalism, but at the high price of propelling many journalists and editors into the pro-democracy protests. In Shanghai, staffers of the *Herald* had drafted an open letter rebutting in detail the Shanghai Municipal Party Committee's account of the sequence of events that had necessitated their actions. Journalists joined the chorus of protests by sending telegrams to the Shanghai Party Committee. On May 3, nearly one hundred members of the press representing approximately thirty media organizations met in Beijing to discuss the preparation of a letter demanding that the Central Committee reinstate Qin Benli and recall the "rectification group" now supervising the paper, as well demanding that the government open a dialogue with journalists. Anger over the *World Herald* matter broadened into a general protest for press freedom on May 4, when an estimated three to five hundred journalists and editors from the nation's leading papers, including the *People's Daily*, the *Worker's Daily*, the *Peasant's Daily*, and the *Guangming Daily*, formed a contingent that joined the mass student march, marking the May Fourth Movement in Beijing. Marching behind banners that proclaimed, "A

Press Blackout Doesn't Help Stability," "Strengthen Supervision [of the Government] by the Press, Push Forward with Political Reform," and "Our Pens Can't Write the Articles We Want to Write, Our Mouths Can't Say the Words We Want to Say," the journalists were warmly applauded by spectators and citizens as they moved toward Tiananmen. Their appearance on the streets of Beijing was historic: never before in the history of the People's Republic of China had members of the press openly protested against the government. It also was a shot in the arm for student activists, a heartening indication that the student movement was on its way to becoming a broad-based movement.

Yet apparently the rising tide of opposition to government censorship did not deter the Shanghai Municipal Party Committee, which was in all likelihood acting with the direct approval of hard-line Politburo members or Deng himself, from additional action against the *Herald*. It forced the *Herald* to remove from its May 8 issue a box containing the text of the following protest telegram by the China World Economics Association. But this proved not to be enough; the entire issue was subsequently suppressed. The *Herald*'s staff would continue to report to work for approximately another month, but no further issues would be printed. After the suppression of the Democracy Movement the *Herald* would be completely shut down.

TELEGRAM TO THE SHANGHAI MUNICIPAL PARTY COMMITTEE

Comrade Jiang Zemin of the Shanghai Municipal Party Committee:

Our association has learned from the April 28 issue of the *People's Daily* that the "Shanghai Municipal Party Committee has decided to reorganize the *World Economic Herald*, has relieved chief editor Qin Benli of his duties, and has assigned a reorganization and guidance working group to the paper. Comrade Qin Benli was appointed by this association and the Shanghai Academy of Social Sciences to manage the affairs of the *World Economic Herald*. A decision to relieve him of his duties should be made only after the persons in charge at this association and the Shanghai Academy of Social Sciences have been consulted on this matter. This association is of the opinion that the above decision of the Shanghai Municipal Party Committee violates the spirit of the work report of the Party's Thirteenth Party Congress (that the Party must operate within the limits of the Constitution and the law, among other points), and does not follow the legally stipulated procedures for the appointment and removal of state cadres. The Shanghai Municipal Party Committee does not have the power to relieve the chief editor of the *Herald* of his duties. For this reason, the Shanghai Municipal Party Committee's decision is without legal effect. Our association raises this serious matter with the Shanghai Municipal Party Committee and requests that the Shanghai Municipal Party Committee revise its decision.

> Respectfully,
> The China World Economics
> Association, May 4, 1989
> *(telegram publicly
> circulated)*

Journalists signalled their determination to pursue the issue of freedom of the press by submitting on May 9 a petition with over one thousand signatures of newspersons to the All-China Journalists' Association, the official body representing journalists—which, like all government-established associations or unions, in reality functioned to ensure the propagation of Party policies. Many of the country's major dailies carried reports mentioning the petition; some of the papers, however, did not elaborate on the reasons behind the reporters' grievances.

MAY 9 PETITION OF CHINESE JOURNALISTS

To the Secretariat of the All-China Journalists' Association:

In accordance with the spirit of the recent remarks [at a news conference] by the spokesman of the State Council, in which it was said that "dialogue can be at all levels," and that dialogue would contribute to "the free flow of thinking and increased understanding," we feel it is imperative to have a dialogue about recent events in the press world with those in the Central Committee responsible for propaganda [and media] matters. [The dialogue should address the following specific issues:]

1. The reorganization of the Shanghai *World Economic Herald* and the dismissal of its chief editor Qin Benli.

2. For a period of time following the death of Hu Yaobang on April 15, due to various restrictions, Beijing news organizations could not comprehensively, fairly, or accurately report the news. In addition, there were some irregularities that appeared in some news reports. These factors resulted in damage to the public's perception of Chinese journalism at home

Illustration 3.6. Satire at Beijing University. The heading at the top states: "Demand for Transparency." The words on the right read: "The Communist Party's Bikini: One Center and Two Fundamental Points." (The One Center and Two Fundamental Points is a Party policy announced in 1988 in which the Center is focused on economic construction, and the Two Fundamental Points are the two policies of adhering to the Four Cardinal Principles and adhering to China's policy of reform and opening up.) The words on the left read: "The Press World's Fig Leaf: Many Different Layers, but All Cut from the Same Cloth."

and abroad. We feel that the various restrictions placed on Beijing news organizations after this major event contravened the basic principle of "letting the people know about important events" expressed in the report of the Thirteenth Party Congress.

3. Yuan Mu, State Council spokesman, said at the dialogue with Beijing university students on April 29, "Our country's news reporting is carried

out under a system in which chief editors are in charge of their papers. Our press is free." We think that these statements are seriously at variance with the actual situation of Chinese journalism.

We hope that we can carry out a dialogue in the near future about the above issues with the comrades in the Central Committee responsible for news and propaganda; with Rui Xingwen, Secretary of the Central Committee Secretariat; with Wang Renzhi, Minister of the Ministry of Propaganda; and Du Daozheng, head of the Party's News and Publishing Department.

We request that the Secretariat of the Journalists' Association pass this request on to the Central Committee.

Respectfully,
(signatures of over 1,000 journalists)

Concerned that the government's stalling had taken the fire out of the student movement, Beijing Students' Federation leaders Wang Dan and Wuer Kaixi seized on the journalists' budding drive for freedom of the press as a new cause. On May 9, however, they were unable to muster more than a thousand students for protests in support of journalists outside the All-China Journalists' Association and the *People's Daily* offices—an event that prior to the movement would certainly have received significant attention was taken instead as an indication that students were weary of demonstrating. The next day, though, in a uniquely Chinese style of demonstrating ten thousand students jumped on their bicycles and rode through Beijing in procession. The two-wheeled protest drew attention anew to the student movement; however, for the first time, some Beijing residents appeared to resent the traffic snarls caused by the protestors.

Mikhail Gorbachev's scheduled arrival in Beijing on May 15 for meetings that were to symbolize the reconciliation of the world's two largest Communist powers after nearly thirty years of often bitter rivalry had become by May 10 a matter of some concern to government and Party leaders. Reports that Beijing University students had sent a telegram to the Soviet leader inviting him to speak at the University were probably not overly alarming; few could have believed that Gorbachev, the consummate politician, would offend his Chinese hosts by accepting the invitation. The possibility of embarrassing demonstrations during the summit meeting must have been more troubling. Yet, despite all the incentives for responding to the students promptly, the conflict between Zhao's moderate faction and the hard-line faction prevented the Party from reaching an agreement on the type of response to be given the students. On May 11, the date of the extended deadline, the government informed the Students' Dialogue Delegation that it was still preparing its response and would give the students its decision by the end of the week.

Students' reaction to the latest delay was mixed. Many, such as the Dialogue Delegation chairman, Xiang Xiaoji, encouraged by the fact that the government had not challenged the legitimacy of the Dialogue Delegation, evinced optimism that a dialogue was only around the corner. More radical classmates, though, suspected that the government was only buying time and would not sit down to talk with them on an equal basis unless additional pressure were brought to bear. Finally on May 12 a concrete reply came from the government. But as the poster below indicates, what the government offered was too little, and too late.

STATEMENT BY THE STUDENTS' AUTONOMOUS UNION OF THE PEOPLE'S UNIVERSITY OF CHINA ON THE GOVERNMENT'S ANSWER TO THE REQUEST FOR A DIALOGUE

On the evening of May 12, the Central Committee, the Standing Committee of the NPC, and the State Council finally announced their "Answer to the [Students' Request] for a Dialogue." The "Answer's" main contents are as follows:

1. next Monday (May 15), an informal discussion meeting (and not a dialogue) will be held;

2. the number of student representatives is to be limited to twenty;

3. only leaders of various ministries and commissions will decide whom to appoint as the representatives of the government;

4. only a partial news report of the informal discussion meeting will be permitted;

5. the students must deliver a list of their representatives to the government by 10:00 a.m. May 13 (today).

The contents of this "answer" amount to nothing but a rerun of the April 29 "informal discussion-dialogue meeting" which Yuan Mu and others single-handedly engineered, and a repetition of their cheap tricks. This response of the authorities only shows that they do not possess even the most minimal sincerity toward the students' urgent demand for a real dialogue between equals! As for the cries for democracy and freedom, the authorities persist in their own ways, turning a deaf ear to these pleas.

The Student's Autonomous Union of People's University vehemently protests the attitude of the government!

As all know too well, from the April 29 "informal discussion-dialogue
meeting" on, the government has time and again put off answering our
classmates' calls for a dialogue. On May 5, the Beijing Students' Federation [sic] submitted a petition [with conditions for a dialogue]. The government declared that it would give an "answer" by May 8; subsequently,
declaring that it "needed to continue thinking over the matter," it pushed
the date for its "answer" up to May 11. But then last week there was no
such answer. It was not until yesterday, May 12, that it concocted the
above so-called "answer." This despicable approach of the government,
which views major affairs of the state as trifling matters, is a fraud on the
people of today, and it brazenly sets the government in direct opposition
to the people!

... What makes people angry is that the authorities persist in their
rigid, hard-line attitude toward this patriotic movement that enjoys such
immense popular support. It is impossible for the people to refrain from
asking: where, where is the sense of mission toward country and people,
and sense of conscience of those officials way up on high?

Youth of passion, rise up once more!

We once again solemnly declare: we vehemently protest this "answer"
of the authorities which is totally devoid of sincerity!

—Students' Autonomous Union of
People's University, May 13
(poster at People's University)

4

THE HUNGER STRIKE

"Fellow Countrymen! All Fellow Countrymen

of Conscience! Please Listen to Our Cry!"

May 13 – May 19

"Deng Xiaoping, My Son Is Going Hungry—
What Is Your Son Up To?"
banner of citizen protestors

"Satellites Have Already Reached Heaven,
but Democracy Is Still Stuck in Hell"
banner of researchers from the Chinese Academy of Sciences

"Without Freedom, What Use Is Knowledge?!"
banner of intellectuals

"The April 26 Editorial Wasn't Written by Us"
banner of reporters

"We Can No Longer Be Silent"
*citizens' and workers' banners on sixth day
of students' hunger strike, May 18*

"Big Brother Has Come"
banner of workers

T he latest delay doomed the careful efforts of the moderate Students' Dialogue Delegation to open a dialogue with the government. Hard-core activists among the students, all along skeptical of the government's sincerity,
could not be held back any longer. Word spread through Beijing that a small group
of students was preparing to begin a hunger strike. The following words of Chai
Ling, an intense, emotional twenty-three-year-old graduate student at Beijing Normal University who would reluctantly become the leader of the student occupation
of Tiananmen, give a glimpse into the feelings of the more militant students who
initiated the hunger strike, as well as the transformation of a nonpolitical young
woman into a passionate student leader.

TAPED INTERVIEW WITH STUDENT LEADER
CHAI LING IN LATE MAY
(excerpts)

On the day of May 4, we once again held a large march. We also released
a declaration declaring that a new movement for democracy and enlightenment had commenced in China. But we had not anticipated that the
day would turn out so badly, that a classmate, acting in his capacity as
a standing committee member of the Beijing Students' Federation, would
unexpectedly announce that after May 4 students would go back to class.
Many classmates were very disappointed. The announcement of our resumption of classes set back [what by then had become a] nationwide
student movement a great deal. Some classmates, upset at the decision,
said that the kind of opportunity we had at the time was something that
even several hundred million American dollars couldn't buy, but with one
sentence uttered by certain people, it was unexpectedly thrown away.
Subsequently, the student movement lost momentum; more and more
students were returning to classes. Arguments over whether we should
return to class or continue the class boycott consumed a lot of the student
movement's time and resources, and the situation was getting more and
more difficult. We felt then that we had to undertake a hunger strike. At
the time, [some] people from the Beijing Students' Federation desperately
tried to dissuade us, but we stood our ground. At the time, there was little
common ground between different groups of classmates.

   In the evening of May 12, I saw a list of students [who had signed up
for the hunger strike]. There were only forty-odd students who had signed
up. We posted the list at the "Triangle" at Beijing University, writing on

197

it a few words: "Send off the warriors." I was very depressed and upset at the time [by the small number of people who had signed up for the hunger strike]. I said, "My hunger strike is for the purpose of seeing just what the true face of the government is, to see whether it intends to suppress the movement or to ignore it, to see whether the people have a conscience or not, to see if China still has a conscience or not, if it has hope or not."

The next day, two hundred—perhaps it was four hundred—classmates signed up at Beijing University. There were also some students from Beijing Normal University among those committed to the hunger strike. That day, we solemnly took an oath in a moving ceremony, tying red headbands around our heads, and writing on the front side of our clothes, "Democracy, Hunger Strike," and on the back side, the character for "Grief" in very large handwriting. Others wrote: "I dedicate myself to my country, but my powers are limited." I also wrote a hunger pledge and made a thousand tapes [of it]. That day, many teachers came to send us off; they also invited us for a last meal. That day, my heart was so heavy. I felt extremely sad; I couldn't swallow a thing. Some teachers specially went far away to buy several large plates of wonton [Chinese dumplings in soup]. I said one sentence then: "With the spirit of the sacrifice of our lives, we fight for life. Death is not what we seek but we contemplate death knowing that the eternal, broad echoes [of our cries] and the cause that we write with our lives will float in the air of the Republic.". . .

I wanted to live a very peaceful life with children and small animals all around. I am not a person who is terribly vain or utilitarian. At the time I got married, the conditions we lived in were very simple and rough, but we very naturally passed a peaceful and serene life. We really lived under difficult circumstances; many people around us were making money [through various means and business deals], but we weren't interested in making money just for the sake of making money. We were involved in our research and study; we all along believed that through knowledge the country could be saved. Then on April 22 [the day of Hu Yaobang's memorial service], I felt some kind of conscience stirring. We were striving for a share of power; we very much felt like telling every worker, Beijing resident, intellectual, even the plainsclothesmen and soldiers: in the share of power that we students were working so hard for, there was also a share for them! If I had not participated in the struggle for this kind of power, and then when it arrived I had said, "Give me a share!" I would have felt very ashamed. I am not capable of doing that kind of thing. I believe fate has decreed that I play this type of role. As long as you have a conscience, you will stand up and step out. . . .

(taped interview)

If we do not achieve our goal, we will not give up!

The last-minute appeal by Chai Ling and her fellow activists for support of the hunger strike worked beyond their expectations. As a groundswell of support for the strike grew, the Beijing Students' Federation endorsed the strike and threw its resources into the strike. On Saturday afternoon, May 13, approximately two thousand students marched or bicycled from Beijing University and Beijing Normal University to Tiananmen to commence the hunger strike. They settled down in groups organized by school in front of the Monument to the People's Heroes on sheets of plastic, clothes, and newspapers that provided little insulation from the hard cement of the Square. The hunger strikers were soon encircled in a protective ring by thousands of students who had come to show their support for their classmates. A small delegation of students also traveled to the gate of the Soviet Embassy to submit an open letter inviting Mikhail Gorbachev to speak at Beijing University. (The invitation would eventually be politely declined.)

Primarily undergraduates from some ten different Beijing universities, the hunger strikers included a sizable number of female students; in previous demonstrations and sit-in protests at the Square, female students had been vastly outnumbered by male classmates. Emotional but clear-headed, these youths saw the hunger strike as a last moral test for the government as much as a pressure tactic carefully timed to win concessions. Compelled to participate in the hunger strike by a strong sense of duty to their country, many of the hunger strikers also felt they were betraying another duty—their obligation to their parents. Despite rapidly changing social mores, the bond between parent and child in China remained strong. Chinese mothers and fathers still thought nothing of making great sacrifices for their children, and in turn, children assumed they would support their parents in their old age.

The statement circulated by the hunger strike group from Beijing University, one of the largest contingents, and other hunger strike documents are presented below.

HUNGER STRIKERS' STATEMENT

In this bright, sunny month of May, we are hunger striking. In this moment of most beautiful and happy youth, we must firmly leave all of life's happiness behind us. We do this ever so unwillingly, ever so un-happily!

Yet [we must do so], for our country has already reached a time when prices are soaring, profiteering by officials runs rampant, power politics hangs high, and the bureaucracy is corrupt. It is a time when large numbers of patriotic, upstanding Chinese willing to devote themselves to the bet-terment of their motherland [instead] live in self-imposed exile overseas, and when social order and public security deteriorate day by day. At this vital juncture of the survival or demise of our people, fellow countrymen, all countrymen of conscience, please listen to our cry!

> This country is our country,
> Its people are our people,
> The government is our government,
> If we do not cry out, who will?
> If we do not act, who will?

Even though our shoulders are still soft and tender, even though death seems to us too weighty, we have gone—we could not but go. History asks this of us.

Our purest feelings of patriotism, our simple and complete innocence, have been called "turmoil," have been described as "ulterior motives," and have been alleged to have been "exploited by a small handful of peo-ple."

We wish to ask all true Chinese citizens, to ask each worker, peasant, soldier, city resident, intellectual, noted figure, government official, po-liceman, and those people who have concocted these accusations against us to place your hands on your hearts, and ask your consciences what crimes we have committed. Are we creating turmoil? Why, after all, are we boycotting classes, are we demonstrating, are we hunger striking, are we giving up our lives? Time and time again our feelings have been ma-nipulated; we endure hunger, we pursue truth, yet we have met with ma-licious beatings at the hands of the army and police. . . . Student represen-tatives have fallen on their knees asking for democracy; they have been seen, but ignored. Our demands for a dialogue of equals have been put off repeatedly. Student leaders face danger.[1]

---

1. At several times in the student movement before the students began the hunger strike, student leaders such as Wang Dan and Wuer Kaixi went into hiding after hearing reports that authorities were on the verge of arresting them.

What are we to do?

Democracy is the highest aspiration of human existence; freedom is the innate right of all human beings. But they require that we exchange our young lives for them. How can the Chinese people be proud of this? We have gone on a hunger strike because we do not know what else we can do; but in this we will continue.

In the spirit of sacrificing our lives, we fight for life. But we are children, we are still children! Mother China, look earnestly upon your sons and daughters; as hunger mercilessly destroys their youth, as death closes in on them, can you remain indifferent?

We do not want to die; we want to live, to live fully, for we are at life's most promising age. We do not want to die; we want to study, to study diligently. Our motherland is so impoverished; it feels as if we are abandoning her to go die. Yet death is not what we seek. But if the death of one or a few people can enable more to live better, and can make our motherland prosperous, then we have no right to cling to life.

As we suffer from hunger, Papa and Mama, do not grieve; when we part from life, Aunts and Uncles, please do not be sad. We have only one hope, which is simply that we may live better; we have only one request, which we ask you not to forget: death is absolutely not what we seek! [Remember that] democracy is not the affair of a few individuals, that the cause of democracy absolutely cannot be accomplished by a single generation.

To die, hoping for the widest echo, an eternal echo.

He will be gone, his words good and wise; the horse will be gone, its neighs sorrowful.

Farewell, colleagues, take care! He who dies, he who survives, are equally faithful.

Farewell, love, take care! I cannot bear to leave you, yet it must come to an end.

Farewell, mother and father! Please forgive me, your child who cannot be loyal [to the country] and [meet the demands of] filial piety at the same time!

Farewell, people! Please allow us to use this means, however reluctantly, to demonstrate your loyalty.

The vows written with our lives will brighten the skies of the Republic!

—The Entire Body of the Beijing University
Hunger Strikers Group, May 13, 1989
(*handbill, poster*)

HUNGER STRIKE DECLARATION

After the huge, sweeping demonstrations of the past few days, today we are once again at Tiananmen Square, [this time] to carry out our struggle through a hunger strike.

[Our] reasons for hunger striking:

First, to protest the indifferent and cold attitude the government has taken toward the boycott of classes by Beijing students.

Second, to protest the government's foot-dragging in [arranging] a dialogue with the Beijing Students' Dialogue Delegation.

Third, to protest the government's continuing tactic of branding this patriotic, student Democracy Movement as "turmoil," and to protest a series of distorted news reports.

Demands of the hunger strikers:

First, we demand that the government promptly carry out with the Beijing Students' Dialogue Delegation a substantive and concrete dialogue based on the principle of equality of the parties.

Second, we demand that the government set straight the reputation of this student movement, and that it give it a fair and just evaluation, affirming that it is a patriotic student democracy movement.

Time of the Hunger Strike:

Depart [from universities for Tiananmen] at 2:00 P.M., May 13.

Site of the Hunger Strike:

Tiananmen Square.

[Slogans of the Hunger Strike:]

"The student movement is not 'turmoil'! Reverse this verdict at once!"

"Dialogue immediately! We won't allow delay!"

"Hunger strike for the people, there is no other way!"

"World opinion, please give us your support!"

"Democratic forces across the world, please support us!"

—Hunger Strikers at Tiananmen
(*handbill*)

PARTING WORDS [OF A HUNGER STRIKER]

If this time I am unfortunate and die, please do not think that my hunger strike was done from a sudden impulse, or was instigated by "those with beards." I have already passed twenty-one years in this world; it has been Chinese soil that has nurtured me. It has been the people who have given me the opportunity to attend primary school, middle school, and university. . . . Now, when they need me, what reason is there for me not to stand up?!

Perhaps I will not be able to fulfill my filial duty. For thousands and thousands of parents and their children, I have tearfully made the choice to go on this hunger strike. . . .

Since time immemorial, it has been impossible to satisfy the demands of both loyalty [to one's nation] and filial duty to one's parents. Papa, Mama, please understand why your son takes this action!

> —A Hunger Striker Named Yu,
> an unfilial son, May 13, 1989
> *(big-character poster next to
> hunger striker at Tiananmen)*

Despite such dramatic statements of their determination to fast until their demands were met, few students had made any provision for an extended stay in the Square. In their street clothes and without any shelter, they were ill-prepared for the blazing sun that beat down over the vast plaza during the day, when temperatures in the Square climbed to well into the 80s Farenheit, or for the chilling Beijing nights. By Sunday, May 14, the second day of the strike, university teachers, who until then had generally watched the movement sympathetically from the sidelines, were actively throwing themselves into the protest, bringing quilts, umbrellas, and extra clothes to the Square and organizing letter campaigns exhorting the government to agree to the students' demand for a dialogue. Even in its first full day, the powerful emotional appeal of the hunger strike was already evident: tens of thousands of city residents went to the Square, out of both curiosity and sympathy, for a glimpse of the fasting students.

For Zhao Ziyang, who had hoped to calm student unrest with a conciliatory approach, the latest and most extreme pro-democracy protest was a serious setback, threatening not only the Sino-Soviet meeting due to begin in less than forty-eight hours but also his already precarious hold on the balance of power in the Party. In a last-ditch attempt to head off the hunger strike, Yan Mingfu, Secretary of the Central Committee Secretariat and an ally of Zhao, along with other high-level Party leaders, suddenly summoned student leaders to a hastily organized "dialogue" meeting in the afternoon of the 14th. The meeting lasted for three hours, but produced no results or prospect for a compromise under which students would leave the Square. The next selection is one student account of the meeting.

RECORD OF THE ABORTED "MAY 14 DIALOGUE"

On the afternoon of May 14, the Beijing Students' Dialogue Delegation suddenly received a notice from the Central Committee and the State Council that Yan Mingfu, Secretary of the Central Committee Secretariat; Li Tieying, member of the Standing Committee of the State Council [and Minister of the State Education Commission]; the Minister of the Ministry of Supervision; and other government leaders would be meeting with the Dialogue Delegation at 4:30 that afternoon in the auditorium of the [Party's] United Front Department.[2] The Dialogue Delegation, after receiving unequivocal assurance that there would be a live broadcast of the meeting, agreed to attend the dialogue meeting.

After the meeting began, both parties expressed their basic views regarding the recent student movement. The first issue which the Dialogue Delegation raised was that the April 26 *People's Daily* editorial, "We Must Take a Firm Stand Against Turmoil," had to be completely repudiated. The Dialogue Delegation maintained that this editorial was completely mistaken and violated the principles of conscience. They argued that this student movement was a great patriotic movement for democracy, and that the movement had received support from Beijing residents and from citizens across the country.

Not long after the dialogue had begun, representatives of the Hunger Strike Group [a newly formed group whose nucleus consisted of the initiators of the hunger strike], who had come over from Tiananmen Square, requested that they be allowed to read aloud a document of "last words" that they had written for their parents. The reading of these "last words" took place against the sound of weeping from all sides. At this moment, the representatives of the students and citizens outside the gate of the United Front Department sent a message to the meeting that they had received no on-site radio report or live television broadcast of the meeting. As soon as the student representatives [in the meeting] learned of this, they were shocked and immediately asked the government leaders to ex-

2. The students were finally meeting—unfortunately under the wrong circumstances—the kind of high-level leaders that their May 2 petition had set forth as a condition of the dialogue: Yan Mingfu, in addition to being a Secretary (a supervising officer) of the Central Committee Secretariat, the office in charge of day-to-day affairs of the Central Committee, was also head of the Central Committee's United Front Department, which oversees the Party's relationships with Taiwan, the eight democratic parties, and overseas Chinese. Li Tieying, Minister of the State Education Commission, was a member of the Politburo and a Vice Premier.

plain what had happened. After they had made repeated inquiries, the government representatives replied that they could not televise the conference because the equipment and facilities of China Central Television and China Central People's Broadcasting were old, so that Central Television was experiencing technical difficulties in making such a broadcast. Upon hearing this reply, the Dialogue Delegation felt that they had in fact been deceived by the other party and that the dialogue could no longer continue. After consultation between the two parties, an announcement was made that the meeting was adjourned, and the Dialogue Delegation withdrew in protest.

This aroused the concern of the representatives from the intellectual community who were waiting for news about the meeting at the United Front Department. Expressing their good intentions and hope for a successful dialogue, they began urgently mediating between the Dialogue Delegation and the government. They suggested two expedients: (1) that the Central Television broadcast an unedited version of the dialogue meeting that had been pre-recorded after either [that day's] news summary or the evening news; and (2) that the Central Broadcasting immediately broadcast the entire dialogue meeting that had been taped thus far, and turn on the loudspeaker system at Tiananmen so that the students, teachers, and people from all sectors of society who had gathered in the Square to give the hunger strikers their moral support could listen to it. After some discussion back and forth, the government representatives held that the first demand was not realistic, and that second demand was beyond their ability to meet. The mediation thus failed.

At midnight, May 14, the entire body of the Beijing Students' Dialogue Delegation left the United Front Department and headed toward Tiananmen Square to give a report to the students and city residents there. Having listened to their report, both city residents and students approved the Delegation's withdrawal from the meeting and expressed anger at the insincere attitude that the government had shown. The Delegation later reviewed Central Television's news report about the dialogue. After doing so, they maintained that the goverment had deceived the people on at least two points: first, the report said that the Dialogue Delegation and the government had discussed several issues concerning the student movement. In fact, the Dialogue Delegation had raised only one issue [before the meeting ended]—the complete repudiation of the *People's Daily* editorial and a correction of the bad name the government had given the student movement. Second, the report said that the Hunger Strikers' Group left Tiananmen Square [for the United Front Department where the meeting was going on] only after the meeting between the government and the Dialogue Delegation had begun [and was well under way].³ The fact is that the dialogue could not even proceed as planned. The Dialogue Delegation confidently believes that if the government had not gone back on its word, the students would have calmly and coolly left the meeting in an orderly manner. As can be seen here, the real reason and responsibility for the abortion of this meeting lie in the government's lack of sincerity.

The Beijing Students' Dialogue Delegation continues to wish to hold a sincere dialogue with the government, so it may express fully the wishes and demands of the students and the general public.

Long live dialogue! Long live the people!

> —The Autonomous Student Union of
> People's University
> (big-character poster at
> People's University, circa
> May 15, 1989)

Throughout the movement, the government would not be the only party guilty of less than candid reporting of events. The above account of the May 14 meeting neglected to mention that serious differences of opinion among the students themselves had contributed to the meeting's failure. Open conflict among the student leaders had broken out when some had suggested that the hunger strikers heed the pleas of Yan Mingfu to leave the Square, to the dismay of student "hard-liners," many of whom were core figures in the newly created "Hunger Strike Group" composed of all the hunger strikers; the hard-liners adamantly refused to abandon Tiananmen. This May 14 discord foreshadowed the disagreement over tactics that would splinter student solidarity later in the month and eventually result in the ascendancy of the Hunger Strike Group over the Beijing Students' Federation. It was also evidence that, contrary to the beliefs of some foreign observers or the later allegations of the hard-line faction in the government, the students were not pawns of Party moderates (though some of the students apparently would subsequently

---

3. The government account of the meeting, as reported in the *People's Daily* on May 15, states that at 4:00 P.M. the dialogue began, and "when the dialogue had continued to 7:00 P.M., student representatives of the hunger strikers at Tiananmen Square came over to the dialogue site. They asked for a live broadcast of the dialogue. The persons in charge pointed out that technical problems and limitations of the facilities rendered this impossible. The student representatives also had different views about how [and whether] to carry out the rest of the dialogue; thus, it was announced that the meeting would be adjourned."

be influenced by them) or "black hands" whose goal was to foment anti-Party unrest.

Similarly, the influence of prominent members of the Chinese intellectual world on the students appears to have been a subtle and limited one. Although in certain cases intellectuals played the role of informal advisor or role model for student leaders—for example, Li Shuxian, Fang Lizhi's wife, was consulted by Wang Dan for advice prior to the movement, and Liu Xiaobo, an outspoken young teacher of literary criticism and an activist, was much admired by Wuer Kaixi—their influence on the larger mass of students was far more limited, particularly before the last stages of the movement, during which students aligned themselves with Zhao Ziyang's faction and the intellectuals who supported it. Thus, the appeal below from twelve of China's most prominent intellectuals and writers for the students to end their hunger strike, which the the group personally read to the students in the Square, went largely unheeded.

OUR URGENT APPEAL REGARDING THE PRESENT SITUATION

In light of the present situation at Tiananmen Square, we twelve scholars and writers, responding to the call of our conscience and a sense of duty, issue the following urgent appeal:

First, we request that persons in charge of the Central Committee publish a statement announcing that this student movement is a patriotic democracy movement, and that they are opposed to any means whatsoever of "settling accounts after the autumn harvest" [that is, retribution] for those who have participated in the movement.

Second, we hold that the student organizations that have been elected and formed by the majority of students through democratic procedures are legal organizations. The government should recognize them.

Third, we oppose any pretext for the use of violence against the students who are hunger striking in protest; we oppose any form or means of violent action against the students. Whoever acts this way shall be condemned by history.

Dear students, yesterday evening, upon learning the news that you all had gone to Tiananmen Square to begin a protest hunger strike, we all felt extremely upset; we were extremely worried. Since mid-April, you have taken to the streets repeatedly to push forward the processes of democratization and reform in China. In an admirable spirit of selflessness and dauntless determination, you have opened a new era in Chinese history. The people will forever remember the historical contribution you have made today, in the year 1989. But democracy is erected gradually; one cannot expect it to be created in the course of one day. We must be completely clear-headed. There are people who will try their utmost to provoke incidents, to intensify conflict, to make the situation worse, for the purpose of undermining the cause of reform and democratization. In order to [protect the] long-run interests of reform in China, in order to avoid incidents that would harm our cause but help those who oppose us, in order that the Sino-Soviet summit meeting can proceed smoothly, we beg that you make full use of the most valuable spirit of the student movement, the spirit of reason, and temporarily leave the Square.

We are confident you will make a wise judgment about what to do. We solemnly reaffirm that should the government fail to do what we request in the three above points, then we will resolutely struggle on together with you to see that they are realized.

—Dai Qing, Yu Haocheng, Li Honglin, Yan Jiaqi, Su Xiaokang, Bao Zunxin, Wen Yuankai, Liu Zaifu, Su Wei, Li Zehou, Mai Tianshu, and Zhou Tuo[4]
*(as reported by the
Guangming Daily News Service,
May 14, 1989)*

4. This distinguished group included a number of China's best-known liberal intellectuals: Dai Qing, mentioned in Chapter 1, note 18, was a *Guangming Daily* reporter; Yu Haocheng was a legal scholar, former editor of the Masses' Publishing House—one of China's largest publishers—and editor-in-chief of *Legal Studies Journal (Faxue zazhi)*, a leading legal journal; Li Honglin was President of the Fujian Academy of Social Sciences; Yan Jiaqi, former Director of the Institute of Political Science of the Chinese Academy of Social Sciences (CASS); Su Xiaokang, one of the writers of the television essay "River Elegy"; Bao Zunxin, an associate researcher at the Institute of History of the CASS and former editor-in-chief of *Walk Toward the Future*, a series of nonfiction books extremely popular with students and young Chinese intellectuals that frequently explored Western ideas; Wen Yuankai, a professor of chemistry at China Science and Technology University and a rising young star in liberal circles; and Li Zehou, a highly respected philosopher at the Institute of Philosophy of CASS. Prior to the Democracy Movement, these individuals were very active in intellectual circles and regularly contributed to influential papers or journals such as the *World Economic Herald*, published articles or books in Hong Kong, and maintained a wide circle of foreign and Chinese acquaintances. Many led intellectuals' protests during the Democracy Movement and were arrested or forced to flee abroad after the suppression of the movement.

The students had intended neither to disrupt the reception of Mikhail Gorbachev nor to humiliate Deng Xiaoping, but their occupation of Tiananmen in the heart of the highly centralized capital, only several hundred meters away from key sites such as the Great Hall of the People, the Forbidden City, and Zhongnanhai had set in motion forces beyond their ability to control. Anxious to see whether authorities would dare to remove the hunger strikers from the Square by force, crowds in Tiananmen had grown to over half a million by the afternoon of Gorbachev's arrival on May 15. To minimize interference with the welcoming ceremonies for the Soviet head at the Great Hall of the People, the hunger strikers and the cordons of students protecting them had shifted to the opposite side of the Square, away from the Great Hall. Yet they could do nothing about the sheer mass of the crowd surrounding them. Though the crowd was well behaved, the atmosphere a curious mixture of festiveness and concern for the fasters, the Chinese government did not wish to take any chances. Greeted at the Beijing airport in a hastily arranged ceremony, Gorbachev was quickly whisked off to the state guesthouse, a safe distance from Tiananmen, before he had an opportunity to deliver a speech he had prepared. That evening, he was brought to the Great Hall of the People for the state banquet through a series of narrow back lanes, finally entering the Great Hall by an inconspicuous rear entrance. The embarrassment for the Chinese hosts would continue throughout Gorbachev's three-day stay in Beijing: schedules would be juggled, sightseeing visits canceled, and motorcades rerouted. Adding insult to injury, the massive foreign press corps covering the Gorbachev visit had found Tiananmen and its idealistic youth a far more compelling story than the summit meeting, and images of scenes in the Square were transmitted to millions worldwide. On May 16, Deng shook hands with Gorbachev in the Great Hall of the People, ending thirty years of Sino-Soviet estrangement—but the meeting was destined to be reduced to an historical footnote by the unprecedented crescendo of anti-government protest rising from all sectors of Chinese society.

Outside, in the Square, only a few hundred meters from Deng and Gorbachev, the hunger strike continued. But now, four days into the strike, the mood of excitement and optimism in the Square had dissipated. In its place was an air of urgency, of uncertainty tinged with anger. Neither citizens nor students had expected the government to allow the hunger strike to go on for so long. Hundreds of fasters had fainted or fallen ill in the hot, increasingly unsanitary encampment in the Square. Medical assistance was promptly rendered to stricken students on the spot by doctors and nurses from volunteer medical teams, while more serious cases were rushed to hospitals by ambulances waiting near a lane into the center of the Square kept clear by student marshals. Yet medical personnel warned publicly that if the strike did not end, lives would be endangered. Their concerns were heightened by

Illustration 4.1. Student protestors welcomed Mikhail Gorbachev with banners written in Chinese and Russian. This banner in Tiananmen declares "Democracy Is Our Common Ideal." Credit: Han Minzhu.

a spirit of martyrdom that had seized many of the fasters: hospitalized hunger strikers were insisting on returning to the Square to resume their strikes; eleven students from the Central Academy of Drama, lying in a row at the west side of the Square without protection from the sun and clad dramatically in white T-shirts specially designed for their protest, had begun refusing all liquids, even water; and some students were rumored to be threatening self-immolation.

Reflecting the grave events of those days, many of the posters, handbills, and speeches from the time are highly emotional, personal statements. Over and over, students asked parents for their understanding, found nobility in the sacrifice of their classmates, and queried the humanity of their government. The next section presents a small sample of the outpouring of writings that appeared during the hunger strike, as well as another short portion of the late-May interview with Chai Ling that was excerpted previously in this chapter.

献给为民主自由而参加绝食团的青年

人民同在

Illustration 4.2. A poster from Tiananmen Square that reads: "The People Are with You: Dedicated to the youth who are participating in the May 13, 1989, Hunger Strikers' Group for democracy and freedom." Credit: October Review.

THE TIME WILL COME WHEN WE CLEAVE THROUGH THE WAVES: FEELINGS AT TIANANMEN SQUARE

We are several female students in the Chinese Department of Beijing Normal University. In the past five days, the scene at Tiananmen Square has made us see more clearly the nature of the government and human life in general. On the 13th, crying, we sent off our classmates. [Over the last few days, whenever we heard] the heart-rending sound of the ambulance sirens at the Square, we wept anew. Now we have cried ourselves into silence. Faced with this kind of government, we feel that we have left the world of mankind; where is their humanity? On the 15th, when our classmates had already suffered through two nights of cold, still the Central Committee leaders casually strolled into the state banquet hall; do they regard us as human beings? We already hold no illusions whatsoever about this kind of government. On yesterday evening's [television] news summary, our respected and beloved Secretary General of the Central

Committee [Zhao Ziyang] declared to Chinese across the nation that all of the Party's leadership power is held by Deng Xiaoping. We feel that no matter what reasons they may have for their actions, the Secretary General and the Premier, simply from a humanitarian viewpoint, can no longer think about their political position and power but must focus on holding a dialogue with the students. They should realize that today's Chinese are no longer humble people who, when faced with a government that will not listen to their pleas, only know enough to kill themselves in grief by ramming their heads against the pillars of the halls of the imperial court [as officials did in the past when emperors rejected their appeals]. We will have our own victory. How can they only think of the Hungarian Incident [the 1956 invasion of Hungary by Soviet troops], the Prague Spring, Polish history? We maintain: now is the time of their awakening. The time will come when we cleave through the waves. We await it.

> —Chinese Department, Class of 1985, Dorm Room XXX, May 17, 9:50, at the Square[5] (*printed in* News Bulletin *No. 7 of the Beijing Normal University Hunger Strikers' Petition Group*)

"FAREWELL": AN OPEN LETTER TO MY RELATIVES

Dear Papa, Mama, and Brother:

How are you!

Today I, together with all the teachers and students who have remained at Tiananmen Square, and millions of people of the capital, pledged to the people of the entire country and the entire world: "We shall sacrifice our blood and lives in exchange for freedom and democracy, and for the bright future of the Republic! What a glorious moment it was! What a magnificent sight! Had you been present, you would certainly have been overcome by the intense emotion of the "Pledge to Struggle to the Death" of our students and the great mass of people of the capital. You certainly would have! This is a new historic milestone for the People's Republic!

5. According to Chinese custom, classes are designated by the year in which they commence studies. Thus, in the spring of 1989, members of the class of 1985 were seniors.

Since the hunger strike began on May 13, I have been fighting [for our demands] at Tiananmen Square (almost) every day; perhaps due to my weak nature, I didn't have enough courage to join the ranks of the hunger strikers. However, I have had sufficient confidence to [participate and] persevere with my great many fellow students [in the fight for our cause] in the heart of the whole nation's struggle for freedom and democracy—Tiananmen Square and the Monument to the People's Heroes. We will fight to our very last breath. "Victory belongs to the people! Long live the people!" . . . This is the rebirth of the Republic. Every day is our day. Often, after we have finished chanting our slogans, I am so excited that I find it hard to calm down!

It seems that university students from almost every field are paying more attention to the fate and future of our motherland than at any time in the past. What is most moving are the acts of the students of the Central Academy of Drama, who have refused water and food for several days now. It takes exceptional courage and willingness to risk one's life to do this. I admire them from the bottom of my heart! Despite the fact that there are not too many students in the Academy of Traditional Chinese Music and the Central Conservatory of Music, the effect of our singing at the Square has been tremendous. The "Internationale," solemn, ringingly clear, is a song familiar to all of us. When we held the last notes of the song, wave after wave of thunderous applause came from the people. At that time I felt proud from head to toe, for we had received the support of the people! Only "the people" deserve the accolade of "the greatest"!

Mama, you are the most loyal veteran Party member, you have been fighting on the battlefront of education for dozens of years. The ravages of time make you look older than your years. Aside from the satisfaction of knowing that you have nurtured and educated several generations of talent, you have nothing. But you feel extremely gratified nonetheless. What you eat is "grass," but what has been wrung from you is "sweat and blood"! So it is that we, as your children, made this pledge at Tiananmen Square. It is also so that you, and the tens of thousand of other mothers, receive what is owed you!

We are shedding our blood for our mothers—our motherland! What is there for us to be afraid of? We are proud just because of this! We also ask our motherland—our mothers—to be proud of her children! . . .

Perhaps people will forget the many, many heroes who sacrificed their lives for this cause, but the glorious deeds of this generation will be recorded in history—a generation that fought for freedom and democracy!

Good-bye, my family!

> —A Patriotic Student from the Academy of
> Traditional Chinese Music, May 21
> *(big-character poster on Beijing Street,*
> *May 25, 1989)*

TAPED INTERVIEW WITH CHAI LING IN LATE MAY
(excerpt)

My father came up to Beijing on May 1. After I got married to my husband, some friction between us developed, we had some fights and whatever, so each time I went back [to visit my parents in Shandong Province], I went by myself. My father was very concerned; he really, really deeply loved me. [When he came to visit me,] he brought a lot of special things for us to eat. He was hoping that we could go around and do some things together. After arriving, he found that both my husband and I had gotten involved in the student movement. We were busy every day at Beijing University doing organizing work and didn't have much time to spend with him. That evening [shortly before he left] he said, "I had better return home, because there isn't much here I can do to help you." He then said, "What will you do? How can I contact you?" I said, "In three days, I'll send you a telegram; after that, I'll ask a friend to do this for me." He said, "In case I cannot receive your telegrams, then what?" I said, "You don't need to come any more. Coming to Beijing won't be any use." I almost threw myself into his arms; I was on the verge of crying. He said, "Don't be like this, there's no need to cry on parting. . . . good-bye, good-bye." He went back to Jinan.

. . . [My father] has devoted all his energies to raising his two daughters; he must be wondering how it could be that both of them have gotten involved [in the student movement]. My younger sister has been influenced a bit by me; she has said she admires her older sister. My father is a person who is eager to excel. He is a doctor. All along, he has cherished the Communist Party. I have said to him, "the Communist Party has duped your generation; you all actually should have received much more [from it in return for your support and sacrifice]." Fine—no point in talking more about the Communist Party. My father said that his generation has its own way of thinking. He is a very open-minded person. He is a Chinese who has endured a great, great deal. I want to go on living for them—my parents—too. My father has placed all of his hope in us (I also have another younger sister and a younger brother). . . .

MAY EVENING

Tonight a girl wearing a white headband
Is the world's loveliest.
Tonight the song we sing,
Heard ten years from now, will bring tears to listeners' eyes.
Tonight we let our hungry stomachs growl,
For China's hunger is greater still than ours.
Tonight we share the same pack of cigarettes,
Because we resemble one another.
The night wind has more than once blown chilling news our way,
Many are the corners where the lamplight is dim and confused.
The heavens keep a long silence,
Their message hard to fathom.
But the moon shows forth a moment's portent—
We can only huddle together tightly.
Tonight the Red Cross sustains many lives—
Our China needs a transfusion, too.
Tonight will be imprinted on frames of film.
Today the dawn of China has yet to come—
This stabs deeply at our hearts.

—(copied from Tiananmen Square)
(big-character poster)

DO NOT ASK MY NAME

—Respectfully presented to those who are hunger striking for truth

May is the busiest season for the police.
They are like cicadas lying low on every street.
They are waving wings,

Waving wings in the sunshine.
On those wings spider webs have grown all over.

Classmate, do not ask my name.
Reach out your hand,
Reach out my hand,
Reach out our hands.
Let our arms coil together—
As branches of a tree weave together death and suffering,
Weave together life and truth.
In May's Square
We use our own bodies
To braid a huge floral wreath—
An everlasting floral wreath.
Yes, May is the season when the green shows fully in the trees,
The time when we pick ourselves from the tree of life.
It is that branch,
It is the countless pale yellow-green stalks beneath the
    Monument to the People's Heroes,
Awaiting the moments of withering and regeneration.
Classmate, do not ask my name.
Reach out your hand,
Reach out my hand,
Reach out our hands,

Let our arms coil together—
As a rock intermingles darkness and light,
Intermingle democracy and freedom.
Under the May sky
We use our own souls
To raise a towering group statue—
That of a group of pioneers.

Search, classmate.
Search, brother.
Search, sister.
Search, friend.
Reach out your hand,
Reach out my hand,

Reach out our hands.
Come, come, come.
Do not ask my name.

—Citizens, May 13, 1989
(*student* News Herald, *special
edition, May 14, 1989)*

"The Children Are Not Wrong"

The Chinese intellectual world was among the first of many groups to organize in support of the hunger strikers. Prior to mid-May, a bold but limited circle of intellectuals had raised their voices in protest; the hunger strike galvanized a far wider spectrum of intellectuals into active participation in the Democracy Movement. On May 15, according to the estimate of the Xinhua News Agency itself, "several tens of thousands" of intellectuals marched from the western end of the Avenue of Heavenly Peace to Tiananmen in a show of support for the hunger strikers. Although the marchers' front lines featured such outspoken critics of the government as Yan Jiaqi, Bao Zunxin, and Wang Luxiang—the latter one of the writers of the controversial television series, "River Elegy"—the marchers also included many from the intellectual and university worlds who had hitherto hesitated to challenge the government publicly. More than one thousand of China's most prominent intellectuals went one step further the next day, committing their names to a united statement, the May 16 Declaration, which called on the government to grant the students' main demands. As the following excerpts of the May 16 Declaration show, the statement was neither radical nor anti-Party nor anti-government. But given the Party's proven intolerance of any challenge to its policies or supremacy, signing the document was risky. Far more critical—and indeed a direct shot at supreme leader Deng Xiaoping—was the May 17 Declaration signed by twelve intellectuals. There appears to be little doubt that the May 17 Declaration was ventured in the knowledge that its signatories enjoyed the direct backing of Zhao's moderate faction.

Like other segments of Chinese society that have been identified as "participant groups" in the Democracy Movement, intellectuals in fact acted from many motivations and held different hopes for the movement. Generally speaking, intellectuals who spoke out during the movement fell into three categories. First, there were those such as Ren Wanding and fellow committed dissidents who wished to see the movement create the basis for a new political force or party that would eventually challenge the one-party system of Communist Party rule. These dissidents, who did not shrink from linking the safer theme of general political reform to the sensitive issue of human rights, did not desire to see the students or the movement become entangled in an internecine Party struggle for power.

Second, there was a group of intellectuals, exemplified by Chen Yizi, an advisor to Zhao and head of the Research Institute for Economic Restructuring—the elite think-tank directly under the Central Committee, which Zhao had loaded with bright, liberal economists and analysts who were closely identified with Zhao's moderate faction. Members of this group were supportive of the student calls for an end to corruption, a dialogue, increased government openness, and freedom of the press, but also sought to use the student unrest to enhance the power of Zhao's moderate faction. They were thus the most aggressive in issuing declarations (which were carefully drafted and timed to accord with Zhao's maneuvers), forming new organizations to promote the goals of the movement, and initiating contacts with the students.

Finally, there was a large, amorphous group of intellectuals who generally supported the students' demands but did not link the movement to any specific political agenda. Some of these intellectuals, such as Dai Qing, the *Guangming Daily* reporter, sympathized with the students but at the same time feared that their radical acts—the hunger strike and the occupation of Tiananmen that would continue until June—would only provide Party conservatives with an excuse to initiate a sweeping crackdown that would roll back the liberalizations won by intellectuals in recent years.

MAY 16 DECLARATION

The "May 16 Circular" of the 1960s is, without doubt, a symbol of dictatorship and darkness in the hearts of the Chinese people.[6] Today, twenty-three years later, we are feeling intensely the call of democracy and light. History has finally reached a turning point: a patriotic democracy movement, with young students as its pioneering leaders, is now emerging throughout the country. . . . This is a great national awakening that both carries on and surpasses the spirit of the May Fourth Movement. This is a momentous historical juncture that will decide the fate of China. . . .

. . . At this very moment, a moment that will decide the fate of the

6. The May 16 Circular issued in 1966 by Mao and his supporters marked the opening of the Cultural Revolution and led to the purge of Peng Zhen, Mayor of Beijing and the Politburo member in charge of cultural and ideological education, and other high Party leaders whom Mao suspected of disloyalty.

people, the country, and the ruling party, we—the Chinese intellectuals at home and abroad who have put our names to this declaration—today, May 16, 1989, do solemnly, by our signatures to this declaration, proclaim to the public our principles.

First, we maintain that, confronted with the current student movement, the Chinese Communist Party and government have not acted sensibly. In particular, there were still signs not long ago that attempts would be made to handle this movement with heavy-handed pressure and force. The lessons of history are worth remembering: the Beijing government of 1919, the Kuomintang government of the 1930s and 1940s, and the Gang of Four of the late 1970s, and other such dictatorial regimes all resorted to violence to suppress student movements, and as a result, all without exception were nailed to history's pillar of shame. History has proven that those who suppress student movements will come to no good end. . . .

Second, a prerequisite for dealing with the present political crisis in a way consistent with democratic politics is the necessity of recognizing the legality of the students' autonomous organizations, which are the product of democratic procedures. Acting otherwise contradicts the freedom of association provided for by the fundamental, basic law [the Constitution] of our country. Labeling in one shot the student organizations "illegal" [as the government has chosen to do] can only result in the sharpening of conflict and in the intensification of the crisis. . . .

Fifth, characterizing the current student movement as anti-Party and anti-socialist political turmoil is wrong. The fundamental meaning of freedom of speech is recognition and protection of the citizen's right to express divergent political opinions. The essence of every political movement since Liberation has been to suppress and attack divergent political opinions. A society with only one voice is not a stable society. It is necessary that both the Chinese Communist Party and the Chinese government review the profound lessons of the Anti-Hu Feng Campaign,[7] the Anti-

7. The Anti-Hu Feng Campaign was waged by the Party in 1955 against Hu Feng, a prominent writer and follower of Lu Xun, one of China's most famous writers, after Hu wrote in 1954 a long letter to the Central Committee critical of Mao's repressive policy toward intellectuals, literature, and culture. In addition to imprisoning Hu, the Party arrested and persecuted many other intellectuals suspected of association with his "counter-revolutionary" clique. Hu spent over twenty years in prison and was not released until after Mao's death. He was finally "rehabilitated," his reputation restored and his case officially reversed, in 1988.

Rightist Movement,[8] the Cultural Revolution,[9] the Anti-Spiritual Pollution Campaign, and the Anti-Bourgeois Liberalization Campaign.[10] It is necessary that they open channels of speech [for the expression of diverse viewpoints]. Only when young students, intellectuals, and people across the country are allowed to participate in the discussion of our nation's affairs will a political environment of true stability and unity emerge. . . .

Sixth, . . . we have arrived at a critical juncture in history. Our people, who have endured so much adversity and disaster, have no more opportunities to lose; there are no more paths of escape. Chinese intellectuals, who have to their name a rich tradition of patriotism and understanding of the bitterness of suffering, must become fully aware of their own ineluctable, historic mission. They must boldly step forth to push forward

8. Declaring in mid-1956, "Let a hundred schools of thought contend; let one hundred flowers bloom," Mao and Party leaders encouraged Chinese intellectuals to air their views of the government candidly in the "Hundred Flowers Movement." Their invitation to speak out produced a torrent of blunt criticism. Mao's response was to initiate in May 1957 the Anti-Rightist Campaign against the regime's critics; over half a million Chinese, primarily intellectuals and cadres, were executed, sent to labor camps in remote areas, or left to languish in jails. Not until 1978, after the ascension of Deng Xiaoping to power, would they be "rehabilitated": released from captivity, their cases reinvestigated and the label of "rightist" removed, and their reputations, jobs, and property restored. Although all but fewer than one hundred "rightists" have been rehabilitated since 1978, the Anti-Rightist Campaign, which marked the beginning of widespread intellectual disillusionment with the Party, has never been repudiated by the Party.

9. The Cultural Revolution, mentioned at numerous points throughout this book, was a mass political movement launched by Mao Tse-tung in 1966 that plunged large parts of China into chaos. Initiated by Mao and his inner group of followers to eliminate political rivals whom Mao perceived to be threatening his power as paramount leader, as well as to resist revisionism or bourgeois tendencies, the Cultural Revolution created deep schisms in Chinese society. Students were encouraged to denounce their teachers, workers to expose their colleagues, and children were even asked to criticize their parents. At the peak of the Cultural Revolution, the excesses of the Red Guards—brigades of high school and college students who had responded to Mao's call to wage "continuous revolution"—not only completely shut down high schools and colleges but also severely disrupted industrial production. During this period of extreme politicization, large numbers of intellectuals and many Party officials were beaten and "struggled"—subjected to humiliating criticism sessions in front of crowds, sent to the countryside for a lesson in manual labor, or killed. Although the Cultural Revolution ended in 1969, its deadening influence on Chinese social and intellectual life was felt until Mao's death in 1976. The Cultural Revolution, now officially viewed as the mistake of a great leader in his waning years, is sometimes referred to as the "Ten Years of Chaos."

10. The 1983 Anti-Spiritual Pollution Campaign and Anti-Bourgeois Liberalization Campaign are described in Chapter 1, note 6.

the development of democracy. They must struggle for the construction of a politically democratic, economically developed, modernized country!

Long live the people!

Long live a free, democratic, socialist motherland!

—Beijing, May 16, 1989
(Signatures of over 1,000 intellectuals)[11]

MAY 17 DECLARATION

Since 2:00 P.M. May 13, over three thousand of our students have been in Tiananmen Square on a hunger strike that has lasted nearly one hundred hours; up to this time, over seven hundred students have fainted. This is a tragic event that has never before occurred in our history. The students have demanded that the April 26 *People's Daily* editorial be repudiated and that the government hold a dialogue with them that is broadcast live. We are facing a situation in which, one after another, our motherland's sons and daughters are falling even as their just demands meet with repeated delay [on the government's part], and go ignored; this [failure by the government to respond positively] has been the reason why the students will not end their hunger strike. Now our motherland's problem has been fully exposed to people in all of China and throughout the world. It is that due to the absolute power enjoyed by a dictator, the government has lost its sense of responsibility and its humanity. Such a government is not truly the government of the Republic—it is a government whose existence is possible only because of the power of a dictator.

The Qing Dynasty has already been extinct for seventy-six years [sic]. Yet China still has an emperor without a crown, an aged, fatuous dictator. Yesterday afternoon, Secretary General Zhao Ziyang publicly announced that all of China's major policy decisions must be reviewed by this decrepit dictator, who is behind the times. Without the consent of the this dictator, there is no way that the April 26 *People's Daily* editorial can be repudiated. After our students have been on a hunger strike for nearly one hundred hours, [matters have reached a point where] there is no choice: the Chinese people no longer can wait for the dictator to acknowl-

11. The signers of this petition include many luminaries of Chinese cultural and intellectual circles.

edge his mistake. Now all depends on the students themselves and on the people themselves. Today, we declare to all of China, to all of the world, that from now on the great fight the students have been waging, their hunger strike of one hundred hours, has won a great victory. The students have used their own actions to proclaim that this student movement is not turmoil but rather a great patriotic democracy movement to bury forever dictatorship and an imperial system.

Let us hail the great victory of the hunger strike! Long live the spirit of nonviolent protest!

Down with the dictatorship of the individual! Those who are dictators will come to no good end!

Reverse the April 26 editorial!

Government by old men must end!

The dictator must resign!

Long live the university students! Long live the people! Long live democracy! Long live freedom!

"Blood Is Flowing from the Students, Tears Are Flowing from Our Eyes; but What Is the Government Doing?—Silence Is a Crime."

The hunger strike was a turning point in the Democracy Movement, a crisis fusing together idealistic students and a citizenry previously noted for its lack of public spirit and for an aversion to risk learned from the bitter lessons of political campaigns in the past. This was not the first time aggrieved students had resorted to a hunger strike: in 1980, more than fifty student activists in Changsha had staged a strike to protest school authorities' interference in elections at Hunan Teachers' College for a representative to the local National People's Congress. That protest, however, had ended after two days, before lives were at stake, and had received little domestic publicity. The idea of people refusing food, though surprising in a society that placed great importance on food and the rite of eating, was not as disturbing to the Chinese as some have suggested. Rather, it was the extremity of the act that shocked ordinary Chinese: influenced by a traditional culture that esteemed moderation, living in a highly repressive society where experience soon taught that individual will or desire had little impact on one's environment, citizens were deeply moved by the youths' willingness to stake their lives, as well as by their faith that the sacrifice would ultimately alter Chinese society.

The first worrisome indications for the government that a Beijing-centered student protest was turning into a nationwide popular protest came on May 15 and

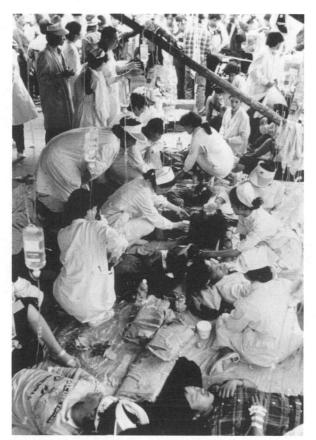

Illustration 4.3. A makeshift emergency aid station in Tiananmen. Credit: Black Star / Peter Turnley.

16. On those days vast crowds had gathered in Tiananmen. Their numbers had been swelled by groups of citizens that had spontaneously marched to the Square in a show of solidarity for the students. University students from nearly all of China's provinces had also begun to pour into the capital to join the tens of thousands already encamped in the Square. All of this, however, was only a prelude to the mass outpouring of support for the students that completely paralyzed Beijing on May 17 and May 18. On the 17th, as Mikhail Gorbachev departed for Shanghai, factory workers, store clerks, private entrepreneurs, high school students, government cadres, and even members of the People's Liberation Army descended onto Changan Avenue in a huge anti-government demonstration. First a stream, the procession on Changan Avenue grew throughout the day until by mid-afternoon it had become an enormous promenade of protest involving over one million participants.

Illustration 4.4. On May 17, students from the University of Communications link hands to form what they call a "moving Democracy Wall" several hundred meters long. The banner in this section of the wall proclaims, "God Is None Other than the People." Credit: Han Minzhu.

The spectacle would be repeated the next day, with a technological upgrade: rather than relying on foot power, demonstrators clambered into and onto vehicles of all types: taxis, company cars, flatbed trucks, buses, even construction equipment. The pace of the protest had quickened—as would the government response.

Few posters or handbills describe the tumultuous events of these two days: for most student and citizen protestors, the events evidently spoke for themselves. But for the Chinese press, still exploring its new freedom, they inspired lengthy pieces, articles that epitomized the peak of press openness during the Democracy Movement.

Illustration 4.5. Students from the Chinese University of Hong Kong join the exuberant mass protest on May 17. Students from Hong Kong had arrived in Beijing by May 4 and actively participated in the Democracy Movement. Credit: Franki Chan.

Illustration 4.6. Young police officials march in Tiananmen in mid-May with a banner declaring that "The People's Police Love the People." Credit: Franki Chan.

HISTORY WILL REMEMBER THIS DAY

—A Record of the Great May 17 March
in Support of the Student Hunger Strikers
by People of the Capital from All Walks of Life

In Beijing, the hearts of thousands and thousands of people hang suspended over Tiananmen Square.

One, two, three, four, five days—about a hundred hours have now passed; tormented by hunger and thirst under the blazing sun, sad and angry, more than a thousand hunger strikers have fainted.

Three days without food marks a critical point for the human body. Beyond this, the cost may well be life itself.

"Save the children!" "Save our country!" Thousands and thousands of people issued these solemn cries from the heart.

On May 17, a huge spontaneous demonstration in support of the hunger-striking students, with over a million participants, finally exploded!

From morning onward, groups of demonstrators surged from all directions onto Changan Avenue. From the Jianguomenwai overpass in the east to the Fuxingmen intersection in the west, the five-kilometer-long avenue was transformed into a tide of people and an ocean of banners.

On a vehicle from the Research Institute of Mathematics of the Chinese Academy of Natural Sciences hung the banner, "Chen Jingrun is concerned about the fasting students," expressing the [entire] intellectual community's concern for the students. Han Dacheng, professor of history at People's University, solemnly told reporters along the march, "I have no doubt that this day will be recorded in the annals of Chinese history."

Among the ranks of the marchers were steel workers, construction workers, postal workers, electronics technicians, machinists, and auto workers. On their banners was written in huge characters: "The Working Class Is a Powerful Backup Force for the Students' Patriotic Democracy Movement."

The peasants came, too. A man from Miyun County by the name of "Old Uncle" Liu told fellow travellers: "I am sixty-seven this year. In the past few days I have been watching television and have seen how the students are suffering. It was too pitiful; I had to come out."

Buddhists also marched into the Square, holding their placards. They came forward to express sympathy and solicitude for the students, and even more to implore people from all walks of life to "cherish mercy in their hearts."

"The Northeast is crying out!"—university students from Shenyang [in northeastern China] appeared with their banners. "Shanghai and Beijing Breathe Together"—university student representatives from Shanghai strode onto Changan Avenue. Tianjin, Hebei, Henan, Zhejiang . . . a multitude of students from outside of Beijing joined the ranks of the marchers. And representatives from the Hong Kong Student Federation, carrying donations from various Hong Kong universities, [also] appeared before the hunger strikers in the center of the Square.

"Save the Students! Sincere Dialogue!" "Oppose Corruption! Eradicate Profiteering by Officials!" "If the Cancer is Not Removed, the Country Will Not Have a Day of Peace"—such were the clear and resounding cries of the demonstrators, which openly expressed their worries and hopes for the future and fate of the motherland.

"Humanity!" a banner with this word fluttered above the monumental edifice of the Museum of the Chinese Revolution, voicing well the heart-felt sentiments of the people.

From morning until evening, millions of people poured spontaneously onto the streets, countless contingents from factories, offices, and institutions. Despite the unavoidable traffic congestion it created on certain streets, the demonstration as a whole proceeded in a well-disciplined, orderly fashion with virtually no unexpected incidents or accidents.

As of 6:30 in the evening, group after group of workers continued to march along eastern Changan Avenue toward Tiananmen Square. "Beijing Automobile Manufacturing Factory," "Beijing Printing and Dyeing Factory," "Beijing Crane Factory," "Beijing Internal Combustion Engine Main Factory," "Capital Iron and Steel Company" . . . the workers prominently displayed their factories' names and shouted out their heartfelt feelings: "We Workers Have Come!" "Salute the Students!" The workers had just come off their shifts; without time to change their clothes, they rushed to join the demonstrators marching in support of the students.

Along North Chongwenmen Avenue, workers from the Beijing Coking Factory got out of their factory buses, unfurled their banners, and set out their placards, quickly forming a contingent of marchers. They had returned to the city from their factory, some fifteen kilometers away in the suburbs, and without first going home or having dinner, they marched, shouting slogans, toward Tiananmen Square. One worker told a reporter, "We couldn't afford to stop production, because then Beijing would have no gas [for heating and manufacturing]. We can only rush to catch up with the marchers after getting off work."

At a bus stop near the Beijing Railroad Station, the dispatcher and bus drivers for the Number 10 and 20 lines said: "Our two routes pass by Tiananmen Square. For a month, since the beginning of the student movement, bus service has suffered some disruption, and the demonstrations have delayed some passengers. The odd thing is that we still haven't heard many complaints. And not one single traffic accident or fatality has occurred. . . .

And now, watching the students who are close to breathing their last, the people can bear it no longer. Thousands and thousands, even cancer patients in the terminal stages of illness, have gone to Tiananmen Square to stretch out to the students hands of support. . . .

All day long, letters of support from the democratic parties, groups and societies, government offices, and individuals have been continuously broadcast in the Square. At this very time, the broadcast station of the Hunger Strikers' Headquarters is reading out a letter of sympathy sent by the staff at the General Hospital of the People's Liberation Army. The letter, filled with emotion, reads, "We are deeply upset by the fact that for five days now the students have not eaten and that many have fainted. We are worried about you as minutes, hours tick by. Dear students, the hearts of the Party members, the hearts of our soldiers, and the hearts of all the people are turned toward you. Victory will be yours. The future belongs to you."

At noon, the sun blazed down. The demonstrators dripped with sweat.

From Jianguomenwai in the east to Dongdan in the west, store attendants from [both] state-owned and collective restaurants and snack shops, as well as housewives who live in the neighborhood, put out large dispensers of tea, offered cups of water, took out ice cream sticks and cold drinks, and offered them free to the marchers passing by.

Holding cups and bowls of tea between their hands, a group of children scurry to and fro delivering tea and refills of hot water, shouting all the while at the top of their voices: "Grandpas, grandmas, uncles, aunts, you have really put yourselves out!"

Such a spectacular and grand demonstration greatly heartened the hunger striking students and their fellow student supporters in Tiananmen Square.

Luo Shijian, a student hunger striker from the Beijing Aeronautics Institute, was asked by a reporter, "Now that the masses have been roused into action, have you thought about whether you need to end the hunger strike and leave Tiananmen Square?" Lifting himself up, Luo said in response, "I don't think the awakening of the people is enough. We would like to see Party leaders take action and stand together with the people. We don't want the Party to be separated from the people. For unity and solidarity between the Party and the people, we will carry on this hunger strike until the end!". . .

Twelve hunger strikers from the Central Drama Academy began refusing water in the afternoon of May 16. At their side stood a gigantic portrait, painted by their classmates from the Drama Department, of a naked mother pleading, "Save the Children." With pain in their voices, doctors from the Beijing Medical Emergency Center told reporters, "The ones in most danger are these. If things continue to drag on in this way, the consequences will be too dreadful to contemplate."

At 2:30 in the morning, upon hearing that his son Mu Feng was one of the twelve who was refusing water, the venerable professor Mu Baisuo of the Academy's Dance Department rushed to the Square to see his son. He pointed to a student lying on the ground, third from the east, and said to us, "That's my son." At the same moment, Mu Feng lifted his head with

Illustration 4.7. Protesting on the streets becomes slightly more hazardous on May 18, with the appearance of an assortment of vehicles. Credit: Magnum / Zachmann.

great difficulty, and saw his white-haired father. Father and son clasped each other's hands.

"I was too moved to say anything. I could only tell my son to listen to the doctors," Mu Baisuo told reporters. "Neither my wife nor I wants to see our son die. We have only two children! But I feel that the sacrifice of a son for a struggle for democracy is a worthy one!"

It is now deep into the night. The demonstrations are still continuing. The hunger strike is still continuing.

Midnight. It has begun drizzling in Tiananmen Square, which for many days now has been roiling with the passion of the people. The temperature in the Square has clearly dropped. But has the heat in the hearts of the people cooled? "We are still waiting, but not much time is left . . ." said one very debilitated student.

Where there is impatience, there too is reason; where there is anger, there too is expectation; where there is pain, there too is hope. . . .

May 17—history will remember this day.

(collective report of People's Daily *reporters, May 17, 1989)*

The impasse in Beijing between the students and the government also set off a string of student demonstrations in dozens of cities across the nation. Marching to show solidarity for the Beijing hunger strikers, students in other cities also vented their own particular grievances: for example, in Shanghai, the Party's take-over of the *World Economic Herald*; and in Hainan, the provincial and municipal government's failure to engage in a meaningful dialogue, as well as the low pay and poor living conditions of teachers. Though peaceful and considerably smaller in size than the massive Beijing protests, the demonstrations nonetheless were distressing evidence to hard-liners that unless decisive action were taken soon, anarchy would reign in all corners of the country. The major national papers also printed stories, albeit less detailed ones, on these demonstrations. The following is an article on developments outside of Beijing that appeared on May 18 in the *Guangming Daily*.

GUANGMING DAILY NEWS REPORT
(May 18, 1989)

University students in major cities across the country continued today their demonstrations and marches in support of the patriotic actions of Beijing university students.

Shanghai: Today, over 100,000 university students and people from all segments of society took to the streets to march in support of the patriotic actions of Beijing university students. In the morning, student marchers from thirty-odd universities set out for Waitan and the People's Square [in downtown Shanghai] from all directions. Along the entire way, many workers perched high on top of construction projects, residents on rooftops, and passengers in buses clapped and cheered the students on.

Guangzhou: Over 10,000 students from . . . over twenty universities and colleges, marching under a hot sun, gathered at the front gate of the provincial government building, where they shouted "Support the Beijing students!" "Long live democracy!" and other slogans. A portion of local teachers, writers, and newspersons also [participated in the demonstration and] carried banners in support of the students.

Wuhan: In the tri-city Wuhan area, marches in support of the Beijing students' hunger strike petition reached their largest size to date. A crowd of over 100,000 university students and people from all walks of life participated in the march. At the Yangtse River Bridge [and] . . . the provincial government and municipal government building gates, tens of thousands of marchers assembled ... The marchers were orderly throughout the demonstrations. An engineer who witnessed the demonstration commented: "This is the greatest patriotic student movement in China since the [1919] May Fourth Movement; it has received the support of all ordinary Chinese with a conscience. This is truly a sign that there is hope for China."

Hefei: Marches in support of the Beijing university students reached their largest size to date today. Students from more than ten universities and vocational schools poured out of their campuses, forming a vast army of over 50,000 who marched forward shoulder to shoulder. . . .

Changsha: Students at universities and colleges all over Changsha held a general class boycott today. Several tens of thousands of university students, state cadres, figures from the intellectual world, and workers took to the streets to march in support of the Beijing students. At the present time, there are over one hundred university students on a hunger strike in the courtyard of the provincial government building.

Xi'an: In a continuation of yesterday's march of several tens of thousands of students and people from all walks of life, today again tens of thousands of students and other people were on the streets in support of the Beijing students' hunger strike petition. At Xincheng Square and major roads leading to the Square in the heart of the city, a steady stream of people flooded in and out, the chanting of slogans rose and fell in the air, and many people delivered water and tea for the student marchers. At present, there are already nearly one thousand university students staging a protest hunger strike. . . .

Harbin: Class boycotts were held today at all universities and colleges in Harbin. More than 30,000 university students, graduate students, and young teachers continued to march on the streets in protest; in addition, nearly one hundred students have announced a hunger strike in support of their Beijing classmates.

In Changchun, Shenyang, Dalian, Huhehaote, Taiyuan, Yinzhou, Chengdu, Chongqing, Guiyang, Fuzhou, Hangzhou, Nanchang, Shenzhen, etc., students also continued their marches [and demonstrations] in support of the patriotic actions of the Beijing students.

The crisis had deepened to the point where disapprobation and despair had also developed in the rank and file of the Party. Even those Party members who had not previously approved of the students' protests—primarily older Party members whose belief in the Party was anchored in the memories of pre-Liberation China and the halcyon years of the fifties, when faith in the transformative power of communism and the leadership of the Party had run strong—and state cadres—now expressed disappointment at the inability of the Party and government to arrange the dialogue sought by the hunger strikers. The following posters by Party members, two of which were written by teachers or students (the third was not signed), do not by any means constitute a cross section of opinion among the Party's urban membership. They do reflect, however, the range of criticism and exasperation directed at the Party and government as the condition of the fasters deteriorated. The poster, "Party Members, Rise Up and Resist Dictatorship," is particularly notable for its four authors' courage in signing their names (which have been deleted here) to a document that so scathingly attacked China's paramount ruler. For this act, the writers may well have been arrested during the subsequent crackdown on the Democracy Movement.

SOME ADVICE TO THE COMMUNIST PARTY AND GOVERNMENT

The fasting students' struggle has received sympathy and support from every level of society. One by one the students have collapsed [faint from lack of nourishment]; according to the dictates of reason, the government should have responded in a sensible fashion. Instead, to our disappointment and frustration, on the morning of the 15th, the General Office of the State Council issued its so-called "Announcement of Concern for the Students," calling on the hunger strikers to return [to school]. What contempt this shows for the intelligentsia! What [do they think] the students are hunger striking for? It is plain to all that at this crucial moment the government must steel itself and make a just assessment of the recent student movement. Are not "criticism and self-criticism" among the Communist Party's proudest traditions?[12] Years ago, Mao Tse-tung dared to acknowledge his own mistakes before seven thousand people at a large meeting. It has been more than twenty years since then—cannot [anyone in the Party or government] yet surpass Mao Tse-tung? If the government continues to deal with the students in this stubborn manner, what will the

12. "Self-criticism," a written or oral declaration in front of an audience in which the confessor avows his errors and professes to understand why his actions or thinking are incorrect, has long been a fundamental Chinese Communist Party method for disciplining wayward members or enforcing political conformity. Punishment for those who offer self-criticism is either waived or reduced, since the statement presumably indicates that the person is repentant and willing to change his ways.

end result be? The student movement has won broad support; moreover, a mood of dissatisfaction is palpable at every level. If things continue as they are, all sorts of political organizations will appear in our society. These organizations may even go so far as to join up with forces of violence, or perhaps establish links with the military. This is not simply alarmist talk. If the government wishes to avoid or put a stop to the development of such a situation, it has the ability and the responsibility to satisfy the just demands of the students. Otherwise the situation will definitely become very difficult to contain. At present the government has three alternatives:

1. continue to deal with the students in a stubborn manner, risking the consequences described above;

2. adopt a military response to the student movement, resulting in the alienation of the entire Chinese people and the evaporation of prospects for modernization (this alternative is tantamount to playing a cruel joke at the expense of the nation's very life);

3. satisfy the student's just demands. This is the best choice, for only in this manner can the fervor of the broad masses' love for their country be directed into positive channels, and the hearts and minds of the people be united with the government so that the crisis facing the country may be met. Of course, for the government to admit its mistakes to the masses may mean that those who have dealt wrongly with the students may be forced to step down. But to these same people I say: you stand at the crossroads of the nation's fate. Ask yourselves which is more important: your own interests, or those of the Chinese nation itself?

I request the government's careful attention to the foregoing.

> —A Communist Party Member Concerned
> about the Party's Future, May 16, 1989
> *(big-character poster at People's
> University)*

COMMUNIST PARTY MEMBERS, STAND UP
—An Appeal to All Party Members

At present, the patriotic Democracy Movement has entered an extremely tense stage: the hunger strike of several thousand classmates in Tiananmen has already entered its seventh day, yet the leaders of our government still have not given a definite reply to the reasonable demands of our classmates. As members of the Chinese Communist Party, we believe that the attitude of the government is not wise. It is mistaken. From April 15 on, we too have been participants in the patriotic Democracy Movement. We have seen how the erroneous judgment [and attitude] of the government regarding this patriotic democracy movement have severely damaged the image of the Party and Party members. We feel deeply grieved by this.

We very much cherish the designation of being members of the Communist Party. We became members of the Party for the cause of communism, which the Communist Party pioneered. Although we only have a few years of Party standing, the education we have received in the Party has taught us the value of the title of "Party member." At Zhazedong, [the infamous prison of the Kuomintang that was in Chongqing], Communist Party members were courageous and dauntless in the face of cruel torture inflicted on them by the reactionary faction. Communist Party members [have a tradition of] taking the lead. Lei Feng, who [always] served the people, was a Communist Party member; Zhang Zhixin, who never wavered from the truth, was also a Communist Party member.[13] The honor of the Communist Party for which the older generation traded their lives and blood has been sullied today by their [opposition to] democratization and [to the installation of a] rule of law. Since April 20, we have been under considerable pressure [to support the Party line], so that we have only been able to join the ranks of the protestors in our individual capacity. When we think about our Party oath, about the duties and responsibilities of a Party member, speaking from our consciences, we can only feel ashamed when we face the broad mass of our classmates. What the true Party member stands up for is the truth, not the personal "face"

13. Lei Feng and Zhang Zhixin are two members of the Communist pantheon of modern heroes and model communists. According to the official Party biography of Lei Feng (over which doubts as to accuracy linger), Lei, an orphan taken in by Communist Party officials, was an exemplar of selfless spirit, courtesy, and dedication to work. In recent years, "Study from Lei Feng" ethics campaigns have appeared whenever conservatives feel it is time to reinforce the populace's communist values. Lei Feng has surfaced again in the post-Democracy Movement assault on bourgeois liberalization. Zhang Zhixin, a symbol of martyrdom, was a graduate of People's University who was executed in 1969 for her criticism of the Cultural Revolution. Before her persecutors killed her, they slashed her throat to prevent her from yelling any defiant words. The writer does not appear to be raising the examples of Lei Feng and Zhang Zhixin in sarcasm.

[reputation] of some individual leaders. To [certain] individual government leaders who have the status of Communist Party membership, we say: you are not true Communist Party members; the image of the Communist Party is not meant to be monopolized by a few individuals, but belongs to every one of us Communist Party members.

We [now] appeal:

1. To protect the honor of the Communist Party and its members, all Party members must stand forth and unequivocally participate as a Party member [rather than as an individual], and in the name of the school's Party branch, in this patriotic Democracy Movement. The interest of the people is paramount.

2. At present the movement has already reached an extremely critical moment. Party members must lead the way by their own example; must assist the students' autonomous unions in schools in organizing classmates; must maintain cool heads; and must work to avoid any unnecessary harm to our classmates.

> —Graduate Students in the Class of 1986
> Materials Department; All Party Members in
> the Party Branch [of the Materials Department]
> *(big-character poster at Beijing Science
> and Technology University, May 26, 1989)*

PARTY MEMBERS, RISE UP AND RESIST DICTATORSHIP
—An Open Letter to the Central Committee and to All Party Members

Central Committee and All Party Members:

At this grim moment we, as ordinary Party members, are compelled by loyalty to the Party and our consciences to stand up and speak out. Deng Xiaoping's remarks of April 25 concerning the student movement completely mischaracterized the nature of the movement; they were followed by the *People's Daily* editorial of April 26 which was based on them. They have led to the present grave consequences, causing the all but complete loss of the Party's prestige. Deng Xiaoping must immediately make

a self-criticism and acknowledge his mistakes! The fact that Deng Xiaoping is not the Chairman of the Party but can still directly issue orders
and commands to it shows [his] scorn for—and harms—democracy
within the Party. This fact is a manifestation of patriarchy and dictatorship. It also reveals that the Central Committee itself disregards Party
discipline and democracy. Facts have proven that it is these practices,
more than anything else, that are likely to trigger power struggles and
turmoil. We absolutely will not recognize any of Deng Xiaoping's individual directives that have been issued without going through formal discussion by the Politburo! We hope that all Party members who are truly loyal
to the Party and who have consciences will stand up and firmly resist
dictatorship. We hope that they will come to the rescue of our country
and the Chinese nation, and advance democracy and reform!

(This letter has been delivered to the university's Party branch.)

> —Chinese Communist Party Members:
> xxx (Associate Professor, Chinese Dept.)
> xxx (Associate Professor, Chinese Dept.)
> xxx (Ph.D. Candidate, Chinese Dept.)
> xxx (M.A. Candidate, Chinese Dept.)

During this critical week in May, China's two main news agencies—Xinhua News
Agency and China News Agency—and major national papers such as the *People's
Daily* and the *Guangming Daily* functioned at the encouragement of Zhao's moderate
faction as public bulletin boards of protest, releasing or publishing a selected portion
of the numerous appeals sent by Chinese citizens and organizations to the papers
and to Party and government offices. The publication of these appeals alongside
articles describing the outpouring of support for the students underscored the new
degree of candor in the Chinese press. Yet relatively objective accounts of events
and statements should not be equated with political neutrality. By giving so much
coverage to the wave of widespread support for the students (on May 18, the
People's Daily devoted all but the lower-right hand corner of its front page to news
of the hunger strike), the news organs bolstered the moderate faction's position.
That this was done with intent seems indisputable; however, the extent of coordination or communication between Zhao's people and the news media is not yet
known.

Regardless of the political uses to which they were put, the calls for immediate
government action—essentially, for government concessions—were remarkably di-

verse. Three such statements, chosen for their disparate sources, appear in the next section. The first is an emotional appeal from Bing Xin, eighty-nine, one of China's most esteemed writers. The next is a letter from Beijing factory managers, which supports the students but urges workers to stay on the job—workers' strikes would have devastated the moderates' chances at resolving the crisis. The last is a statement from four of China's "democratic parties."[14] Only once in forty years had the democratic parties broken out of their docile roles as "little brothers" to the Communist Party: in the "Hundred Flowers Movement" of 1957, leaders from the various parties had criticized the Party. However, the subsequent persecution of these figures in the ensuing Anti-Rightist Campaign and the Cultural Revolution had reduced the parties into their present state of unswerving obedience to the Party's policies.

LETTER FROM BING XIN

"I hereby call upon the parents of the people
For the protection of my sons and grandsons."[15]

These two lines are from a couplet that I saw once on the pillars of the temple of the local god in the countryside near Yantai [in Shandong Province] during my childhood.

At this moment, there are several hundred thousand of "my sons and grandsons" suffering at Tiananmen Square. When will this suffering end?

I cannot agree more with what the presidents of ten universities in Beijing have said in their open letter [of May 16, which was widely publicized], "We hope that the leading officials of the Party and government will as quickly as possible meet with the students and hold a dialogue with them."

I believe that if right now one or two top leaders of the Party and government could just show up at Tiananmen Square and speak to the huge crowd of hundreds of thousands, and say one or two sentences of sincere sympathy and understanding, this would move the present state of affairs

14. See Chapter 3, note 7, regarding the democratic parties. In addition to the four democratic parties that signed this letter, at least two others made similar public statements.
15. The language of this couplet, which is apparently a prayer to a local god, is ambiguous. An alternative translation of *minzhu fumu* could be "parents of democracy"; however, given the circumstances in which the couplet originally appeared—in a rural area some eighty years ago—it has been translated as "parents of the people."

toward reason and order. Then our sons and grandsons will not have to pay an unnecessary and grievous price [for their patriotism].

I hereby plead with today's "parents of the people": please hasten to protect our sons and grandsons!

—Written in haste, May 17, 1989
(released by China News Service,
May 17, 1989; published in People's Daily,
May 18, 1989)

URGENT APPEAL FROM NINE FACTORY MANAGERS

At this historical moment that impinges on the fate and future of the country, we urgently ask that the Party and government agree on one position, and that the main leaders in charge of the Party and government, Zhao Ziyang and Li Peng, personally stand up and go out to meet and talk with the students. [We urgently ask that our leaders] carry on the distinguished tradition of the Communist Party of criticism and self-criticism; that they carefully reflect on certain methods that were used to handle the student movement in the previous period; and that they agree to the constitutional demands put forth by the students. Only in this way will the present impasse be broken; if it is not, the Party, the country, and the students alike will suffer. We also call at this time for people in the entire nation to exercise their powers and functions to prevent any further deterioration in the situation.

To avoid the occurrence of social turmoil, we appeal to all the masses of workers in industry and in communications, to people in each and every profession, to stay on your jobs, and to continue your work. To show support for the students it is not necessary that everyone takes to the streets; we can use many [other] effective means, [including] the media, to express our common minds and hearts.

—[Managers of Nine Beijing Factories][16]

16. The story carried in the newspapers and news services reported that ten factories had issued the statement, but it appears the actual number was nine.

LETTER TO SECRETARY GENERAL ZHAO ZIYANG FROM FOUR OF THE DEMOCRATIC PARTIES

Secretary General Zhao Ziyang:

The hunger-strike protest of Beijing university students is still continuing. The situation has now reached the point where the health and the lives of many students are in great jeopardy. This grave situation has made us extremely anxious. For the protection of the students and for overall stability, we hereby make this urgent appeal to you:

First, we hold that the recent actions of the students constitute a patriotic movement, and that the reasonable demands raised by the students do [in fact] accord with the positions of the Central Committee and the State Council. We hope that the issue of the students' reasonable demands can be resolved through democratic and legal avenues.

Second, we propose that the main leaders of the Central Committee and the State Council meet with the students as soon as possible and hold a dialogue with them.

At the same time, we sincerely hope that for the sake of the state and the Chinese nation, and for their own health, the students who are hunger striking in protest cease the hunger strike, and return to their schools.

Respectfully,

> Fei Xiaotong, Chairman,
>   China Democratic League
> Sun Qimeng, Chairman,
>   China Democratic Construction Association
> Lei Qie, Chairman,
>   China Association for the Promotion of Democracy
> Zhou Peiyuan, Chairman,
>   September 3rd Society[17]

But resolving the crisis was not as simple as Bing Xin, the factory managers, and most citizens perceived. On each side, moderately inclined leaders found their hands tied by hard-line forces within their camp. Zhao, through his principal representative, Yan Mingfu, frantically tried through the week of the 15th to persuade

---

17. The heads of the democratic parties are sometimes well-known figures from intellectual or cultural circles. Fei Xiaotong is China's leading sociologist; Zhou Peiyuan is a former President of Beijing University.

the students to end the strike. On the 16th, Yan had once again gone to Tiananmen to plead with students, going so far as to offer himself as a hostage. Yan had said many of the right things—that the student movement was a patriotic one, that a real dialogue must be initiated immediately—but not enough: he had not acknowledged the legitimacy of the students' autonomous organizations, and he had not taken a position on the students' demand that the April 26 editorial be repudiated.

Yan and even Zhao were in fact powerless to do anything about the *People's Daily* editorial. The Party's position on this issue had been decided by Deng, acting, it appears, with the solid support of the "group of elders": there was to be no retreat. Zhao, searching desperately for a political chink in the armor of Deng's supreme authority, tried on May 16 to shift responsibility for the crisis wholly onto Deng: in his meeting with Gorbachev, he revealed that by an earlier Party decision, Deng Xiaoping had been formally given ultimate decision-making authority and that all major policy-making decisions had to be approved by him. What Zhao did not bother to say, since it was obvious to all, is that the April 26 editorial stood because Deng refused to reconsider it. The ploy by Zhao would fail: support for Deng and his hard-line position would hold firm, and Deng himself would be enraged by his former protégé's insubordination.

In the case of the students, although leaders such as Wang Dan, Wuer Kaixi, and Wang Chaohua (a female graduate at the prestigious Chinese Academy of Social Sciences and the oldest of the leadership of the Beijing Students' Federation) appear to have believed that continuing with the hunger strike would provoke a hard-line response and possibly lead to bloodshed, they were unable to persuade the majority of the hunger strikers, who voted on several different occasions to persist until the government made the concessions they sought—concessions, it is clear in retrospect, that could never be made.

Zhao had had his chance. Party conservatives saw his failure as a vindication of their position that only a show of government force would end the pro-democracy protests. In emergency meetings on the 17th and 18th, the Party's top leadership agreed to take firm measures against the protesters. Zhao, outvoted, refused to go along and offered his resignation instead; Deng, however, refused to accept it. Meanwhile, Li Peng and hard-liners assumed the lead within the Party. On May 18, it was not Zhao but Li who called student leaders into a meeting that would be the government's last attempt to avert an action the hard-liners had been preparing for: the imposition of martial law in the capital. The encounter, however, only underscored the great gulf between the government of hard-liners and the hunger strikers. Excerpts of the meeting, in which most Chinese obtained their first glimpses of the student leaders, and in which Wuer Kaixi attracted the attention of millions by impudently cutting off Premier Li Peng before he had finished his opening remarks, follow.

TRANSCRIPT OF MAY 18 MEETING
BETWEEN PREMIER LI PENG AND STUDENTS
(excerpts)

[Premier] Li Peng: I am very glad to meet you all. For today's meeting, we are going to talk about only one subject: that is, how to get the hunger strikers out of their present plight. The Party and the government are very concerned about this matter. We are also deeply disturbed by it and fear for the health of these students. Let us solve this problem first; afterward, all matters can be easily settled through discussion. We say this not out of any ulterior motives, but mainly because we are concerned. You are all very young; the oldest among you is no more than twenty-three. Even my youngest child is older than you all. I have three children and none of them is involved in profiteering by officials. But all of them are older than you. You are like our own children, our own flesh and blood.

Wuer Kaixi: [interruping] Premier Li, it doesn't seem that we have enough time for this kind of talk.[18] We must enter into a substantive discussion as quickly as possible. Now, I would like to say what we have to say. Just now you have said that we were going to talk about only one subject. But the real situation is not that you invited us to this discussion, but that we, all these many people in the Square, asked you to come and talk. How many subjects to discuss, therefore, ought to be up to us. Fortunately, our views here happen to be in agreement. . . . We have heard and read Comrade Zhao Ziyang's talk that came out in writing yesterday [in which Zhao, on behalf of the Politburo, stated that the students' demands for democracy were reasonable and patriotic, and promised there would be no retaliation]. So why haven't the students gone back [to their campuses]? Because we believe that it was still not enough, far from enough. I am sure you are aware of the conditions that we have put forth [for ending the hunger strike] as well as developments in the Square.

Wang Dan: Let me give a report on the situation in the Square. More than two thousand people have already lost consciousness. As for how to make

18. This translation is based on the official Xinhua News Agency transcript of the meeting. Hong Kong papers published transcripts that differed slightly from the Xinhua account and were somewhat more embarrassing to the Chinese government. Most notably, Wuer Kaixi's opening remarks are recorded as: [interrupting Premier Li Peng] "We don't have much time. We are sitting very comfortably here, but outside the students are suffering from hunger. So excuse me very much for interrupting you. . . ."

them end the hunger strike and leave the Square, all the conditions we have stipulated must be fully met. . . . In this regard, our position is very clear: the only way to make the hunger strikers leave the Square is to satisfy the two demands that our students have presented to you.

Wuer Kaixi: For your age, sir, I feel it might be appropriate if I call you Teacher Li. Teacher Li, the issue at this time is not at all how to persuade the group of us present here. We would very much like to have the students leave the Square. [But] right now, what's happening in the Square is not so much a case in which the minority follows the majority, but one in which 99.9 percent follow 0.1 percent—so if a single hunger striker refuses to leave the Square, then the other several thousand will not leave either.

Wang Dan: Yesterday, we conducted a poll among over a hundred students, asking whether or not they would agree to withdraw from the Square after our conversation with Secretary Yan Mingfu. The poll showed that 99.9 percent of the students voted against withdrawing from the Square. Here, we would like to make clear once again what our demands are: one, that the current student movement be recognized as a patriotic Democracy Movement, not a disturbance, as it has been called; and two, that a dialogue be arranged as quickly as possible and broadcast live. If the government can quickly and satisfactorily respond to these two demands, we then will be able to go and work on the students, to get them to leave the Square. Otherwise, it will be very difficult for us to do this task.

Wuer Kaixi: . . . Up to the present, still no one has stated that the student movement is not turmoil. The nature of this movement must be [properly] defined. Then, we can work out several [specific] methods for [conveying this message]: (1) Comrade Zhao Ziyang or Comrade Li Peng—Zhao Ziyang would be best—could go to the Square and speak directly to the students; or (2) the *People's Daily* could print another editorial repudiating the one published on April 26, one that apologizes to the people across the country and acknowledges the great significance of the current student movement. Only if this is done can we make our best efforts to persuade the students to convert the hunger strike into a sit-in protest. After we reach this point, we can proceed to solve other problems. We on our part will try our best to persuade the students, but we cannot say for sure that we will succeed.

[Student leader] Xiong Yan: We believe that whether or not the government or some other party acknowledges that this is a patriotic democracy movement, history will recognize it as such. But why do [we] especially need the acknowledgment of the government and the others? Because this represents a desire of the people; that is, [a desire] to see if our government is, after all, our own government. . . . Second, we are people who are struggling for the sake of communism, people of conscience, people with humanity. To resolve this kind of problem, [the government] ought not to care about "losing face," or whatever other thing. . . .

Li Peng: Let me raise one point. When we are talking, I hope you will be kind enough not to interrupt. When we are finished, whomever has more to say can speak again, there will be plenty of opportunities. . . .

Yan Mingfu: . . . The only issue that I am concerned with is that of saving the children who are hunger striking in the Square, who are now in a very weakened state, their lives gravely threatened. In my opinion, the final resolution of the issues [between us] and the issue of the hunger strike should be separated. In particular, those students who have not participated in the hunger strike must show care for the hunger strikers. I am confident that in the end we can solve all our problems. . . . We should reach an agreement that these two issues ought to be discussed separately, for the evolving situation, as I pointed out to Wuer Kaixi and Wang Dan on the evening of May 13, has already gone beyond the good intentions of those who initiated the hunger strike. They are already out of your control. . . .

Li Peng: Now, let me make a few points. Since you said you would like to discuss matters of substance, I will begin by discussing a matter of substance. I suggest that the China Red Cross and Beijing Red Cross be put in charge of getting the students who are participating in the hunger strike safely to hospitals. I hope that other students in the Square will support and assist this operation. This is my specific proposal. In the meantime, I will ask all the medical personnel under the jurisdiction of the Central Committee and Beijing Municipality to do their best to rescue and take care of the student hunger strikers, so as to ensure the absolute safety of their lives. Regardless of how many common points of view, or disagreements, we have, saving human lives is our top priority for the moment. . . .

Second, neither the government nor the Party has ever stated that the masses of students were creating turmoil. We have always regarded the patriotic enthusiasm and wishes of the students as positive and good. Many of the things you have done are quite correct; many of your criticisms correspond to what the government sees as problems and hopes to resolve. To be frank, you have definitely provided impetus for finding solutions to these problems. . . . Now that our students have so sharply pointed out these problems, [their criticisms] can help the government overcome obstacles on the road to progress. This I think is positive. However, the way the present situation is developing does not depend on your good intentions, your idealistic visions, or patriotic enthusiasm. The fact is that disorder has already appeared in Beijing and is spreading across the entire country. I do not mean to pin responsibility for disorder onto our students, absolutely not. The present state of affairs is already objective reality. Let me tell you, my students, yesterday the Beijing-Guangzhou railway line around the Wuhan area was blocked for more than three hours; this caused one of our major railway transportation lines to cease operation. And right now, all sorts of idlers and riff-raff from many cities are descending on Beijing in the name of the students. In the past few days, Beijing has basically fallen into a state of anarchy. Let me just reiterate, I do not mean to pin responsibility on our students. I just hope that our students will turn this over in their minds and think about what consequences will follow if things [are allowed to] go on like this.

The government of the People's Republic of China is one responsible to the people, and we cannot sit and watch idly. We must protect the safety of our students, protect our factories, protect the achievements of socialism, and protect our capital. Whether or not you are willing to listen to these words, I am very glad to have had such an opportunity to tell everyone. China has experienced many episodes of turmoil. Creating turmoil was not the original intent of many people, but in the end, turmoil was what occurred.

Third, presently there are some government employees, city residents, workers, even staff from certain departments of our State Council who have taken to the streets to show their support for the students. I hope you will not misunderstand why they are doing so. It is out of their concern for you and out of the hope that you will not harm your health. However, I do not completely approve of the methods of many of these people. If they try to persuade you to eat and drink a little, in order to protect your health, if they try to persuade you to leave the Square and express whatever you have to say to the government by way of discussion, that [kind of behavior] is completely correct. But there are also many who have gone to the Square to encourage you to continue with the hunger strike. I will not say what their motives are, but I do not approve of this kind of behavior. As Premier of the government, I must make my position clear. . . .

[Student] Wang Zhixin: This is not a dialogue but a meeting.

Yan Mingfu: Correct, a meeting.

(based on Xinhua News Agency transcript)

The hard-liners had given the students their final warning. In the comfortable meeting with the students, an exasperated Li Peng had stated, "Beijing in the last few days has basically fallen into a state of anarchy. . . . We [the government] cannot sit by and idly watch. . . . We must protect . . . our factories, the achievements of socialism, and our capital." Now Zhao made his final plea. Defying his colleagues' directives, Zhao, tailed by an impassive Li Peng, hastened to Tiananmen in the small hours of the morning on the 19th to visit the hunger strikers. On the verge of tears, Zhao beseeched the students to give up the hunger strike. Hinting at the division in the Party leadership, he told them, "We have come too late. I am sorry, my students. You can criticize us. This is justified. You have already been hunger striking for seven days. Does it have to be eight, nine, or ten days? . . . Many problems can be resolved. . . . The door to dialogue will not be shut. But resolving these problems requires a definite process . . . all matters and situations are always very complicated, they need a definite process [to resolve]."

Zhao's personal, emotional appeal reached many of the hunger strikers. Reading between the lines of Zhao's brief comments, they began to feel for the first time that it made more sense to return to campuses and prepare to assist Zhao and his moderate supporters than to remain in the Square. And further sacrifice seemed pointless, given the hard-liners' indifference to their suffering. Students also realized their ranks had been depleted by illness; increasing numbers of hospitalized or weak students were yielding to the pleas of parents and friends to take food.

The shocking news that the government was about to put the capital under martial law, leaked to the protestors sometime Friday by Zhao's associates, suddenly added new urgency to the debate over whether or not to continue the hunger strike. Various proposals circulated through the student camp: to leave the Square, to end the fast but remain where they were, to have the students from the provinces return home; to concentrate efforts on blocking the troops' entry into Beijing, and so on.

As the students argued among themselves, a last desperate attempt by Zhao's faction to challenge the hard-liners was taking shape. Outvoted in the Politburo, Zhao's last hope was to seek support from a wider political base, the National People's Congress. Under the Chinese Constitution, the National People's Congress was the "highest organ of state power" with the power "to recall or remove from office the Premier"; furthermore, the Standing Committee of the Congress was

Illustration 4.8. A banner in Tiananmen during the hunger strike: "Save the Children." Credit: October Review.

granted the power to "annul those administrative rules and regulations or orders of the State Council that contravene the Constitution or statutes." Such a strategy for checking the power of the Party had been proposed and discussed in the past by liberal thinkers, but this was the first occasion on which it would actually be put to the test.

As early as May 4, Zhao had suggested resolving the crisis of the student protests "through legal and democratic avenues"; yet it is unlikely that at the time he actually expected to be forced to turn to the National People's Congress. Zhao and his supporters must have known that in normal circumstances, the odds were nil that the rubber-stamp Congress, or even its executive body, the Standing Committee, would act to negate a Party decision. But these were no ordinary times: millions of citizens, including workers and Party members—citizens who had never before dared to challenge the Party—had demonstrated against the hard-line government. Even the moderates had come to think that "people power" might make a difference.

Zhao's faction thus shifted tactics to focus on making public the rift between Zhao and the hard-liners. Casting the rupture as primarily a struggle between Zhao and Li Peng, the unpopular Premier, they sought to build support inside and outside the Party for the convening of a special session of the National People's Congress. To reach the public, Zhao's supporters relied on contacts with student groups (and possibly with workers' organizations that were forming at this time), and used the organizational force of these groups to spread word of the rupture between Zhao and the conservatives (for example, a student declaration on the 19th called for the convening of the National People's Congress); they also used the organizations they directly controlled, such as the Research Institute for Economic Restructuring, an influential think-tank that Zhao had loaded with bright young economists and analysts committed to reform that was directed by Chen Yizi, an advisor to Zhao, and the State Commission for the Restructuring of the Economic System, the government body that had spearheaded reform.

Two handbills released by supporters of Zhao divulging details of Zhao's break with the hard-liners and the imminent announcement of martial law are printed below. Although not all of the information provided in the first one, written by an unidentified group of apparently high-level officials, may be accurate, its account of the Politburo meeting essentially conforms with reliable reports from other sources. The second handbill, which was read several times over the students' broadcasting station in Tiananmen, was released by the Research Institute for Economic Restructuring and three other liberal organizations closely associated with Zhao. Reports by the government after the crushing of the Democracy Movement condemning the maneuvers of Zhao's faction would mention these handbills.

A LETTER TO THE PEOPLE

Citizens of the Republic, fellow compatriots, dear students, members of the Communist Party, members of the People's Liberation Army:

With deepest grief and the greatest indignation, we make public to you news that is absolutely true: Secretary General Zhao Ziyang has been recalled; Li Peng now presides over the Politburo; and a decision has been made to take extreme measures against the students tonight. The following is a brief account of the events leading to these decisions:

On May 13, at a Politburo Standing Committee Meeting, Zhao Ziyang proposed that the April 26 editorial in the *People's Daily* be immediately repudiated. His proposal was overruled. On May 15, Zhao Ziyang decided to go to Tiananmen Square and make public his personal views, but was stopped by the General Office of the Central Committee, the reason being that such an action violated Party discipline. On May 16, at a Politburo Standing Committee meeting, which Deng Xiaoping attended, Zhao Ziyang set forth six proposals:

1. that the April 26 editorial be repudiated;
2. that he take personal responsibility for the editorial;
3. that the National People's Congress establish a special organization for the investigation of profiteering activities by the sons and daughters of high-ranking officials, including his own son;
4. that official résumés and personal backgrounds of officials with the rank of vice minister and above be made public;
5. that the income and benefits of high-ranking cadres be made public; and
6. that the special privileges of high-ranking cadres, such as "special supplies," be abolished.

The above proposals were overruled. On May 17, the Politburo Standing Committee passed by a slender majority the decision that Zhao step down and Li Peng take over the Politburo. Now the imposition of martial law is imminent, and the dark days following the April 5 crackdown in 1976 are about to be repeated.

But times are different now. History will not be reenacted. As has been reported, Wan Li had firmly supported Zhao Ziyang; he called a meeting of the Deputy Ministers of the National People's Congress, which unanimously passed a resolution refusing to accept the above decisions of the Politburo. Li Peng threatened to impose Party discipline to punish Wan Li. According to another reliable report, [staff from] the Commission for the Restructuring of the Economic System and nine other commissions and ministries have decided to stage a protest hunger strike. In light of these grave developments, we urgently appeal to people from all walks of life:

1. Under no circumstances must you resort to violence in opposing [the Li Peng government and martial law].
2. Workers, students, professors, and citizens, begin a nationwide boycott.
3. The People's Liberation Army is an army made up of your brothers and children. Under no circumstances must we massacre one another.

We vehemently demand:

1. Immediately convene [a special meeting of] the Standing Committee of the National People's Congress—dismiss Li Peng!
2. Immediately convene a special meeting of the National Party Congress[19] [of the Communist Party] to choose a Secretary Gen-

19. According to the Chinese Communist Party Charter, the National Party Congress is the

eral—put an end to the conduct of state affairs from "behind the screen" and to rule by old men!

Fellow citizens, compatriots, and dear fellow students—

The Chinese nation is once again at a time of crisis. Our Republic and the Chinese Communist Party face a life-or-death choice, a choice that will determine whether they survive or perish. Let us take action at once and, with whatever nonviolent means possible, put up firm resistance!

—Some cadres from central organs,
May 19, 1989
(*handbill*)

SIX STATEMENTS CONCERNING THE PRESENT SITUATION

1. The current patriotic Democracy Movement, led by university students and widely participated in by people from nearly all social sectors, has written the brightest chapter ever in the history of Chinese democracy movements.

2. The degeneration of the situation to today's grave state is due entirely to the Party's and government's procrastination and errors in their policies.

3. Since the founding of the People's Republic, the top leadership of the Party and the government has never in this manner divorced itself from the people, violated the dictates of wisdom, and directly opposed itself to the wishes of the people. The reason for this lies in the traditional political structure, one that is incapable of operating under a system of law. The absence of openness in politics has led to a situation in which those in the Party and the government are obsessed with power struggles at the top and do not consider the interests of the nation and the future of the country to be of foremost importance.

4. At present, the situation is still deteriorating. [The top leadership's] insistence on standing by its wrong decisions and committing new mistakes that result in extreme measures (such as the imposition of martial law) will lead to real turmoil, even division of the nation. This dark pros-

---

"highest organ" of the Party; however, it is a rubber-stamp body that meets only once every five years. Its primary function is to validate the resolutions of intra-Party conflicts.

pect is something that the Chinese people, who have gone through the ten-year Cultural Revolution, can by no means accept.

5. Therefore:

We call for the disclosure of the behind-the-scenes maneuvers and the disputes within the top leadership; let the people of the entire country make a judgment and choice [about what they want];

We call for the immediate convening of a special meeting of the National People's Congress to exercise the supreme power granted it by the Constitution and intervene [to end martial law];

We call for the immediate convening of a special meeting of the National Party Congress to review the work of the Politburo during this most recent period;

We call for all those who are active in support of the students in all quarters to observe reason and order; we call for all to protect the achievements that this student movement has already made;

We call on people from all walks of life to organize and assist the students in maintaining order and in logistical work;

We call on the hunger strikers to take special care of themselves, and to end the hunger strike at the earliest opportunity. You have already won a significant victory. Our country needs you to win new victories through newer, more enduring means!

6. Our country is the people's country; our government is the people's government; and our army is the people's army. The historical tide of modernization in China is something no force whatever can block!

> —Research Institute for
> Economic Restructuring
> Rural Development Research Center
> of the State Council
> China Trust Company Research Institute for
> International Issues
> Beijing Young Economists' Association
> 4:00 P.M., May 19
> (handbill)

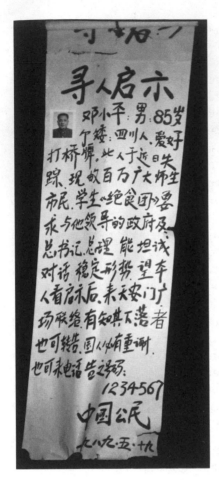

Illustration 4.9. A poster in Tiananmen on the eve of martial law reads: Missing Person Notice: Deng Xiaoping, male, 85, short, from Sichuan Province. Hobby: bridge. This person has recently disappeared. Presently, several million students, teachers, Beijing residents, and the student "Hunger Strikers' Group" are asking for a frank and sincere dialogue with the government he heads, the Secretary General of the Party, and the Premier of the government. [Such a dialogue] will calm down the situation. We hope that after seeing this notice, the above person will come to Tiananmen Square to get in touch with these groups. Those aware of his whereabouts can also notify us. The citizens will be most grateful for any assistance. Contact can also be made by phone at the following number: 1234567.

—Chinese citizens,
May 19, 1989

Credit: Han Minzhu

5

THE DECLARATION OF MARTIAL LAW

AND THE ARMY'S

ATTEMPT TO ENTER BEIJING

"Rescind Martial Law!" "Down with Li Peng!"

May 19 – May 27

"To maintain social order in the capital and restore normal routine, we have had no alternative but to move to Beijing some troops from the People's Liberation Army. . . . This action is absolutely not directed at the students."
President Yang Shangkun, May 19, 1989

What Are You Lacking?

The newspapers are in your hands,
Broadcasting is in your hands,
Guns are in your hands,
Prisons are in your hands.
So what are you lacking, oh Emperor?
You lack only the hearts of the people.
You lack only the truth.

from the student News Herald, *May 22, 1989*

he end of the hunger strike that had triggered the most serious political
crisis of Deng's rule proved to be both anticlimactic and irrelevant. The
Hunger Strikers' Group declared at 9:00 P.M. on the 19th that the hunger
strike had been converted into a sit-in protest, but the announcement was overshadowed by growing fear of martial law and possible violence. It also did little to
alleviate government fears of losing control of the capital; indeed, hard-liners only
viewed the decision, perhaps with some justification, as part of Zhao's strategy to
muster public support for his forces by making martial law appear no longer necessary.

Only one hour after the students' announcement, Li Peng and President Yang
Shangkun addressed high Party and army officials at a special meeting. Also present
were members of the Politburo Standing Committee and Vice President Wang
Zhen; only Zhao was conspicuously missing. Stiffly punching his fist into the air, Li
delivered a tough speech that echoed the inflammatory *People's Daily* editorial of
April 26. Martial law over all important districts of Beijing would be formally declared at 10:00 the next morning. Excerpts from Li's speech, as well as one by Yang
that followed it, are presented below.[1]

SPEECH OF PREMIER LI PENG AT SPECIAL MEETING OF CENTRAL AND BEIJING MUNICIPAL PARTY, GOVERNMENT, AND ARMY CADRES ON MAY 19, 1989
(excerpts)

Comrades!

Today, in accordance with the decision of the Standing Committee of
the Politburo of the Communist Party of China, the Central Committee
and the State Council have convened a meeting of central and Beijing
Municipal Party, government, and army cadres to ask that everyone urgently mobilize, take firm and forceful measures, take a clear stand to halt
turmoil, restore social order, and protect stability and unity, to ensure
that [our policy of] reform, opening, and socialist modernization can be
smoothly carried out.

The briefing that Li Ximing, Secretary of the Beijing Municipal Party
Committee, has just given shows that the situation in the capital is quite
grave. Anarchy is becoming more and more serious; law and discipline

1. About half of Premier Li's speech is translated here. The full text of the official Xinhua
News Agency translation is reprinted in the *New York Times*, May 20, 1989, p. A-6.

are being violated. Before the beginning of May, the situation had begun to calm down, due to our concerted efforts. But entering May, turmoil again began to rise. More and more students and other people became involved in demonstrations, many universities were paralyzed, traffic was jammed everywhere, leading offices of the Party and government were rushed, and public security deteriorated. This seriously interfered with and upset the normal production, work, and school schedules, and daily routines of the people of the whole city. Also because of this, arrangements for some of the activities for the Sino-Soviet summit meeting, which attracted worldwide attention, had to be changed or cancelled, greatly damaging our country's international image and prestige.

The hunger strike being carried out by some of the students on Tiananmen Square is continuing. Their health has already been seriously damaged, and the lives of some are in danger. In fact, a minority is using the hunger-striking students as hostages, and they are trying to threaten and coerce the government into responding to their political conditions. They do not possess even a drop of humanitarianism. The Party and government have taken every measure they can to treat and rescue the fasting students, have repeatedly engaged in dialogue with representatives of the hunger strikers, and have solemnly declared that they will continue to listen to their opinions in the future, in the hope that they would immediately stop their hunger strike, but this has not obtained the hoped-for results. With extremely excited crowds packing Tiananmen Square, shouting inflammatory slogans continuously, the representatives of the hunger strikers even indicated themselves that they were no longer able to control the situation. Now, if we do not promptly bring this situation to an end, and instead just let things keep developing, a situation that no one wants to see will very likely emerge. . . .

As our Party and government have stated many times, the intentions of the great majority of the students are good and honest; the students themselves do not wish to create turmoil. They are patriotic; they hope to advance democracy, to fight corruption in the government. These desires are consistent with the objectives that the Party and government want to try their hardest to achieve. Some of the issues and views that they have raised have already played a constructive role in improving the work of the Party and government. But irresponsibly resorting to methods such as marches, demonstrations, class boycotts, and even hunger strikes that have harmed social stability has not only impeded the resolution of problems, it has also caused the situation to develop along lines other than those the students themselves desired. In fact, the situation is moving more and more toward the opposite of what they seek.

It is becoming clearer and clearer that an extremely small number of people want to achieve through turmoil their political goals, which are to negate the leadership of the Communist Party and to negate the socialist system. They openly come out with slogans negating opposition to bourgeois liberalization. The goal is to achieve an absolute freedom which brazenly opposes the Four Cardinal Principles. They spread masses of rumors, and attack, slander, and insult the principal leaders of the Party and government. Now they are concentrating their attack on Comrade Deng Xiaoping, who has made immense contributions to the cause of reform and opening. Their goal is to undermine organizationally the leadership of the Communist Party of China, overthrow the government legally constituted by the National People's Congress, and totally negate the people's democratic dictatorship. They stir up trouble everywhere, secretly link up with others, encourage the establishment of all sorts of illegal organizations, and attempt to force the Party and government to recognize them. What they want to do is lay a foundation for the establishment in China of opposition factions and an opposition party. If they should achieve their goals, reform and opening, our democratic legal system, and socialist modernization would all go up in smoke, and China would undergo a reversal of history. A China with great hope and a great future would become a China without hope or future.

An important purpose of our taking a clear stand against turmoil and exposing the political plotting of an extremely small number of people is to distinguish the masses of young students from an extremely small number of people who are the ones inciting turmoil. This is because we care for the young students. The same desire and goal was the reason we previously took such an extremely tolerant, restrained attitude in dealing with the student movement. We didn't want to harm good people, particularly not young students. But that extremely small number hiding in the background, plotting and fomenting turmoil, thought the Party and government were soft and could be pushed around. They constantly manufactured rumors, deceived the masses, and exaggerated the situation. As a result, the situation in the capital and in many places throughout the country has become more and more grave. We are forced to take decisive, firm measures to halt the turmoil. . . .

Comrades! Our Party is the governing party; our government is a people's government. To fulfill our responsibilities to our sacred motherland and to the entire people, we must take firm, decisive measures to put a swift end to the turmoil, protect the leadership of the Party, and protect the socialist system. In so doing, we are confident of the support and approval of all members of the Communist Party and Communist Youth

League, workers, peasants, intellectuals, democratic parties, people from various walks of life, and the broad masses. . . .

SPEECH BY PRESIDENT YANG SHANGKUN ON MAY 19, 1989
(excerpt)

. . . I completely stand behind the statements made by Comrade Li Peng as a representative of the Standing Committee of the Politburo. Recently Beijing's normal work and production, order, and daily routines have all been thrown into chaos; in essence, in many aspects, [Beijing] is already in a state of anarchy. To maintain social order in the capital and restore normal routine, we have had no alternative but to move [to Beijing] some troops from the People's Liberation Army. This is entirely for the purpose of assisting the People's Armed Police and public security police to carry out their duties. It absolutely is not directed at the students. I hope that every sector of society and the broad masses of the people will show full understanding and support for this action. . . .

"Military Control Is an Insult to Beijing Residents"

Once more Deng and the hard-liners in the government had grossly misread—or blatantly chosen to ignore—the mood of the populace. No move could have more provoked the residents of Beijing. During the day on Friday the 19th, the streets of the capital had been somewhat quieter, as if the majority of citizens had collectively discharged their anger in the giant demonstrations of May 17 and 18. The deployment of troops, however, stirred them into action once more on the night of the 19th. At key intersections around the city, often alerted by members of the "Flying Tigers"—a motorcycle squad formed by Beijing's nouveau riche, its young, swaggering private entrepreneurs—residents young and old swarmed onto the streets to block army trucks, tanks, and armored personnel carriers. Surrounded by thousands of peaceful but determined citizens, the convoys full of armed soldiers stalled, unable to move forward or turn back. In some cases, they were able to advance to within the city's perimeters before running into the human blockades; in others, they were stopped far away from Tiananmen in outlying counties. As news that the army had ground to a halt filtered back to Tiananmen in the deep hours of the night, students there breathed sighs of relief: Tiananmen was evidently safe for the time being.

Most of the citizen resistance arose spontaneously out of anger and shock that the government would resort to military force to regain control of the capital. Beijing residents were also determined to protect the students; Yang Shangkun's assertion that the army was not being sent in to suppress the students had been greeted by universal disbelief. Those responding to the reports of army (or People's Armed Police) sightings, reports as often false as accurate, ranged from young parents with a child in tow to "dare-to-die" groups of young students and workers. The first wave of citizen resistance was soon reinforced by a strong propaganda campaign to mobilize the entire city. The activists, who by now included not only students and associates of Zhao but also workers, seized on any means available to get their messages across: big-character posters, typed or handwritten flyers, broadcasts at Tiananmen and from campuses (at People's University, students had set up a station to broadcast out toward the street), and speeches at street corners. Some of the materials hastily drafted in reaction to martial law exhorted the people to organize and maintain a state of vigilance; others appealed to the People's Liberation Army soldiers to not force their way into the city; and still others defiantly expressed outrage at the government's manner of ruling the country.

EMERGENCY DECLARATION FROM THE PEOPLE OF THE CAPITAL TO THE PEOPLE OF THE NATION

The capital is in danger! China is in danger! The nation is in danger! The Republic is in mortal danger!

Faced with the democratic struggle of millions of patriotic students and people from every level of society [which has blossomed in] the past weeks, the current ruling clique in the government has brazenly stirred up disturbances, announced military control, and branded the patriotic movement of the millions in the capital as "turmoil." All this stands in flagrant violation of the Constitution of the Republic. They have placed themselves in diametric opposition to the people, becoming traitors to and enemies of the Republic. They may no longer be said to represent Party and country.

Now is the darkest, bloodiest, and most inhuman time in the history of the Republic, a time that like none before causes one billion people to completely despair. The Republic now faces its most severe trial ever. . . .

The people of the capital, in their opposition to bloody oppression and high-handed terrorism, have already mentally prepared themselves to fight to the last drop of blood. They have begun an emergency mobilization, preparing to throw themselves into the struggle, and hereby issue this emergency declaration to the people of the entire nation:

1. [We] call upon the people of the nation to initiate a "national movement of noncooperation" in resistance to the government. Since the present ruling clique no longer represents the country and the government, do not cooperate with it, follow its orders or implement its directives, or heed it.

2. Begin emergency nationwide activities in support of the Democracy Movement, and assist the capital with emergency medical facilities and medication.

3. Begin a movement to obtain the signatures of delegates to the People's Congress from all over the country on a petition to remove from office Yang Shangkun, Wang Zhen [Vice President and a conservative member of the "group of elders"], Li Peng, and Yao Yilin [member of the Politburo Standing Committee and conservative economist]—members of the ruling clique of the present military government—in order to forestall great bloodshed among the people and to rescue the Republic.

4. Launch an emergency effort to encourage troops from all over the country to declare publicly their solidarity with the people, to strengthen their protection of the lives of the people of the capital, and to mete out punishment to the prime culprits in the government.

5. Launch an emergency effort to encourage all provincial, municipal, and autonomous regional governments, as well as military districts, to declare their support for the people of the capital and condemn the ruling clique; to promote and protect political stability in all [other] places; to oppose publicly the ruling clique of the present military government; and to declare it a bogus governing regime.

6. Use every possible means to call upon the governments and peoples of the world for support, assistance, and aid. . . .

10. The people of the capital, along with all the patriotic students, are determined to protect with their blood and their lives the Republic and the dignity of the constitution, even if the price is the loss of their freedom, the beautiful blue sky, their very lifeblood.

Unite, people of China!
The people shall triumph!
Long live the people's democracy movement!

—May 20, 1989
(handbill)

RESPECTFULLY SUBMITTED TO ALL THE OFFICERS AND SOLDIERS OF THE PEOPLE'S LIBERATION ARMY WHO HAVE RECEIVED ORDERS TO ENTER BEIJING

I am the daughter of a veteran, the wife of a middle-aged military man. I am at the same time a university instructor. At this moment, our students are in Tiananmen Square protesting the Li Peng government that has lost its mind. I have heard about your arrival in the suburbs of Beijing. I gather you must have seen what attitude the millions of Beijing citizens hold toward this patriotic democracy movement of the students. If the Li Peng government has deceived you, then the masses will tell you what the true situation is. The action of the masses has already declared to the entire world that this movement in Beijing is a great patriotic democracy movement, one that has received the support of people across the nation, including officers and soldiers of the People's Liberation Army who know what has been going on. Now the millions of citizens of Beijing, together with the hundreds of thousands of university students, are prepared to resist to the end the Li Peng government, which has already become the enemy of the people. Because over the past month the people have been observing the words and actions of the Li Peng government, they have completely lost hope in it.

Truth, I believe, will eventually defeat evil. These last few days, what has worried me most is that you might appear here; I am worried because you have no idea what is really going on. Now you have indeed followed your orders and come, and I can hardly control myself. I only want to tell you all how we feel at this very moment. I have deep love for you, but I have deeper love for my sincere, lovely students and for the millions of Beijing residents who have, acting out of a sense of justice, bravely stepped forth and given the students resolute support at this critical time when their struggle has become one of life or death. Because I only want to tell you that I absolutely do not wish you to fight [for this government], I am standing right in front of you. I just want to tell you that if you dare to raise your hands against the people of the capital, against my students, history will forsake you. You will be called "the men most hated" rather than "the men most loved."[2]

As one who is a relative of yours, I beg you with my tears: do not under any circumstances touch our students and do not under any circum-

2. A reference to a movie called "The Men Most Loved" about People's Liberation Army soldiers.

Illustration 5.1. Beijing residents surround and block army convoys attempting to move into the capital. Credit: Ming Pao Newspapers, Hong Kong.

stances anger the people. It is already wrong of Li Peng to have told you to come. Now the people can still forgive you. But if you raise your hands against them, you will all remain condemned through the ages.

I am standing in front of you, with my son in my arms. If you decide to advance, you will have to drive your tanks over my body.

> Respectfully yours,
> A Soldier's Wife, May 21, 1989
> (distributed by the Qinghua University
> Propaganda Team, May 25, 1989)
> *(handbill)*

THE PEOPLE OF BEIJING DO HAVE "QUALMS" ABOUT THE ARMY'S ENTRY INTO THE CITY!

Because of blockades and various protective measures that the people of Beijing have used in the past few days to exert pressure and halt them, the military troops ordered by Li Peng to carry out the martial law decree are still trying to enter the city of Beijing. To account for this situation, a few government newspapers have explained that the people of Beijing are uneasy about the army's entrance into the city because they have never experienced such military control before, and that they have "qualms" because they fear that once the troops are in the city, they will kill students.

Following the line of logic laid down in these news reports, it would seem that once these "qualms" were dispelled, the people of the capital would welcome the troops into the city without any "qualms or hesitations."

The fact is that the people of the capital have already taken a clear stance in the matter; with regard to the army's entrance into the city, they do not in the least have "qualms or hesitations."

The people of the capital resolutely oppose what Li Peng has called "a martial law decree," and oppose military control. They do so because this "martial law decree" represents to them that utterly contemptible and primitive form of power politics—dictatorship; because this "martial law decree" is intended to nip China's democracy in the bud and, by military force, frighten the people into submission to Li Peng's foolish, feudalist rule of autocracy; because this "martial law decree" is nothing but an excuse that Li Peng and his gang uses to vindicate their abuse of power over the people. The people of Beijing are totally capable of self-government. Until now, all has been well in Beijing; the people have lived and worked in peace, and no turmoil has existed at all. Beijing has no need for any type of military control.

Now, in the closing years of the twentieth century, the people of Beijing are not about to allow the wheels of history to turn backward. The people have come to understand that if China is truly to develop, the entire nation must unite under the banners of democracy, freedom, the rule of law, and human rights. Each person's wisdom and talents must be allowed full play while power must be subject to checks, and the people must be encouraged to participate in the government, so that government by the few may be changed to government by the many, and a lively political culture may emerge.

History has reached the end of the twentieth century. At a time when the majority of the world's nations are brave enough to open up and move ahead, continually and creatively doing the best they can to develop their countries, the Chinese people are still fighting for rudimentary democratic rights. Given this contrast, how can the people of the capital not be enraged at the Li Peng gang's reactionary, villainous action of threatening the people with military force? How can this fail to awaken the people's courage and stiffen their resolution to fight their last battle against the Li Peng gang in order to protect their own rights and to prevent our motherland from further depredations at the hands of autocrats?

He who underestimates, he who defies the awakening of the Chinese people will be cast aside by the people.

The people will triumph!

—Some Beijing University Teachers,
May 25, 1989

Students played a leading role in the citizen resistance. In particular, Beijing students, most of whom had left Tiananmen to return to their campuses, helped to maximize the blockades' effectiveness by spreading word of the latest army movements and overseeing the erection of barricades. Where troops were hemmed in by crowds, students worked to maintain calm and order. They also stepped into the shoes of the Beijing police, who had vanished from sight during the mass demonstrations the week before, assuming responsibility for keeping traffic flowing to the extent possible. Throughout martial law, students called on their classmates and Beijing residents to exercise restraint and avoid provocation of the army. In the handbill below, prepared by Beijing University students, the people are urged to understand the difficult position of the troops confronting them.

AN OPEN LETTER TO BEIJING RESIDENTS CONCERNING THE ENTRY OF THE ARMY INTO THE CITY

To our comrades, the residents of Beijing:

For more than a month you have actively participated in every possible way in the patriotic Democracy Movement, and have made a tremendous contribution that has moved our nation to song and to tears. In the past few days, however, a few people in the Central Committee, usurping the name of the Party and the government, have deceived the officers and soldiers of the People's Liberation Army (PLA), and have attempted to use military force against the people in a bloody act of suppression. In view of the current situation, we call upon the masses of the city residents who are at all avenues blocking the entry of the PLA to keep in mind the following points:

1. The PLA is not our real antagonist. The PLA is an army made up of the people's own sons and brothers. Unaware of the true state of affairs, they have been tricked into coming here. In the past few days, some

troops have had no access to newspapers or television, and thus have been unable to obtain complete and unbiased information about the current Democracy Movement. For this reason, we must explain the facts to them and tell them what the true situation is so that they can understand what the people want. However, in disseminating our views, we must use reason and not force; we must persuade them rather than force our ideas on them. We must understand and respect the officers and soldiers of the PLA.

2. Those who have usurped the name of the Central Committee and the government and have deceived the PLA into coming to Beijing have now adopted a completely irresponsible attitude toward the troops, deliberately making inadequate provision for their food supplies. There are troops who have hardly eaten anything for several days. The usurpers' intention is none other than to provoke conflict between the army and the people. In response to this situation, we must demonstrate our concern for the people's army and do everything possible to make sure that they have adequate supplies of food and drink.

3. We must understand that it is a soldier's duty to obey orders. Yet we will explain to them that a soldier has the right to resist or oppose orders that contravene the will of the people. It is of even greater importance to explain to the troops that the people have no alternative but to block their way, but that in so doing the people will avoid any violent confrontation. At the same time, we must be on our guard against undercover police or others with ulterior motives who might attack the troops as an act of provocation.

4. If the troops break formation to withdraw or rest, let them pass unhindered.

> *(Beijing University handbill,*
> *May 20, 1989;*
> *title added by editors)*

"We Don't Want Order Imposed at Knifepoint"

Through the weekend and into the beginning of the next week Beijing residents acted as if their city was under siege—from their own government's army. At some sites Beijing's lumbering articulated buses were driven up and parked across primary access routes into the city. Lorry drivers abandoned their vehicles, sometimes still loaded, after conferring with students about the proper spot to leave them. Traffic dividers were dragged onto the roads. The city's subway system, with a station at

Illustration 5.2. At Hujialou, a major Beijing intersection, a local student updates a crowd that has stopped army trucks on developments across the city. Foreign military analysts later reported that the trucks blocked here were transporting anti-aircraft missile fuel; no missiles, however, were detected. Credit: Han Minzhu.

Qianmen at the southeastern corner of Tiananmen, was shut down; unconfirmed reports stated that subway workers had done this to prevent troops from sneaking in underground.

Residents and students felt reasonably secure during daylight hours. But tension across the metropolis, particularly in the Square, mounted as the sun went down; it was common belief that if the army were to move, it would do so between midnight and 5 A.M. At night, Beijing streets, normally quiet even on sultry summer evenings, were filled with thousands of bicyclists, a citizenry turned volunteer nightwatchmen. In the Square, protestors, now heavily dominated by students from outside Beijing, remained calm and remarkably disciplined, yet an edge of nervousness occasionally verging on paranoia was unmistakable: rumors abounded of electrified subway grills or of tear gas attacks by paratroopers, and at one point, students lofted homemade kites in the hope that the lines would entangle parachutes bearing tear gas canisters or soldiers.

As the handbill below reveals, their stunning blockade of the army, which reduced martial law to a hollow proclamation, filled the people of Beijing, from store clerks to Party cadres, with a great deal of pride, and led many to believe overoptimistically that their actions would bring about the downfall of Li Peng.

THE HEROIC PEOPLE

—A Record of the May 20, 1989 Incident

(excerpts)

It was surprising, Chernyshevsky [the Russian revolutionary and writer] once said, that during the time of revolution the common people who ordinarily appeared to be apathetic and indifferent could show an enthusiasm never before seen in them.

The Chinese people today, and the residents and workers of Beijing in particular, are revealing an enthusiasm and courage that astonish the world. They have shown no fear in what they do or think, only an amazing ability to understand a righteous cause. They have moved the world with their indomitable revolutionary spirit, one of absolute selflessness in the face of all kinds of danger as they fight for justice—a spirit that they have never been able to express under normal circumstances (and which may well lie low after today). The revolution occurring at this very moment in China depends on the masses, who every day strike us as ordinary, and whose vigorous efforts will save us from total destruction.

At this moment, soldiers are all around the city; it is highly possible that the Democracy Movement will be suppressed. This revolution is facing a critical moment, and can be saved by nothing other than the courage and passion of the people. . . .

The army's trucks, tanks, and armored personnel carriers have been kept in the suburbs by public buses and garbage cans, and other objects used as road blocks, and by people who are willing to let their bodies— bodies made of flesh and blood—be crushed by the tanks. The martial law that Li Peng and his gang has issued has thus far been rendered as useless as a blank sheet of paper. The soldiers are being persuaded by excited people and students; some of the persuaders are choking with sobs, while some soldiers shed tears in return. Quite a number of soldiers have driven their trucks away.

The workers are on strike, and the people are in the streets. Traffic is being directed not by policemen but by students and city residents. The demonstrators and their trucks continuously march and drive by Tiananmen. There are several hundred thousand people gathered at the Square, where red flags and banners emblazoned with slogans flutter in the air. The streets are filled with passersby, leaflets, and knots of people continually forming and reforming. People are exchanging news, discussing the development of events, and expressing their opinions. Nowhere

Illustration 5.3. A workers' bicycle brigade patrols the streets at night. Credit: Franki Chan.

can one find a supporter of martial law, but leaflets cursing the Li Peng gang and the government are visible everywhere. By the street under the Gate of Heavenly Peace [facing Tiananmen Square], the banner of the "Capital Workers' Autonomous Union" has appeared; public buses have now stopped running, and the subway has been closed by the workers, who cut off the power supply for fear that the subway might be used by the troops. It is said that the students have ended their hunger strike (the people have opposed continuing the hunger strike), because it has already been proven that the hunger strike can never move that bunch of "bastards," "whose conscience has been eaten up by dogs. . . ."

On the ruins of the autocratic system, we will rebuild a great China!

Mao Tse-tung was like the sun that shone everywhere.
Deng Xiaoping is like the moon, never the same on the first and fifteenth of the month.
Hu Yaobang was like a shooting star, a flash of light in a time of darkness.
Li Peng, that inferior brother of theirs, is more like a black hole.

—A Cadre of a Central Committee Office,
morning, May 21
(poster on a Beijing street)

From the very beginning of the protests, the government had linked student activism to "turmoil" (*dongluan*). The charge of creating "turmoil" was a serious one in China. "Turmoil" was not just troublemaking; turmoil was the destroyer of social stability and unity, a threat to the fabric of Chinese society, for it was closely associated in the minds of Chinese with the trauma of the Cultural Revolution, when young Red Guards had terrorized citizens and when Chinese feared betrayal by neighbor, colleague, or even family member. In *People's Daily* editorials and speeches by government leaders, the specter of the Cultural Revolution, now officially termed the "Ten Years of Turmoil" (or alternatively, the "Ten Years of Chaos") had been raised: the takeovers of campus broadcasting stations, the appearance of big-character posters, the forming of nonsanctioned student organizations, and the initiation of contacts with workers and students in other cities had all been compared to the activities of students at the opening of the Cultural Revolution.

Students responded to the government's attempt to associate them with "turmoil" by writing posters that compared and distinguished the pro-democracy protests from the turbulence of the Cultural Revolution. Other poster writers acknowledged that there had indeed been many upheavals in China since 1949, but asked people to consider who bore responsibility for this turmoil. One such poster follows.

FOR FORTY YEARS, WHO HAS BEEN CREATING TURMOIL?

1957: In the 1957 Anti-Rightist Campaign launched by Mao Tse-tung, hundreds of thousands of intellectuals were condemned as rightists.[3] The number of people who were either exiled or driven into committing suicide was countless.

1958-1962: The Great Leap Forward launched by Mao Tse-tung resulted in a depression of a severity never before experienced.[4] Countless people died of starvation, and edema could be found everywhere.

3. See note 14 below.
4. Under the slogan of "catch up with Great Britain within fifteen years," in the winter of 1957 the Party introduced the "Great Leap Forward," a grossly overambitious program to propel China into the ranks of developed nations. Acting out of the belief that economic development could be achieved through the sheer musclepower of the mobilized Chinese masses, leaders implemented policies that within a year brought the economy to the brink of collapse. Workers were ordered to work round-the-clock shifts to the point of exhaustion, machines were run nonstop until they broke down, hundreds of thousands of acres of

1966-1978: Mao Tse-tung's Cultural Revolution, "unprecedented in history," plunged the Chinese people into a disaster also unprecedented in history.

1983-1984: The campaign launched by Deng Xiaoping in the name of "a nationwide attack on criminal offenders" led to a countless number of unjustified, fabricated, and erroneous convictions.[5] This was followed by great numbers of people all over the country appealing to, lodging complaints with, and demanding redress from higher authorities.

1987: The Anti-Bourgeois Liberalization Campaign launched by Deng Xiaoping resulted in a nationwide ideological confusion, which forced Hu Yaobang to step down, caused a large number of intellectuals to leave the country, and hindered the nation's progress in areas of science, technology, and culture.

July-October, 1988: Misjudgments in the central government's economic policies led to depreciation of the Chinese yuan, which then led to drastic withdrawals of savings and panic buying across the country; all of this caused tremendous anxiety among the populace.

May 20, 1989: Deng Xiaoping, Li Peng, Yang Shangkun, raping the will of the people, ordered the imposition of martial law in Beijing. Deploying thousands of troops equipped with tanks, aircraft, artillery, armored cars, and chemical weapons, they planned a bloody crackdown against the people. The city of Beijing, the entire country, and the entire world responded to this with outrage and with vehement support of the demonstraters; residents of Beijing and students tried to block the troops.

---

forestland were cleared, and peasants in the newly formed communes were forced to try to meet totally unrealizable grain quotas. The folly of the Great Leap Forward was perhaps best epitomized by the call for citizens to manufacture steel in their own "backyard furnaces." With the economy in tatters as a result of the Great Leap Forward, an estimated twenty million Chinese died of starvation when a series of natural disasters struck the country in 1960 and 1961.

5. In the fall of 1983, the Party commenced a harsh crackdown on criminal elements that led to the arrest and imprisonment of at least six hundred thousand suspected criminals. Responding to the Party's directive that criminals be severely punished, the Standing Committee of the National People's Congress passed two laws permitting courts and the procuratorates to bypass the usual procedures contained in the Chinese Law of Criminal Procedure. They also provided that regardless of the provisions of the Criminal Law, which limited the applicability of the death penalty to certain crimes, all persons guilty of violent crimes or sex crimes could be sentenced to death. An unknown number of persons were put to death during the campaign; it is believed that under the cover of the campaign, scores of political prisoners were also executed.

These facts are evidence enough: none of the various episodes of turmoil which has erupted in the forty years since the founding of the Republic was created by the students, or the democratic parties, or the populace. Nor was such turmoil created by Taiwan, the United States, or the Soviet Union. Rather, all the turmoil was the doing of an extremely small number of individuals. Take a look and count up the bad persons in the Politburo (you've got all types): some with a beard, some without; some bald, others with long hair; hooligans, profiteers, bullshitters with low IQs, hypocrites, those who say yes when they mean no . . . As is evident from these facts, the very origin of turmoil can be traced to an extremely small number of individuals in the Politburo who have usurped the power of the Party, of the government, and of the military.

(handbill at Beijing University)

"As Long as Li Peng Hasn't Returned Home, the Workers Aren't Going to Return Home Either!"

The appearance of workers on the streets during the tumultuous week of May 15 may well have been the decisive factor in the hard-liners' deliberations over whether or not to impose martial law. Student unrest alone was troubling—and to the most authoritarian leaders, intolerable. Far more feared, however, was any sort of uprising among the workers. Students did not pose an immediate, direct threat to the government's control over the country; workers, who could halt production and cripple transportation and communications, did. Students had, with rare exceptions, hewn to their declared principle of nonviolence; workers were less likely to show such discipline. The leadership was aware that worker dissatisfaction had been on the rise in recent years. Urban workers, more than any other segment of Chinese society, perceived themselves to be the losers in the decade of economic reform. Some workers in factories and companies that had flourished under the reforms had prospered with their units. But for many more, the benefits of reform had been far less substantial, and the double-digit inflation of the mid- and late eighties had hit them harder than other Chinese. In a country where workers were beholden to their units for everything from housing to job assignments for their children, no labor movement had ever developed; the official worker unions, like the official student unions, were merely extensions of the Party. But by 1988 and 1989, signs of restlessness had appeared among workers: wildcat strikes or work slowdowns, unreported in the official press, had broken out in different areas of the country.

Contingents of marchers with banners bearing the title of various "workers' autonomous unions" had appeared during the mid-May demonstrations. The groups behind such appellations, however, were a loose assortment of worker activists who had temporarily banded together rather than organized workers' groups with an identifiable membership. But the threat of military action spurred these activists into founding workers' organizations for the protection of the students. Information about the nature and activities of these various workers' groups (as well as on the persecution of workers who participated in the Democracy Movement) is scanty because workers had neither extensive foreign contacts nor an informal domestic network of friends and acquaintances that allowed activists to keep in touch with each other, such as the one intellectuals had. It is not even clear how many different organizations existed. In Beijing, three organizations' names appeared on handbills or in news reports from the period of martial law: the Capital Workers' Autonomous Union, the Beijing Workers' Union (which appears to have been established in mid-April), and the Beijing Workers' Autonomous Union. These may have been entirely separate groups or simply one organization using inconsistent names. Banners of workers' organizations were also raised in Xi'an, Guangzhou, and Hangzhou. In any event, even after their formal establishment, workers' organizations remained rather amorphous, loose-knit groups composed of a limited number of activist workers, rather than tight organizations with a broad worker base. Members included workers from the Capital Iron and Steel Company, the Beijing Bureau of Railroads, newspapermen, and lawyers. Although their initial raison d'être was the physical protection of the students occupying the Square, the organizations also envisioned themselves as spokesmen for workers' interests; however, their leaders neither sought nor believed official recognition possible. Yet even these embryonic, extremely weak organizations would be branded illegal and their members persecuted during the suppression of the Democracy Movement.

Rumors that workers would walk off their jobs in an anti-government, anti-Li Peng protest were rife in Beijing during the first weekend of martial law. On the eve of martial law, May 19, the Beijing Workers' Autonomous Union had threatened a general strike for the next day if the government did not meet the hunger strikers' demands. No general strike appears to have occurred, however; the work slowdowns that did take place in factories across Beijing were generated spontaneously by a severely distracted and anxious populace. In Beijing, as in other major cities, work disruption during the height of the demonstrations in May, whether prior to or after martial law, was due primarily to the paralysis of traffic, not workers' refusal to report to their jobs.

A selection of handbills distributed by the workers' organizations in Beijing is presented below.

BEIJING WORKERS' AUTONOMOUS UNION PREPARATORY OFFICE PUBLIC NOTICE (No. 1)

The Beijing Workers' Autonomous Union is a transitional organization that the workers of the capital have spontaneously created during an extraordinary period. Its aims include: fighting for democracy; opposing dictatorship; supporting the students on hunger strike; and advancing, with university students and all other classes of people throughout the country, the course of democratization in the country. To this end, the Autonomous Union calls for:

1. at 12:00 on May 20 all Beijing workers from every occupation (excluding power, water, gas, and telecommunications) to go on strike until the troops that have been brought to Beijing have all withdrawn;
2. workers to block troops from entering the city, to protect the achievements attained so far during the Democracy Movement, to safeguard order in Tiananmen Square, to use vehicles from every work unit [factory, office, etc.] to block main transportation arteries and subway exits, and to ensure the normal operations of the China Central Television and China Central Broadcasting stations;
3. workers to cooperate citywide with people from all sectors of society in disseminating information about the true situation the numerous officers and soldiers who have entered Beijing.

> —Beijing Workers' Autonomous Union
> Preparatory Committee, May 20, 1989
> *(handbill)*

BEIJING WORKERS' AUTONOMOUS UNION PUBLIC NOTICE

We hereby declare:

This afternoon the standing committee of the Beijing Workers' Autonomous Union held an emergency meeting regarding the organizing work we must immediately undertake in light of the present situation. The members of the standing committee improved the leadership group by establishing a leadership group, a secretariat, a propaganda department, a logistics department, and a liaison office.

1. The Beijing Workers' Autonomous Union is a spontaneous organization of workers in the capital formed in response to the current situation. . . . It welcomes all workers of the capital and the unions in the capital's industrial enterprises to participate actively in our union organization.

2. In accord with the present situation, the Union has specially decided that:

    a. the current task of the worker-marshals is to cooperate closely with the Beijing Students' Federation to protect the students' lives and safety and the stability of social order in Beijing;

    b. the worker-marshals, while preserving public order, should protect the transport of all types of material goods and articles of daily use for ordinary citizens, such as vegetables and grain.

> —All Members of the Standing Committee of
> the Beijing Workers' Autonomous Union,
> May 21, 1989
> (*handbill*)

NOTICE TO ALL CHINESE COMPATRIOTS

The tyranny of the corrupt officials is nothing short of extreme! The ruthlessness of officials is nothing short of extreme! As vast as the Chinese mainland is, there is no place for the truth to stand. There is no reactionary force, however, that can stem the tide of the Chinese people's rage. The people will no longer believe the lies of the authorities, for on our banners appear the words: science, democracy, freedom, human rights, and rule by law.

The Beijing Workers' Union was officially established in Beijing on April 21, 1989, to protect workers' interests. On the same day, it issued two documents: "Notice to All Beijing Residents" and "Ten Questions," which were slandered in an April 26 [*People's Daily*] editorial as reactionary.[6] So we would like to ask you: since you lack the courage to answer our ten questions publicly in the newspaper, then why don't you publish the two documents in full in your newspaper? Could it be that you don't have even this much courage? Isn't it true that you have

---

6. The *People's Daily* editorial did not in fact mention these two documents; it did allege that people had usurped the names of workers' organizations to spread reactionary leaflets.

shouted for forty years, "believe in the broad masses"? We solemnly demand a full retraction of the editorial of April 26, and the severe punishment of whoever concocted the article, and of his backers.

We have conscientiously documented the exploitation of the workers. The method of exploitation is based on the method for analysis given in Marx's *Das Kapital*. After deducting the following from the total value of output—workers' wages, welfare, medical care, social accumulation funds, depreciation of equipment, and the costs of expanding production—we were astonished to find that the "people's public servants" have devoured all surplus value created by the people's blood and sweat. The total value of this exploitation comes to an amount unmatched in history! Such ruthlessness! and replete with "Chinese characteristics"! These "people's public servants" have used the blood and sweat of the people to build palatial retreats all over China (guarded by soldiers and labeled as "restricted military zones"!); to buy foreign luxury vehicles; and to go abroad on pleasure trips with their children, and even with the children's nannies! Under the pretext of carrying out "observation and research tours" abroad, both male and female officials have illicit affairs. Their scandals and crimes are too numerous to record!

The opinions of Mr. Fang Lizhi in "How to Attract Foreign Capital,"[7] proceeding from the interests of the nation and the people, are correct. We firmly support his ideas, because otherwise borrowed foreign capital will end up—"legally"—in the same place it has in the past: transformed into the private wealth of corrupt officials, as has been the case repeatedly in recent years. While the country suffers, a tiny handful benefit, and the people end up shouldering the debt.

We oppose the continued compulsory purchase of state treasury bonds,[8] a barbaric practice that violates human rights. We demand the public posting of national revenues from and expenditures of these funds,

7. An article by Fang Lizhi suggesting that foreigners bear in mind China's poor record on human rights when considering investment in China appeared in the *Asian Wall Street Journal* on April 25, 1989.

8. Since 1981, the Chinese government has been issuing several billion yuan of state bonds every year for the purpose of supplementing government coffers. Theoretically voluntary, purchase is in practice compulsory. Thus, according to Article 8 of the 1989 Regulations on State Bonds, "Issuance of state bonds will use the method of assigned purchase quotas. The purchase quotas are to be based on a certain proportion of a citizen's income." The annual purchase quota for each person has usually been one month's income, and the bond payment is often deducted directly from wages. Bonds issued after 1984 are not redeemable for six years. Since the suppression of the Democracy Movement, citizens have been forced to increase their investment in bonds.

including the purpose for which the money is used, and the complete and immediate repayment by the government to the people of the capital and interest represented by all bonds currently held by the people. Simultaneously, we demand that the state treasury bond market be closed, because it is a big market for officials, and a source of great wealth for the corrupt among them. We reiterate: raise salaries and stem inflation; it is time to end the system under which two and even three generations of workers have received the same wage. We demand the investigation of officials at the level of the Central Committee, the Central Advisory Commission, the Central Military Commission, and ministerial officials of the State Council.

The first group to be investigated with regard to their material consumption and use of palatial retreats should include: Deng Xiaoping, Zhao Ziyang, Li Peng, Chen Yun, [Chairman of the Central Advisory Commission], Li Xiannian [former President of the PRC and now Chairman of the Chinese People's Political Consultative Conference], Yang Shangkun, Peng Zhen [former member of the Politburo], Wan Li, Jiang Zemin, Ye Xuanping [governor of Guangdong Province], and their family members. Their assets should immediately be frozen and subjected to the scrutiny of a National People's Investigative Committee. The results of the investigation should be made public as soon as possible.

University students have matured! This is evidenced by the maintenance of revolutionary order while hundreds of thousands gather before the Gate of Heavenly Peace [facing Tiananmen Square]. The people have acquired [political] consciousness! They have recognized that in any society, in any historical period, there are only two classes: the rulers and the ruled. Those classes, political parties, social organizations, and individuals who conform to historical trends are progressive and revolutionary; others are backward and reactionary. This is the basic reason why Chinese people, who have lived in a society in which the word of a man [rather than the rules of law] determines all, have loved, wanted, praised, and cherished "upright officials" ever since the era of Qin Shi Huang [the first emperor of China]. The political movements of the last forty years have served simply as political means of oppressing the people. History has shown that the authorities are good at storing up retribution for grudges; however, historical truth cannot be altered.

We must now be on our guard against political careerists within the Chinese Communist Party who will use the current Democracy Movement to usurp power for their own purposes. Deng Xiaoping used the people's movement of April 5, 1976, to obtain power. Afterward, his evil intentions were exposed. The "achievements in reform" that he has announced are false and superficial. The reality is that the living standard of ordinary people has declined, and a large foreign debt has accrued which will be paid by the people.

Working comrades, rally around the Workers' Union! Under the leadership of the Union, the Democracy Movement will advance to new levels. The Union has decided that at 2:00 P.M. sharp on May 22, there will be a major demonstration of workers of the city in front of the Gate of Heavenly Peace, with the peaceful presentation of a petition and [expressions of] support for the university students' movement. The slogan of the demonstration is: "As vast as the Chinese mainland is, there is no place for the truth to stand!"

—Beijing Workers' Union, May 17, 1989

TEN QUESTIONS

We request that the Central Committee answer the following questions:

1. How much money has Deng Pufang [Deng Xiaoping's son] spent placing bets at the horse races in Hong Kong? Where did this money come from?
2. Do Mr. and Mrs. Zhao Ziyang pay the golfing fees when they play every week?[9] Where does the money for the fee come from?
3. What evaluation has the Central Committee made of the [progress of] reforms in the recent past? Premier Li Peng acknowledged during the official Lunar New Year's festivities this year that there had been errors in the current reform process. What were these errors? How can he account for the actual situation of difficulty we are in?
4. The Central Committee has promised to take measures to control general inflation and pricing. In fact, prices have risen without respite as the living standards of the people have dropped precipitously. May we ask the reason for this?
5. Beginning next year, [China] must begin to repay its foreign debt. We would like to ask the size of the burden in national per-capita terms.

9. It was widely reported in Hong Kong that Zhao Ziyang regularly played golf at one of China's few golf courses, a Japanese-managed course outside of Beijing, where fees are extremely high. Zhao's expensive passion has rankled many Chinese, who have come to regard it as a symbol of the gap between the living standards of the ordinary people and those of Party leaders.

Will the people's basic standard of living be affected? Please answer. . . .

7. How many houses and palatial retreats do Central Committee leaders have scattered about the country? What are the rates of their material consumption and expenditures? May these figures be made public? Please give an answer.

8. Make public the personal incomes and expenditures of Central Committee leaders.

9. What comment does the Central Committee have on the three preconditions for peaceful negotiations set forth by the authorities in Taiwan[10]? How will the Central Committee answer?

10. Please have the Central Committee provide precise explanations of the definitions and connotations of the following three terms: (a) political party; (b) revolution; (c) reactionary.

We request that the Central Committee publish the responses to the above ten questions in the newspapers.

—Beijing Workers' Union, April 20, 1989
(handbill)

By May 18, buoyed by the chain of mass demonstrations that had broken out throughout the nation, Beijing student leaders had been able to announce to Li Peng in their meeting that their movement had become a "people's movement." By the criterion of broad citizen participation, the mid-May national protests and the subsequent resistance to martial law in all quarters of the capital lent credence to this claim. Though not all sectors of Chinese society rose up in protest—demonstrations did not break out in the countryside (although there apparently were protests by high school students in some small towns in rural areas), and were noticeably smaller and tamer in the prosperous southern province of Guangdong—an extraordinarily large cross section of the urban citizenry participated in the protests and resistance. But the "people's movement" was a relatively short-lived, emotionally driven phenomenon that never had an identity separate from the students' cause. When citizens first took to the streets en masse, it was to express concern for the fasting students rather than to voice independent demands for wage hikes, democratic

10. The Kuomintang government of Taiwan has for years had a policy of "three nos" in regard to relations with the Communist government of the PRC, which it still refuses to recognize: "no compromise, no negotiation, and no contact." In the last several years, however, there have been signs of a slight thawing in the hostility between the two states; in 1989, a high-ranking official of the Taiwan government appeared in an official capacity in the PRC for the first time as a delegate to the Asian Development Bank meeting.

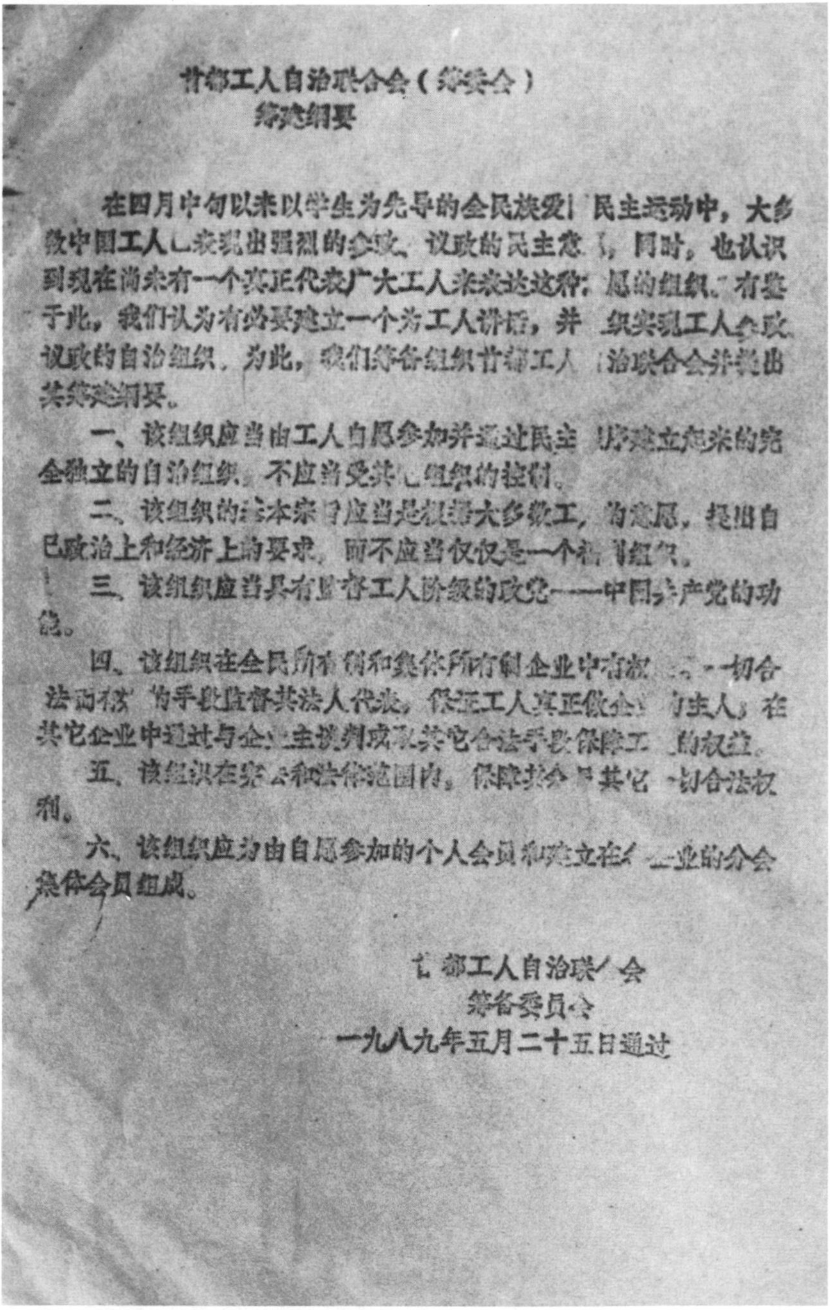

首都工人自治联合会（筹委会）
筹建纲要

在四月中旬以来以学生为先导的全民族爱国民主运动中，大多数中国工人已表现出强烈的参政、议政的民主意识，同时，也认识到现在尚未有一个真正代表广大工人来表达这种意愿的组织。有鉴于此，我们认为有必要建立一个为工人讲话，并组织实现工人参政议政的自治组织。为此，我们筹备组织首都工人自治联合会并提出其筹建纲要。

一、该组织应当由工人自愿参加并通过民主程序建立起来的完全独立的自治组织，不应当受其它组织的控制。

二、该组织的基本宗旨应当是根据大多数工人的意愿，提出自己政治上和经济上的要求，而不应当仅仅是一个福利组织。

三、该组织应当具有监督工人阶级的政党——中国共产党的功能。

四、该组织在全民所有制和集体所有制企业中有权[illegible]一切合法而有效的手段监督其法人代表，保证工人真正做企业的主人；在其它企业中通过与企业主谈判或采取其它合法手段保障工人的权益。

五、该组织在宪法和法律范围内，保障其会员其它一切合法权利。

六、该组织应为由自愿参加的个人会员和建立在各企业的分会集体会员组成。

首都工人自治联合会
筹备委员会
一九八九年五月二十五日通过

Illustration 5.4 Text of a flyer distributed by workers announcing the preliminary manifesto of the Capital Workers' Autonomous Union. Credit: Toby Feldman.

changes, or the like; when citizens blocked the army, it was to protect the students from harm as well as to protect their own city. Thus, while the mass protests and defiance of martial law were an unprecedented kick of sand in the face of the Party, they hardly represented the birth of new political forces to challenge the existing order. The newly formed workers' and intellectuals' organizations did contain the seeds of such new political forces. But during their brief existence, their focus was very immediate and narrow: to prevent the hard-line government from crushing the student movement and, as part of that effort, to build support for Zhao.

Beijing students enthusiastically welcomed the support of Chinese from other segments of society, which they realized had become essential to their movement's survival. Yet there was also ambivalence in their ranks about close association with nonstudent organizations, particularly workers' groups. Although some of their leaders were eager to link up with forces allied with Zhao, other prominent student figures such as Chai Ling, who believed in the purity of the student movement, resisted entanglement in the political struggle between the moderates and hardliners. Others were more concerned about maintaining order and control over protest activities; students feared that workers were less disciplined and more prone to violence.

Solid pragmatic reasons for safeguarding the integrity of the students' organizations did exist at the time. In addition to these, however, there may have been a strain of elitism. For centuries, Chinese intellectuals have viewed themselves, with justification, as an enlightened class, one whose duty was to counsel authorities or, when need be, to remonstrate with those in power. Many intellectuals presently cite the low educational level of the population as one of the barriers to implementing full democracy in China. The appeal of "neo-authoritarianism" to some intellectuals in recent years can also be traced to their conviction that the masses cannot be trusted with self-governance.

In posters such as "China's Only Way Out" in Chapter One and "Meditations at the Foot of the Monument to the People's Heroes," which follows later in this chapter, student writers take pains to remind their readers that intellectuals, including students, are not superior to any other Chinese. Yet the two posters below reveal a different perspective, one in which intellectuals are elevated to the position of prime importance and are viewed as the class that will cleanse the country of bureaucracy. Neither of these posters is convincing in general: their proposals for reform are superficial, if not naive, suggestions that do not begin to address the deep-rooted causes of China's problems. Nonetheless, the tenor of their comments cannot be completely ignored.

A DISCUSSION OF
HOW SCIENCE CAN SAVE CHINA

. . . It has been forty years since the founding of the People's Republic, fully twenty of which the Communist Party has wasted carrying out various political movements. Now the gap between China and the other countries of the world is widening; China's gross national product lags among the world's lowest, and China is in danger of losing her global citizenship. We are aware that the guiding ideology of the Party is Marxism-Leninism. As a science, Marxism-Leninism is really quite progressive, but now we are in the eighties, the Information Age, when every month—every day, even—sees new developments in science and technology. If our Party refuses to consider our time, our place, and our conditions, and continues to cling desperately to a philosophy more than a hundred years old, then it has definitely ossified. Marxism-Leninism is not a magic panacea; in fact, there is not one socialist country in the world that has been able to make a good job of it. None of the socialist countries has a standard of living as high as that of the Western countries. Where is the way out for China? This is a question which must be confronted by every single one of China's sons and daughters.

Comrade Deng Xiaoping once said, "It doesn't matter whether a cat is black or white; if it can catch mice, then it is a good cat." In this writer's humble opinion, the Communist Party and the Kuomintang should both try to be more tolerant and, taking the interests of all China's people to heart, should put away their various political agendas and prejudices and join hands to take care of China's affairs instead of stubbornly sticking to their "isms" and their "x number of cardinal principles." Just think: if they go on like this forever with their endless internecine political squabbles, what will happen to China?!

A guiding group must be established, a group unique in the world, comprising specialists and scholars. This group should be completely free of political prejudice, and science should be the standard by which the policies they formulate are judged. As soon as they issue a policy, it should undergo repeated scientific testing and proving by specialists and scholars. (When necessary, computers may be used as a planning aid.) The experience of the developed countries in enterprise management should be brought into play, and China should be managed as one vast enterprise. Because science would be its sole guiding ideology, the government would base its judgments on science, not the [power] of individuals.

It would draw up its policies on the basis of scientific directives derived from computer programs, not the network of personal relationships that exists at present. Only in this way can every last bit of corruption be swept clean away. If we dismantle the bureaucracy entirely, then the bureaucrats naturally will find no more market for their activities. Because the new guiding group would be composed exclusively of intellectuals, it would naturally place great emphasis on education and the rule of law, and therefore would undoubtedly receive the support of the Chinese people.

> —"A Small Handful" of "Scoundrels"
> Concerned about Their Country and People
> *(small-character poster at*
> *People's University)*

UNDER THE BANNER OF THE PEOPLE'S REVOLUTION, LET US MAKE A FINAL EFFORT TO SAVE THE CHINESE NATION

Seventeen refuse water, three thousand fast, hundreds of thousands take to the streets, and the hearts of 1.1 billion are united in one truth. To what hour now point the hands of history's clock? The policies of economic retrenchment have come to a dead end, while Li Peng's Cabinet stakes the last bit of capital left over from ten years of reform on a single roll of the dice. Corruption has become the tacitly understood prerogative of government officials at every level. Again we are witness to the disintegration of organizing forces that marks the end of a dynasty. The prelude to a people's revolution is in the air!

Our intention is not to attack the Communist Party organization nor the individuals therein. We believe that people's revolution is the only ray of light illuminating the death struggle of the Chinese nation; moreover we believe that people's revolution is the only avenue through which the members of the Communist Party may restore the tremendous prestige they enjoyed in the historic year 1949. We issue a solemn call to all the members of the Communist Party, and to all patriotic citizens of the Republic: under the banner of people's revolution, let us make a final effort to save the Chinese nation, now at its last gasp!

This entails the following:

(1) Revising the Constitution of the People's Republic of China and delet-

ing its preamble [in which the leadership of the Communist Party, China's adherence to Marxism–Leninism–Mao Tse-tung Thought, and China's adherence to the socialist path are put forth]; announcing the creation for posterity of a united and democratic Chinese Republic; adopting a mixed economic system; rendering inviolable the property of individual citizens; abolishing all laws that contradict the principle of the freedom of citizens; providing for the designation of the country's leaders through general elections, and the direct election of delegates to the National People's Congress; truly bestowing supreme judicial authority on the Supreme Court; and allowing the free formation of political parties.

(2) Taking the following decisive measures to extricate the country from its financial crisis and to strive for economic recovery:

(a) divesting all bureaucrats of their supra-economic powers [that is, privileges founded on political power rather than economic strength] and special privileges, and auctioning off all national property [practical ownership of which is] enjoyed by political leaders by virtue of their position;

(b) putting up for public auction, open equally to all individuals, Chinese and foreign, [all] state-owned large, medium, and small enterprises;

(c) enacting laws encouraging workers to purchase medium- and small-sized enterprises, so as to realize worker self-management;

(d) using the proceeds from these auctions to augment bank reserves and to pay off domestic and foreign debts;

(e) implementing price reform, and creating a unified market (and at the same time, taking measures to allay urban unemployment).

(3) The only hope for the resurgence of the Chinese nation lies in the few millions of intellectuals. Under economic conditions that preclude large-scale literacy campaigns, there is only one road to the preservation of civilization: first, the pay scale of all intellectuals employed by the government, from assistant professors to full professors, must be raised so that monthly salaries fall between 500 yuan [sic] (the amount sufficient to maintain a family of three) and 7,000 yuan (the international standard for a research assistant). Second, citizens must be encouraged to leave the country and live overseas. Expelling the old and embracing the new is the only plausible remedy for a China on the brink of death.

The continued existence of the Chinese Communist Party must be predicated on its acceptance of a thoroughgoing people's revolution. If our beloved fellow comrades in the Party miss this once-in-a-millennium opportunity, the inevitability of the people's revolution, which alone will determine the fate of the people, will nevertheless remain unaltered.

History will remember this historic time, these historic lives, these historic heroes! . . .

—123/43
(big-character poster, mid-May, 1989;
original title: "Advice to All My
Fellow Chinese in Light of the
Recent News of the Position Taken
by the Reformist Faction")

"China's Walesa—Where Are You?"

The government's June 4 killing of hundreds, perhaps thousands, of civilians in the name of suppressing "turmoil" was to be a watershed in the political thinking of liberal intellectuals. Demolishing for many the hope that the impetus for democratic reforms could come from within the Party, the shock of June 4 and its chilling aftermath forced them to conclude that only the development of independent political forces would bring fundamental change to China. Yet, as the poster below shows, some members of the intellectual community had reached a similar conclusion long before June 4. There are reasons to doubt that the proposal outlined in the poster for intellectuals to withdraw from the Party and form their own association, a nascent political group, would have come to fruition. For all their disenchantment with the Party and their newfound boldness, intellectuals by and large neither were prepared to nor desired to sever their ties with it. Involvement in such an association, even if it purported to be nonpolitical, created definite risks for members; in recent years, even theoretically oriented symposiums organized by reformist intellectuals had drawn the attention of Party watchdogs. On the other hand, even if intellectuals were not quite ready to form an independent association, there were signs prior to the Democracy Movement that the Party was in deep trouble among intellectuals: a number of Beijing University teachers were reportedly preparing to withdraw from the Party, and a secret political party had been formed by graduate students at Beijing University.

WITHDRAW FROM THE COMMUNIST PARTY

—A Proposal to Organize an Association for the Promotion of the Chinese
Democracy Movement

To the broad masses of patriotic Chinese intellectuals:

In view of the fact that the top leadership of the Chinese Communist
Party is corrupt and incompetent, that it treats the people like dirt and
regards democracy as heresy, that it has turned a deaf ear to the reasonable demands of patriotic youth, and that it has adopted a hostile attitude
and an exploitative strategy toward intellectuals, we propose that the
broad masses of intellectuals unite and withdraw, in groups and stages,
from the Communist Party to which we have hitherto dedicated our lives.
We propose that our intellectuals build a new organization representing
the interests of the people, to be called the Association for the Promotion
of the Chinese Democracy Movement, APCDM for short.[11]

1. The Necessity of Withdrawing from the Party

1. While engaged in the overthrow of the old regime, the Communist
Party was a progressive force. However, due to the ingrained conserva-
tism, narrowness, and ignorance of the small farmers [among whom it
found its base] it gradually deteriorated into a reactionary force.

2. Before establishing itself as a governing power, the Communist Party
viewed intellectuals as its allies. After coming to power, however, it began
to treat them as antagonists requiring containment and totalitarian control. All the anti-rightist campaigns waged one after another have been
aimed at repressing intellectuals. Even at times when the Party has chosen
to be respectful of intellectuals, it has merely used them, rather than putting them in important positions.

3. In response to the present pleas to improve teachers' conditions and
to increase funds for education, the top leadership of the Chinese Communist Party has shown not the least bit of sincerity in pledging to take
action. One reason is that paying attention to education brings no credit
in the arena of the power struggle.

4. Intellectuals can no longer rely on the Party as an organization to
protect their own interests and those of the people. Moreover, the Party's

---

11. The name chosen for the proposed organization may have been chosen for its closeness
to the name of one of the democratic parties, the Association for the Promotion of Chinese
Democracy, which has traditionally drawn its membership from academics and professionals.

reputation has plummeted at home and abroad; remaining in the Party tarnishes the good reputation of intellectuals.

2. *Methods and Procedures for [Mass] Withdrawal from the Party*

We propose that a few hundred noted public figures from the educational, theoretical, literary, and artistic communities take the lead in withdrawing from the Party. After handing in their withdrawal applications, following the procedures laid down in the Party's charter, they will, on a certain date, hold a press conference in Beijing and declare to the public their reasons for withdrawal.

Next, intellectuals will withdraw from the Party in groups and stages, and publish withdrawal statements. Should it prove impractical for well-known public figures to withdraw in groups, we propose that they unite with a few hundred enthusiastic young and middle-aged teachers and graduate students from Beijing University, People's University, Qinghua University, Beijing Normal University, the Chinese Academy of Social Sciences, the Chinese Academy of Sciences, or other units, and withdraw together with these people.

3. *Organization of the APCDM*

As the CCP cannot represent the interests of the people, and as the existing political parties are mere vassals of the CCP, intellectuals have no choice but to form once again an organization or political party of their own that does represent the people's interests. We may call it the Association for the Promotion of the Chinese Democracy Movement. In its preparatory stage the APCDM can simplify admission procedures so as to recruit members broadly and allow far-sighted people from other parties to join. The advancement of democratic government, the realization of freedom of the press and of an independent legal system, the punishment of corrupt officials, and an emphasis on education should be among the aims that the APCDM struggles to achieve.

4. *Striving for the Legalization of the APCDM*

One can be sure that at this moment the CCP will not approve of our preparations for the organization of the APCDM. Therefore, it is necessary that intellectuals join the APCDM by the tens of thousands and make our Association an objective reality. We will then be able to wage a continuous struggle against the ruling party, as did Poland's Solidarity, until we achieve legal status. History has shown that in China's democracy movements past and present, without the organization and support of a political party, the Chinese people—common masses and students alike—are always, like a pile of loose sand, swept away by the existing regime.

Therefore, the most urgent task of Chinese intellectuals is to initiate a party organization that can stand up to the challenge of the CCP. This is the demand of the people. This is the hope of democracy. Let us act!

> —Some Party Members on the Faculty of People's University (*big-character poster at People's University, mid-April*)

A few extraordinary intellectuals did not stop at words. Upon the imposition of martial law, declaring that they could no longer identify themselves with the Party, its acts, and certain of its leaders, they publicly announced their withdrawal from the Party. Such extreme acts, virtually unknown in forty years, attracted much attention and required great courage. In the eyes of many intellectuals, criticism of the Party was one matter; total renunciation quite another. Complete rejection of the Party was seen as not productive: by removing oneself from the Party, one lost any opportunity to influence the Party from within. Nor was it seen as necessary: one could remain in the Party and retain the practical advantages and security of membership while divorcing oneself from its ideology or policies. Withdrawal from the Party, while theoretically permitted under the Party charter, would politically mark an individual for life. Indeed, as a speech by Song Ping, Politburo member and head of the Party's Organization Department, would illustrate in August 1989, withdrawals from the Party were regarded as threats to the Party.[12] Thus, in a move of self-deceit, the Party has preempted the initiative of members who declare their intention to resign by expelling them first.

The declaration immediately below was posted on a Beijing University bulletin board on May 20. The personal courage of its writer is underscored by a comparison with the second statement below, which also expresses total disgust with the Party—yet which is unsigned and stops short of actually announcing any resignation from the Party.

DECLARATION OF WITHDRAWAL FROM THE PARTY

I [hereby] clearly and unequivocally withdraw from the Communist Party, which has been violated and sullied by Deng Xiaoping and Li Peng. This Party has betrayed the confidence and high expectations I originally

12. Song Ping's speech appears in the *People's Daily* (Overseas Edition), August 23, 1989, p. 1.

placed in it, and has placed itself in opposition to the people. If Deng Xiaoping is the Party, and Li Peng represents the Central Committee, then I absolutely refuse to be tainted by association with them.

This is my solemn declaration.

> [signed] Zhu X X
> Instructor in the English Department and former Party member, May 20, 1989
> *(handwritten declaration posted at Beijing University)*

RECOMMENDATION OF WITHDRAWAL FROM THE COMMUNIST YOUTH LEAGUE

In view of the corruption in the Party, and of its actions and behavior during the present student movement, actions that are the source of despair, we, as members of the ranks preparing for entry into the Party—the Communist Youth League—propose to all members of the Communist Youth League at Beijing University (that is, all members possessed of reason and conscience): do not entertain false hopes any longer. Let us withdraw from the Youth League to express the awakening of our consciousness, our true intentions, our support of the hunger-striking students, and our opposition to the inhuman silence with which the government has chosen to respond!

> —May 18, 1989
> *(big-character poster at Beijing University)*

The Beijing residents' frustration of martial law plans gave new momentum to the efforts by Zhao's supporters to use the National People's Congress—or, more precisely, the Standing Committee of the NPC—to shift the balance of power from the hard-liners, whose control over the Politburo was indisputable, to Zhao. Pulling off such a feat would require a number of steps, each one calling for sufficient backing from high-level Party officials or influential members—backing that Zhao's faction was gambling it could muster. The first step was to build support for an emergency meeting of the Standing Committee of the NPC; although constitutionally stipulated procedures for convening an extraordinary session of the entire NPC existed (such a meeting could be called if one-fifth of the NPC members—approximately 600 representatives—demanded one), the real hope for Zhao's supporters lay not in the huge, essentially powerless NPC but in its executive organ, the 155-member Standing Committee. The power to call an emergency meeting of the Standing Committee lay in the hands of its Chairman, Wan Li, eighty-three. Details of Zhao's attempts to reach and persuade Wan Li can only be speculated on; whatever form they took, they were complicated by the fact that Wan Li was abroad on state business at the time.

Had Wan Li agreed to call an emergency meeting of the Standing Committee, Zhao would have focused next on getting the Standing Committee to annul the declaration of martial law. Whether the Standing Committee, a body of individuals with some influence but generally outside the inner sanctum of Party power, would have dared to defy the top leadership of the Party, is very uncertain. Quite certain, however, is that the hard-liners would not have tolerated Zhao's insubordination without attempting to intervene; as Chinese critical of the political system had repeatedly noted, power politics respects no procedure. But had Zhao and the moderates succeeded in firming up support in the Standing Committee, the third and final step, dismissal of Li Peng through the mechanism of the entire NPC, would probably have been a foregone conclusion; the entire NPC had never been more than a rubber stamp for decisions taken by its Standing Committee.

Zhao's principal agents in this last-ditch struggle were apparently the Research Institute for Economic Restructuring; the private Stone Corporation led by Wan Runnan, one of China's best-known entrepreneurs; and also possibly supporters in government and Party offices. The Stone Corporation, the country's largest computer company, had previously given invaluable support to the students by donating equipment for a broadcast station in the Square, as well as funds. A research institute it had set up, the Stone Social Development Research Institute[13]—headed by Cao Siyuan, a liberal reformer who had been one of the principal architects of the country's first bankruptcy law—now assumed a crucial role in Zhao's efforts to use constitutional means to derail Li Peng and the hard-liners.

13. The Social Development Research Institute of the Stone Corporation is the outstanding example of the nongovernmental research institutes that have recently sprung up in China. Another prominent private research institute was the one at the Capital Iron and Steel Company; according to some reports, it was shut down after June 1989. The existence of such private institutes, whose nongovernmental status affords them a considerable amount of independence, has become possible only within the last few years with the loosening of state control over enterprise management and the emergence of private enterprises. These organizations generally have met state requirements for the registration of all institutions, economic units, and social organizations because of their affiliation with an existing legal entity. But the winds of liberalization in the last decade have also led to the appearance of many other organizations and associations that are not clearly attached to a legally recognized institution. After the crushing of the Democracy Movement, the Chinese government moved to reassert state control over such associations—the seeds of a "civil society" in China—by promulgating a new law tightening the regulation of all social organizations.

The following petition calling for an emergency meeting of the NPC Standing Committee, which was closely associated with Hu Jiwei, the editor-in-chief of the *People's Daily* from 1977 to 1982, but which by Hu's own account was drafted by the Stone Social Development Research Institute, reportedly began circulating in Beijing prior to martial law, on May 17. The petition campaign, spearheaded by the Stone Social Development Research Institute, would intensify in first days of martial law.

PROPOSAL FOR THE IMMEDIATE CONVENING OF AN EMERGENCY MEETING OF THE STANDING COMMITTEE OF THE NATIONAL PEOPLE'S CONGRESS

To the members of the Standing Committee of the National People's Congress:

In recent days the situation in the city of Beijing and in the rest of the country has made it clear that our country has reached a state of extreme crisis. As members of the highest organ of state power, elected by the people, we bear great responsibility toward the People's Republic in this time of emergency. It is necessary that we immediately reflect the will of the people through legal procedures. Therefore we propose that a special emergency meeting of the members of the Standing Committee of the National People's Congress be called for the 24th through the 26th of May to discuss the current grave situation and to try to find a correct solution to the crisis through legal channels. Should the convocation of the entire Standing Committee prove impossible on such short notice, we propose the calling of a special emergency meeting of those members who are in Beijing.

—May 21, 1989

"Protect the Square!"

As Zhao's faction and the hard-liners engaged in a deadly game of political survival, students and residents of Beijing continued their blockade of the streets. For the better part of a week, from the evening of May 19 to Thursday, May 25, they would ride an emotional roller coaster, climbing to new hope or plunging into despair and anxiety with each new set of rumors. For example, on Monday the 22nd, citizens were encouraged by an unsubstantiated report that seven retired top-level officers of the People's Liberation Army had sent a letter to Party leaders urging that martial law be rescinded, only to be subsequently dismayed by an official report that a number of provincial Party committees had expressed support for the martial law order. News coverage in the *People's Daily* reinforced the perception that Zhao was down but not out: on the front page of the May 22 issue, a single picture of residents exuberantly waving off withdrawing army trucks seemed to be a small but potent counterpunch to government-inserted announcements from Martial Law Headquarters and articles reiterating the hard-liners' position that order had to be restored.

Tiananmen, once the symbol of protest, had become the last stand of the Democracy Movement. The numbers of students encamped in the Square had fallen to somewhere between twenty and forty thousand, with another several hundred students and teachers from the University of Politics and Law entrenched at Xinhuamen; but the students who remained were no less determined than the hunger strikers had been. Workers, too, had joined the occupation of the Square; in the northeastern corner, the banner of the Capital Workers' Union fluttered above a tent that served as its headquarters. Although the time for speechmaking in the Square had passed, citizens continued to express their feelings through posters and banners posted in and around the plaza. Some of those voices from Tiananmen follow.

IT'S ABOUT TIME, MY FELLOW CHINESE!

. . . We have never cast off the specter of authoritarianism which, either in the form of naked tyranny or in the cloak of idealism, never ceases to hover above our heads, sucking away the vitality of our nation and leaving our creativity sucked dry. Under the authoritarian system, the leaden weights of totalitarian politics and an unfree economy have suppressed the talents and wisdom of this most gifted people in the world. Mired in this stagnation, our nation becomes poorer and more backward with each passing day. China can be saved only if our political system is fundamentally transformed. Only democracy can save China. Our ancestors missed many opportunities for cultural regeneration. We cannot afford to miss another such opportunity. . . .

"There is never such a thing as a Savior." Let those who think themselves intelligent for advocating "old" authoritarianism or "new" authoritarianism [realize the impotence of their schemes] in the face of the people's immense power, and crawl off to console themselves. The realization

Illustration 5.5. Premier Li Peng is portrayed as a "fascist pig" in this poster at Tiananmen. Surveillance cameras affixed to lampposts, such as one visible at the right, were permanent fixtures in the Square and also along Changan Avenue. Students did not attempt to dismantle them. Credit: Melissa McCauley.

of democracy cannot be dependent upon the benevolence of any person, as no dictator has ever shown a benevolent heart. Receiving alms while sitting locked in a cage is not democracy. Democracy can only be obtained by the struggle of the people themselves. It's nonsense to say that "the people would not know how to exercise democratic rights" or "democracy is not suited to the national conditions." Democracy has always been given to the government by the people, and *not* the other way round.

Democracy is not a mystical concept; it is a concrete way of conducting your life. It means that you can choose your own path in life. It means that you have the right to improve your government, the right to express your thoughts freely, and the right to write books and spread your beliefs. It means that every single person must abide by the law, while at the same time each may use your intelligence to the fullest to have a [bad] law rescinded. Under democracy, you can be free from the terror of a government which acts without the least regard for human life. In other words, if democracy is trampled upon, then the dark shadows of authoritarianism will be cast into the life of every individual. In China, it has always been the case that the officials are allowed to get away with arson while the people may not even light their lamps. In China, no one has ever valued the individual—"a human life isn't worth a cent." In China, no one has ever heeded the groans of the common people. It's about time, my fellow Chinese! We do not want to live our lives in this manner any more! . . .

It's about time, my fellow Chinese. Let us break our chains and become free human beings. Let us rise and free our country from the vicious cycle of its history.

With the blood of our devotion let us light the torch of truth, and let it illuminate this dark wilderness at this last moment before daybreak. The power of democracy is like a spring tide bursting through a tiny opening—once it starts coming there is no way to counter its force. This is where the hearts of the people lie. This is the march of history. How then can we let this hope be stifled?

—Ye XX
May 25, 1989, at Tiananmen Square
(*essay written on a banner
posted at Tiananmen*)

I STILL FEEL LIKE REPAYING THE FAVOR HE DID ME

Since my arrival in the capital, some intangible thing or matter has made me feel this nameless pressure. At first, I could not figure out from which quarter this pressure came, nor what could be its source. There were just these feelings of restlessness and discomfort, accompanied by a burning resentment. Afterward, when I was able to calm down and think through the matter, I realized that the pressure came from fear. But fear of what? Of death. And fear of whom? Of Deng Xiaoping, even though he is an eighty-five-year-old man! Now, if it came to using my fists, a fifty-one-year-old like me could certainly handle three or five like him. And if it came to wrestling, I could certainly tumble him a dozen times, until he was bruised and swollen all over. But physical combat and political struggle are, after all, two quite different things. Instead of physical strength, the latter depends on the difference in status and power between the two sides. While I'm just a crew-cut common guy, that old man has over the last eleven years been the big man up there, controlling every change in the political climate. His position as the Chairman of the Central Military Commission gives him even the power to bestow life or death. So, if you think about it, you might say that I am totally incomprehensible. You may think that I'm a lunatic, or at least a rash bloke whose brains are not quite developed yet. No, comrades, I'm not what you think I am. In truth I'm a descendent of Wen Tianxiang, the honest official who lived at the end of the Song dynasty. His famous saying, "Since antiquity no man has escaped death; let me but leave a loyal heart to shine in the pages of history," is etched into my mind and blended with my blood. You know, life is just like that—my life belongs to me, and I can do whatever I wish with it. It is nobody else's business. Deng Xiaoping may be powerful, but this is one thing beyond his control. If I want to fight with Deng, can he change my mind? Can he stop me from doing it? Well, at this stage I only want to challenge Deng on the political front. I do not plan to destroy him physically just yet. You know why? Because I still owe him a favor. It was only because of him that I was rehabilitated.[14] At the moment I'm exposing his true character and trying to take away his power; that's because I have the interests of the country at heart. But I will admit that deep down I still feel like repaying the favor he did me, and that's why I'm shouting, "Comrade Deng, turn back before it's too late!" Student movements cannot be suppressed. Chairman Mao saw early on the fate of those who would try: "Those who suppress student movements will come to no good end." . . .

No matter how I regard Deng, I still urge him from the bottom of my heart: Comrade Deng! Lay down the butcher's knife, and you shall be-

14. Beginning in 1978, hundreds of thousands of intellectuals who had been persecuted as "rightists" during the 1957 Anti-Rightist Campaign were "rehabilitated": released from labor camps after more than twenty years and their rights, property, and reputation officially restored. Deng Xiaoping was instrumental in introducing the policy of rehabilitation and ideologically paving the way for intellectuals to join Chinese society by asserting that they were members of the working class.

come immediately a Buddha. Although it can be said that you are guilty of many evil deeds, you still are one who can become a saint. What course to follow?—let Deng decide! But I am afraid that this is the last opportunity. There will be none after this. . . .

Forget it! Let's not talk about it anymore!

—May 20, 1989, 1:30 A.M.
(small-character poster at
Tiananmen Square; original title:
"Deng Xiaoping Is a Conspirator")

MADWOMAN

Crouched hidden all the day long in the box that is China
   washing the infants' diapers   these last few thousand years
Now   I spread out my body
And hammer it into a metal knife   to slit open this world's ugly face
These men's ugly faces

China   the filicidal father[15]
Has this night
   now gone and ravished his daughter   China   China
A living coffin   in vain have I been buried
     the grave-companion of you all
     these last few thousand years
My two breasts   have become my grave-mound
My body overgrown with a mossy mold

In this nation rife with stiff corpses
     my naked body has steeped in

15. The inspiration for this poem appears to be "Diary of a Madman," a famous short story published by Lu Xun in 1918. In "Diary of a Madman," the narrator suffers from a persecution complex and imagines all those he meets to be "man-eaters," cannibals waiting to prey on not only him but on each other as well. Official PRC interpretations of the tale assume that the dehumanizing society Lu Xun so chillingly describes is the old culture that was initially attacked by the May Fourth Movement and subsequently swept away with the new socialist society created by the communists.

The blood- and pus-like trickle

                                    of the Yellow and the Yangtze
                                        rivers
                                    several thousand years now

They cannot wash my skin white
I lie on the bed
                                    with sobs I caress myself
                                    degrade and destroy myself
    China   those respectable gentlemen
                                    never fail to disappoint me

In all these thousands of years

                                    I am the only one to crawl alive
                                    from this living coffin
And abandon the boredom and death that fill this place
                                    I have broken the darkness
Black are my eyes   black my hair   black my
                                                        clothing
Blackened my feet   and my soul is blackest of black
But my gloves are white
These two white hands can kill our father

I am a hysterical woman of China
The first madwoman well so what
In the deep of night   I left my home   came running
                                                            out
Only then did I fling aside my husband
Well what of it
I am a madwoman   gone stark naked
I stand in the tree branches searching for the sun
At all the men's meetings   I cast a dissenting vote
Well so what

A nation overrun with peasants
A nation overrun with bourgeoisie
A nation overrun with bureaucrats
Stuck in their countless wars
Stuck in these thousands of years of history and time they
    still await deliverance
Where death turns the corner   in the enmeshment with the soil
They progress from slavery into slavery

The arms that once waved now at last hang down
  like funereal ribbons
And become plants

The newspaper built on lies
Is the same as the Great Wall built on ashes
The scholar of refined erudition
                    The old man unwilling to be buried[16]
Are the same as the youth who doesn't give a damn
The famous poet squatting in the public latrine is the same
  as the child run by computers
The ubiquitous teahouses and the offices and research
  institutes are the same

I hate them all	Confucius	Chuang Tzu[17]
	Stalin	Marx
They make me sick	I will swallow all crimes	
	and deceptions	
I have died	I have become immortal	
	Yet still I cannot fly to the moon	
	as in the fairy tale[18]	
The night	Chinese	filthy
	tattooed with stars	
Yet again like a rapist	spreads himself across my shoulders	
Humiliating my beloved	I will kill you	
From now on	no longer may you sully my body	
I am no madwoman	I am human	
	I will gladly suffer the punishment	

(unsigned poster at Tiananmen
Square, mid-late May)

Students' repeated defiance of authorities' orders against demonstrating, and the willingness of individuals to step forward to lead organizations condemned by the government, indicated that Chinese youth were no longer easily intimidated by

16. An apparent reference to Mao Tse-tung, whose embalmed body still lies enclosed in a glass coffin in the Mao Memorial Hall in Tiananmen Square more than a decade after his death.
17. Chuang Tzu (369-286 B.C.), one of the fathers of Chinese Taoism and author (or partial author, along with his disciples) of the Taoist classic bearing his name.
18. In the Chinese fairy tale, Chang E flees to the moon after stealing and drinking the elixir of immortality.

Party authority. Their posters revealed that many questioned the right of the Party to lead the nation, going so far as to term the Party's rule a "dictatorship"; a few also sharply faulted socialism for China's present backwardness. Yet, in spite of students' refusal to bow to Party authority and in spite of the blunt critiques of the Party and of socialism, the student movement was not a radical one. From the very first demonstrations to the last hours in Tiananmen, students insisted on nonviolent protest. At no time did the students (aside from a very few extremists) consider storming government buildings, taking over the television and radio stations, or arming themselves. Participants in the protests neither sought to topple the Party from power nor to do away with socialism. Only with the imposition of martial law did the protestors directly place themselves in opposition to the government; and even then, their objectives were confined to bringing down hard-line figures rather than the entire ruling order. Some continued to believe in the idea of Party leadership but felt absolute power had corrupted it; those who had rejected the Party, seeing no alternative to it in the near future, desired incremental change that would diminish its power. And while clearly a great many students believed that the route to prosperity lay in more private enterprise, wholesale rejections of socialism were rare.

Within the bounds of moderation, however, significant differences of opinion could, and did, arise over how far to go in confronting the government. No student leader wished to see blood shed or lives lost in the protest for democracy, but some were more willing than others to risk violent confrontation; indeed, as a selection that appears later in this chapter shows, Chai Ling (but not only Chai Ling) felt deeply that only bloodshed would awaken the Chinese people. And leaders found that moderation won few supporters from among the most active protestors—the students who turned out for marches or who occupied Tiananmen. Both Zhou Yongjun and Wuer Kaixi suddenly lost favor with students after making announcements that they believed would save lives: Zhou after calling off at the last minute the April 27 march, Wuer Kaixi on May 23 after telling students to retreat from the Square to the embassy district. (In both cases, however, the two also brought their own downfall by making the announcements without first consulting other student leaders.) Thus, from throughout the movement, moderate voices, though always present, frequently did not prevail.

The declaration of martial law had convinced many students of the futility of attempting to establish channels of exchange with the government. Angered and threatened, they now felt that only the dismissal of hard-line leaders such as Li Peng, Yang Shangkun, and Chen Xitong, the Mayor of Beijing, would suffice. Furthermore, as the statement below of the Beijing Students' Federation shows, students wanted to challenge the "emperor" himself: Deng Xiaoping. But even in this period, when the battle lines had seemingly been irrevocably drawn, there were also students inclined to conciliation: the tone of the second statement below, also released by official student organizations, could not contrast more sharply with the antagonistic one of the first.

LETTER TO CHINESE ACROSS THE NATION

Compatriots Across the Nation:

The situation in Tiananmen Square is deteriorating daily. Due to the fact that any kind of development may occur, we believe that it is imperative for the university students of Beijing to announce to Chinese across the entire nation the following:

1. The current situation is entirely the result of erroneous decisions committed by the [top] leadership of the Central Committee. The cruelty and inhumane indifference they showed in their handling of the university students' hunger strike protest aroused righteous indignation in Chinese across the nation. The leading decision makers of the Central Committee and the State Council must bear full responsibility for any terrible consequences that may be caused by those decisions.

2. Given the attitude and behavior of state Yang Shangkun and State Council Premier Li Peng during the handling of the hunger strike protest, we maintain that they have completely lost [any claim of possessing] the moral character demanded of a Communist Party member and the fundamental qualities state leaders must possess. Thus, we propose that the Standing Committee of the NPC immediately relieve Yang Shangkun and Li Peng of all their posts in the government, that the Central Committee relieve Li and Yang of their posts in the Party, and furthermore, that they be expelled from the Party. Aritcle 187 of the Constitution of the PRC provides: ["Any] state employees whose dereliction of duties causes harm to common property or to the interests of the state or people shall be punished." The acts of Yang Shangkun and Li Peng already constitute dereliction of duties; therefore, we are filing a complaint with the Supreme People's Procuratorate requesting it to bring proceedings against them.

3. Deng Xiaoping, as Chairman of the Central Military Commission, has placed himself above the state and the Party, fundamentally violating Clause 3 of Article 10 [of the Party Charter] which states: "The supreme leadership organ of the Party is the National Party Congress and the Presidium it establishes." He has been practicing feudal rule and one-man

dictatorship in violation of Article 16 of the Party Charter, which states: "It is not permitted for any leader whatsoever arbitrarily to make decisions by himself or to place himself above the organization." In the course of handling the student hunger protest, he contrived an anti-people, anti-revolutionary plan to suppress the student movement with military force in violation of Article 131 of the Criminal Law of the PRC: "The personal rights, democratic rights, and other rights of citizens are protected by law and shall not be unlawfully infringed by any person or organization." [In light of such] direct contravention of the Charter of the Chinese Communist Party, we propose that the Central Committee relieve him of all of his Party duties and expel him from the Party. Furthermore, we are filing a complaint with the Supreme People's Procuratorate requesting that it bring proceedings against him. . . .

4. We will not take part in any factional struggle within the Party, [for] we believe that the construction of a democratic political system [built on] sound democratic processes and a solid legal system is the problem that China urgently needs to address. There is no need for us to leave the future of China in the custody of one or two people. We must thoroughly do away with the mentality, passed down over [hundreds of years of] history, of "placing all our trust in an upright official." For these purposes, we urgently call for the creation of an autonomous organization, one built on the principles of democracy, by intellectuals, workers, and urban residents who have united together. Such an organization is completely constitutional; it represents fundamentally the wishes of the people. It shall effectively function to supervise and check the government and the Party in power. Only when this is done can we say that our students' struggle for democracy has achieved it goal. . . .

—Beijing Students' Federation
(handbill, circa May 22, 1989)

AN OPEN LETTER TO DENG XIAOPING

Hello, Xiaoping!

. . . Some leaders of the central government, refusing to comply with the will of the people, have failed to examine themselves to see if they are the cause of problems. Instead, they have labeled this patriotic movement "turmoil" and have already deployed troops to enter Beijing. Yet although more than a day has passed since the announcement of the martial law orders, the marches and demonstrations have continued unabated in Beijing. The army is simply unable to enter the city. . . .

You are an intelligent man; it is impossible that you should not understand the current situation. The wishes of the people have been made very clear. Although some of the people marching have shouted slogans unfavorable to you, we believe that for the majority these are merely words spoken in anger. In this letter we will not take the time to list the outstanding contributions you have made to our country; however, the people will not forget your achievements. Everyone is complaining that up to this point you, who are recognized in this country and abroad as the most powerful politician in China, have been incapable of making a sensible assessment of our patriotic movement for democracy, an assessment that your sharp mind should be able to make.

We admit that there is a certain degree of disorder in Beijing. We also ardently hope that this disorder will cease as soon as possible. What is even more important is that we are unwilling to clash with the People's Liberation Army, an action that would lead to real turmoil. But the pursuit of democracy and the fight against corruption are the fervent demands of the public at large. The vast numbers of people who have already begun to take action will not compromise with the current government, which has made an incorrect evaluation of this patriotic movement and which does not enjoy popular support. In this way, the antagonism between the current government and the masses will persist, the disorder will not subside, and the prospects for restoring stability will grow ever more remote.

In light of this situation, we feel that you must once again shoulder a great historical task (or should we say opportunity): to bring about the peaceful resolution of this movement for democracy in this country of ours where real democracy still has not been completely realized. We sincerely ask you to use your prestige and your great influence in the Party, government, and military to force certain highly unpopular leaders to step down and to reestablish an honest and law-abiding government which is responsive to the people and which truly serves the people wholeheartedly.

This movement for democracy can be viewed as a turning point for China. We believe that you will come to a full understanding of this hard-fought popular movement for democracy, assess it correctly, and take proper measures that conform to the wishes of the people. The way this segment of history will be written depends most heavily on you. We sincerely hope that your handling of this matter will greatly advance Chinese democratization in a nonviolent way, and that in your late years you can once again perform a great deed for the Chinese people, enabling China to soon become a truly democratic, free, prosperous and strong nation. Conflict is imminent. We earnestly request that you, Comrade Xiaoping, make a decision as soon as possible.

—Tiananmen Square Command Center
—Command Center of the Non-Beijing
Students in the Capital
—Beijing Students' Federation
—Recovering Leaders of the Hunger Strikers
(open letter, circa May 21, 1989)

"Beijing Is Still in the Hands of the People"

By Tuesday, May 23, "people power" appeared to have triumphed over the orders of Party leaders. In the capital and its suburbs, army convoys were turning back; some disappeared to unknown sites, others to camps on the outskirts of the city, where they settled down, apparently to await orders. Although the first reported violence since the beginning of martial law had occurred in a confrontation between students and soldiers in Fengtai, a village in the Beijing suburbs, it had arisen in the confusion caused by troops pulling back, not advancing. Tension was abating across the city: for many Beijing residents, life was returning to normal. Rubbing salt in the wound of the Martial Law Command Headquarters, one hundred thousand people turned out on the 23rd for an anti-Li Peng, anti-martial law protest march organized by intellectuals, students, and journalists.

But Deng Xiaoping, Li Peng, Yang Shangkun, and the group of veteran revolutionaries did not see people power in the scenes of blocked army trucks, surrounded troops, and the takeover of the streets. They saw only turmoil, chaos, a "state of anarchy"—threats to their vision of China and to their power. And they perceived those threats to be greater than ever before, for the enemy included not only an "extremely small number" of bourgeois liberals, but one whom they had originally counted as one of themselves—Zhao Ziyang. No retreat was possible; no wavering in the ranks would be tolerated. The following speech by Yang Shangkun, given at an emergency meeting of the Central Military Commission on May 24, makes clear that for the government there would be no turning back. It also provides a fascinating glimpse of Zhao's fall in the Party. Evidently, not all of those in Yang's audience agreed with his views; copies of the confidential Party document with his speech would be leaked to Zhao's supporters, and excerpts posted in Beijing.[19]

REMARKS OF PRESIDENT YANG SHANGKUN ON MAY 24 AT AN ENLARGED EMERGENCY SESSION OF THE CENTRAL MILITARY COMMISSION

The reason the Military Commission has decided to call an enlarged emergency session, inviting leading comrades from all the largest [military] units, is to speak about a certain matter. At present Beijing is still in a state of chaos. Although martial law has been announced, in fact there are some martial law tasks that have not yet been carried out. Some of the troops supposed to carry out these tasks have been obstructed, and in order to avoid direct conflict they have not forced their way through. After working at it, however, most of the troops have been able to take up their assigned positions. A few days ago it was even more chaotic; no vehicles bearing military plates were being allowed through [the road-blocks]. Can such a situation still not be called "turmoil"? This turmoil has yet to be put down.

. . . The wish of the Central Committee has consistently been to mitigate the [restive] mood of the masses, and to help calm things down. But the more trouble they made, the bigger it got, so that now [the entire city of] Beijing is out of control. Meanwhile, in the provinces [it's been the same]: after a relatively calm period, they've started making trouble again; now there's trouble in almost every major city of every province. In sum, every time we retreat a step, they advance a step. At the moment they are concentrating on one slogan: "Down with Li Peng!" They've decided among themselves that this is the slogan to use; they've gotten rid of the other ones. Their purpose is precisely to overthrow the Communist Party and the present government. It was calm for awhile, and then as soon as someone from the Central Committee made a speech or an article appeared in the newspaper, they started up again. Then they calmed down, and then started up yet again. In the end, they pushed things to the point where it was necessary to announce martial law in Beijing.

Why should such a situation appear? Why has the [situation in the] capital gotten out of control, and [why have] marches and demonstra-

---

19. It has been reported that the Army officers who provided copies of Yang's speech to the students have been arrested.

tions taken place throughout the country? And why have the slogans people are shouting been directed exclusively at the State Council? Recently some highly respected senior comrades, among them Comrade Chen Yun, Comrade [Li] Xiannian, Comrade Peng Zhen, and moreover Comrade [Deng] Xiaoping, Comrade Wang Zhen, and Elder Sister Deng [Yingchao].[20] How could things have come to this? After analyzing the course of events, we arrived at this conclusion: this matter took place among the students, but its roots are in the Party. What I mean is that there are two voices in the Standing Committee of the Politburo [which comprises five members, including Premier Li Peng and Secretary General Zhao Ziyang], two different voices. As Comrade Xiannian put it, it is the same as having two headquarters.

The spirit of the [*People's Daily*] editorial of the 26th was one of resolute opposition to turmoil; this was decided upon after discussion in the Standing Committee, and was approved by Comrade Xiaoping. At that time Comrade [Zhao] Ziyang was not in Beijing; he was in [North] Korea, and the decision of the Standing Committee and the approval of Comrade Xiaoping were cabled to him there. In his return cable, he wholly approved of and supported [this decision]. But upon returning to China on the 29th of April, the first thing he did was to assert that the tone of that editorial was too strident, and its assessment [of the student movement] incorrect. Now, this editorial spoke about opposing turmoil, and pointed out that this turmoil was well organized and had its own program; that its nature was anti-socialist and anti-Party. Yet [Zhao Ziyang] still felt this was a patriotic students' movement; he would not even admit it was turmoil. As soon as he came back he demanded that the Central Committee act according to his opinion and announce that the editorial was erroneous. Among the five voices of the Standing Committee there rose another, different voice. . . . The revelation to the students of all these different opinions in the Standing Committee added fat to the fire, and the students became even more active. This was why we began to see the slogans, "Support Zhao Ziyang," "Down with Deng Xiaoping," and "Down with Li Peng."

During that time, the Standing Committee had a number of meetings [and decided] we could not change our tone. But [Zhao Ziyang] persisted in his opinion. [Even] when Comrade Xiaoping came to one of the meet-

---

20. These octogenarians form the core of the conservative "group of elders" that continues to dominate Party affairs. See page 276 for the background of Chen Yun and Li Xiannian, and page 260 for Wang Zhen's position. Peng Zhen is the former Chairman of the National People's Congress; Deng Yingchao is the wife of the deceased Premier Zhou Enlai.

ings Zhao stuck to his guns, saying he couldn't bring himself round to our way of thinking, and that as far as the question of the essential nature of the student movement, he could not maintain agreement with the opinions of Comrade Xiaoping and the other members of the Standing Committee. So then he proposed that he resign, saying he couldn't go on. Later I advised him that this was a very serious question, and that if we changed our position on the nature [of the student movement] it would be the end for all of us. All of the teachers, school presidents, and students active [in the Party] would suffer a blow; the very ground would be swept out from under them. All those students, teachers, cadres, and others who had been working hard [on getting the students to calm down and to see the Party's point of view] would lose their power. Around this time the students proposed the organization of a new students' federation, and set themselves in opposition to the old [official] student union. They also wanted their own elections. Certain things reminiscent of the Cultural Revolution began to appear in Beijing: for instance, at Beijing University they seized the school's public address system and smashed the sign at the [official] students' union. It happened at the University of Politics and Law, too; it happened at many schools. At some places they even broke windows to get into the public address station. Now our problem is that, since we have revealed to the public these two different voices within the Party, the students now think there is someone in the Central Committee who supports them; so now the more they stir up trouble, the worse it gets. They've demanded an emergency meeting of the Standing Committee of the National People's Congress and even of the whole Congress itself: clearly their purpose in this is to use these organizations to pass resolutions refuting the editorial of the 26th, as in their eyes the student movement is a spontaneous, patriotic movement. Just think: if the Standing Committee of the NPC were to pass such a resolution, wouldn't that mean the complete overthrow of [everything] that editorial [stood for]? Right now they are actively working on this project, circulating a petition [among the delegates]. Confronted with such a situation, what are we to do? Comrades Xiannian and Chen Yun have hurried back to Beijing from the provinces and demanded a meeting be called immediately to map out a policy for the right way to deal with this. Naturally the rest of us, including Peng Zhen, Wang Zhen, Elder Sister Deng, and we two old commanders, are also very concerned about this state of affairs. Should we advance, or retreat? If we retreat, that means conceding [the students'] point of view; if we don't retreat, then we must hold fast and implement the policy laid out in the editorial of the 26th.

This is the first time in many years now that [such a group of] elders of eighty years and older have sat and discussed Central Committee matters. Xiaoping, Chen Yun, Peng Zhen, Elder Sister Deng, Old Wang—we all feel that there is no path for retreat, that retreat would mean defeat for us all, defeat for the People's Republic of China, the restoration of capitalism, just as that American, [John Foster] Dulles,[21] wished. After a few generations, our socialism would become liberalism. Comrade Chen Yun said something very important: this would mean the complete destruction all at once of the People's Republic, which was formed only after decades of war, and the loss of all the achievements gained with the blood of tens of thousands of revolutionary martyrs; in essence, it would mean the negation of the Chinese Communist Party. The comrades in Beijing saw quite clearly what sort of things Comrade Ziyang said when he visited the hunger strikers on Tiananmen Square early in the morning of the 19th of May. What did he say? Anyone with half a brain would agree that the things he said were nonsensical. First he said, "we've come too late," then started crying. Next he said that the situation was very complex, that there were many problems which could not be solved right away, but which would be solved after a certain period; he said, "you all are still young and have a long road before you" [and also] "we are old, so it doesn't matter about us." He said all these depressing, gloomy things that made him sound not only as if he had a guilty conscience but also as if he was suffering wrongs that he couldn't openly talk about. When most of the cadres in Beijing heard about these words of his, they remarked how his disregard for the principles of organization and [Party] discipline was really too much. That same evening there was a meeting of Beijing municipal [and Central-level] Party, government, and military cadres that he was supposed to attend. But when meeting time rolled around, he suddenly said he wouldn't go. For the Secretary General to miss such an important meeting makes it easy for everybody to see there's some sort of problem. He'd been supposed to speak at the meeting, but he didn't go, and at meeting time everyone was still waiting for him. Just then the troops began their advance on Beijing. Originally the announcement of martial law had been planned for midnight the morning of the 21st, but

21. Whether or not his speeches from the 1950s are memorialized in the West, John Foster Dulles left a lasting impression on Chinese ideologues with a series of speeches made between 1953 and 1957 in which, in the words of the official *Beijing Review*, he "repeatedly averred that it was the established policy of the United States to promote 'liberalization' in the Soviet Union, China, and other socialist countries" (*Beijing Review*, February 12-18, 1990, p. 18). Dulles' prediction that there would be evolutionary change away from socialism to capitalism and freedom is often raised in Chinese government allegations that the West is actively supporting bourgeois liberalization in China.

because the situation made the imposition of martial law essential, it was proposed to move it up to the 20th. Originally I wasn't supposed to speak that night, but time was pressing and the announcement had to be made, because the troops were blocked at various spots, so how could we just not say anything? So I said that the troops were ordered to enter Beijing in order to maintain security, and that they were absolutely not for the purpose of suppressing the students—and that if people didn't believe me, they should wait and see. . . .

Today I'd like to touch base with all the comrades from all the major military units. After deliberating back and forth, the Central Committee determined that it was necessary to make a change in the leadership, because [Zhao Ziyang] could not carry out the Committee's directives, and moreover he had his own program. He wanted to use [the] legislative process to achieve his own objectives, because within the Party, in the Politburo, most of the comrades didn't share his opinions, and he only had one vote in the Standing Committee—his own. When the news that Zhao Ziyang had offered to resign leaked out . . . they began blowing hot air out there, saying, "How can seven eighty-year-olds solve problems?" I say, this question is an easy one to answer. [First,] this decision was taken by a majority in the Standing Committee of the Politburo, in accordance with established Party procedures; and second, these few elder comrades enjoy the greatest prestige in the Party, they have the longest membership, and they have made important contributions to Party and country. I don't even need to mention Comrade Xiaoping; Xiannian, Chen Yun, Commander Xu, Commander Nie, Elder Sister Deng, Peng Zhen, and Old Wang all have made important contributions, so how can they keep silent when the Party and country are at such a crucial pass? They can't simply sit by and stare as the country goes down the drain. This is the bounden duty of a member of the Communist Party. There are people spreading talk that there is really no Party, that it's all decided by one person. Nothing could be further from the truth; the disposal of this matter was undertaken through the correct decision of a majority in the Politburo and the Standing Committee, with the full support and endorsement of the senior generation of revolutionaries including Chen Yun, Xiannian, and Comrade Xiaoping. When Gorbachev came to China, Zhao Ziyang explained to him Comrade Deng Xiaoping's historical position in the Party; this was certainly the right thing to do. But when [Zhao] got on the news, the first thing he talked about—and he talked about it for quite some time—was that all important decisions were taken by Comrade Xiaoping. All the comrades with any sense at all felt that [Zhao] was sloughing off responsibility by talking in this way, putting Comrade Xiaoping at the forefront to take all the blame for any mistakes. Lately he's done a whole series of this kind of thing; I think you all have a feeling for what I'm talking about.

Now the whole Party must unite, and act with one mind to carry out the spirit of the editorial of April 26th. We can only advance; we can not retreat. Today I'm touching base with all of you so that you'll be psychologically prepared. It is particularly important that, no matter what, the military be kept under our control. Has everyone in the military brought his thinking into line with ours? This depends on you and how you do your work. I think that we don't have any problems with the officers [at the top] in the military commands, but will there be any persons who cause problems in the army corps level and below? Some people are still saying that there are three chairmen on the Military Commission, and they wonder why Deng Xiaoping can act on his own to mobilize troops to implement the martial law order. These people don't understand the military in the least; the only people they can fool are the students. The military is a system based on the responsibility of senior officers; the only thing we do is assist the Chairman [of the Military Commission] in his work, acting as military advisors. . . . Please cooperate, everyone, in carrying out the following tasks:

1. Please clear your minds [of any hesitations] and set your thoughts on what must be done.

2. Upon your return [to your units], hold Party committee meetings and explain [the situation] to everyone. In the military, make sure this message reaches cadres at the regimental level; they are very important.

3. [Members of] the Party committees must unify their thinking; no matter what, you must set your thinking in line with that of the Central Committee, especially those of you in the military. Those of you who do not carry out orders will be dealt with according to military law.

4. Please pay particular attention to educational institutions. Cadres, department heads, professors: you must carry out your tasks among the students. Military schools must absolutely not hold parades and demonstrations, nor express support for them.

5. Those troops which have now arrived at their designated positions are to hold those positions, and they must be assured of sufficient rest. You must mobilize among the lower levels, and explain to the cadres at the grass-roots level what's happening. . . .

*(based on internal Party document
as reprinted in Hong Kong sources)*

Illustration 5.6. Army troops withdrew to camps at the outskirts of Beijing to await further orders. Credit: Franki Chan.

Pro-Zhao activist intellectuals such as Yan Jiaqi, Su Xiaokang, and Bao Zunxin openly rose to the fight between Zhao's forces and the hard-liners upon the declaration of martial law. By expressing their opposition to Deng and Li in public statements— for example, the "Intellectuals' Vow" that follows here—they joined the front lines of the battle. They also fought to rally support for the Hu Jiwei petition with open letters to the NPC Standing Committee and declarations such as the one below, which was circulated in the capital and also released to a Hong Kong paper. It was not the only time Zhao supporters, faced with hard-liners' control of the Chinese media, would resort to the Hong Kong press to spread news of their efforts—and to build the impression of gathering momentum. On May 25, an article appeared in the Hong Kong daily *Wenhuibao* reporting that fifty-seven Standing Committee members had signed the petition. That article, which Hu himself would later criticize for a number of errors (including an inflated total name count when the number of signers had in fact only reached 38), as well as an open letter calling for an emergency session signed by twenty-four Standing Committee members published in the *Science and Technology Daily* on May 22, led foreign observers and well-connected Chinese to think for a brief period that perhaps Zhao would succeed in having a meeting called.

INTELLECTUALS' VOW

As intellectuals, we solemnly swear on our honor, on our entire conscience, on our bodies and souls, on every shred of our dignity as human beings: we shall never betray the struggle for democracy built on the lives and blood of the patriotic students; never seek any excuse whatsoever for our own cowardice; never again allow our past humiliations to be repeated; never sell out our own consciences; never surrender to dictatorship; and never acknowledge the present last emperor of China as our lord and master.

> —[signed] Yan Jiaqi, Bao Zunxin, Su Xiaokang,
> and seven other intellectuals
> *(open declaration)*

RESOLVE CHINA'S CURRENT PROBLEMS THROUGH DEMOCRATIC AND LEGAL CHANNELS
—A Response to Li Peng

When a head of state is being spurned by the people, if he does not resign the people may remove him from office via means provided by the Constitution.

Article 57 of the Constitution states that the National People's Congress is the highest organ of state power. The National People's Congress has the power to remove the Premier of the State Council from office. The Standing Committee of the People's Congress, as a permanent institution of the National People's Congress, has the power to repeal administrative regulations, decisions, and orders of the State Council that contravene the Constitution and the laws.

Now what must be done first and foremost is to convene immediately an emergency meeting of the Standing Committee of the National People's Congress, which will make the following decisions with respect to two issues at hand:

1. to rescind the "Order of the State Council Regarding Enforcement of Martial Law in Certain Districts of the Municipality of Beijing" signed by Li Peng on May 20; and

2. to call for an interim assembly of the National People's Congress at the earliest possible time. . . .

Article 29 of the Constitution states that the armed forces of our nation belong to the people. The army can be mobilized only when foreign invasions or serious domestic armed riots have occurred. At present, Beijing is neither being invaded by foreign troops nor being disturbed by armed riots; the deployment of the army to Beijing in the name of "enforcing martial law" is an action that contravenes the Constitution. Therefore, we strongly call for an emergency meeting of the Standing Committee of the National People's Congress to be convened to rescind the martial law order. . . .

Democratic politics is the politics of responsibility. Article 63 of the Constitution states that the National People's Congress possesses the power to remove the Premier of the State Council. Article 61 of the Constitution states that "an interim assembly of the National People's Congress may be convened if the Standing Committee of the National People's Congress deems it necessary, or if one-fifth of the representatives of the National People's Congress adopt such a proposal." We fervently hope that the National People's Congress will be convened as soon as possible to investigate the actions of Premier Li Peng in April and May which betrayed and antagonized the people, and to strip Li Peng of his office as Premier.

For a long time, the usurpation of government functions by the Party and the lack of distinction between Party and government have practically invalidated the constitutional provision that the National People's Congress is the highest organ of state power; it has been turned into a blank sheet of paper. Now the time has come to find the roots of the problem and do away with the Party's presumptuousness in overriding the highest organ of state power. Meetings of the National People's Congress and the Standing Committee of the National People's Congress, as long as they conform to the provisions of the Constitution, may be convened without the permission of Li Peng or anyone else who holds an important position in both the Party and the government at the same time. Indeed, could it be that a meeting of the Standing Committee to rescind Li Peng's martial law order or a meeting of the whole Congress to remove him from office can be convened only with the approval of Li Peng or someone else [like him]? In order to resolve the serious political crisis now occurring in our country, the only course to take is to go through democratic and legal channels. To this end, we appeal to every member of the Standing Committee of the National People's Congress and every delegate to the National People's Congress to cast a sacred vote to rescind the martial law order and to remove Li Peng from the office of Premier. When the Chinese people see that the National People's Congress has become truly worthy of being the highest institution of state power, each one of you will have made an unparalleled, monumental, and historic contribution to the construction of democratic politics in China.

Now the time has come for Li Peng to decide what course to follow; if Li Peng chooses to adopt the policy of suppression by force, if he decides to use force at all cost to maintain his dwindling authority, then the millions of Chinese people will vow, with their blood and their lives, to forge a democracy for China.

(article published in Ming Pao
newspaper, Hong Kong, May 26, 1989)

Students had risen to the challenge of martial law with discipline and calm determination. Whether directing traffic, acting as sentinels at Tiananmen, keeping crowds away from soldiers at blockades, or exhorting residents to turn out to protect Tiananmen, they comported themselves well under crisis conditions. The poise and patience of individual students did not, however, translate into organizational coherence. Student organizations, from the beginning of the movement rather unstable in nature, began to fall apart under the great pressure brought by martial law to make quick decisions of life-and-death import. The Beijing Students' Federation, whose influence had already been overshadowed during the hunger strike by the more extreme Hunger Strikers' Group, held limited sway over the students from the provinces who in numbers dominated the occupation of the Square. An organization of non-Beijing students had been formed, with representatives from almost every province, but it had yet to assert itself convincingly. Still other student groups were appearing and disappearing overnight.

The problem within the student ranks was not just one of leadership. Complaints of bureaucratism and waste—the same charges that the students leveled against the Party hierarchy—had also surfaced. Favoritism and arbitrariness could be found in the Square as elsewhere in the country: one's chances of obtaining a pass through a series of security checkpoints often depended on one's connections; possession of a pass did not guarantee that student guards would honor it. Student leaders were even suspected of corruption: thousands of (U.S.) dollars of contributions, mostly from Hong Kong, had been flowing into the student organizations' coffers, but no accounting had been done. With the immediate threat of the army entering Beijing apparently past, cooperation among student groups evaporated. Friction between Beijing students and non-Beijing students was particularly noticeable: Beijing students complained that the outsiders were undisciplined and lacked initiative; the students from the provinces expressed annoyance that their Beijing classmates refused to share leadership of the Square.

Such phenomena have prompted many observers, foreign and Chinese, to conclude that the fighters for democracy did not themselves practice or understand democracy. It is not entirely true that the students did not run their organizations according to the principles they espoused: on campuses and in Tiananmen, student groups tried, to the extent possible under chaotic circumstances, to reach decisions and select leaders through a process of open discussion and voting. Certainly, however, they were guilty of many nondemocratic practices such as intimidation of those who did not wish to boycott classes in the early stage of the movement, and later, favoritism in access to leaders or resources. Such failings had many causes: the authoritarian and bureaucratic environment they had grown up in; their lack of experience in the politics of compromise; the sheer logistical problems presented by the sudden descent of tens of thousands of students onto Tiananmen in a nation that was, for all its development over the past decade, still at the level of third-world countries in terms of material amenities, communications, and transportation; and perhaps most fundamentally, the fact that the movement was, beginning with the first marches hours after Hu Yaobang's death, essentially one of spontaneous protest; the movement was suppressed before students could make, or attempt to make, the transition from impromptu or hastily organized protests and temporary associations to long-term objectives and permanent organizations.

In light of these factors, a more important question than the one of whether the students implemented democratic principles within their movement is whether they were aware of defects in their practices and in their thinking. There are several reasons for believing so. By late May, a significant segment of the protestors were suggesting that they return to their campuses not only to consider tactics but also to strengthen their theoretical bases. Clearly, these students sensed their own unpreparedness for sustaining a serious, long-term democracy movement. In addition, the next posters illustrate that some students, disappointed by what they saw in Tiananmen, had already begun to voice criticisms and to call for introspection.

MEDITATIONS AT THE FOOT OF THE MONUMENT TO THE PEOPLE'S HEROES

. . . The current movement has so far gained a considerable victory. It has opened an important, epoch-making chapter in China's history. Despite this fact, however, we cannot help but remark that over the last several days a series of phenomena have appeared on Tiananmen Square, signs that are disorienting, that are anger-provoking, and above all, that make one anxious. Fixing our gaze at the heavily enforced defense lines around the Monument, and at the people bustling about on the Monument, everyone who truly has a democratic consciousness will realize that a potential crisis is impending. Gusts of the odor of decay and of all sorts of stale mentalities and attitudes, ready for the grave yet still prevalent in the current system, have assumed new forms to threaten our cradle of democracy with rot and deterioration.

While myriad urgent calls for help ring in your ears, you can see that the waste in every school's camp is astonishing. Highly nourishing food is strewn about, countless bottles of drinking water have been set aside and left to sit for days, countless steamed buns and loaves of bread have been thrown on the ground.

Under the Monument, the layers of sentries and the tight patrols are immediately awe-inspiring. But after going through three checkpoints holding a special permit in your hand, it is certainly disappointing to find no trace of anyone from the Beijing Students' Federation.

Time is passing, minute by minute, second by second. The ceaseless quarrels of the standing committee of the Beijing Students' Federation provide an interesting comparison with its loss of direction and its loss of control over the Square.

Faced with these oddities and absurdities, people can't help asking why, in this central zone of the Democracy Movement, are the demonic shadows of feudalism, bureaucracy, and corrupt politics making their appearance? Why, under the great banner of democracy, are there people so practiced in role-playing, being wolves in front of sheep and sheep in front of wolves? Why do none of the tens of thousands of students on the Square seem to notice this or do anything about it? Traced back to its source, we feel that all this shows our neglect of democratic consciousness, our blindness toward the deep inner meaning of the Democratic Movement, our compromise with our old mentality, and our deeply ingrained feudalistic habits. Even though young students have been the fighters in the avant-garde of this movement of the entire nation, the dead weight of long feudal dictatorship has made us still unused to viewing our own actions and our own demands in terms of a citizen's consciousness and rights. We are still not used to assessing others and ourselves by the standards of equal, democratic "persons." The appearance of the above phenomena is due to our having neglected to sweep away the old vestiges of feudal, totalitarian consciousness and to nourish democratic consciousness in ourselves. Very obviously, if we condone these phenomena, this student movement will in the end necessarily lead to the appearance of a new dictatorial class, a new bureaucrat class, and will cause the Beijing Students' Federation, in a paroxysm of feverish excitement, to slide toward being the antithesis of the Democracy Movement. It will of necessity aggravate some of the blindness, disorientation, alienation, and exhaustion that have already been seen among the students and people of the city. In order to prevent this latent danger from derailing the entire Democracy Movement, in order to foster the real appearance of democratic consciousness in this movement, we think that from now on all of us involved in this movement should, with a highly rational spirit, engage in profound reflection and self-examination with respect to our own behavior and the goals and significance of this Democratic Movement. The point of departure for this reflection and self-examination should be: does all the work we are engaged in, everything we think, everything we do, really promote the spread of democracy? Does it really promote a democratic spirit? . . .

Concretely speaking, we must first have a completely clear awareness that the people of the city—which includes students, newspersons, people involved in legal work, and people from the democratic parties—are all equal, and that given their common goal, the existence of relationships among them of mutual help and support is natural and necessary. However, since they comprise two relatively independent classes and are factors of pluralism in a democratic society, this is not really the main or most important thing. They all have their own particular interests and demands, have the right to realize these interests and demands, and should have a full understanding of their interests. They should therefore not be dependent on or [totally] compliant with each other. The people owe us nothing, be it material or spiritual. No one should be comfortable soliciting or demanding contributions from the people because he sees himself as already having done great things for the movement. No one should take responsibilities and duties that originally were theirs and shift them onto others to be carried out.

Second, all of you who are involved in this movement must be absolutely clear and aware that you are promoters of this movement precisely because it is a movement for each person to realize his self-worth, to achieve and uphold the dignity of the person. No one should just sit around and enjoy the fruits of others' efforts. No one should look to others to save them and plan strategies for them. In particular, each of the university students, who form the central force of this movement, should have a clear democratic consciousness, should make an effort to get rid of the master-slave mentality. There is no need to live contentedly in the shadow of leaders one has put in place; neither can one force one's own demands and will on others, making oneself into a new aristocracy that lives off the flesh and blood of the people. To this end, we call upon all students who have thrown themselves into this movement to take a stand for the promotion of democracy, for independent thinking, and for active participation; and for each in his daily work to bring about broad and deep dissemination of the spirit of democracy by adopting a spirit of self-responsibility and assuming a commitment to the purity of democracy. Thus shall we lay the first firm cornerstone for the establishment of [a truly] modern Chinese society.

(published in Democracy Forum)

THE AWAKENING OF PEOPLE'S CONSCIOUSNESS IS A PREREQUISITE FOR DEMOCRACY
—Reflections on the Nankai Phenomenon

During the spring and summer of 1989, when the students of Beijing, defying the high-handed policy of the goverment, marched in the streets to declare war against authoritarianism and ignorance, the students of Nankai University [one of China's leading universities, in Tianjin, a major city 140 kilometers from Beijing], a campus just one step away from the capital, were the first to declare, in the spirit of true brotherhood, their support to their fellow students in the capital. . . . The students in the capital were deeply moved by the sincerity of the Nankai students, who in turn were proud of their own fortitude.

Beneath the banner of Nankai, however, I have seen placards such as the following:

Carry out Premier Zhou Enlai's behest;
Carry on the Nankai Spirit.[22]

A wire came from Premier Zhou: "Li Peng is not the son I adopted."

When I read these lines, feelings of anxiety surged up in me; I sighed because these are signs indicating that the consciousness of the Nankai students is still steeped in authority worship, and that their ways of thinking are still enveloped in the dark shadow of servility.

As much as they have thrown themselves, body and soul, into the current earth-shaking Democracy Movement, our Nankai students have yet to think through the causes and aims of this Democracy Movement from the conscious standpoint of participants who constitute the main body of the movement. They lack democratic consciousness and a real need for

22. Zhou Enlai was a graduate of Nankai University.

democracy; for this reason, they have been vague about what they are "rebelling" against, uncertain about what they "hope" for.

Putting up Zhou Enlai on their sign differs little in essence from crying, as the common masses have cried for thousands of years, for a Judge Bao, an upright official who will right all wrongs.[23] In feudal times, officials, whether clean or corrupt, were in essence lackeys who swore loyal service to the Emperor, the only difference being that corrupt officials were more near-sighted characters of less than lofty morals, with the tendency to place personal interests above the larger interests of the feudal government, while the clean officials tried, by their loyal service and by leading pious lives, to harmonize the relationship between the ruling classes and oppressed masses. Since they played a pivotal role in ensuring the control and enslavement of the people, in a certain sense these clean officials were even more loathsome than the corrupt ones. In short, regardless of whether feudal officials were clean or corrupt, the goals dictating their actions were none other than protection of the security of the feudal system and of the interests of the rulers, and thus it was not possible for them, whether clean or corrupt, to be truly responsible toward the people. The fact that people cherish the memory of Zhou Enlai reflects their hatred of corruption and their yearning for an honest government. But no matter how I try, I cannot see the connection between Zhou Enlai and our present Democracy Movement. What we are striving for is democratic politics, not "clean official" politics, and Zhou Enlai is far from being a modern combatant for democracy before whom we should prostrate ourselves in worship. Nankai students' worship of Zhou Enlai, the psychology of their taking pride in him, has prevented them from examining and criticizing their own slavishness; more tragic still is the fact that they consciously glorify and worship this slavish mentality. . . .

The Nankai phenomenon clearly illustrates the slavishness and apathy ingrained deep in the consciousness of the university students who make up the main body of the Democracy Movement. It is not, therefore, just the general masses who need to be awakened to modern democratic consciousness, but first and foremost the students themselves, who stand in the forefront of the movement. It would do us good to examine ourselves from time to time, to see in what form the dark shadow of feudal authoritarianism still lurks within ourselves. It would do us good to ask ourselves from time to time: are we citizens—or slaves?

We must recognize that democratization in society and politics can

23. "Judge Bao" was the popular name for Bao Zheng (999-1062), an official known for his honesty and integrity.

only be realized by the modern-minded. In China, only when every individual aspires to be a citizen and not a slave will there be true hope for the rejuvenation of our people.

> (*article in* Democracy
> Forum, *No. 2)*[24]

Three poems composed in mid to late May reflect powerfully the feelings of students facing the prospect of a violent suppression. "I Have a Dream" first appeared at Nanjing University as a poster. Its origins are unknown, but there is a good possibility that it was inspired by Martin Luther King's speech of the same name: many university students were familiar with the story of Martin Luther King, and a videotape of "Eyes on the Prize," a television documentary series on the 1960s civil rights movement in the United States, was available at Nanjing University.

I HAVE A DREAM

I have a dream.
I dream that the flowers of democracy
Will one day bloom everywhere.
I have a dream.
I dream that the banners of freedom
Have eclipsed the swords of the dictators.

O, our 5,000 years of history
Filled with 5,000 years of yearning.
Now at the end of the twentieth century
We finally have the right to dream.

I have a dream.
I dream that the vastness of the heavens
Becomes the windows of our prison.
I have a dream.
I dream that our sacred peaks and mountains
Turn into walls against our despots.

---

24. *Democracy Forum* was a Democracy Movement journal published by graduate students of Beijing Normal University. Its first issue appeared on May 25.

So let the song of this sorrowful and woeful people be tears.
So let us stand firm at the final front and fight again.
Our heads will be bullets
And our bodies, the guns of justice.

I have a dream.
I dream of blazing, raging flames.
I have a dream.
I dream of weeds growing wildly.
As the weeds survive in the raging flames,
We can then see,
See a phoenix of Nirvana.

As these phoenixes fly by
We will cry out.
This is China's eternal dream.

I have a dream.
Deceit is buried beneath the sea.
Despotism is banished to a distant land.
There are no longer struggles for power;
No more violent fantasies;
No more sons of the Republic prostrate on the ground;
No more sham public servants haughtily above;
No more of the looting from a century of chaos;
No more of the vicissitudes of dynastic change.

The people will be able to be their own masters
They will be able to speak.
They will be able to stand without hindrance on
Tiananmen Square.

I have a dream.
For this dream I'm willing for my blood to be shed.
For this dream
Let me endure hunger and exhaustion;
Let my heart be filled with anger and despair;
Let the guns of evil with murderous intent
Be aimed at my bare breast,
For behind me, never failing,
Are generations of China's sons and grandsons,

A dream of democracy and freedom
As beautiful and moving as fresh blood.

So for our sorrowful and woeful people
Let tears be our song.

Let us stand firm at the final front and fight again.
Our heads will be bullets
And our bodies, the guns of justice.

—Jie Fu, May 21, 1989
(poster and
handbill in Nanjing)

WITH OR WITHOUT OUR HEADS, IT'S PRETTY MUCH THE SAME

—Impressions of Martial Law in Beijing

It's you who snatched away our grocery baskets,
It's you who so considerately built us these tiny dovecotes,
It's you who supplied the boxcars—
Only our heads can we call our own.

Once again you blindfolded our eyes,
Once again you stuffed our ears,
Once again you gagged our mouths,
Once again you bound our hands and feet,

What's left for us common folk?
We've lost all our pep, we have nothing left—
Still you say we are rioters.
Well, what the hell, we might as well give you our heads.

If we keep our heads or lose 'em—
It's pretty much the same.

(published in student News Herald,
No. 5, May 22, 1989)

I NEVER KNEW

I never knew
that above the red flag stood the law,
that below the brows there were eyes,
that within the heart a world was enclosed,
that beyond sincerity there was evil.

I never knew
that there was a China within the Middle Kingdom,
that anger's flame raged behind the tears,
that there were living souls buried in this grave,
that it was a lifeless mummy sitting in the chair.

I never knew
that the nation's emblem was nothing but a face,
that truth was defined by a few individuals,
that a moment of silence could mean laughter,
that among the singing voices there was a way out.

I never knew
whether the world was large or small,
whether there were too many people or too few,
whether a blank sheet of paper was light or heavy,
whether slogans were good or bad.

I never knew
that to be carefree could mean apathy,
that serenity was glee,
that generosity and forgiveness foreshadowed disaster,
that storms and tempests were felicitous.

I never knew
that before the Cutural Revolution came May Fourth,
that after the Cultural Revolution would come April Fifth,
that before tomorrow there is today,
and that when today is over, there will be tomorrow.

—Ji Nan
(published in student News Herald,
No. 5, May 22, 1989)

Demonstrations involving hundreds of thousands of people—considerably smaller than those at the height of the protests during the hunger strike, but still quite large—continued in Beijing and other cities during the remainder of the week. In the capital and elsewhere, however, citizens felt that the fate of the Democracy Movement was no longer in their hands, but lay in the resolution of the internecine struggle taking place in Zhongnanhai. With each passing day the signs that the hard-liners had rebuffed Zhao's last challenge multiplied. Under the leadership of Li Peng, a propaganda group was tightening the hard-liners' grip over the contents of the major papers. On Wednesday, May 24, six of the seven military commands in the country announced their support of Li's declaration of martial law, as did the general offices of the army, navy, and air force. On Thursday, May 25, Wan Li, cutting short his state visit abroad, returned early to China. But he did not fly to Beijing; instead, he stopped in Shanghai, where he was met by the Shanghai Municipal Party Committee. Citing "health reasons," he remained in Shanghai, a severe if not fatal blow to Zhao, who desperately needed him in Beijing. That same day Li Peng appeared in public for the first time since the 19th to receive some foreign ambassadors; Zhao remained invisible. On Friday the 26th, the Beijing military command, the only command that had not yet endorsed martial law, fell in line, burying any lingering hope that martial law would be rescinded.

The students in Tiananmen had taken advantage of the interlude to consolidate leadership in one unified organization: on May 23, sixty-nine schools represented in the Square voted to transfer leadership from the Beijing Students' Federation to a temporary group; the next day, a permanent organization, the "Protect Tiananmen Headquarters," led by Chai Ling, was established to direct the occupation of Square. Despite its name, the new organization faced an uncertain future, for students were in the midst of a heated debate over whether or not to persevere in the occupation. As the fact that martial law would stand became increasingly evident each day, the arguments grew more and more intense, pushing aside all other organizational concerns. Some of the rationales and emotions underlying this fateful debate are captured in the pieces that follow.

ANALYZING THE CURRENT SITUATION AND ITS CONSEQUENCES

... Li Peng's speech [on May 19] was a signal that the government has finally reached the limit and decided to declare war against the people. This has placed the two forces in the struggle between democracy and dictatorship into direct opposition. The situation is now white-hot.

. . . The government in which the people used to have hope and which they thought to be their own is no longer their own, nor does it represent their will. Facing the people now is a government the nature of which has fundamentally changed, a force of brutality and dictatorship. The struggle that began by demanding democracy now aims at overthrowing the modern emperor and a few [other] individuals and taking back the power which they have held so tightly in their hands. Democracy has cleared the people's vision; democracy has enabled them to identify their enemies; democracy has facilitated the exposure of the enemy's identity.

Our past experiences as well as the history of China tell our people that bloodshed and turmoil have been the cost of overthrowing emperors, and that between two opposing sides, the side that sheds more blood is always the side that falls. As the situation now stands, any blood shed will be the blood of the people; no imperial throne will crumble of its own accord.

However, in view of the lessons learned by peoples or organizations of other countries in the world who have won final victory through nonviolent struggles, one may hope to see another scenario: the [consciousness] of the masses is fully wakened, and the great majority of the people grasp its truth. This will surely isolate those few individuals [in power] and make them an absolute minority bereft of supporters. Their power will be reduced to nothing. Yet the quality and character of our nation [the low level of education in China and the established political tradition] make the possibility of this scenario remote indeed!

Perhaps we will see yet another scenario: fresh blood, shed to protect justice and truth, will show its might, stirring the people's hearts and stimulating their minds with its tragic heroism. Quickly and fiercely, it will awaken in all of the people a democratic consciousness and a desire to see truth triumph. Without any doubt, however, the awakening of such consciousness can only be achieved at the cost of much blood, turmoil, and disintegration of the nation, and will entail protracted struggle. Furthermore, dictators will occasionally clothe themselves in the robes of democracy, which may prove sufficient to deceive some people.

In view of the above, one may propose two different ways to end the current struggle:

1. Immediately end the struggle at Tiananmen Square so that bloodshed and real turmoil are avoided. Employ other, more long-term methods to disseminate the ideas of democracy and truth, which will eventually, to the greatest extent possible, truly bring forth a democratic consciousness in the minds of the entire nation.

2. Bloodshed. Bloodshed will mean quick gains, but only at great cost.

Given the quality and character of our nation, however, it is possible that any gains won by such a process might be usurped by opportunists.

[3.] Compromise. Compromise entails a long process, but any gains would be solid ones. The cost would be equal on both sides. Real and substantial results, however, would be guaranteed.

(small-character poster on a
Beijing street, circa May 23, 1989)

A LETTER TO THE STUDENTS IN TIANANMEN SQUARE

Dear Fellow Students:

We are former graduates of the classes of 1966, 1967, and 1968, who were [among the first to be] sent [by the Party] to the countryside in the Cultural Revolution.[25] Some of us now work in government offices, Party and government organizations, news agencies; others work in institutions of higher education, scientific research institutes, hospitals, and [industrial and commercial] enterprises. . . .

As your elder brothers and sisters, we would like to say to you what is on our minds. . . .

Given the current situation, we feel that your determination to hold out in Tiananmen Square may not necessarily help you achieve your final goal. The reasons are as follows:

1. Since April 15, the students of Beijing have continued a nonstop struggle for almost forty days now, which has consumed a great deal of your physical and emotional energy. The hygienic conditions on Tiananmen Square are extremely poor; in another few days, you may well be defeated by your own physical exhaustion. Moreover, if student supporters from outside Beijing are to join you in the Square, such logistical problems as food and lodging will only become worse.

25. Many Red Guards and other high-school and college students from China's cities were packed off to the countryside toward the end of the Cultural Revolution in 1968-1969 to be "educated"—to learn firsthand about manual labor, which Mao extolled. This tactic also ensured that the Red Guards, who had lost power to the army, would not rise up once more. Some of the youth sent to the countryside managed to obtain permission to return to their city residences after a short stay in the countryside; others were not able to return for years.

2. We have been trying to remind the soldiers that they are the people's army and persuade them to turn back; as of tomorrow morning, this work will have lasted two days and three nights. Our success in this is due to the wholehearted support of Beijing residents. Such support, however, is not well organized, and someone with ulterior motives may well find a way to use the crowd to his own advantage. If that happens, it will give the government reason to act against you, will it not?

3. Disruptions and difficulties have already been caused in the life of Beijing residents (especially old people and small children). Should there occur shortages of grain, vegetables, gas [for healing], etc., the people will then blame not only the government but you as well. You cannot afford to lose the popular will, the support of the people who have identified with you, and who have been fighting by your side, can you?

It is said that Beijing is now in a state of "anarchy," and that it is you who will return "government" to the city. Who will be the winner then, and who the loser?

In addition to the reasons above, we have a few more words to say. As everyone knows, in today's China, doing away with the leadership of the Chinese Communist Party will only leave us with no other political force capable of filling the leadership vacuum. Now if the government enforces martial law and if there is large-scale bloodshed, as much as we, and the people of the entire country as well, will admire your spirit of sacrifice for the sake of democracy, we cannot help but ask you, dear fellow students, have you ever thought of the possibility of such an outcome, or thought of the severe consequences that might result from it? It is our belief that once such a situation occurs, it is highly possible that it would lead to an open split in the Party and in the army, to a complete loss of public order, to the loss of lives, to the drastic deterioration of our economy and our livelihood, and even complete national disintegration. All this will spell long-term disaster for the entire nation. Such a result would run counter to your original goal. Any gains you have so far made will end up, if not completely destroyed, then certainly puny in comparison to the severity of the aftermath. Democracy in China cannot come overnight. At about 5:00 P.M. on the 22nd of April, a comrade of our number heard one of your representatives making a speech in front of the Monument, in which he said: "Just as a meal is eaten mouthful by mouthful, the struggle has to be fought battle by battle." This is a basic understanding that we all share. . . .

Dear fellow students, please assess the situation coolly and rationally. Discuss these opinions of mine among yourselves. Lenin once said that if truth takes one step too far it becomes falsehood; political activities will succeed only if they are carried out with the correct strategy, and struggle will succeed only if it is carried forward in an orderly fashion. How right he was!!

Again we suggest: you have already achieved great and epochal victories. The people will carve the date you voluntarily left the Square on the richly inscribed monument of history, alongside April 22, April 27, May 4, and May 13.

> History is with you,
> The people are with you,
> Truth is with you,
> Glory is with you,
> We are with you;
> Please accept our most respectful salutations!

> —A Group of "Educated Youth" from the
> Classes of 1966, 1967, and 1968,
> May 24, 1989
> *(big-character poster)*

EDITORIAL FROM *NEWS FLASHES*
(excerpt)

. . . The heroic actions of the hunger-striking students at Tiananmen have turned the Square into a symbol of Chinese freedom and Chinese democracy! The magnificently heroic expressions of support for the students by all the people of the capital have turned Beijing into a new model of freedom and democracy for the entire contemporary world! The movement of wholehearted support for the students among people in every part of China, including Hong Kong and Macao, as well as overseas Chinese, has revealed the Chinese people to be the nation with the brightest prospects in the twenty-first century! The entire body of Chinese people absolutely must not allow the Li Peng regime to turn back the clock! We must swear to defend Tiananmen with our lives! We must swear to defend the capital city of Beijing with our lives! We must swear to defend the Republic with our lives! We shall erect a new Great Wall of the Chinese nation with our bodies!

Resolutely quash the martial law order! Immediately call an emergency meeting of the National People's Congress! Defend the Constitution! Oppose turmoil! Down with Li Peng! Long live the people! Long live freedom!

—*(editorial from Democracy Journal*
News Flashes (Xinwen kuaixun),
No. 1, May 22, 1989)

EXCERPT FROM INTERVIEW WITH CHAI LING IN LATE MAY

. . . The blackest day has not yet come, yet still many of our fellow students do not understand that our presence here and now at the Square is our last and only truth. If we withdraw, the only one to rejoice will be the government. What goes against my inclinations is that, as commander-in-chief, I have again and again demanded the power to resist these capitulationists, while the Beijing Students' Federation and the Non-Beijing Students' Federation are also anxious to have the power to make decisions. Once, at a meeting with figures from the academic world, I felt great frustration because I felt these people were trying to use the student movement to place themselves in the limelight once more. I have resisted such tendencies from the beginning. I have also been irritated at Wuer Kaixi all along; he has at times used his own influence and position in ways that have caused great damage. Some people are now trying to put him in the limelight again. My criticisms of him are directed chiefly at some of the methods and angles from which he considers things. I feel that the best days, the days of greatest unity, were when the group of hunger-strikers was just starting out. . . .

Some fellow students asked me what our plans are, what our demands will be in future. This made me feel sick at heart; I started out to tell them that what we were waiting for was actually the spilling of blood, for only when the government descends to the depths of depravity and decides to deal with us by slaughtering us, only when rivers of blood flow in the Square, will the eyes of our country's people truly be opened, and only then will they unite. But how could I say that to my fellow students? The saddest part is that in order to achieve their own objectives, some students—people from higher-up levels—have asked that the government take no measures, but simply wait until our [movement] collapses. If we withdraw from the Square, that will be exactly what happens. Everyone who was not destroyed in previous political movements will be swept away with one flick of the broom. Deng Xiaoping said it correctly: there really is always a small handful, be they in the Party, in society, or among the students. If they get their way, then what will happen in China will actually be a sort of restoration of the monarchy. Forty or seventy years afterwards, there will be a great massacre, and who knows how many years it will take after that before democracy dares to stand up again. The methods they use are assassination, disappearance, and [the sowing of] spiritual dissension; these are exactly the methods they used against Wei Jingsheng. There is no way I can tell these things directly to my fellow students; it's hard for me to tell them we must awaken the masses with our blood. The students would definitely be willing to do this, but others are still just little kids! [bursts into tears] . . .

(from a tape of interview with Chai Ling, late May)

Debate over whether to leave Tiananmen intensified on May 26, after reports spread through Beijing that Li Peng and the hard-liners had consolidated control of the Party. Most Beijing students, including the leadership of the Beijing Students' Federation, favored withdrawing and returning to their campuses to prepare for the next stage of the movement. Students talked of continuing their democracy journals, expanding contacts with workers and people in the countryside, and exploring the ideas represented by democracy in further discussions. But few students from the provinces shared their views. An estimated 170,000 students had arrived in Beijing in the period between May 16 and May 26; although more than half had since returned home, they were being replaced by new arrivals each day. Having traveled far to the capital, and camped only a stone's throw away from center of power in China, the pro-democracy activists from the provinces were reluctant to give up Tiananmen.

On May 27, though, it appeared that the students in the Square had finally reached a decision. At a meeting to which the press had been invited, Wang Dan, Wuer Kaixi, and Chai Ling announced that the students would leave the Square on May 30. A last rally was scheduled for that day. After two tumultuous weeks, the occupation of the Square had entered its final hours.

6

THE CRUSHING OF THE
DEMOCRACY MOVEMENT

"We Possess Nothing—Except Wisdom and Truth"

May 27 – June 9

"Subsequently the situation developed into a counter-revolutionary rebellion. ... They had primarily two fundamental slogans: overthrow the Communist Party, and do away with the socialist system. ... We never will forget how savage and ruthless our enemies were. We should not show them an iota of forgiveness. ..."
Deng Xiaoping, June 9, 1989

"Those who suppress student movements will come to no good end."
Mao Tse-tung, September 1966

"Deng Xiaoping, Are You in Fashion Any More?"

The Beijing student leaders had underestimated the will of the students from outside Beijing and overestimated their ability to influence matters in Tiananmen. Their suggestion—which had actually been presented as an announcement—that the students leave Tiananmen was rejected by the students in the Square in less than twenty-four hours. On the morning of the 28th, a joint conference of the Protect Tiananmen Headquarters and student, worker, and citizen organizations announced that unless an emergency session of the National People's Congress were convened immediately, the occupation of Tiananmen would continue at least until June 20, when the Congress was scheduled to meet in regular session.

Many of the students who refused to leave Tiananmen were not naive. They expected the government to resort to force to end the occupation. Undaunted, however, these student activists had vowed not to return home empty-handed; unless the government made some concession, they were determined to stay in Tiananmen. Beijing students had successfully used Tiananmen as a public stage for the hunger strike and other demonstrations for freedom and democracy; now it was their turn to claim the historic Square symbolically and physically. The relatively small number of worker activists who also remained in Tiananmen must likewise have been aware of the dangers of occupying the Square. But they, too, had made a vow—to defend the students to the end.

What the students may have miscalculated were the benefits of staying. Undeniably, their presence in Tiananmen lent the movement visibility, and the Square was a powerful rallying site. Yet their primary rationale for remaining—the belief that their presence in Tiananmen would bring pressure on the National People's Congress to remove Li Peng from office and rescind martial law—seems to have been unrealistic, given the indications at the time that the hard-line faction already had an iron grip on power. The moderates' last real hope for convening the National People's Congress had lain in winning the support of Wan Li, Chairman of the Standing Committee of the NPC. On May 27, however, Wan Li had declared unequivocally his support for the Central Committee's decision to impose martial law.

Li was so scorned and hated by Beijing citizens that his dismissal alone, without any government concession to the students' basic demands—government recognition of the Beijing Students' Federation, a dialogue with the students' own representatives, retraction of the April 26 *People's Daily* editorial, and freedom of the press—would have been regarded as a significant victory for the democracy cause. Li was an object of hate for a multitude of reasons. Many residents believed Li was a man of ordinary talents who had reached his present position of power only because he was the adopted son of former Premier Zhou Enlai. Furthermore, Li, with his cautious economic philosophy, represented a threat to the economic reforms initiated by Zhao and supported by many Chinese. Li's lifeless, bureaucratic manner also did not endear him to the ordinary people. Finally, Li had played the preeminent role in representing the hard-line government position throughout the Democracy Movement; Li had delivered the May 19 speech sealing the movement's fate and had signed the martial law decrees in his capacity as state Premier. Attacks on Li often went beyond the political to the personal, and occasionally verged on the puerile: for example, students at a Shanghai university painted Li's name on the floor at the entrance to the student's autonomous union headquarters for visitors to wipe their feet on.

In contrast to the vicious attacks on Li, attacks on Deng Xiaoping were considerably more restrained. Initial reluctance to criticize the country's supreme leader— or fear of doing so—evident in the early days of the Democracy Movement had been overcome by anger at Deng's intractability. Yet Deng's psychological hold over people was still powerful and undeniable. Banners attacking Li proclaimed "Overthrow (dadao) Li Peng!"; those attacking Deng usually declared more mildly "Step Down (xia tai), Deng Xiaoping!" or only obliquely attacked him by demanding "Oppose Autocracy!" Thus, while Li Peng was being depicted as a fascist, Deng was drawn as the doddering emperor.

The appearance of anti-Deng posters and banners must have come as a shock to the eighty-four-year-old Deng, a vivid confirmation of what he had been hearing for some time: that he could no longer count on support from the ordinary people. The attacks on Deng represented the culmination of a gradual turnaround in public opinion. Deng had taken over the leadership of the Party in 1978, riding a crest of great popular support. Intellectuals had quickly become disenchanted with him after his harsh suppression of the Democracy Wall movement in 1979. Subsequent ideological campaigns against "spiritual pollution" and "bourgeois liberalism," repression of the 1987 student movement, and his sacking of Hu Yaobang had confirmed their belief that Deng, despite his willingness to loosen the economic straitjacket of state planning, was still an autocratic ruler who brooked no dissent and distrusted intellectuals. But Deng and his reforms had remained fairly popular among many Chinese until 1985 or 1986, when rampant corruption, soaring inflation, and shortages of goods had started to undermine confidence in him. The sense of malaise that would give birth to the Democracy Movement had set in, and as it deepened in the succeeding years, Deng's popularity plummetted.

The first two selections below reveal the total disillusionment, indeed bitterness, many Chinese intellectuals, particularly younger ones, harbored toward Deng. A far more benevolent viewpoint emerges in the third selection, but the conclusion of all three writers is the same: Deng must go.

HAVE A LOOK AT TODAY'S OVERLORD

He's the biggest hypocrite in China today: he mouths "reform" while nursing evil designs, everywhere and always posing as the emperor who has abdicated.

He used the contemptible means of a palace coup to force out Hu Yaobang, the hero of reform, putting a puppet in his place.

He proclaims his support for education, but in fact takes the teeth out of the policy so that our intellectuals are hard-pressed for their three daily meals, yet still must endure society's contempt.

He calls out for democracy, yet ruthlessly crushes democracy movements and extinguishes the students' patriotic and democratic fires. And what is most grievous is spiritual oppression.

He speaks of respect for the rule of law, but what he does is pack the public security department, procuracy, and judiciary with hundreds of thousands of soldiers turned legal officials of the lowest quality who serve as his hatchet men.

He treats the Constitution like a toy, amending in the morning, deleting in the evening, fixing it so that only the Chairman of the Central Military Commission is given a lifetime appointment.

On the surface he proclaims his desire to turn around the Party's work style, yet behind our backs he practices all kinds of nepotism. Social mores thus get worse and worse, and the cozy relationship among the Party, government, and military stinks to high heaven.

Every year he talks of retiring, but he still hasn't stepped down. Acting as the behind-the-scenes ruler is not satisfaction enough. He must at times appear in all his hideousness, defiling public opinion, claiming that the people won't allow him to retire.

Enough! Today's China is not the China of the Yuan family's warlord rule.[1]

1. Yuan Shikai was a powerful northern warlord who in 1912 assumed the presidency of the newly formed republic from Sun Yat-sen, on the understanding that he would work with the Revolutionary Alliance (*T'ung-meng hui*) republicans who had led the revolution against the Manchu emperor; they were to lay the foundation for a parliamentary form of government. However, Yuan quickly betrayed the republicans by assassinating one of their

It is not the China of Empress Dowager Cixi either. We absolutely will
not let him go on sitting in the palanquin of the emperor who has
"abdicated."

(big-character poster at Beijing University)

O MY KING

You once called for democracy,
Built Democracy Wall,
Ended an era of prostration to idols.
Tramping on the people's trust,
You climbed to the top.
Democracy Wall collapsed—
How great you were indeed,
O my king.

For many years now,
A multitude of student movements
Have come together at one point: democracy and freedom.
You have always bestowed a caress followed by a slap;
Thus have you effortlessly pacified such "turmoil"—
But this time you're wrong.
Do you feel it,
O my sagacious king?

You all have said it ten thousand times:
The people are the masters of the state.
But the freedom you dole out to these "masters"
Is no better than that of a caged bird.
Controlling the mass media,
You opt for obscurantism,
Ten thousand lies—
And yet you do not blush,
O my majestic king!

---

leaders, and consolidated his own power by appointing his generals to important positions.
Yuan then made the fatal mistake of trying to increase his power further by manufacturing
a popular movement to declare him emperor; overwhelming opposition from other warlords forced him to abandon this scheme, and he died soon after.

You want the China of the nineties
To copy your doddering gait,
And when Party rules don't suit you
You have them changed.
Now you want to change the Constitution again.
What else will you want to change tomorrow,
O my supreme king?

You may live in the clouds,
But today the cry of the people
Has surged like a wave toward your throne.
You have begun to totter.
All the thrones in the world
Are made of the same stuff—if not paper, then mud.
Do you understand,
O my Kaiser, O my king?

—XXX, May 15, 1989
(*big-character poster*)

LET'S TALK ABOUT DENG XIAOPING

The great service of Comrade Deng Xiaoping cannot be erased. Certainly, the writer here has no less reverence for him than a Christian has for God.

Since the end of 1986, however, the radiance of his image has dimmed a great deal. The statements he made at the expulsion of Liu Binyan, among others, from the Party and his remarks about how to handle the students have dumbfounded all his Party comrades. In front of my eyes now is no longer the image of a great, kind elderly man, but that of Empress Dowager Cixi, a tyrant, or a fascist—and even more so when he said that in suppressing the students, the Party should not be "afraid of bloodshed."

Well truly, perhaps he alone is not to blame. When Mao Tse-tung was three years younger than he is now, didn't he often cry: "Hey, those few counter-revolutionaries! Put them all in jail!"

For this, one can only blame the laws of nature; how could they have let vigorous young lads of forty or fifty years ago, of fifty or sixty years ago, become today's old mules with muddle-headedness written all over their faces?

Illustration 6.1. In a poster near Tiananmen, Deng is caricatured as Empress Dowager Cixi, the power-hungry dowager who controlled real power in China for more than twenty-five years during the Qing Dynasty. The poster on the right urges citizens to come to Tiananmen that night to protect the students because military action is expected. Credit: Franki Chan.

You want to know what "rule of invalids" is? Just look at the political arena in present-day China.

When I look at Deng Xiaoping, I feel that our Party has aged. When I look at Yang Shangkun, I feel that our Republic has aged. And when I look at that crowd of "Noble Lords on High" in the Central Advisory Commission [one of the most powerful Party committees], I feel that our government suffers from an unclear mind, blurred vision, and impaired dexterity. I feel it is gasping for breath; it is drooling and raving, strapped to a respirator and an I.V. for dear life.

Xiaoping enjoys great prestige. If he steps down, the "group of elders" will have no choice but to step down, too. Then a group of comrades in their prime, like [Zhao] Ziyang and Li Peng, will be able to hold up the government on their own, and, with assurance and boldness, lead China to new achievements. In this way, our Party and government will always remain young and vigorous.

Allow me to say this, Xiaoping: if only you had laid down your great responsibility on the day celebrating the thirty-fifth anniversary of our nation [October 1, 1984], your radiant image would have rivaled even

Mao Tse-tung's. You should now go to the most beautiful spot in our motherland to build a villa. There you could fish, do a little gardening, or teach your grandchildren to read from picture books. Or you could invite other elders over for a game of bridge, and have the losers crawl under the table.[2] Wouldn't it be great really to enjoy your last heavenly years without worrying about other people's business?

You have exhausted all your energy for the people. It's past time for you to rest. (Tears are flowing as I write.) Immortals also grow old, you know.

And when people grow old, they become as simple as children. Don't we have that saying "we are honest even with children and old people"?[3]

Mind you that Lin Biao's entire life had boasted no less illustrious service and glory, but he went down in disgrace.[4] Why? If plotting the murder of a "Glorious Leader" was a heinous crime, plotting the murder of a glorious people is an even greater crime.

Xiaoping, it is for your sake that I have said this much.

—XXX, An Observer, April 30, 1989
*(excerpt from small-character
poster, "April Outline," April 30, 1989)*

"Our Pens Cannot Write the Articles We Want to Write"

Since the imposition of martial law on May 20, the Chinese press had been compelled to revert to its familiar role of reporting only the official government line. Editors and journalists, a good number of whom support the students' cause, had little choice but to comply with Party orders: Party authorities reviewed articles before they could be printed, and army troops were stationed at the *People's Daily* offices, the Xinhua News Building, and other key communications points such as the China Central Television (CCTV) station. Many journalists, however, refused to cave in completely to Party and government pressure. With open defiance impossible, they resorted to indirect ways of criticizing the government. For example, on May

2. A Chinese joke is for the losers at a card game to crawl under the table in a show of humility.
3. A sign with these words was traditionally displayed in Chinese stores to indicate that the shopowner was impeccably honest.
4. Lin Biao, Mao Tse-tung's closest aide and his heir apparent, died in a mysterious plane crash over Mongolia in 1971. Mao subsequently declared that Lin had in fact been fleeing from Beijing after his plot to assassinate Mao and seize power was uncovered. Some Chinese suspect, however, that Lin's plane was sabotaged on Mao's orders.

22, *People's Daily* editors inserted an article on the front page about the rapidly changing situation in Hungary in which the Hungarian Premier was quoted as saying, "no political force whatsoever should be permitted to use the army to resolve internal government problems. ... The most odious characteristic of Stalinist-style [rule] is the use of military force to manage the people of one's country." They also introduced a daily news feature, a box bearing the heading: "Martial Law: Day X," which summarized the situation in Beijing each day. The brief summaries were fairly objective—which was embarrassing for the government, since "people power" had temporarily blocked the advance of troops into the city—and the name of the box seemed to suggest that the Beijing residents were withstanding a siege. After May 30, editors were forced to drop the feature; on June 4, the newspaper printed a letter attacking the box for distorted, inflammatory reporting.

The next selection, a piece from the students' *News Herald*, relates reporters' responses to the government's physical takeover of the Chinese media after martial law was imposed.

NOTES FROM AN INTERVIEW ON MAY 25

Following Li Peng's speech of May 19 declaring martial law in Beijing, large news organizations in the capital have reduced the coverage of events in the square and on the streets of Beijing, which had been considerable during the two days preceding the speech. Most of the important pages of the newspapers and key time slots on the radio are being used to report decrees and circulars of the government and the Martial Law Command Headquarters, as well as so-called "positive responses" from various circles. Troops have successively occupied the stations of China Central Broadcasting, China Central Television, and Central International Radio, the offices of *People's Daily* and *Beijing Daily*, and other news organizations.

At noon on the 25th, in the northwest corner of the Square, a *People's Daily* reporter who requested anonymity indignantly said to this writer, "What kind of people's government is this anyway? Since the 20th, the government has sent in soldiers of the People's Liberation Army and People's Armed Police to establish military control. Whenever you enter or exit the newspaper bureau or go to the restroom, they goddamn follow you in your tracks and interrogate you. Those of us in the business call the office our home. But now, without even personal freedom, how can we speak of any home?"

At this moment, a colleague of this reporter told this writer, "The majority of the people in our newspaper bureau have been on the side of the students all along and have been supporting them in various ways. However, before the students began a hunger strike, many of the objective reports we wrote about the student movement were consigned to limbo and replaced with government instructions. On the 15th, we witnessed the courageous act of the students. When we saw people from all walks of life marching in support of the students and censuring us, we could not remain seated any longer—we were being treated too unjustly. So for the next few days, many reporters and editors from our office, holding up a banner with the words, 'The Scapegoats are Coming,' joined the ranks of the marchers."

After pausing for a moment, he added, "The government keeps on insisting that it will not 'settle accounts' [after the movement dies down]. But in reality, after the troops entered the office on the 20th, the authorities began to pay special 'attention' to those of us who participated in the marches and flashed at us a 'yellow card' as a warning. Later, the authorities recklessly tampered with our articles so that they were distorted beyond recognition when they appeared in print. Moreover our 'boss' issued an explicit order prohibiting us from covering the student movement or the support for it in various circles, and warned that violators would have their wages and bonuses withheld or receive other punishment. But who cares about that stuff? When we go out each day, the only place we head for is among the students."

This writer then asked, "But in the last few days the *People's Daily* hasn't had many reports on the student movement, and . . ."

Looking very embarrassed, the two reporters threw up their hands and sighed, saying, "You're too naive. Our articles have to pass tests every step of the way. Furthermore, after the imposition of martial law, each article must be sent up for inspection by persons at every level and finally approved by the authorities before it is typeset. We have no control over the newspaper!" "But—" the reporters seemed to be consoling this writer, "even though this is the situation, many reporters in our office who support the students still want to use every method possible to report on the student movement. If 'down with Li Peng' doesn't work, we change it to 'oppose the Premier of the State Council.' If that doesn't work, then we change it to 'the main target of the attack is the Premier of the State Council.' "

So that's the way it is. I couldn't help feeling great admiration for the reporters. I flashed the revolutionary "V" sign as I bid the two farewell.

It is reported that similar events are occurring in other newspapers.
We believe that black clouds can never hide the sun.
Justice always prevails! Long live journalists with a conscience!

(article published in News Herald
No.6, May 27, 1989)

Workers' Daily editors planned to print the following article on the third page of the May 26 issue. The piece had already been typeset when Party censors ordered it pulled. The censored article was reprinted in *News Flashes (Xinwen kuaixun)*, a news report edited by intellectuals and journalists that began appearing in late May.

THE PRESS MUST HAVE THE COURAGE
TO SPEAK THE TRUTH

Beginning from no one knows when, a kind of "mouthpiece mentality" has become the master of the Chinese press world. The press function of "service" has been elevated to supreme status, while the press function of "supervision" appears to have been extremely debilitated. Moreover, the imbalance between the two has caused the press to sink gradually into the status of being merely an appendage to political power holders. This is particularly true when, in times when certain political exigencies require the sacrifice of truth, our press often shamelessly, indeed tragically, plays the role of the rumor-monger and trumpeter [of a political cause].

[Today, under reform,] an "open-styled" press has appeared, but it can only be described as "two papers, one pattern" [that is, papers have become independent entities in name only; in fact, they all echo each other]—just another example of a situation in which the press continues to be subordinate to politics. It cannot be denied that after experiencing ten years of turmoil, after lessons learned from bitter experience, the Chinese press has progressed a great deal in the way it thinks about itself. In the meantime, however, we see another fact, and see it not without feeling a chill. From time to time, the dark shadow of the "mouthpiece theory" hangs over the heads of the press like the sword of Damocles. Although the press has had the honor of banging the drum for other circles when they show ideological liberation, it continues to perplex us that the press itself has not, up to today, cast off various types of restrictions and restraints. In a suffocating atmosphere such as this, the human dignity of many in the press world has been warped. Newspapermen no longer possess single-minded ardor for the pursuit of the facts, the impulse to fight for freedom of the press, or the religious-like zeal for the story that pays no heed to personal safety.

As an ordinary person, one wants to figure out what the real facts are; but as an editor or reporter, one wants to know what the political safety coefficient is, to figure out how the winds are blowing in the official arena. One press person has remarked, not without a sigh of emotion, that "previously, reporters were termed 'free-lancers'; nowadays, they have become persons without any freedom."[5] Owing to this reality, the prestige of the press has declined. Ordinary folks say, not without a sharp edge to their voices, "In our papers, except for the year, month, and day, everything else is false." This sentence deserves the attention of all those who work in or are in charge of journalism.

What is meant by "having the courage to speak the truth"? Put simply, it means that one must seek truth from facts and speak according to the facts. It means that one must not violate the precepts of the heart and say false words. It means one must be objective and just. And the press must free itself from various types of submissiveness to power. On the other hand, what is meant by social stability? Does it mean that all of our media should go around singing loudly the same false tune of peace and prosperity, of the fine situation? That our ordinary people meekly and submissively play the role of tamed subjects? That our officials possess "iron authority," where their words are sacred, and once spoken settle all matters? No! Real society is certainly not this kind of superficial stability. Marches are certainly not so terrifying; neither is a diversity of opinions. What is truly frightening is when people have grievances but cannot find any normal channels for discharging them. . . .

It is undeniable that there still exist various types of external constraints that determine whether or not the press can speak the truth. Whether the press will be able to speak the truth depends on how the present newspaper system is reformed and on the entire process of democratization in China. It also depends on whether or not our press people possess the dedication of the faithful and the courageousness of martyrs. There are some words that are far from difficult to say; they require neither a scholar's erudition nor a politician's savvy. All that is needed is courage and insight. If the press's voice of courage merges with the heartfelt sound of the people, such papers and articles will need no salesmen

5. "Free-lancers" (*ziyou zhiyezhe*, independent professionals) is a term used for people who before 1949 did not work for a unit but were self-employed.

and will circulate in a flash. Were all our press people to possess this kind of character, then there would be hope for China's press—and also hope for Chinese democracy.

(in News Flashes, *No. 5, May 31, 1989)*

Entering the last week of May, the Democracy Movement appeared to have sunk to its nadir. The number of students in the Square continued to decline. Those remaining seemed to have no clear leadership; Chai Ling, tired and disheartened by the difficulties of keeping the Movement together, had resigned from her post as commander of the Protect Tiananmen Headquarters on the 29th. The Square, which even during the days of tightest student organization had resembled a makeshift encampment, now had degenerated into a shantytown, strewn with litter and permeated by the stench of garbage and overflowing portable toilets. Life in Beijing had essentially returned to normal; Tiananmen, once a magnet pulling in huge throngs, had become only an unkempt campground of little interest to citizens, many of whom considered the struggle for democracy lost.

But as had happened in the past, fresh initiatives by enthusiasts of democracy would reinvigorate the fading movement. First, a crudely sculpted thirty-three-foot-high statue would bestow the struggle for democracy with a memorable symbol. On May 30, students from the Central Academy of Fine Arts in Beijing unveiled in Tiananmen the "Goddess of Democracy." The statue, hastily constructed from plaster and styrofoam, was far from beautiful, but it attracted thousands of spectators to the Square and angered the authorities, who condemned it as an "illegal, permanent" structure that would have to be torn down. The Goddess of Democracy would stand for only five days before being destroyed by soldiers in the assault on Tiananmen that would end the Democracy Movement, but it has become an internationally recognized symbol of the students' spirit and hopes. The following account of the birth of the Goddess of Democracy was written by a young woman who witnessed its construction, a former student in the Sculpture Department at the Central Academy of Fine Arts, after the Democracy Movement was crushed.

THE BIRTH OF THE GODDESS OF DEMOCRACY

Nothing excites a sculptor so much, ordinarily, as seeing a work of her own creation take shape. This time, however, I was watching the creation of a sculpture that I had no part in making, and feeling the same excitement. It was the Goddess of Democracy statue that stood for five days in

Tiananmen Square, from May 30 to the morning of June 4. I witnessed the making of it, and want to put the story on record for the world to know. . . .

Students and faculty of the Central Academy of Fine Arts, which is located only a short distance from Tiananmen Square, had from the beginning been actively involved in the demonstrations. It was students in the Oil Painting Department who in the first days, when a major objective of the movement was to honor the recently deceased Hu Yaobang, had made a huge oil portrait of him and propped it against the Monument to the People's Heroes in the Square. On May 27, a representative of the Beijing Students' Federation came to the Central Academy to ask that they produce another large-scale work of art, this time a statue, and that it be ready by the time of the great demonstration on the 30th. That gave them three days in which to do it. The Federation offered them 8,000 yuan (over $2,000 U.S. by the official rate) for materials and other expenses. The undergraduate students in three of the four studios of the Central Academy's Sculpture Department agreed to take on the job. There were about fifteen of them, all young men in their early twenties.

The Federation suggested that the sculpture be a replica of the Statue of Liberty in New York, like the smaller one that had been carried in a procession by demonstrators in Shanghai two days earlier. But the Central Academy sculpture students rejected that idea, both because it might be taken as too openly pro-American and because copying an existing work was contrary to their principles as creative artists. They rejected also the suggestion of a "Chinese-style" work, because there is no tradition in China for sculpture that powerfully expresses a political concept. . . .

What was called for, the students felt, was a new work of universal appeal, Chinese only in the eclectic way that today's China sometimes borrows what it needs from foreign cultures. But apart from style, they had another problem: the short time in which they had to complete it. . . .

Their solution was ingenious, and explains some features of the statue as it took shape: its slightly off-balance look and its posture with two hands raised to hold up its torch, whereas the Statue of Liberty in New York needs only one. The students, with the strong academic training that young artists receive in China, chose a thoroughly academic approach to their problem: they decided to adapt to their purpose a studio practice work that one of them (or perhaps it was several of them) had already made, a half-meter-high clay sculpture of a man grasping a pole with two raised hands and leaning his weight on it. It had been done originally as a demonstration of how the distribution of weight is affected when the center of gravity is shifted outside the body. . . . This was the unlikely beginning from which the Goddess of Democracy was to grow, by a remarkable process of transformation. The students cut off the lower part of the pole and added a flame at the top to turn it into a torch; they leaned the sculpture into a more upright position; they changed the man's face for a woman's, added breasts and long hair, and otherwise made him into a her.

I did not witness this transformation of the model myself, but was told about it afterward by the sculptors. They were a bit embarrassed in relating how it happened; they thought of it more as an emergency expedient than as an ingenious or admirable solution. Their aim was to portray the Goddess as a healthy young woman, and for that, again, the Chinese sculpture tradition offered no models. What they turned to was the tradition favored within the Central Academy's Sculpture Department, the Russian school of revolutionary realism, and specifically the style of the woman sculptor Vera Mukhina, whose monumental statue of A Worker and Collective Farm Woman, originally placed atop the Soviet Pavilion at the 1937 Paris World's Fair, is still much admired in China; the head of the farm woman in this work was the principal inspiration for the face and head of the Goddess.

This transformed model was then made the basis for the ten-meter-high statue. It was divided (marked) into four horizontal sections, and teams of young sculptors transferred the measurements of these, by a process well known to academic sculptors, to the corresponding parts of the huge work that would be assembled on the Square. The main material was styrofoam plastic; this had not, so far as I know, been used before in China for monumental sculpture, but perhaps the idea had come from foreign sculptors who had used it, or from the use of that material in advertising displays, store windows, and so on. Large blocks of it were carved into rough approximations of the shapes desired and then wired together, with plaster added to the surface to join the pieces more strongly and to allow finer modeling. Constructed in this way, the four sections were fairly light: each could be lifted by five or six students.

One young Central Academy faculty member was openly supportive of the students and served as go-between to help them get materials and facilities that they could not otherwise have obtained, even with money. Others on the faculty were certainly giving their support behind the scenes, persuading the political leaders in the Academy and protecting the students. Without their help, the sculpture could not have been made openly, as it was, in the Sculpture Department's outdoor workspace within the Central Academy compound. . . .

Illustration 6.2. On the night of May 29, students from the Central Academy of Fine Arts transport the three sections of the Goddess of Democracy to Tiananmen. Fearing that the authorities would send forces to prevent the statue from reaching the Square, other students link arms to form a protective escort. Credit: Franki Chan.

When the time came to transport the pieces of the statue to the Square, another problem arose: the students had intended to carry them in one of the Academy's trucks, but the State Security Bureau, hearing of this, sent word that any driver daring to take them would lose his license. In the end the students hired six of the familiar Beijing carts, made like a bicycle in front with a flat cart with two wheels behind; four of these carried the sections of the statue, with tools and materials on the other two. Students from the Central Academy, along with others from seven other academies of crafts, drama, music, dance, and so on, who were cooperating, accompanied the carts to guard them.

The route had been announced: turn left outside the Academy gate, then westward to Donghuamen, the east gate of the Forbidden City, and so around the road between the wall and the moat to the Square. But this was to deceive the police, in case they were waiting to stop us; in fact, we turned right out of the Academy and followed the shorter route, down Wangfujing, the well-known shopping street, turning right along Changan Avenue, past the Beijing Hotel.

The place on the Square where the statue was to be erected had been chosen carefully. It was on the great axis, heavy with symbolism both cosmological and political, that extended from the main entrance of the Forbidden City, with the huge portrait of Mao Tse-tung over it, through the Monument to the People's Heroes, which had become the command headquarters of the student movement. The statue was to be set up just across the broad avenue from Mao, so that it would confront the Great Leader face to face. When we arrived around 10:30 at night, a huge crowd, perhaps fifty thousand people, had gathered around the tall scaffolding of iron poles that had already been erected to support the statue. The parts were placed one on top of another, attached to this frame; plaster was poured into the hollow core, locking it onto a vertical iron pole which extended from the ground up the center to hold it upright. The exposed iron supports were then cut away, leaving the statue free-standing. It stood on a base also made of iron rods, about two meters in height, which was later covered with cloth. The statue was deliberately made so that once assembled it could not be taken apart again, but would have to be destroyed all at once.

The work continued through the night. . . . By noon on the 30th, the statue was ready for the unveiling ceremony. Actually, only the face was "veiled," by two long pieces of cloth, bright blue and red—the students could never have collected enough cloth to cover the whole figure.

The ceremony was simple and very moving. A statement had been prepared about the meaning of the statue, written on a long banner stretched on poles near the statue, and was read over the loudspeaker by a woman, probably a student at the Broadcasting Academy, who had a good Mandarin accent. Like the sculpture itself, the statement was a piece of passionately dedicated improvisation; it was written on the banner in rather crude calligraphy. Here is a rough rendering of it:

Dear Compatriots and Fellow Students:

We, as proud citizens of China, have broken the autocracy of the government and now stand welcoming the Democracy Movement of 1989. All the people are of a single mind: to combat bravely the feudal autocracy. Fighting tirelessly through the days and nights of the past weeks, we have achieved victories one after another, because the people are invincible.

Now this autocratic government, possessing only animal characteristics, lacking all human feeling, has used the most shameless and scurrilous methods, violence and cheating, in their attempt to kill the Goddess of Democracy as a newborn infant in her cradle. But this coming of darkness proves only that they have reached the end of their road; the day of their doom has already arrived. They will be judged by all the people.

At this grim moment, what we need most is to remain calm and united in a single purpose. We need a powerful cementing force to strengthen our resolve: that is the Goddess of Democracy.

Democracy, how long has it been since we last saw you . . . ?

You are the hope for which we thirst, we Chinese who have suffered decades of repression under feudal autocracy!

You are the symbol of every student in the Square, of the hearts of millions of people!

You are the soul of the 1989 Democracy Movement!

You are the Chinese nation's hope for salvation!

Today, here in the People's Square, the people's Goddess stands tall and announces to the whole world: A consciousness of democracy has awakened among the Chinese people! The new era has begun! From this piece of ancient earth grows the tree of democracy and freedom, putting forth gorgeous flowers and a bountiful harvest of fruit!

The statue of the Goddess of Democracy is made of plaster, and of course cannot stand here forever. But as the symbol of the people's hearts, she is divine and inviolate. Let those who would sully her beware: the people will not permit this!

We believe strongly that this darkness will pass, that the dawn must come. On the day when real democracy and freedom come to China, we must erect another Goddess of Democracy here in the Square, monumental, towering, and permanent. We have strong faith that that day will come at last. We have still another hope: Chinese people, arise! Erect the statue of the Goddess of Democracy in your millions of hearts!

Long live the people!
Long live freedom!
Long live democracy!

The statement was signed by the eight art academies that had sponsored the whole project: the Central Academies of Fine Arts, Arts and Crafts, Drama, and Music; the Beijing Film Academy; the Beijing Dance Academy; the Academy of Chinese Local Stage Arts; and the Academy of Traditional Chinese Music.

When the time came for the actual "unveiling," two Beijing residents, a woman and a man, were chosen at random from the crowd and invited into the circle to pull the strings that would remove the pieces of red and blue cloth. As these "veils" fell the crowd burst into cheers, there were shouts of "Long live democracy!" and other slogans, and some began to sing the Internationale. A musical performance was given by students from the Central Academy of Music: choral renditions of the Hymn to Joy from Beethoven's Ninth Symphony, another foreign song and one Chinese, and finally the Internationale again. A planned performance by students in the Central Academy of Dance had to be cancelled, since with the pressure of the crowd there was not enough room for them to dance.

. . .

On the terrible night of June 3rd to 4th I was out around the Square for some forty hours without sleep; that is another story. Afterward I could no longer go on living at the Central Academy—it was too dangerous—and most of the students and faculty had fled when I returned there the day after the massacre. But I found a few of the sculpture students, and quickly questioned them about matters to do with the planning and making of the statue that were not clear to me. Before, there had seemed to be no urgency about getting the whole story; now there was. That was the last I saw of them; they were frightened, with good reason, and dispersed to safer places. I have not heard anything about any of them since then. . . .

—Tsao Hsingyuan
(Berkeley, late June 1989)

At the same time, plans for a "Democracy University" furnished students with a long-term focus for the occupation of the Square. Many students and intellectuals had been arguing for some time that the Movement was doomed unless students strengthened their theoretical understanding of democracy and formulated programs that would broaden its political base. Beijing student leaders had proposed returning to campuses to organize theoretical work and to plan the next stage of the movement. The students in Tiananmen, working closely with students from the Chinese University of Hong Kong, proposed instead to start a "Democracy University" right in the Square. In their vision, Democracy University would be a type of "open university" where people from all walks of life could meet and discuss their ideas on democracy, freedom, and reform in China. Democracy University would transcend political boundaries—intellectuals from not only China, but Taiwan, Hong Kong, and the West would be invited to lecture. And finally, Democracy University was both a means and an end: a means of exploring and developing democractic reform for China, and the embodiment itself of the practice of democracy. Plans for Democracy University went ahead rapidly: an organizing committee was established, intellectual activist Yan Jiaqi and journalist Liu Binyan were invited to be the honorary presidents, and the date for the inauguration ceremony set for 8 P.M. on June 3.

Finally, a new hunger strike by a pop star and three young intellectuals revived for a brief time public interest in the movement. On June 2, Hou Dejian, a popular singer and composer who had left Taiwan for China in 1983, and Liu Xiaobo, one of China's leading young scholars of literary criticism, joined by two friends, commenced a hunger strike in Tiananmen. Their strike was an important show of solidarity for the students; although the Capital Cross-Sector Federation, a recently formed alliance encompassing students, intellectuals, workers, and other citizens, had been attempting to organize a large-scale hunger strike, it had not produced any action to date. Yet the attempt to keep the movement alive seemed to be a largely symbolic statement that implicitly acknowledged the waning of the protests: it was to last only seventy-two hours, and Hou Dejian's participation would be limited to forty-eight hours to enable him to meet recording obligations in Hong Kong. The enthusiastic rally at which Hou Dejian and his friends announced the start of their hunger strike was to be one of the last in Tiananmen; in fewer than thirty-six hours, thousands of army troops and dozens of tanks would control the Square.

The hunger strike manifesto of the four, written by Liu Xiaobo and translated below, is notable for its appeal to fellow citizens to leave behind, once and for all, the Maoist mentality of class struggle that had taught them to categorize Chinese as either part of the "people" or a member of the "enemy," and to attack enemies with violence. Declaring, "take class struggle as the key link," Mao had brought the nation through a series of tumultous movements, most notably the Anti-Rightist Campaign in 1957 and the Cultural Revolution in the late 1960s; the results in each case had been years of violent conflict between Chinese and Chinese during which tens of thousands had been killed. Although in the eighties Deng the pragmatist had deemphasized class struggle in favor of economic development, the Party's ideological campaigns against the encroachment of "bourgeois liberalism" were still waged in the name of class conflict; following the suppression of the 1989 protests, the Party would again invoke the concept of class struggle, declaring, "the bloody lesson of this struggle has made us realize the objective existence of class struggle."

HUNGER STRIKE MANIFESTO

We are on a hunger strike! We protest! We appeal! We repent!

Death is not what we seek; we are searching for true life.

In the face of the irrational, high-handed military violence of the Li Peng government, Chinese intellectuals must dispose of their age-old disease, passed down over centuries, of being spineless, of merely speaking and not acting. By means of action, we protest against military control; by means of action, we call for the birth of a new political culture; and by means of action, we express our repentance for the wrongs that have been the doing of our own age-old weakness. The Chinese nation has fallen behind; for this, each one of us bears his share of responsibility. . . .

Our hunger strike is no longer a petition, but a protest against martial law and military control! We advocate the use of peaceful means to further democratization in China and to oppose any form of violence. Yet we do not fear brute force; through peaceful means, we will demonstrate the resilience of the democratic strength of the people, and smash the undemocratic order held together by bayonets and lies. . . .

The thousands of years of Chinese history have been a story of violence met with violence, of learning to hate and to be hated. Entering the modern era, this "enemy consciousness" [where one separates the enemy from the people] has become the legacy of the Chinese. The post-1949 slogan: "Take class struggle as the key link [to all human struggles and as the motive force of history]" has pushed to the extreme this traditional mentality of hatred, this enemy consciousness, and the practice of meeting violence with violence. This time, the imposition of military control is but another manifestation of the political culture of "class struggle." It is because of this that we are on a hunger strike; we appeal to the Chinese people that from now on they gradually discard and eradicate [our] enemy consciousness and mentality of hatred, and completely forsake [our] "class struggle" form of political culture, for hatred generates only violence and autocracy. We must use a democratic spirit of tolerance and cooperation to begin the construction of democracy in China. For democratic politics is a politics without enemies and without a mentality of hatred, a politics of consultation, discussion, and decision by vote, based on mutual respect, mutual tolerance, and mutual accommodation. Since as Premier, Li Peng has made grave mistakes, he should be made to resign according to democratic processes.

However, Li Peng is not our enemy; even if he steps down, he would still enjoy the rights that citizens should have, even the right to adhere to his mistaken beliefs. We appeal to all Chinese, from those in the government down to every ordinary citizen, to give up the old political culture and begin a new one. We ask that the government end martial law at once. We ask that both the students and the government once again turn to peaceful negotiation and consultative dialogue to resolve their differences.

The present student movement has received an unprecedented amount of sympathy, understanding, and support from all sectors of society. The implementation of martial law has turned a student movement into a national democracy movement. Undeniable, however, is the fact that many of those who have supported the students have acted out of humanitarian sympathy and discontent with the government; they have lacked a citizen's sense of political responsibility. Because of this, we appeal to all [members] of [Chinese] society gradually to drop the attitude of [merely] being onlookers and simply expressing sympathy. We appeal to you to acquire a sense of citizen consciousness. First of all, this citizen consciousness is the awareness that [all citizens] possess political rights. Every citizen must have the self-confidence that one's own political rights are equal to the rights of the Premier. Next, citizen consciousness is a consciousness of rationalized political involvement—of political responsibility—not just a sense of justice and sympathy. It means that every man or woman cannot only express sympathy and support, but also must become directly involved in the construction of democracy. Finally, citizen consciousness means self-awareness of one's responsibilities and obligations. In the construction of social politics bound by rationality and law, every one of us must contribute his part; likewise, where social politics are irrational and lawless, each bears his share of responsibility. Voluntary participation in the political life of society and voluntary acceptance of one's responsibilities are the inescapable duties of every citizen. The Chinese people must see that, in democratized politics, everyone is first and foremost a citizen, and then a student, a professor, a worker, a cadre, or a soldier.

For thousands of years, Chinese society has followed a vicious cycle of overthrowing an old emperor just to put up a new one. History has shown that the fall of a leader who has lost the people's support or the rise of a leader who has the backing of the people cannot solve China's essential political problem. What we need is not a perfect savior, but a sound democratic system. We thus call for the following: (1) all [sectors of] society should establish lawful, autonomous citizens' organizations, and gradually develop these organizations into citizens' political forces that will act to check government policy making, for the quintessence of democracy is the curbing and balancing of power. We would rather have ten monsters that are mutually restrained than one angel of absolute power; (2) by impeaching leaders who have committed serious errors, [we should] gradually establish a sound system for the impeachment of officials. Whoever rises and whoever falls is not important; what is important is how one ascends to, or falls from, power. An undemocratic procedure of appointment and dismissal can only result in dictatorship.

In the course of the present movement, both the government and the students have made mistakes. The main mistake of the government was that, conditioned by the outmoded political ideology of "class struggle," it has chosen to take a stand in opposition to [the position of] the great majority of students and residents, thus causing continuous intensification of the conflict. The main mistake of the students is that, because the organizing of their own organizations left much to be desired, many undemocratic elements have appeared in the very process of striving for democracy. We therefore call on both the government and students to conduct level-headed self-examination. It is our belief that, on the whole, the greater fault for the present situation lies with the government. Actions such as demonstrations and hunger strikes are democratic ways through which people express their wishes; they are completely legal and reasonable. They are anything but "turmoil." Yet the government ignored the basic rights of the people granted by the Constitution; on the basis of its autocratic political ideology, it labeled the student movement as "turmoil." This stand led to a series of wrong decisions, which then led to the growth of the movement and rising antagonism. The real catalyst for the turmoil is therefore the government's wrong decisions, errors of a gravity no less than [those committed in] the "Cultural Revolution." It was only due to the great restraint shown by the students and people of Beijing and to impassioned appeals from all sectors of society—including the Party, the government, and the military—that wide-scale bloodshed has been avoided. In view of this, the government must admit to and examine these mistakes it has made. We believe that it is not yet too late to correct the mistakes. The government should draw some painful lessons from this major movement. It should learn to become accustomed to listening to the voice of the people, to allowing people to express their desires through the exercise of the constitutionally granted rights, and to governing the country in a democratic way. This nationwide movement for democracy is a lesson for the government in how to govern society by means of democracy and the rule of law.

The students' mistakes are mainly manifested in the internal chaos of their organizations and the lack of efficient and democratic procedures. Although their goal is democracy, their means and procedures for achieving democracy are not democratic. Their theories call for democracy, but their handling of specific problems is not democratic. Their lack of cooperative spirit and the secretarianism that has caused their forces to neutralize each other have resulted in all their policies coming to naught. More faults can be named: financial chaos; material waste; an excess of emotion and a lack of reason; too much of the attitude that they are privileged, and not enough of the belief in equality; and so on. In the last hundred years, the great majority of the Chinese people's struggles for democracy has remained at the level of ideological battles and slogan shouting. Enlightenment is much talked about, but little is said about the actual running of a democracy. Goals are discussed, but not the means, the procedures, or process through which they will be achieved. We believe that the actual realization of a democratic political system lies in the democratization of the process, means, and procedures of operating such a system. For this, we appeal to the Chinese people to forsake this tradition of "empty democracy," a democracy of only ideology, slogans, and [abstract] goals, and begin the construction of the process, means, and procedures for the operation of a democracy. We ask you to transform a democratic movement focused on ideological enlightenment into a movement of democracy in action; this must be done by starting with each specific matter. We call for the students to begin a self-examination that should focus on the overhaul and reorganization of the student groups in Tiananmen Square.

The government's grave mistakes in its approach were also reflected in its use of the term "a handful of persons" [to refer to participants in pro-democracy protests]. Through our hunger strike, we would like to tell the media, home and abroad, who this so-called "handful of persons" [really] are: they are not [a bunch of] students, but citizens with a sense of political responsibility who have voluntarily participated in the present nationwide democratic movement led by the students. All we have done and all we are doing is lawful and reasonable. In this combat of opposing political cultures, of character cultivation and of moral strength, the hunger strikers intend to use their wisdom and actions to make the government feel shamed, to make it admit and correct its wrongdoings. We also intend to encourage the autonomous student organizations to improve themselves daily in accordance with democratic and legal procedures.

It must be acknowledged that democratic governance of the country is unfamiliar to every Chinese citizen. And every Chinese citizen, including the highest officials in the Party and the government, must learn it from the bottom up. In this learning process, mistakes by both the government and the people are inevitable. The key is to admit mistakes when they become evident and to correct them after they appear; to learn from our mistakes and turn them into positive lessons; and, during the continuous process of rectifying our mistakes, to learn gradually how to govern the country democratically.

We don't have enemies!

Don't let hatred and violence poison wisdom and the process of democratization in China!

We all must carry out a self-examination!
Everyone bears responsibility for the backwardness of China!
We are above all citizens!
We are not seeking death!
We are searching for true life!

> —Liu Xiaobo, Ph.D. in Literature, Assistant Professor, Chinese Department, Beijing Normal University.
> Zhou Duo, former Assistant Professor, Sociology Research Institute, Beijing University; Director, Comprehensive Planning Division, Beijing Stone Corporation Group.
> Hou Dejian, well-known composer and song writer.
> Gao Xin, former Chief Editor of *Normal University Weekly*, Party member.

"We must use a sharp knife and cut the tangled rope." With these words, spoken in late April, Deng Xiaoping had made clear his position: the student movement was to be suppressed, quickly and decisively. But for nearly seven weeks, Deng's will had been frustrated—by hesitation within the Party about using force to suppress student unrest, by the presence of international guests, by a power struggle that had threatened to cleave the Party, and finally, by overwhelming citizen support for the protestors. However, in late May, with Zhao's challenge extinguished, and with the support of the military lined up, all obstacles to a crackdown appeared finally to have been cleared away.

One of the first signals of the impending crackdown was the May 30 detention of at least three members of the Capital Workers' Autonomous Union by the Beijing Security Police. On the same day the government also detained eleven members of the "Flying Tigers," a motorcycle brigade of young men that had been assisting the students by conveying messages and acting as scouts.

Worker activists were the government's first targets, probably because it feared that the struggling Democracy Movement would find a reincarnation in the form of worker unrest, which it feared even more than student restiveness. Additionally, workers were more vulnerable to government intimidation than students. As junior members of the intellectual class, students enjoyed slightly more latitude than other citizens to criticize the Party or government—not necessarily because Party leaders had any special respect for the intelligentsia but only because their persecution would have drawn much more attention at home and abroad. In comparison to workers, intellectuals had far greater access to more liberal-minded Party officials and foreign journalists and friends. Moreover, workers were far more economically dependent on the state than were students. Workers could not afford to lose their jobs in a state-controlled economy, particularly if they had families to support. Denial of a state job assignment was less threatening to students, who for several years (until the state reversed its policy in 1989) had actually been encouraged to arrange independent employment. Expulsion from a university, while a severe blow in degree-conscious China, would not have been devastating.

The following handbill was distributed on May 30 by the Capital Workers' Autonomous Union to inform citizens and foreign journalists of the abduction of one of their leaders by the Beijing Security Police. On the same day, several thousand workers and students protested at the Beijing Security Bureau headquarters for the release of the arrested workers. As a result of these efforts by workers and students, the detention of the workers was widely reported outside of China. According to the Chinese government, the workers were released within several days. After the June crackdown, however, the government again moved against workers, issuing arrest warrants for their leaders and arresting many other workers.

EMERGENCY NOTICE OF THE PREPARATORY COMMITTEE OF THE CAPITAL WORKERS' AUTONOMOUS UNION

At 2:00 this morning, at a news conference called by the [Beijing] Students' Federation, an eyewitness confirmed that at a little past 1:00 this morning in the vicinity of the Beijing Hotel, two police jumped out of a Beijing jeep with police license plates and forced a bicyclist to get off his bicycle. This bicyclist yelled at them, "why are you taking me?" The police did not respond, but forcibly pushed him into the jeep. Before being forced in, the kidnapped person threw two notebooks onto the ground. The witness immediately brought the notebooks to the Bejiing Students' Federation.

The name Shen Yinghan was written on the cover of the notebooks. Inside the books was written this sentence: "Yesterday (all of the) 200 yuan that was raised was deposited in the [xxx]. The Capital Workers' Autonomous Union cites this evidence as proof that the kidnapped person was none other than Mr. Shen Yinghan, a member of the Executive Committee of the Preparatory Committee of the Capital Workers' Autonomous Union. After learning of the news of his kidnapping, the Capital Workers' Autonomous Union immediately sent a person to Mr. Shen's home to get more information and discovered that he had indeed not returned home.

The Capital Workers' Autonomous Union was established on the basis of the constitutional provision of "freedom of assembly." It has done absolutely nothing illegal. This Preparatory Committee will go to the Beijing Security Bureau this morning at 9:00 to take up this matter with them. In addition, we call on the great mass of workers to take action and demand that workers' representative Shen Yinghan be released at once. Workers also have the right to be patriotic. Save our compatriot! Save our workers' representative!

> —[The Preparatory Committee of the] Capital Workers
> Autonomous Union, May 30, 1989
> *(handbill distributed in Beijing)*

Many Chinese, both in and out of the Movement, foresaw the inevitability of bloodshed if the students refused to yield Tiananmen. None, however, was prepared for the carnage and destruction of the army takeover of Tiananmen on June 3. During the long night of the 3rd, as troops fought pitched battles at key city intersections with crowds of furious and unbelieving residents determined to halt their advance to Tiananmen, Beijing finally descended into the chaos that the government had time and again warned of. The soldiers' weapons were AK-47s, truncheons, tear gas, tanks, and armored personnel carriers; the citizens' weapons were rocks, steel bars, crude barricades, and Molotov cocktails—and anything else found on the streets that could be hurled at the soldiers. Before the army's subjugation of Beijing was complete, hundreds—possibly thousands—of civilians lay dead; scores of soldiers had also been killed.[6]

6. All foreign observers have agreed that although it is impossible to determine with any certainty the number of deaths between June 3 and 7, the Chinese government's figure of two to three hundred deaths is far too low. The most conservative non-Chinese estimates place the civilian death toll at more than four hundred. Many analyses have estimated the number of civilians killed to be at least in the high hundreds and quite possibly into the thousands. See, for example, Amnesty International, "People's Republic of China, Preliminary Findings on Killings of Unarmed Citizens; Arbitrary Arrests and Summary Executions Since June 3, 1989" (calling the official figure of two hundred a "gross underestimate"); International League for Human Rights, "Massacre in Beijing: The Events of 3-4 June 1989

Illustration 6.3. On the afternoon of June 3, the People's Armed Force attack a crowd at the entrance to Zhongnanhai with electric batons and tear gas. The crowd fights back with rocks and bricks; many are injured. The characters proclaim, "Long Live the [Chinese] Communist Party!" Credit: Franki Chan.

The army's first attempts to penetrate to Tiananmen in the middle of the night of June 2–3 had been less than threatening. In a maneuver that may have been intended to deliver arms surreptitiously to soldiers who had managed to slip into the center of the city, army convoys loaded with weapons had begun driving into the city from its western outskirts, only to be blocked by barricades of buses and trucks, and surrounded by thousands of residents. This time the mood of the crowds was much more ugly than in the first days of martial law: soldiers were threatened, tires slashed, and vehicles overturned or looted. At about the same time, several thousand unarmed soldiers had tried to approach Tiananmen from the east. They too were halted by angry crowds in front of the Beijing Hotel; after being taunted and pushed around, the young, obviously green soldiers retreated in disarray.

---

and Their Aftermath" ("most probably that the number of people killed . . . was well into the thousands"). Some Hong Kong papers and magazines have reported death tolls as high as seven to eight thousand. The actual number of deaths during the suppression will probably never be known, since evidence and records may well have been destroyed by martial law commanders.

Illustration 6.4. On June 3 tension increases further when thousands of troops emerge from the west side of the Great Hall of the People and attempt to seal off part of Changan Avenue. They are quickly prevented from moving by a huge crowd. Credit: Magnum / Stuart Franklin.

In the afternoon of the 3rd, however, aggressive military action led to violent clashes. Near Xinhuamen, the entrance to Zhongnanhai, the Party headquarters just west of Tiananmen, dozens were injured in the worst violence yet of the Democracy Movement when corps of the People's Armed Police indiscriminately attacked people on Changan Avenue with electric truncheons and fired tear gas. Additional fighting occurred when several hundred other paramilitary personnel attempted to reach Tiananmen in order to recapture weapons that had fallen into the hands of students and citizens during the night; students had placed the weapons on display near the Square, but would later try unsuccessfully to return them to military authorities. In another encounter, five thousand troops who emerged from the west side of the Great Hall of the People, which they had apparently reached through underground passages, engaged in a tense standoff with a huge crowd of at least fifty thousand. What would certainly have been large-scale bloodshed was avoided only by the troops' decision not to force their way through to Tiananmen. Throughout the afternoon, however, isolated patches of violence broke out when soldiers beat or whipped people who tried to enter the troops' ranks to plead with them to withdraw.

At Tiananmen, students and other protestors remained calm despite the escalating tension elsewhere. Plans for the inaugural ceremony for Democracy University remained unchanged. Throughout the day, the students' broadcast stations had been waging a "battle of speakers" with the more powerful government speakers mounted in the Square, countering government propaganda announcements and warnings with their own propaganda and news updates. Sometime in the afternoon or early evening, amid multiplying reports of clashes between citizens and soldiers, the Protect Tiananmen Headquarters issued the following urgent appeal.

URGENT CALL TO MOBILIZE FROM THE PROTECT TIANANMEN HEADQUARTERS

Today is the third of June, 1989. . . . History will show that this day will be a symbol of shame, a day that the people will always remember. On this day, the government has ripped off the last shred of the veil covering its hideous visage. It has dispatched thousands of brutal troops and police, who have frenziedly attacked totally unarmed students and people, to suppress the students and people. They have used every type of weapon, from tear gas to electric truncheons. We no longer hold out any hope whatsoever for this government. We now solemnly declare: if Li Peng's government is not brought down, China will perish and the people will no longer have any right to existence whatsoever. Thus, we solemnly state that our rallying cry is: Down with Li Peng's government!

We call on the entire people to take action: Workers, strike! [People of Beijing,] go on general strike! Resolutely resist the ruthless rule of Li Peng's government! We appeal to all of our classmates to return quickly to Tiananmen Square to defend our position. In the future, the Square will become the clearest banner of the triumph of truth over evil, of the people's triumph over fascism. We appeal to all patriotic soldiers with a sense of justice: please arise! Resolutely refuse to be the sacrificial objects of dictators! Do not open fire on the people!

We also appeal to all patriotic, peace- and freedom-loving people and nations across the world: please give your utmost support and aid to the Chinese people's struggle for justice.

The people will be victorious! Truth will be victorious! Long live democracy! Long live the people!

Long live the Chinese nation!

All Beijing residents and students, join together!

Victory is near!

(broadcast, June 3, 1989)

"With Blood Write the Preface to China's Future"

The government's efforts to clear Tiananmen had been stymied once again by the defiant people of Beijing. But this time the government would not hold back the army: the Democracy Movement was to be suppressed at all costs. By evening, troops from various Chinese army commands were moving into Beijing from all directions under orders to reach Tiananmen, with force if necessary. As they advanced, they met with stiff opposition: barricades of all sorts lay across street intersections and in some sites, crowds of young men, sometimes assisted by women and older people, hurled bricks and Molotov cocktails at troops and their vehicles. Beginning at around 10 P.M., troops moving east on Changan Avenue toward Tiananmen unleashed a savage and often random barrage of firepower as they slowly progressed against fierce resistance, mowing down not only workers and students defending barricades, but also any persons moving within their range. Bloody battles also occurred to the south of Tiananmen before troops pushed their way through to the Square.

By approximately 1:30 A.M., Tiananmen was surrounded by troops. The full story of the next hours may never be known. It is generally agreed that between 1:30 and 6:00 A.M., the army proceeded to clear the Square, first sealing it off and then forcing thousands of students and their supporters to withdraw through its southeast corner. But details of the operation are not clear; many outside of China question the Chinese government's official account, which states that no persons were killed in the Square. According to that account, troops permitted students and citizens to leave the Square peacefully before tanks knocked down the Goddess of Democracy and the demonstrators' tents; a few "obstinate" persons who refused to leave were forcibly removed. However, eyewitness accounts of firing in the Square, the sound of heavy gunfire from in the Square between 5:00 and 6:00, and self-contradictory government accounts, have all cast serious doubts over the veracity of the government's version.

If soldiers did fire on and kill people in the Square, as appears likely from independent eyewitness accounts, the number of casualties probably was small in comparison to the many deaths on western Changan Avenue. For many Chinese, however, the question of whether people died in Tiananmen has assumed a special importance, becoming the issue in which they seek the ultimate proof of their government's moral bankruptcy and of the democracy protestors' sacrifice. This may explain why the taped account of Chai Ling, the head of the Tiananmen Command Center, and other eyewitness accounts of what happened in the Square have been published over and over again in Hong Kong and in Chinese-language books on the Democracy Movement. Excerpts of Chai Ling's taped account, which was made by her on June 8 and smuggled out of China to Hong Kong, where it was broadcast by the Hong Kong Television Corporation, are presented below. As of winter 1989, Chai Ling was rumored still to be in hiding somewhere in China.

"I AM CHAI LING . . . I AM STILL ALIVE"
(excerpts)

It is 4:00 in the afternoon on June 8, 1989. I am Chai Ling. I am the General Commander of the Tiananmen Command Center. I am still alive.

I think I am the most authoritative commentator to speak on the overall situation in the Square during the period from June 2 to June 4. I also have an obligation to tell the true story to each of you, each and every citizen, each and every compatriot.

After around 10:00 P.M. on June 2, the first signal [of the impending repression] was that [we heard that] a police car had hit four innocent people, and three of them had already died. Then immediately following this, the second signal came: [we learned that] entire truckloads of soldiers had abandoned their guns, uniforms, and other weapons, letting them fall into the hands of the citizens and my classmates who were blocking the trucks. The students, very vigilant about this sort of behavior, immediately collected these objects and turned them into the Public Security Bureau, as our receipt proves. The third signal came at 2:10 in the afternoon on June 3, when a large force of soldiers and People's Armed Police beat students and local residents at Xinhuamen and Liubukou [the streetcorner just west of Xinhuamen]. At the time our classmates were standing on top of a bus yelling through megaphones, "the people's police love the people," "the people's police don't beat people." Just as one of our classmates was yelling out the first sentence, a soldier charged forward, kicked him in the stomach, and swore at him, "who in the hell loves you!" This was promptly followed by a truncheon, and the boy fell over immediately.

Let me explain a bit about our positions. I am the General Commander [of the Protect Tiananmen Headquarters]. We had set up a broadcast station in the Square. It was [originally] the hunger strikers' broadcast station. I always stayed there, directing the activities of all the students in the Square through broadcasts. Of course there were other students in the Headquarters, such as Li Lu, Feng Congde, and others. We frequently received emergency reports about various developments. There were continued reports of students and residents being beaten, of being cruelly injured. . . .

At precisely 9:00, all the students at Tiananmen Square rose, and raising their right hands, took an oath: "I swear that for the sake of advancing the democratization of our motherland, for the true prosperity of our nation, for our great motherland, I pledge to use my own youthful life to protect Tiananmen and defend the Republic, not to overthrow a small clique of conspirators but in order that 1.1 billion people do not lose their lives amid a white terror. Heads may be cut off and blood may flow, but the people's Square cannot be lost. We are willing to use our youthful lives to fight down to the last person."

At precisely 10:00, the Square's Democracy University officially opened for classes. The Vice General Commander [of the Headquarters], Zhang Boli, was appointed its president. People from all quarters expressed warm congratulations on the establishment of Democracy University. At the Headquarters, where emergency reports were being received continuously, the situation was extremely tense, while at another section of the Square, in the north, applause thundered for the founding of Democracy University. The university was located near the Goddess of Liberty [in the northern part of the square], and to its east and west on Changan Avenue, blood flowed like a river.

The slaughterers, the soldiers of the 27th Army, used tanks, assault weapons, and bayonets (the time for tear gas had passed) on people who had yelled only a lone slogan or only had thrown a single brick. They used automatic guns to mow them down so that the chests of all of the dead were soaked in blood. Our classmates ran to the Headquarters. Their hands, chests, and legs were covered with blood, their compatriots' last drops of blood; they had held their [dying] classmates in their own arms.

Since April, when the movement was a student-led patriotic democratic movement, all the way to the present, when the movement has grown into a nationwide movement, our guiding principle has been [to engage in] peaceful protest; our principle for struggle has been peaceful protest. Many students, workers, and citizens came to our headquarters to tell us that since the situation had reached this state, we should take up arms. Male students were also extremely agitated . . . [but] we at the Headquarters said to everyone: "our struggle is one of peaceful protest, and the highest principle of peace is sacrifice."

In this spirit, we all emerged from our tents slowly, one by one, hand in hand, shoulder by shoulder, to the sound of the "Internationale," and walked over to the northern, western, and southern sides of the Monument to the People's Heroes. Everybody sat there quietly, awaiting with

Illustration 6.5. Hundreds of injured or dying civilians are rushed to hospitals by flatbed tricycles during the bloody night of June 3 and morning of June 4. Ambulances are sometimes blocked by troops from reaching the wounded on the streets. Credit: Franki Chan.

calm expressions the butcher knives of the slaughterers. We were carrying out a war of love and hate, and not a battle of military force. . . .

The students just sat there quietly, lying down to await the [moment of] sacrifice. At this time, megaphones inside the headquarters tent and loudspeakers outside played the song, "The Descendants of the Dragon" [a popular song about the Chinese race by Hou Dejian]. Our classmates sang along with the music, their eyes welling up with tears. Everybody hugged each other and held hands, for each person knew the last moment of his or her life had arrived, the moment had come to sacrifice our lives for the Chinese people. . . .

At around two or three in the morning [as troops in the Square began moving in toward us], we had no choice but to abandon the Headquarters and retreat to the broadcast station at the foot of the Heroes' Monument. As General Commander, I mobilized the students for one last time, directing them to encircle the Heroes' Monument. The students [in the first row] sat there calmly. They said to me, "We'll just sit here quietly. We in the first row are the most determined." [Behind them], other students said, "We in the back will also sit here quietly. Even if the classmates in the first row are beaten and killed, we will just sit here calmly. We will not move and we absolutely will not kill."

I said a few words to everyone. I told them, "There is an ancient legend. According to this legend, there was once a colony of about 1.1. billion ants. One day the mountain the ants lived on caught on fire, and the ants had to escape down to the foot of the mountain if they were to live. At that point, the ants formed a ball and rolled down the mountain. The ants on the outside burned to death, but even more ants survived. . . .

"My fellow students, we in the Square, we already stand at the outermost layer of the Chinese people, for each of us in our hearts is clear: only the sacrifice of our lives will suffice for the life of the republic."

The students began singing the "Internationale," over and over again they sang it, hands clasped tightly together. Finally, our four compatriots who were hunger striking, Hou Dejian, Liu Xiaobo, Zhou Duo, [and Gao Xin] could no longer restrain themselves. They said, "Children, do not make any more sacrifices."

Each and every one of us was utterly exhausted. The hunger strikers went to negotiate with the military and found a military representative who claimed to be responsible for the Martial Law Command Headquarters. They said, "We will withdraw from the Square, but we hope you will guarantee the safety of the students. We will withdraw peacefully." At the same time, our Headquarters was soliciting the opinions of the students, asking them whether they wanted to stay or to withdraw. We decided that all the students would withdraw. But at that moment, that bunch of slaughterers violated their promise: as the students were leaving, soldiers wearing combat helmets and armed with machine guns charged to the third tier of steps at the platform of the Monument. Before the Headquarters had a chance to announce the decision to withdraw, our loudspeakers had been strafed into shreds. This was the People's Monument! It was the Monument to the People's Heroes! They were actually shooting at the Monument. Most of the rest of the students retreated, crying as they retreated. . . .

Some say more than 200 students died; there are also others who say 4,000 have already died in the Square. Up to now, I still don't know the exact number. But every one of the people at the Workers' Autonomous Union near the [northern] edge of the Square perished. There were at least 20 or 30 of them. . . .

As we went around Mao's mausoleum [immediately south of the People's Monument] hand in hand, heading west from the south end of the Square, we saw a dark mass of some 10,000 helmeted soldiers seated at

Illustration 6.6. Tanks and thousands of troops occupied Tiananmen Square by the morning of June 4. During the next few days, helicopters would move between the Square and points to the west, leading to rumors that they were ferrying away bodies to be burned in a large crematorium located to the west of Beijing. Although these rumors have never been substantiated, it is quite possible that some helicopters were flying to a top-secret military compound in Beijing's Western Hills, where Deng and possibly other high Party leaders were sequestered during the assault on Tiananmen. Credit: Franki Chan.

the southern side of the Monument. The students screamed at them, "Dogs!" "Fascists!"...

We wanted to stick out our chests and march back to the Square. But all the residents stopped us. They said, "Children, do you know, they've set up machine guns, don't make any more sacrifices." So we could only continue heading [west] toward the Xicheng District from Xidan. On the road we saw four corpses of residents. The farther north we went, the closer we got to our schools, the more citizens' eyes were filled with tears. ...

When the last ranks of students who had withdrawn from Tiananmen Square arrived at Beijing University, this marked the forced end of our Movement, which had started on May 13 with a hunger strike and then had become a peaceful sit-in protest. Later we obtained information which said that at 10:00 on the night of June 3, Li Peng had given three orders: first, army troops were permitted to open fire; second, military vehicles were to enter the city at full speed and recover the Square before dawn on June 4; and third, the organizers and leaders of the movement were to be killed, without exception.

Compatriots, this is the ruthless, crazed, bogus government that continues to deploy troops [around Beijing] and to rule China. The Beijing Massacre is happening at this very moment; massacres all over China will also slowly commence if they are not already occurring. But my dear compatriots, as the night darkens, dawn approaches. As this regime becomes increasingly fascist, crazed, and oppressive, [the Chinese people will awaken,] and a true people's democratic republic will be born. This is the final juncture for the survival of the Chinese people. Compatriots, all citizens with a conscience, all Chinese, awaken! The final victory will be yours! The day is fast approaching when the Central Committee that pretends to speak for the Party—Yang Shangkun, Li Peng, Wang Zhen, and Bo Yibo—will be annihilated!

> Down with fascism!
> Down with military rule!
> The people will be victorious!
> Long live the republic!
>
> *(based on the Hong Kong Television Corporation's broadcast on June 10 of Chai Ling's tape of June 8, 1989)*

Chinese across the country reacted to the June 3 massacre with rage and anguish. On streets and campuses, paper mourning wreaths hung in somber contrast to militant posters demanding "blood for blood." Yet even those who advocated violent resistance to the army's occupation in Beijing recognized the futility of an unarmed citizenry challenging tanks and machine guns. Student leaders refused to abandon the principle of nonviolence. They placed their last hope for bringing down the government on general strikes that would paralyze China's cities. The first selection below, a broadcast from the student broadcast station at People's University, is an example of the emotional appeal for unity that went out to citizens in the first days after the massacre. The second selection, a student poster from Nanjing, reveals in contrast the kind of rage felt by many students after the killings.

"THE VOICE OF BEIJING WILL BE ONE WITH THE PEOPLE"

Dear listeners and friends, the entire staff of the Voice of Beijing has already passed twenty nights together with all of you. Last night we could not help wiping the tears from our faces as we cried out: farewell! farewell, our dear people! Although we have met with a slaughter, the voice of truth will be eternal among the people! But today, our classmates, our elder brothers, our teachers, our respected and dear people of Beijing, as you innocently fell under the butcher's knife, you became the cannon fodder for the power struggle among the Central Committee's top leaders.

Your blood will absolutely not be shed in vain! We must respond with a citywide strike: workers must strike, students must boycott classes, and there must be a general strike; we must stop the entire country from functioning. . . . We must clear-headedly see just how base the vicious intentions of the authorities have become. In the several days before the repression, the authorities maliciously tried to provoke clashes between soldiers and the people. In the course of one night, they provoked [the soldiers] into becoming beasts. But let us think calmly for a moment. The true beasts are those who encourage conflict from behind the scenes! The soldiers also have their loved ones; they too are people. We thus should unite all the patriotic soldiers whom we can unite, and isolate the beasts lurking behind the scenes—they are the true provocateurs of murder! Repay our debts of blood! Repay our debts of blood!

We thus ask the people in this grave moment to maintain calm and wisdom. The people will fight the authorities to the bitter end or perish in the struggle. No matter what the outcome, the entire staff of the Voice of Beijing will always stand with the people! As long as martial law is not enforced here in the district of Haidian [the university area], we will not leave. As long as People's University is here, we too will be here. With pools of our compatriots' blood around us, we cannot continue living as if nothing has happened. Believe us, dear people, the Voice of Beijing will fight with the great people of Beijing until the very last breath. The Voice of Beijing will be one with the people! Now and here, we urgently appeal to all Chinese who love their country: rise up! rise up! We have no choice. All people of Beijing, take action! Workers, go on strike! Students, boycott classes! Begin a general strike! The people's blood cannot be shed in vain; it absolutely cannot be!

(broadcast from the student broadcast station at People's University, circa June 4, 1989)

HANG LI PENG ON THE GALLOWS

The people are bleeding,
The heroes have fallen,
The air overflows with the wailing of a billion,
   death, massacre . . . his doing
—Hang Li Peng on the gallows.

Evil crime and shame fill his life,
The look in his eyes pollutes the air,
His black blood makes the rich earth rot
—Hang Li Peng on the gallows.

Heroic martyrs,
Your blood has already poured into
   our guts,
Our chests are like the ocean,
   let them roar!
—Hang Li Peng on the gallows.

(poster at Nanjing University, June 5, 1989)

The general strikes students hoped for never materialized. For two days following the army takeover of Tiananmen, Beijing residents continued to resist military rule, erecting barricades, attacking small groups of soldiers, and setting fire to vehicles. By Tuesday June 6, however, resistance had collapsed in the face of the army's overwhelming force. A new fear gripped the city—fear of civil war. According to rumors sweeping through the shaken capital, the 38th Army based in the Beijing military district had refused to participate in the Tiananmen operation and was now preparing to challenge the hated 27th Army, which Beijing residents believed had been primarily responsible for the assault. Some news sources reported that heavy gunfire had been heard at Nanyuan Airport, a military facility south of Beijing. On June 7, fears grew when the 27th Army rumbled out of Tiananmen to take up defensive positions at the eastern part of the ring road circling Beijing, as if preparing for an attack. A mass exodus of foreigners had already begun; Beijing residents, who could not flee, stockpiled essentials and anxiously waited.

Adding to the tension was uncertainty over who was in charge of the country. Only Li Peng had appeared on television since the Tiananmen takeover; Deng had not been seen in public since May 16. Rumors of Deng's death had begun to circulate in a city which for several days had lived on nothing but rumor.

On June 9, the fear and uncertainty ended. Deng appeared on television in a meeting addressing top military and Party leaders. Though his gait was a bit unsteady and his speech slightly blurred, Deng appeared healthy. At his side were all of China's highest leaders—with the exception of Zhao Ziyang—including Wan Li, the moderate president of the National People's Congress whom the students had vainly hoped would oppose martial law. There was no indication at all that the military had been, or still was, divided.

Excerpts of Deng's June 9 speech are presented below.

DENG XIAOPING'S REMARKS TO MARTIAL LAW OFFICERS ON JUNE 9

(excerpts)

Comrades, you have been working hard! . . .

This disturbance was bound to come sooner or later. It was determined by the international macro climate and China's micro climate. It was definitely coming and was something that could not be diverted by man's will; it was only a matter of time and scale. For it to occur now is advantageous for us. The biggest advantage for us is that we have a large group of old comrades who are still living and healthy. They have gone through many disturbances; they understand the complexities and subtleties of matters. They supported taking firm steps against the upheaval. Although there were some comrades who for some time did not understand, in the end they will understand, and they will support this decision of the Central Committee.

The April 26 *People's Daily* editorial defined the nature of the problem as "turmoil." This word "turmoil" exactly describes the problem. What some people opposed was this word; what they demanded revised was this word. [But] as our experience has proven, the judgment was correct. Subsequently, the situation developed into a counter-revolutionary rebellion; this was also inevitable. . . . It was relatively easy for us to handle the present explosion. The main difficulty in handling the matter is that we have never before encountered this kind of situation in which a small handful of bad persons were mixed into the masses of so many young students and onlookers. For a while, we could not distinguish the good from the bad; this made it difficult to take many steps that we should have taken. If there had not been so many elder comrades in the Party who gave us their support, then even grasping the nature of the matter would have been difficult. Some comrades do not understand the nature of the problem and believed that it was purely a problem of how to deal with the masses. In reality, the opposing side is not only a mass of people who exchange truth for lies. It is also consists of a group of people who have created an opposition faction, and many dregs of society. They want to subvert our country and subvert our Party: this is the [true] nature of the problem. . . .

Was the general conclusion of the Thirteenth Party Congress of "One Center, Two Fundamental Points" correct? Are the "Two Fundamental Points"—namely, supporting the Four Cardinal Principles and continuing the policy of reform and opening up to the outside—wrong? Recently, I have been pondering this question. We are not wrong. Adhering to the Four Cardinal Principles [adherence to socialism, adherence to the "people's democratic dictatorship," leadership of the Chinese Communist Party, and adherence to Marxism, Leninism, and Maoism] was not in itself a mistake; if there has been any error, it has been our not adequately implementing them. We have failed to make the Four Cardinal Principles the basic framework for educating people, students, and all officials and Party members. The nature of this incident is the antagonism between bourgeois liberalism and adherence to the Four Cardinal Principles. . . .

Was the basic policy of reform and opening up a mistake? No. Had there not been reform and opening up, how could we be where we are today? In the last ten years, there has been a relatively big improvement in the living standards of the people. It should be said that we have climbed up a step; even though inflation and other problems have appeared, the accomplishments of the last ten years of reform and opening up are more than enough. Of course, the policy inevitably brings with it many [negative] Western influences; we have never underestimated this [danger]. . . .

Our basic approaches, from [overall] strategies down to [specific] policies, including the policy of reform and opening up, are all correct. If there is anything that has been insufficient, it is that there is still not enough reform and opening up. We will encounter more challenging problems in the course of reform than in the course of opening up. In the reform of the political system, there is one point that can be affirmed: we will adhere to implementing the system of the National People's Congress rather than the American-style system of the separation of three powers. In reality, Western nations also do not carry out a system of separation of powers. The U.S. condemns us for suppressing the students. But when they handle domestic riots and student demonstrations, don't they send in the police and the army? Aren't there arrests and bloodshed? They suppress students and people; on the contrary, we are putting down a counter-revolutionary rebellion. What credentials do they have for judging us?! From today on, when we handle this kind of problem, we must pay attention to see that when unrest appears, we cannot allow it to spread.

Deng's speech in effect marked the end of the 1989 Democracy Movement. The unrest that had erupted in China's other cities had already begun to decline before he addressed his military lieutenants. Even in Shanghai, where reaction to the massacre had been particularly strong, opposition was beginning to fade. Student organizing strength had been fatally weakened by the earlier decision to abandon the campuses and have students return to their home towns. A restrained but firm response by the mayor of Shanghai, Zhu Rongji, had also helped to quell unrest. Appearing on television to reassure Shanghai's citizens that he would not call in the army and impose martial law, Zhu succeeded in calming passions. At the same time, he made it clear that authorities would not allow further disruptions. By promising money in return for cooperation, Shanghai authorities also convinced workers to assist the police in maintaining order on the streets, thus forestalling the possibility of a workers' strike.

In his remarks to his military officers, Deng reiterated the official verdict on the recent events: the turmoil had been a "counter-revolutionary rebellion" led by "a small number of bad elements." No more serious charge against the Democracy Movement could be made; counter-revolution is the Chinese Communist ideology's equivalent of sedition, punishable by death under Chinese criminal law.[7] By so labeling the pro-democracy protests, Deng and the Party signaled their intention to deal harshly with democracy activists.

In the weeks subsequent to June 9, security police issued a most-wanted list of twenty-one student leaders, with Wang Dan, Wuer Kaixi, and Chai Ling at the very top. The most-wanted list for intellectual activists included Yan Jiaqi, Bao Zunxin, Su Xiaokang, Wan Runnan, and Chen Yizi. More than twenty prominent intellectuals were also publicly attacked for advocating "bourgeois liberalization"—the Party's code word for Western democratic ideas of individual rights, freedom of speech, political pluralism, and human rights. Fourteen workers were also named in a workers' "most-wanted" list. Police arrested thousands of Chinese in the most sweeping repression of Deng's era. To impress upon citizens the gravity of the charges and the futility of attempting to evade arrest, Chinese television repeatedly broadcast newsclips of detainees, some handcuffed to trees and obviously beaten, as well as stories of co-workers or family members turning in persons sought by the government.

Estimates by a U.S. State Department report and by human rights groups place the total number of persons arrested during the post-June 4 suppression at between twenty and forty thousand. Official Chinese sources had reported that approximately two thousand arrests had been made in Beijing alone during the first two months of the crackdown. Although some of the persons detained have been

---

7. Article 103 of the Chinese Criminal Code (promulgated July 1, 1979 at the Second Session of the Fifth National People's Congress) states that with a few exceptions, counter-revolutionary offenses of a particularly heinous nature are punishable with the death penalty. Counter-revolutionary offenses are generally defined as acts for the purpose of overthrowing the political power of the dictatorship of the proletariat and the socialist system or jeopardizing the country. On June 20, 1989, the Chinese Supreme People's Court issued a notice directing all courts to punish severely "counter-revolutionaries who staged the counter-revolutionary rebellion and created turmoil." In addition, a 1983 law, the "Decision of the Standing Committee of the National People's Congress on Procedures for Swiftly Trying Criminals Who Seriously Endanger Public Security," provides that expedited procedures may be used in cases where the crime is that of seriously endangering public security. This law could be applied to Democracy Movement "counter-revolutionary" cases through a simple directive of the Party.

accused of acts of violence during the resistance to martial law, or protests after June 4 outside Beijing, the majority of those arrested have been charged only with peaceful acts of protest, such as distributing handbills or speechmaking; to avoid arrest, many students and citizens who did no more than write posters or sign open letters during the Democracy Movement went into hiding once the suppression began. Many of the arrested were workers—the easiest targets of persecution. According to some reports, workers who were accussed of attacking soldiers and army vehicles were often beaten by security police.

There have been forty officially confirmed executions of individuals accused of seriously endangering public security or engaging in counter-revolutionary crimes such as fomenting rebellion,[8] many of these were summary executions carried out within days of the accuseds' arrests. It is quite likely that additional executions have been carried out without any public announcement.

The notices translated below appeared in Beijing several days after the army takeover of Tiananmen.

BEIJING MUNICIPALITY PEOPLE'S GOVERNMENT MARTIAL LAW COMMAND HEADQUARTERS

Public Notice (No. 10).

The Federation of Autonomous Student Unions of Beijing Universities and Colleges (*Gaozilian*) and the Beijing Workers' Autonomous Union (*Gongzilian*) are illegal organizations that have not been registered in accordance with the law. They must immediately disband of their own accord.

The members of the two illegal organizations must immediately cease all illegal activities.

The heads of the "Gaozilian" and the "Gongzilian" are the main instigators and organizers in the capital of the counter-revolutionary rebellion. From the day of this public notice, these persons must immediately sur-

---

8. Closed trials and unannounced executions make it impossible to determine the total number of executions that have been carried out by the Chinese government for Democracy Movement-related activities. At least forty officially confirmed executions have been reported in various cities, including Shanghai, Beijing, Chengdu, and Wuhan, for crimes such as arson, destroying government property, inciting riot, and attacking soldiers. Hong Kong papers have reported that many additional executions of protestors have been carried out in secret. Most if not all of those executed appear to have been workers and other citizens rather than intellectuals or students.

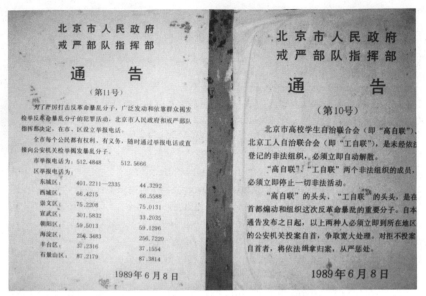

Illustration 6.7. Public Notices No. 10 and No. 11. Credit: Kaoru Ono.

render themselves to public security organs in their location; the policy will be to try to treat these people leniently. Important members who refuse to surrender voluntarily will be apprehended and brought to justice in accordance with the law, and will be severely punished.

—June 8, 1989

BEIJING MUNICIPALITY PEOPLE'S GOVERNMENT MARTIAL LAW COMMAND HEADQUARTERS

Public Notice (No. 11)

In order to strike back severely at counter-revolutionary rebels and to widely encourage and rely on the masses to expose and denounce counter-revolutionaries' criminal activities, the Beijing Municipality People's Government and the Martial Law Command Headquarters have decided to set up in the city and its districts hotlines for calling in information.

Every citizen throughout the city has the right and duty at any time to expose and denounce counter-revolutionary rebels by calling the hotlines or directly contacting the public security organs.

City hotline numbers:	512.4848	512.5666
District hotline numbers:		
Dongcheng District	401.2211-2335	44.3292
Xicheng District	66.4215	66.5588
Chongwen District	75.2208	75.0131
Xuanwu District	301.5832	33.2035
Huyang District	59.5013	59.1296
Haidian District	256.3843	256.7220
Fengtai District	37.2316	37.1554
Shijingshan District	87.2179	87.3814

—June 8, 1989

"Seeds of Fire Cannot Be Extinguished; the People Will Be Victorious"

But if the post-Tiananmen crackdown sent thousands to jail and silenced all dissent in China, it also failed to capture many of its most important targets. A good number of the student and intellectual leaders sought by the government evaded capture and fled to the West, somehow eluding discovery despite a nationwide security alert and a pervasive Chinese social system of monitoring by co-workers, neighbors, and local "neighborhood committees," composed of volunteers, usually retirees, whose function is to keep a watchful eye over activities in the residential area where they live and to mediate minor disputes. The Chinese government at first chose to suppress news of their flight; the escapes, which must have been accomplished with the help of many sympathizers, seemed to belie its claim that only a "small number of bad elements" had led the disturbances. It would later change its tack, blaming Hong Kong, the United States, France (which gave leading dissidents refuge), and other foreign governments for aiding and abetting fugitives and stirring up unrest in the country.

At least two students on the government's "most-wanted" list of student leaders managed to flee safely: Wuer Kaixi, the former chairman of the Beijing Students' Federation, and Li Lu, the student leader from Nanjing University, who had served in the last weeks of the Tiananmen occupation as Deputy Commander of the Protect Tiananmen Headquarters. Like most Democracy Movement figures who made it out of the country, Wuer Kaixi followed an escape route to southern China and across the porous border there to Hong Kong. On June 28, two weeks after his name appeared on the most-wanted list, Wuer Kaixi defiantly renewed the call for the struggle for democracy in a videotape shown on Hong Kong television. Excerpts of the tape follow.

"AS SURVIVORS, OUR LIVES NO LONGER BELONG TO US ALONE"
(excerpts)

I speak to all you compatriots who hold freedom and democracy dear, to the entire Chinese people. I am Wuer Kaixi of Beijing Normal University, a representative of the Beijing Students' Federation and of the Beijing student movement. I am also one of the twenty-one "counter-revolutionary rebels" on the so-called "wanted" list circulated by the pretender government. . . .

I would like to state simply that on June 4, one of the blackest days in the history of the People's Republic, our motherland became sick. In the early hours of the morning of that day, the reactionary warlords, reactionary government, and fascist military, directed and headed by Li Peng and Yang Shangkun, and controlled from behind the scenes by Deng Xiaoping, revealed themselves as the cruelly bestial fascists they are by firing upon tens of thousands of students who had gathered peacefully to petition for the redress of grievances. I must tell you all that although I naturally cannot at this time give precise figures for the number of dead and wounded, still I may tell you that that night at Tiananmen Square there were at least several thousand people killed. . . .

Our fervent hope was for peace; how innocent we were! The fascists' violence was completely beyond our conception. When we started out we never so much as imagined that these beasts would descend to such depths! . . .

The presence of our fellow students will linger forever on Changan Avenue and Tiananmen Square. How many souls there must be howling with anger all along Changan Avenue! May they rest in peace!

As survivors, our lives no longer belong to us alone: our lives now include those of our fellow students and compatriots who gave their lives for democracy, for freedom, for our beautiful motherland, and for her strength and prosperity. Their lives have been melded together with ours.
. . .

I believe that the memory of these martyrs will live forever. They are like the laborers on the towpaths [of the Yangtze Gorges]: they gave their lifeblood in an effort to keep the sinking ship of China away from dangerous shoals and lead her toward the bright and open ocean.

Compatriots! Comrades! Warriors of patriotism and democracy! I am Wuer Kaixi, and I wish to say that although the great massacre is past, and events in China are temporarily at a low ebb, I still believe that our movement will be victorious in the end. Our demands must be realized in the motherland; we will most certainly launch another much larger movement for democracy and completely overthrow the reactionary warlords. . . . On this basis, we must ensure that every Chinese person has democratic consciousness. What is democracy? Many people have asked me this. Democracy means that the people control governmental power, and not the other way around. It means that people are free to choose a political-economic system that accords with their own wishes. This is democracy; it means implanting a glorious democratic consciousness into the mind of every citizen of the People's Republic of China. In the past we have failed to do this; our education has been very poor. The level achieved by our children has been very low, and the average level among our citizens is very low. Our true task is to raise the quality of our citizenry! . . .

Our purpose is not simply the overthrow of Li Peng. Whether we overthrow him or not is unimportant; but whether or not we can shout, "Down with Li Peng!" is very important. What we want is not simply the overthrow of the man, but the establishment of governmental checks and balances in China, so that we have real democratic institutions in China. I think that all of us, including our patriotic compatriots overseas, have the duty and the responsibility to join themselves with grass-roots political forces that can constitute such checks and balances, to join with these forces that can speak for the people. This is our ultimate goal! At present our task is to break the news blackout and cultivate democratic consciousness among the Chinese people; our long-range task is to build grass-roots political forces that will serve as the basis for governmental checks and balances.

(videotape broadcast in
Hong Kong, June 28, 1989)

"TO FIGHT WITHOUT FIGHTING, THAT IS THE RAZOR'S EDGE OF NONVIOLENCE"

. . . To fight without fighting, that is the razor's edge of non-violence.

This is what I believe happened in the American Civil Rights Movement. I am here to learn as well as to inform, so you must teach me. But I know that this definitely happened during the spring of 1989 in Beijing's Tiananmen Square.

My first encounter with the concept of nonviolence was in high school when I read about Martin Luther King, Jr. and Mahatma Gandhi. At the time, this method of nonviolence seemed—to my superficial understanding—extremely logical and beautiful. Here was a method which would clearly win in the end, no matter how long the struggle may last. Although the process may take longer, you get the true result—a real and lasting change—not a fake result.

At the time, Dr. King's ideas seemed very idealistic to me—from my simple understanding of his principles. Just like the sense of nonviolence which Albert Einstein gave to me, which Gandhi gave to me.

But that was the first step in my life. And that was the first step in the lives of many young Chinese seeking some beautiful way for China. We were exposed to the principles of nonviolence and it gave us inspiration. It was something very pure, very idealistic in our minds.

There is one thing you must know, however, to understand China's nonviolent movement—and the principle of nonviolence within the Chinese individual: China has suffered through more than four thousand years of violence and revolution. The Chinese people have suffered oppression and tyranny for over four thousand years. One dynasty after another was established and then violently destroyed. And always the people suffered. The most recent dynasty, with its most recent set of emperors, is the Communist Party. I say this without bitterness or ill will. It is a statement of fact. The Communist Party leaders have followed in the footsteps of all other violent, oppressive dynasties in China. And soon they too will fall.

As we moved closer to the demonstrations in the spring, we took the second step toward nonviolence. In the universities, the student organizations and salons studied and discussed the future of China—the culture, history, and psychology of the Chinese people. And we realized quite clearly that China cannot suffer any more. China cannot possibly live through any more violent revolution, or any more "national salvation." This myth of "national salvation" plays into the cycle of dynasty after dynasty. Those who carried out the revolt knew only what they wanted to destroy, not what they wanted to achieve or build up. "Destroy the empire," they said "and we will be saved." But saved from what? To what goal? The end result is violence and tyranny again—perhaps more terrible than the tyranny which was destroyed. Just look at Mao and the so-called "Cultural Revolution"—a grand name for the national salvation that jailed, persecuted and terrorized a generation.

The "universal truth" for the Chinese people is that government comes from the barrel of a gun.

In the light of this Chinese reality, we had to find a good way for China—a good way to achieve true change. First of all, we came to the conclusion that individualism—that self-awareness which recognizes the value of every human life—this individualism was the only way for the Chinese to break out of the dynastic cycle. And I feel that these two are the same thing—nonviolence and individualism

But also this confuses me. I am still unclear. How can this nonviolence and this individualism come to some reality, to some practical skill or method in social revolution? It is still a question for the Chinese. Perhaps you can help me to understand this. So many nonviolent struggles succeeded—like the Civil Rights movement, and Eastern Europe. But the question still remains for the Chinese youth—How? It is time for us to really learn, and practice the principle. To learn from the examples of struggles like yours.

But personal learning—learning through experience—came to us through our third nonviolent step—the actual movement itself.

We know that the one thing necessary to achieve real democracy and human rights in China was peace. China could suffer no more violence. Peaceful revolution was the only answer.

Early on, we leaders were approached by several high-ranking military generals. They wanted to support us and stand with us against the other part of the army. We knew this would lead to civil war. We knew that. So we refused to even meet with them

We did not want to give the government any excuse to crack down on the demonstrations. So we tried to prevent anything from confusing our principles or our goals. We prevented not only violence, but even people saying some bad slogans against the Communist Party. We tried to prevent this to keep our goals and principles very clear. Even if people wanted to support us and join us we said, "OK, you can stand beside us and support us and cheer and protect us, but you cannot join in our march." We wanted to be sure that the people participating were those dedicated to our goals and nonviolent principles with full understanding. And those people were primarily the students from Beijing.

And the more strict we were in this path, the more support we received from the people. Until finally, almost four million people supported us. And they began to have their own demonstrations—the workers, the intellectuals, the journalists, even the peasants held their own demonstrations. It was beautiful and moving.

Also, we were dedicated to making these demonstrations absolutely peaceful. We controlled traffic, policed the Square and surrounding areas to be sure no violence or crime would happen. Actually, during those months, the crime rate in Beijing dropped tremendously because the thieves declared something of a strike in support of our movement. They didn't want to give the government any excuse to crack down, either.

I would also like to talk about the reasons why our movement failed. There are many reasons. The primary one is that sight of our goals was lost. Our original plan was to return to the campuses, regroup, and continue our movement through the broadcasting stations, the newspapers, and the tremendous support we had gained from the people. But the movement got out of control. So-called conservative leaders—like me— lost power, and so-called radical leaders gained it. Rather than moving to achieve something positive, the students started merely to react. If the government did nothing, the students remained in the Square doing nothing. If the government made some statement, or did something, then the students proposed another hunger strike. Some students even proposed to set themselves on fire in protest. For no constructive reason. We prevented this.

But the new leadership chose reaction over creation, and lost sight of why they were there. Oddly enough, when this new leadership was voted into power, the Beijing students had been joined by many students from other cities. These students had not been "educated" in our goals and principles. And so more than 70 percent of those supporting the new leadership were from outside Beijing. And most of them left a few days after the vote.

Nevertheless, after all these experiences, we knew there was no way to use violence in this revolution. No radicalism ever took the students to that stage. And not only the students but the people themselves realized that nonviolence was the most important skill for social change.

At the time, quite honestly, I did not see clearly how important this nonviolent principle was to the future of China. Only after I escaped and had time to reflect could I see that nonviolence is the only hope for the future, for the real Chinese beautiful future. And one thing I truly believe now, after all these experiences, is that beautiful goals can only be reached through pure and beautiful means. This is my lesson from Tiananmen Square.

I still see in my heart all the beautiful and heart-breaking examples of nonviolence displayed by the students. On June 3 and 4, the students returned guns to the authorities and did not use them. They tried to persuade the citizens to hold back, to be peaceful. They shouted at the crowds, "Stop throwing stones! Don't hurt the truck! Don't hurt the soldiers!" The students took wounded soldiers to the ambulances. . . .

And the most moving picture I have in my mind is a schoolmate of mine trying to return a rifle to the soldiers. He was just trying to return it, but they did not listen to him. They began to beat him to death with billy clubs, and he was kneeling. He had the gun in his hand, he held it over his head and never used it. And he was beaten to death.

All these memories show me that once you practice nonviolence, it becomes rooted in your heart.

I do not fully understand the theory of this nonviolent principle. But I feel I know its spirit. I know that it is the only way for China. And the only way for the world if we are to survive. Our various communities struggle to achieve justice and equality, freedom and human rights. We must join hands and stand as one. As Dr. King once said, "Injustice anywhere is a threat to justice everywhere. Whatever affects one directly affects all indirectly."

We must learn from each other. All our communities must learn peace from each other. And there is much, so much I must learn from you, and from Dr. King. Please teach me. Please help China and the Chinese find that crystal way which will lead to the crystal goal. And together, as one movement for human rights and peace worldwide, we will be able to look at the tyrants and oppressors of history and say to them—in Dr. King's words—"We have matched your capacity to inflict suffering with our capacity to endure suffering. We have met your physical force with soul force." We are free.

(speech by Shen Tong at Martin Luther King Center, Atlanta, Georgia, January 13, 1990)

China after June 4, 1989, has once again returned to the state of stability and unity desired by her rulers. Tiananmen Square's vast space is bare; no banners break the eye's clean sweep from east to west. Those who would raise their voices in protest—who did raise their voices in protest—have been silenced. To ensure unity, Chinese newspapers speak with one voice; discordant ones such as the Shanghai *World Economic Herald* have been shut down or reorganized. In the interest of stability, the size of entering classes in the universities has been drastically reduced, and students sent off for military training before commencing their studies. To ward off the influence of bourgeois liberalization that undermines socialist character and values, new university graduates are being assigned to work in organs at the grassroots level rather than being given jobs in higher-level government and Party offices.

But, as in the months before the outbreak of the 1989 pro-democracy protests, widespread discontent in China's cities simmers below the deceptive surface of stability and unity, a reminder that the Party's control over Chinese society is not completely secure. Workers in some thirty cities have petitioned authorities for permission to stage marches, to no success; morale among students and young teachers is extremely low.

And for the first time, the Party faces a distant but unified challenge from a coalition of Chinese—prominent intellectuals, students, dissidents, businessmen, and overseas Chinese—who reject the notion that China's present "national conditions" preclude the introduction of democracy and that democracy would threaten stability and unity. The Federation for a Democratic China (FDC), founded in France on August 1, 1989, by Yan Jiaqi, Wan Runnan, Wuer Kaixi (all of whom managed to escape to the West) and dissident journalist Liu Binyan (who was in the United States in 1989 on a fellowship) has made clear that overthrowing the Party is not its objective. It has also made it known, however, that it seeks democratic reforms based on a fundamental overhaul of the Chinese political system, including an end to the Party's monopoly on power. Born in the horror and outrage that followed the bloodshed of June 4, the FDC, which includes students but is dominated by liberal intellectuals or figures from the Party's reform wing who fled China, has been actively building contacts with East European opposition groups. With its four high-profile founders of entirely different backgrounds, the FDC has been able to unite Chinese from the People's Republic of China and overseas Chinese to an extent no other Chinese dissident organization had achieved heretofore. Yet tensions within the group have already appeared. Whether it can surmount them to forge a coalition that will effectively carry on the struggle begun in the 1989 Democracy Movement remains to be seen. Our final selection from the 1989 Chinese Democracy Movement is the manifesto of the Federation for a Democratic China.

DECLARATION OF THE FEDERATION FOR A DEMOCRATIC CHINA

Today, in Paris, we proclaim the Federation for a Democratic China Front [FDC]. The aim of the FDC is to establish a system of democracy in China. . . .

The surging waves of the Chinese Democracy Movement of 1989 provided China with a golden opportunity for political reform. To this, China's dictators responded with a bloodbath, plunging the whole country into barbarous terrorism. It is the most atrocious reactionary act ever committed by China's autocratic system since the fall of the Manchu [Qing] Dynasty; it is an act against China's modernization drive.

Once again, China's catastrophe demonstrates that, without the arousing democratic consciousness in all sectors of society, without the development of diverse independent political forces, and without a resilient and maturing democracy movement, it is unthinkable that this one-party regime will ever yield to democratic politics.

The search for freedom and dreams of happiness are with mankind from the moment of its birth. In the world today, the democratization of politics and an orientation toward a market economy are forceful trends. Violating the will of the people and defying history, the decaying members of the Chinese Communist Party are heading into an impasse.

When they deprived the people of the legal right to seek freedom and democracy, they also deprived themselves of a legitimate claim to govern.

When they spoiled the fruits of reform of the past ten years, they also forfeited the last chance that history had given them.

When they tightened their political, economic, and ideological controls, they also tightened the ropes around their necks. The fetters on which their rulership of the Chinese people depends are now beginning to weigh heavy on those who [are supposed to] hold them.

The one-party system of autocracy has embedded in it evils that cannot be eradicated without destroying the system itself. Now, China's autocrats are painfully chewing on the bitter fruits of their own creation. To remove the evils of the system, they must first eliminate themselves. In the meantime, to prevent the regeneration of those evils, we must first end the one-party autocracy on which their existence relies. Our mission, bestowed upon us by history, is to eliminate these dictators, along with the soil of autocracy in which they grow. Only then will the Chinese people be able to enjoy, for generations to come, a life of democracy and freedom, of vitality and creativity.

The June 4 massacre has facilitated the awakening of the Chinese people, home and overseas, and helped to meld an alliance of all the Chinese democratic forces.

The FDC is an inevitable product in the course of Chinese democracy. "To oppose the June 4 massacre" and "To continue the 1989 Democracy Movement" are its basic starting points.

The FDC is an independent political force, a political organization, founded by Chinese compatriots at home and overseas who are devoted to the cause of democracy in China.

It is our goal to establish the most extensive alliance and [to promote] cooperation; to fight for a China built on freedom, democracy, law, and human rights; and to fight for the promotion of progress and peace in the world. To achieve these goals, the FDC stands together with the workers, peasants, and soldiers who live at the bottom of Chinese society. It stands together with the Chinese intellectuals and students who have always committed themselves to the cause of democracy and freedom. It stands together with the emerging entrepreneurs, the private industrialists and businessmen who rose during the last ten years' reform. It stands together with those within the Chinese Communist Party and the People's Liberation Army who are democratic, open-minded, and who have promoted reform. It stands together with our patriotic fellow countrymen overseas, in Taiwan, Hongkong, and Macao. It stands together with the peoples in the world who will stand up for justice and fight for democracy and who love freedom.

To end the one-party system in China, to defend basic human rights, to promote a market economy, and to build a democratic China—these are the guiding principles of the FDC.

The FDC will maintain that peace, reason, and nonviolence are its criteria for action. We strongly condemn the autocratic regime for its use of terrorism against the people. We understand that in the middle of the bloodbath threatening to annihilate humanity and in the face of terror exercised by the tyrannical government, the Chinese people on the mainland are burning with indignation and anger. We understand, too, that all kinds of resistance are difficult to prevent. We are determined, however, to use only truth, justice, and the will of the people as our weapons, and we disapprove of any form of terrorism and any terrorist organization. We will carry out our battle in broad daylight. . . .

We are confronted with brutality and a bloodbath as formidable as the mountains. Responsibilities and expectations of the people as heavy as the mountains press down on our shoulders. We possess nothing, except wisdom and truth.

Yet, siding with us are human justice and human morality, the will and spirit of the Chinese people, and truth, whose authority only history can tell. Time and the immutable laws of history are on our side.

Watching us with earnest eyes are the martyrs of June 4, whose bodies are buried in the netherworld and whose souls have ascended to the highest of heavens.

We cannot afford to wait. We must set to work—with solidarity and resilience, with wisdom and courage, with our pain and our sacrifice.

Fellow compatriots:

In our hearts, on our hands, and under our feet, we bear the future of a new China. Ahead of us are the first gleams of a new day.

The twentieth century will be the century of a democratic China!

Long live a democratic and free China!

—Drafted by
the Preparatory Committee of
the Federation for a Democratic China,
Paris, August 22, 1989

Credit: Franki Chan.

INDEX OF DOCUMENTS

with other universities, 134; loses
leadership of movement, 206, 312,
322; quarrels within, 314; refusal to
recognize, 186, 331; support for
hunger strike, 199
Fei Xiaotong, 240
Feng Congde, 80, 361
Fengtai, 302
feudal system, 155, 157
"Fifth Modernization—Democracy"
(poster), 23
Flying Tigers, 258, 354
foreign debt, 31, 277, 283
foreign exchange, 29
Four Big Freedoms, 108
Four Cardinal Principles, 144, 162–
70, 191, 257, 370
Four Modernizations, 14, 23, 75
France, 375, 382
freedom, call for, 124–25, 126, 127
French Revolution, 25
Fuzhou, 232

Gandhi, Mahatma, 378
Gang of Four, 107, 219
Gao Panlong, 8
Gao Xin, 354, 364
Gaozong, Tang Emperor, 166
Goddess of Democracy, 342–48, 360
Gorbachev, Mikhail, visit by, 192,
199, 208, 209, 210, 223, 241, 256,
307
government officials, corruption
among, 26, 31, 39, 184. See also
nepotism; profiteering by officials
graduate students, 81–82, 114, 120,
170, 236, 284, 286
Great Hall of the People, 209
Great Leap Forward, 269, 270
Great Wall, 20
"group of elders," 175, 186, 241, 260,
304, 336
Guangdong, 278
Guangming Daily, 188, 218, 231–32,
237
Guangzhou, 134, 231, 272
Guiyang, 232

Hainan, 231
Han Dacheng, 227
Han Hua, 111
Han Wudi, 166
Hangzhou, 134, 232, 272
Harbin, 232
He Dongchang, 117, 163
Hefei, xiv, 232
Hehai University, 8
Henan University, 44, 45
historical materialism, 168–69
Hong Kong, 19, 30, 326, 375; funding
of protestors, 312; press reports,
242, 309, 312, 361, 373; student
activism in, 134; student protestors
from, 225, 227, 348
Hong Kong Television Corporation,
361
Hou Dejian, 349, 354, 363, 364
"How to Attract Foreign Capital"
(Fang Lizhi), 275
Hu Deping, 124
Hu Jiwei, 161, 290, 309
Hu Qili, 69
Hu Yaobang, 8, 332, 333: death of, 5,
9, 15, 190; fall from power, 5–6,
78–80, 146, 270; and mass
campaigns, xv, 10; meaning of
name of, 7; memorial services for,
61, 84, 97, 198; poetry for, 46; and
the press, 108, 111; replaces Hua
Guofeng, 147; student support for,
9, 13, 14, 78–79, 83–84, 140, 178,
268, 343
Hua Guofeng, 146–47
Huang Xiang, 23
Huhehaote, 232
human rights, 23–24, 25, 218, 275,
381
Hunan Teachers College, 149, 222
Hundred Flowers Movement, xii, 220
Hungary, 212, 338
hunger strike, 209–16, 221–22, 226,
234, 237, 242, 244, 249, 268, 299,
326; ended, 255; intellectuals call
for end to, 207–208; Li Peng
statement on, 256; reasons for, 198,
202; renewed, 348–59; students'

/